Arthur Ransome, 1949

# THE
# AUTOBIOGRAPHY
# OF
# ARTHUR
# RANSOME

edited,
with prologue and epilogue,
by

RUPERT HART-DAVIS

JONATHAN CAPE
THIRTY BEDFORD SQUARE LONDON

FIRST PUBLISHED 1976
TEXT © 1976 THE ARTHUR RANSOME ESTATE
PROLOGUE AND EPILOGUE © 1976 RUPERT HART-DAVIS

JONATHAN CAPE LTD, 30 BEDFORD SQUARE, LONDON WCI

ISBN 0 224 01245 2

SET IN 12PT BEMBO SOLID
PRINTED IN GREAT BRITAIN BY
EBENEZER BAYLIS & SON LIMITED
THE TRINITY PRESS, WORCESTER, AND LONDON

# Contents

# CONTENTS

# *Illustrations*

# *Prologue*

Arthur Ransome wrote the bulk of his autobiography between 1949 and 1961, from the age of sixty-five to seventy-seven. He several times made me promise that, if necessary, I would edit and see it through the press. This would have presented few difficulties, had it not been for the unusual way in which he wrote his books.

With *Swallows and Amazons* and its eleven successors it was his habit to prepare an extremely detailed synopsis, complete with chapter-titles, so that he knew exactly what was to happen in each chapter. He then began writing whichever chapter took his fancy or seemed easiest, leaving the most difficult to the last. Thus a surviving page of his work-sheet for *Pigeon Post* shows that at one point he had written and revised nineteen of the first twenty-nine chapters, leaving Chapters 2, 4, 7, 10, 11, 13, 18, 19, 23 and 25 still to be written. Reading the smooth-flowing narrative, building up to a climax, it is difficult to believe that the book was written in this extraordinary way, but so it was.

When it came to his autobiography, written over more than a decade of his old age, this idiosyncratic mode of composition left many problems for his editor. Characters introduced in later chapters were often introduced again and again in earlier chapters, written years later. A great deal of repetition had to be removed, and passages transposed, so that people were introduced on their first appearance.

For many years after 1917 Ransome planned to write a history of the Russian Revolution and he amassed a large quantity of notes and memoranda, apart from his memories. Time and again in the autobiography he was tempted to devote several pages to discussion of Russian political parties, contemporary theories of the future, and a great deal of other material irrelevant to his own story. There have been many histories of those days, and I have restricted Ransome's narrative to events in which he was involved as actor or eyewitness.

The most difficult chapters were missing from the typescript, but the author's drafts of them required only minor revision. Except for a few linking sentences and some of the chapter-titles, all the words in the book are Ransome's.

He was remarkable in many ways, but chiefly because in himself he combined two very different characters. Half of him was a dedicated man of letters, with a passion for language and literature. He had read everything and was always deeply concerned with all branches of the literary life. His early writings were all literary, and though he later looked on most of them as false starts, they served one all-important purpose—they helped him to shape and perfect that lucid and seemingly effortless prose which he was to use in the work he always wanted to do above all, the writing of stories.

The other half of him was a perpetual schoolboy, with all the zest, fun, enjoyment and enthusiasm of youth—always ready to watch cricket or Rugby football, to sneak off to his beloved Garrick Club for a game of chess or billiards or simply to drink a little Burgundy with his cronies. The two greatest delights of his life—fishing and sailing—he enjoyed long after his doctors had told him to give them up, and to accompany him on any of these enterprises was like sharing them with a most articulate, knowledgeable and amusing boy.

It was the amalgamation of these two characters—the man of letters and the schoolboy—that produced his enduring memorial, his twelve books for boys and girls. He was as fond of children as the next man, but not excessively fond. The unique quality of these books is simply explained by the fact that their author was always partly a child. (Notice the exactitude of his early memories in the pages that follow.) All the best books are written to please and satisfy one person – their author; not an unseen and incalculable public—and Arthur Ransome's children's stories fully satisfied both his literary and his boyish ambitions.

As the books became more and more popular, he began to be deluged with letters from children—hundreds and thousands of them—varying from the enchanting and the droll, through the prosaic to the idiotic. (He answered them all courteously.) But of all the questions that his young readers asked him, one was predominant and recurring—the question 'Is it real?'

The stories seemed so lifelike that the children couldn't be sure if they were fact or fiction. And with this question they touched the heart of Ransome's secret. For everything in those books *is* real—every technical detail of sailing, camping, bird-watching, every aspect of the Lake District, the Norfolk Broads, the North Sea passage. They are all things that Ransome had seen and done and enjoyed, and continued to enjoy, so that he was able to turn them into fiction of such verisimilitude that his readers took it as fact.

No storyteller could hope for a richer reward, and Arthur Ransome seems assured of exactly the kind of immortality he would have chosen—not the writing of learned theses on his work, nor critical assessments of his talent, but the voices of generation after generation of children, delightedly asking their parents 'Is it real?'

But before he came into his kingdom he had many bizarre and unexpected adventures by the way, as readers of this book will discover.

*Marske-in-Swaledale*                    RUPERT HART-DAVIS
*February 1976*

# BOOK ONE

# CHAPTER I
## *Early Memories*

Some thirty years ago, in Moscow, I was asked by a young Russian writer what was the first thing I could remember. He explained that he was writing his autobiography and was collecting early memories from his friends as he had none of his own. I have no need to do that. Some of my memories go back a long way, indeed to my second year. I can remember being held up in my father's arms on the deck of a steamship, after a night-crossing, to see the pigs being loaded into gaily painted schooners in Belfast harbour. I remember, a few weeks later, sitting hard on the road after slipping through a rolled tube of blankets out of my mother's arms when she was sitting at the back of a wagonette that had stopped in an Irish village and suddenly started forward. Then I remember seeing snowdrops in the grass under some trees and, far away, a man driving along in a two-wheeled side-car through an avenue on the further side of a wide stretch of grassland. Long afterwards I was told that I had imagined this, but I described the event in great detail, enquiry was made, and the place and time identified. The park was that of Sir Nathaniel Staples. It had a drive on either side, and the two drives and the snowdrops under the trees were exactly as I had remembered them.

My next early memory (if indeed autobiographies need such things) is of Queen Victoria's Golden Jubilee in 1887. I was then three-and-a-half and carried a blue mug with me on my way to the Jubilee tea in a big tithe-barn at Wold Newton in Yorkshire. I can still see the raised floor at one end of the barn where the old people who had shared in the Coronation festivities of fifty years before were sitting in their smock frocks, the women all wearing linen sunbonnets. There is some point in recording such memories if the recorders live to a great age, and I am glad that I was taken by my father to have my head patted by a grey old man, one of the Baineses, who had been born in 1798, the year of the *Lyrical*

*Ballads*, could remember Trafalgar, had been a youth of seventeen at the time of the Battle of Waterloo and, like Sir Walter Scott, had spoken with persons who could remember the Highlanders coming into England in 1745. This may seem interesting to some young friend of mine who in the year 2024 may like to say that he once knew an old fogey who had as a child seen one who had been born in the year when Coleridge was finishing *The Ancient Mariner*. But the memories that seem important to the rememberer are not of these chance touchings of the skirts of history, but of quite simple things, drifting snowflakes seen through a melted peephole in a frosted nursery window, the sun like a red-hot penny in the smoky Leeds sky, and the dreadful screaming of a wounded hare. That last I can never forget.

I was born on January 18, 1884, in Leeds, where my father was Professor of History. Long afterwards my mother showed me the house in which I was born, a mean, ugly little building, one of a row, not far from Woodhouse Moor. The first house I remember living in must, I think, have been pulled down to make room for the growth of what was then the Yorkshire College and subsequently became Leeds University. I remember little of it but hearing *Sylvie and Bruno* read aloud, and that winter peephole through the frost on the nursery window. From there we moved to a house half way between the Skyrack Inn and the Three Horseshoes at Headingley on the outskirts of Leeds. I remember that house by a bush of white guelder roses and my own small garden of pansies with a border of Virginia stock. But I well remember the Shire Oak, the ruin of which remains enclosed in an iron paling, and the old horse-drawn omnibus that used to start from the Skyrack and had straw on the floor to keep the passengers' feet warm. For a long time it kept up its hopeless competition with the horse-drawn trams, in which, sometimes, I used to go into Leeds with my mother. The trams started from their stables by the Three Horseshoes, and they were valued neighbours when we moved to our last Leeds house, 3 St Chad's Villas, opposite St Chad's church and the vicarage where the Hoyles (very distant connections of ours) kept sand-lizards in a glass vivarium. The horse-trams did not hurry, and a small boy could keep pace, trotting level with them along the pavement. My mother used to tell of her shame when she had set out for Leeds leaving me, not ready, at home and, sitting in the tram, looked back and saw me running steadily down the hill from the Horseshoes a very long way behind. She said nothing, hoping that I would give up and turn back. The tram went on and on until at last the conductor saw that he was being pursued. Kindhearted man, he stopped his tram. I panted up, plumped myself down on the seat beside my mother and remarked happily 'Just in time' to the unfortunate passengers whom I had thus delayed.

I was born in Leeds, but the Ransomes are an East Anglian family. Thomas Ransome, my grandfather, was the son of John Atkinson Ransome, who late in the eighteenth century left his brothers to discover ways of chilling steel and making plough-shares and other agricultural implements, and to found the Ipswich firm of Ransome & Rapier, while he went north to Manchester and became a surgeon celebrated in his day. His bust was to be seen over the Manchester Medical School of which he was one of the founders, and he was the surgeon brought from Manchester on the footplate of an engine too late to save Huskisson after he had been run over at the opening of the Liverpool and Manchester Railway. He gave his son the best possible scientific training and his friend Playfair took my grandfather as a young man into his own laboratory. But my grandfather never carried anything through or profited by his exceptional gifts. For example, being interested in photography and finding the wet plates then in use both troublesome and messy, he devised dry plates for himself. Then, when other photographers were using cumbrous stand-cameras, he invented and built for his own use a camera that could be used in the hand. He made not a penny from either of these inventions but grew interested in large-scale chemical processes and, with no business sense whatever, set up as a 'manufacturing chemist'. The results of this were disastrous and my father (his eldest son), who had won himself a series of scholarships (at Merton and elsewhere), handicapped himself for many years by paying off his father's debts. When my grand-mother died, leaving my grandfather with children in the nursery, he married the young woman who was looking after them and proceeded to raise another family, the youngest of whom was about the same age as myself. My grandfather became interested in boats (another early memory is of being held up in the arms of my step-grandmother to see a flickering light far out in the dark-ness over Morecambe Bay, and hearing her say 'Do you know what that is? That's your grandfather late with the tide and stuck on the sands again.'). Then he became interested in electricity, in mechanical inventions of all kinds, and was always very busy at what he was doing, but never at anything that would keep his family in bread and butter. He was a first-rate field-naturalist, as interesting a companion on a country walk as any small boy could wish, and a very good, ingenious fisherman. He early saw the advantage of stiffer, shorter, quicker-striking rods over the long whippy things then in use, and the disadvantage of quicker-striking rods to anyone who, like himself, always fished with horsehair casts. He therefore made a practice of adding a foot of whalebone to the tip of his stiff rods, with very good results, the stiff rod giving quickness in the strike and the little bit of whalebone providing just enough elasticity to save the horsehair from too rugged a pull. He was acute in considering all business except his own, and when I first came to fish the Beela (my father's and my grandfather's favourite river) in 1930 or thenabouts, the old keeper, Tom Stainton, told me of a remark of my grandfather's sixty years before. Tom was appointed keeper on the Beela by the little club that controlled the water, and one of the committee raised the question as to what was to be done about a superannuation fund. 'Superannuation!' exclaimed my grandfather. 'No man appointed beck-watcher on the Beela will ever want to be superannuated.' 'And by gum,' said old Tom to me, 'I never have and never will.'

Unluckily for me, indeed for us both, my father thought that he saw in me signs of the irresponsibility, carelessness and flibbertigibbet inability to stick to anything for long that had made my grandfather so heavy a burden on his own shoulders as a young man. I cannot but recognise now that I gave him plenty of cause so to think. I was for ever after some new thing and, much worse, for ever planning that it should be the occupation of a lifetime. I spent every penny I had on coloured paper, made spills in dozens and grosses and formed a one-man company that should make spills for all Leeds, for all Yorkshire, for all the world, and put the match-factories out of business. In this my father saw at once a foreshadowing of something like my grandfather's disastrous venture as a manufacturing chemist. It seemed to him (and indeed was) a miserable, mercenary ambition, and in the small boy of six or seven he saw already the man who threw away in exchange for empty husks the prospect, open before him, of a useful scientific career. When I had glutted the spill-market and loaded his own mantelpiece and those of his friends who, not seeing the dread implications of my activities, annoyed him by paying pennies for my merchandise, spills were forgotten and I was practising day in day out the simpler conjuring tricks that were to lead me to the prideful moments of a professional magician who, before vast audiences, should produce rabbits out of a hat (for the moment I was content to produce white mice). My father was still more disheartened. His hopes rose a little when I showed a deep interest in caterpillars and found and identified some of the rarer hawk-moths, but fell again on learning that I proposed to breed them on a gigantic scale and sell them sordidly to collectors. Then I had plans for making a fortune out of the monstrous multiplication of Belgian hares, which came to nothing because of my unwillingness to kill them. He was pleased when, after a visit to the Leeds museum in the Philosophical Hall, I set about making one of my own, but was once more disheartened when he heard that I saw my museum, temporarily housed in the drawer of a washing-stand, as already the nucleus of a collection that should fill a building something like the Leeds Town Hall and attract pilgrims, at sixpence a head, from all parts of the world. It was a very good museum for a washing-stand drawer. There was a bronze token struck by Wilkinson the ironmaster who built the first iron vessel, sunk and I suppose rusted away by now at the bottom of Helton Tarn in the Winster valley. There were sharks' teeth in it, and cowries from the South Seas. There were ammonites, belemnites and other fossils collected by myself, and there was an acorn from Tasso's garden at Ferrara, given me by J. R. Mozley, poet and inspector of schools, that was highly valued by me as a sort of totem, long before I knew who Tasso was or what he was doing with a garden in a place of so strange a name. Alas, in almost everything I did with such enthusiasm my father saw not so much the enthusiasm as the traits which in his own father he had most deplored.

My maternal grandfather Edward Baker Boulton was just as incapable of self-help, and as interesting to small boys. He had owned enormous areas of sheep-lands in New South Wales until the break-up of the big estates brought about by legislation. However, though he had spent most of his life in Australia his heart had never been in his sheep-farming. He was a good water-colour painter and cared for nothing else. He settled my grandmother in Tilly House at Wem in Shropshire while he went off to Australia for years at a time. My mother was the eldest of his second family and inherited his gift for water-colour painting. Sometimes, leaving the second family in the care of the not much older daughters of his first wife, he and my grandmother used to go to Australia together. I owed to them the shark's teeth and the tropical shells that enhanced my museum. He and my grandmother had endless stories of blackfellows, bushrangers, kangaroos, laughing jackasses and such, and used to bring back with them emus' eggs of vast size, the skins of snakes they had met and killed in their Australian garden, and tales of storm and calm, petrels and albatrosses, that, when I first read *The Ancient Mariner*, made me feel that I had sailed those seas before. I can see my grandfather now, skipping nimbly out of the way of a boomerang flung by himself when it came spinning back to him with greater speed and accuracy than he had expected. That must have been at Wem. I remember him later at Clifton, where in the basement of the house in Apsley Road that seemed to be mainly occupied by my grandmother and many aunts he had made for himself a private Bohemia of his own where he drew and planned pictures and rolled innumerable cigarettes with a small machine, the handle of which he allowed me to twiddle. From Clifton I was taken to the Bristol docks, and saw sailing ships alongside the quays, to the Suspension Bridge over the gorge with tiny steamers moving on the river far below, and to the Zoological Gardens where I was allowed to hold in my arms a lion-cub, then only a little smaller than myself, which grew up to be the famous Hannibal.

That grandfather died when I was very young and the aunts were ruled by my formidable grandmother. She was a Gwynn but would never admit that she had a drop of Welsh blood, though with that name she could hardly escape it, and my father used to tease my mother with pretended proofs that he could trace her ancestry back to Caractacus. My grandmother taught me the moves of chess when I was little more than a baby, so that I owe to her what has been a pleasure all my life. Chess is a form of argument without words. Players who do not know each other's language can find each other very good company. They are freemasons of a kind and are everywhere welcomed by their peers.

Both my grandfathers married twice and each of them had two large families, so that I began life with a vast number of uncles and aunts. On the one side were the Ransomes, with in the past a strongly Quaker and East Anglian background and, by the time I was born, an almost unbelievable number of parsons and complex North Country connections with Butterworths, Jacksons, Remingtons and Binyons. On the other side were the Boultons from Shropshire, mixed up with Boutflowers and Tailleurs and, for me, enhanced by that romantic shadowy Australia, from which they appeared now and then bringing strange gifts, and into which, after farewell visits, equally exciting, from time to time they vanished. A young Boulton uncle, revolting from the sheep-station of Bergen-op-Zoom (not far from Sydney), went for a visit to British Columbia and remained there for the rest of his life. Another Boulton uncle, while working as a boy in Liverpool, chose to live in a lighthouse at the mouth of the Mersey, joined a cotton firm, made his fortune in Bombay, kept the rest of his family going, became a noted pig-sticker, won the Bombay Hunt Cup on a horse called Gownboy and soon afterwards died of a fever.

# CHAPTER II

## *Lake Country Holidays*

My father and I had an early conflict over politics. He was a
Liberal Unionist and an Imperial Federationist. At the same time
he was a pioneer in working men's education and founded a
working men's club in Leeds that was for a long time named after
him. His closest friend, from his Oxford days, was Arthur
Acland who had been Minister of Education under Gladstone. My
father loathed Mr Gladstone and all his works, and could never
forgive him the death of Gordon, but characteristically, though
disagreeing on politics, and holding views almost exactly
opposite, he and Arthur Acland were so far tolerant of each other
that they were able to combine in writing a political history of
England in which every sentence was an agreed sentence, a really
gallant attempt at impartiality. Indeed his hatred of Gladstonian
views did not prevent my father's choice of Acland as my godfather, though he thought the idea of Home Rule a betrayal that
promised the break-up of the British Empire.

I was a very small boy at the time of a General Election and,
when my father's party were wearing blue favours, I bought for
myself and appeared at the dinner-table with a yellow rosette, at
that time the badge of Mr Gladstone's supporters. My father saw
it at once.

'Why are you wearing that beastly colour?' he asked.

'Because I am a Gladstonian.'

'And why are you a Gladstonian?' asked my father.

'Because he wants to give Home Rule to Ireland.'

'And why do *you* want to give Home Rule to Ireland?'

'To save us the trouble.'

'Go on being a Gladstonian!' exclaimed my father in disgust,
less at my political creed than at the unworthy motive that
explained it.

I think now that my yellow ribbon displayed in the midst of

favours unanimously blue was probably less the result of inheriting my grandfather's inclination to take the line of least resistance (to which my father was inclined to attribute it) than an early manifestation of my ineradicable tendency to disagree with any majority wherever I happened to be. Years afterwards, in Russia, it was always the same. With Radek, with Bukharin and even with Lenin, I used to find myself arguing until I became almost White, and then spend time at the British Mission, arguing on the other side until I became once more not Red, but at least a reasonable pink.

I was a sad disappointment to my father in other ways. He was a very good shot and a notable fisherman. In these activities he was wholeheartedly at one with his father and he hoped from the first that I should be the same. As a small boy he had enjoyed going shooting and fishing with his father. But when he took me with him to the Wharfe I was never content to watch him catching trout and so to learn to do as much myself when old enough to have a rod. He would turn, on hooking a trout, to make sure that his pupil was alert and watching, only to find that he was alone, and that his pupil had gone off down the river and was paddling in the water, turning stones, to catch loaches by himself. It was different on Coniston where I had a rod of my own and an almost equal chance of catching perch. But for him trout came first, and my unwillingness to learn the mysteries by mere watching seemed to him little short of sacrilege. He took me shooting, and I learned to be a tolerable spaniel, struggling noisily through a thicket to put up an unwilling pheasant and learning to 'Mark Cock!' when a woodcock went skimming through the trees. But after the dreadful affair of the wounded, screaming hare, when I burst into tears and would not and could not stop, he never took me out shooting again until not long before his death when he let me carry a gun (with no cartridges), trained me to do so in such a way as not to be a danger to my neighbours in the field. But he died before teaching me actually to shoot. I have never become an even tolerable shot, except with a rifle, and that not until I was nearly sixty.

I was a disappointment to my father in many ways, but shared to the full his passion for the hills and lakes of Furness. He had been born on the shores of Morecambe Bay within sight of the hills, held himself an exile when in Leeds and, to make up as far as he could for his eldest son's being born in a town, carried me up to the top of Coniston Old Man at such an early age that I think no younger human being can ever have been there. Leeds in those days was a good place for a country-bred professor. My father fished or shot every week-end while he lived there. This was in term-time when he was lecturing five days a week, and busy in the evenings with his working men's club, his Conversation Club and with the ground-work of his history-books. The moment term was over he was off to the North, taking his family with him. Every Long Vacation he was no longer a professor who fished, but a fisherman who wrote history-books in his spare time.

Preparations began long before the end of term. There would be an orgy of fly-tying. My father tied for his friends and for himself the delicate Yorkshire wet flies that T. E. Pritt pictured in his famous book, lightly hackled and dressed on short lengths of fine gut or horsehair. My father was one of the first to introduce Halford's methods in the North and to fish with dry fly, but after a year or so he gave up tying dry flies because he had no time to spare for them and he was himself first of all a wet-fly trout-fisher. Long before the day of the journey the wooden candle-sticks in his study were festooned with new-made casts, his rods were ready, his landing-net mended, an inspection held of our perch-floats, and our shotted casts for perch-fishing hung beside his own. Meanwhile my mother was busy day after day patching and mending our clothes, replacing used half-pans of water-colour (she used to run short of cobalt blue) and buying (we used to remind her) sheets of transfers to keep us happy on the rainy days that we knew, in the Lake District, to be inevitable. A huge supply of ginger-nuts was bought for the train journey. At last came the great moment of Sitting on the Bath. The bath was a large, deep, tin one, painted a mottled orange-brown. It had a flat lid, a staple, a padlock and a huge leather strap over all. The bath, used at Christmas for a bran-pie, stuffed with presents, with a cotton-wool crust that was cut with a monster paper-knife, was now crammed with bedding and clothes that filled it and rose high above it. The lid was pressed down on the top and my mother began to wonder what could be left out. We children climbed on and slid off and climbed again. With the weight of all of us together the lid sank but never far enough. The end of the strap (which at first would not reach so far) was put through its buckle, and mother and nurse gained on it, one hole at a time.

Still, blankets, sheets and underclothes oozed from beneath it and we went officiously about it and about, poking them back. Then, when we had done our utmost one of us was sent down for the cook, a big, cheerful, brawny Armstrong from Northumberland who allowed us in the kitchen but once a year, to wish while we stirred her Christmas pudding with a long-handled spoon, her own huge hands engulfing our small ones and providing the force to drive the spoon round and round through the stiff, currant-spotted mass of uncooked pudding. The cook would wipe her vast forearms, come up to the nursery, laugh at the sight of us waiting, defeated, round the bath, seat herself solidly on the lid and another half-dozen holes were gained in a moment. But even with the weight of Molly Armstrong I can never remember the lid closing far enough to let my mother use the padlock. 'It'll have to do now,' she would say, and that was that.

Then next day there was a hurried run round to say farewell to the hole in the grubby evergreens (Leeds was a smoky city) that only we knew was a robbers' cave. Then came the drive down into Leeds in an old four-wheeled cab, the bulk of the luggage having gone before. The railway journey through the outskirts of Leeds, through smoky Holbeck, past the level crossing that we knew from our 'walks', and on by Wharfedale to Hellifield, my father's gun and rods on the rack, ginger-nuts crunching in our mouths, noses pressed to the windows to watch the dizzying rise and fall of the telegraph wires beside the track, was a long-drawn-out ecstasy, and not for children alone. By the time we reached Arkholme we could feel my father's mounting excitement (he had been pointing out to us one by one the rivers we crossed). At Carnforth we had to change from one train to another unless, as in later years, my father had been able to book an entire 'saloon' carriage for us and our luggage, so that we could sit in it until it was coupled to the other train, on the Furness Railway that we always counted as peculiarly our own. There were well-known landmarks as the train ran slowly round Morecambe Bay. There was the farmhouse that was built like a little fortress against raid-ing Scots. There was Arnside Tower. There were our own Lake hills, and Coniston Old Man with a profile very different from the lofty cone it showed to us at Nibthwaite. Then at last we were at Greenodd, where the Crake and the Leven poured together to the sea not a stone's throw from the railway line. There would be John Swainson from Nibthwaite, or Edward his son, with a red farmcart and a well beloved young lad with a wagonette. We climbed, or were lifted, down to the platform to be greeted by my father's old friend, the station-master, with the latest news of the two rivers. We watched the train go on without us across the bridge and away up the valley of the Leven. Anxiously we watched the loading of the cart, holding our breaths lest the bath should burst its strap before being roped down on the top of all. Then came the slow drive up the valley of the Crake, always halting at the Thurstonville Lodge for a word with the keeper there. Up the winding hill and down again by Lowick Green, over the river at Lowick Bridge, where my father had a look at that streamy water just below, as I have so often had a look sixty years later. We stopped again by a little wooden bridge close to one of my father's favourite places, and again by the Hart Jacksons' cottage, had a glimpse of Allan Tarn, rumbled over Nibthwaite Beck at the entrance to the tiny village, turned to the right up the road to Bethecar, a steep short pull between barn and orchard, for which we all got out, and there we were at the farm, being greeted by Mrs Swainson and her daughters, and getting our first proper sight of the lake itself—Coniston Water.

Tea was always ready for our arrival, and after the long journey we were always made to get that meal over before doing anything else. Then 'May I get down?' and we were free in paradise, sniffing remembered smells as we ran about making sure that familiar things were still in their places. I used first of all to race down to the lake, to the old stone harbour to which, before the Furness Railway built its branch line to Coniston village, boats used to bring their cargoes of copper-ore from the mines on the Old Man. The harbour was a rough stone-built dock, with an old shed or two, and beside it was a shallow cut, perhaps six feet across and twenty long, where the Swainsons' boat, *our* boat, was pulled up half way out of the shallow, clear water which always seemed alive with minnows. I had a private rite to perform. Without letting the others know what I was doing, I had to dip my hand in the water, as a greeting to the beloved lake or as a proof to myself that I had indeed come home. In later years, even as an old man, I have laughed at myself, resolved not to do it, and every time have done it again. If I were able to go back there today, I should feel some discomfort until after coming to the shore of the lake I had felt its coolness on my fingers.

After the solemn secret touching of the lake I had to make sure that other things were as they had been. I used to race back to the farmhouse, to find my father already gone with a rod to the river, my mother and our nurse busy unpacking, and (though the younger ones might be detained) nothing wanted from me except to keep out of the way. I had to make sure that the butter-churn was in its old place, and the grandfather clock in the kitchen still whirring wheezily as it struck the hours. I had to glance into the earth closet in the garden, with its three sociable seats, two for grown-ups and one small one for a baby in the middle, to see that there had been no change in the decoration of its walls. These were papered with pages from *Punch* bearing the mystic word 'charivari' and with pictures from the *Illustrated London News*, including portraits of Mr Gladstone, of whom (after the affair of the yellow ribbon) I was an obstinate supporter. The newspapers, no doubt, had been left by other visitors, and the pictures showing Conservatives and Liberals alike impartially pasted up by the farmer.

Then I had to have a look at the cowsheds, and the hayloft above them, the blue and red haycart, the damson orchard, and from a safe distance the bee-hives and the muckheap in the farmyard that had a top that looked solid but was not, as I had learnt by jumping down on it from the orchard wall. From there it was only a few steps to the beck, and I had to make sure that I could still crawl through under the bridge. Then up to the farm again and through the gate behind it. Through that gate went the rough fell-road to Bethecar and Parkamoor, winding and climbing through a wild country of rock and sheep-cropped grass, purple heather and bracken (much less then than now). Here was the Knickerbockerbreaker, a smooth precipitous rock easy to climb from one side for the pleasure of sliding down its face to the damage of my knickerbockers which, when they were threadbare, kind Annie Swainson used to darn *in situ*. Sharp to the right through the gate a grass track led up the steep sides of Brockbarrow (Badger Hill) and not far up that track was a group of rocks making something like a boat. This we called the Gondola. Seated in it, we could look out high above the lake to the pier on the further side at which the real Gondola called, giving a warning whistle just before it came into view round the trees on the Waterpark promontory. This was a steam vessel, shaped like an Italian gondola, with a serpent figurehead, formally approved by Mr Ruskin who lived at Brantwood and, a legendary figure, was sometimes to be seen slipping furtively off the road, taking refuge behind a tree from the very few strangers who walked along it.

Those holidays at Nibthwaite I owe to my father's passion for the lake country. They bred a similar passion in me that has lasted my life and been the mainspring of the books I have been happiest in writing. Always that country has been 'home', and smoky old Leeds, though well beloved, was never as real as Swainson's farm, Coniston lake and the valley of the Crake. There, in the heavy farm boat, with its oars that worked on pins instead of in row-locks (so that a fisherman could drop them instantly if a pike or a char took his trailed spinner) I learned to be at home on the water. My father had rowed at Oxford and from the beginning taught his children to row with their backs and to regard their arms merely as strings connecting the oars to the part that did the pulling. 'In ... Out! What are you doing with those elbows? ... Keep your eyes on stroke's shoulders ... Now then ... Ten strokes both together ... In! ... Out! ... In! ... Out! ... (Crash!) You again, Arthur!' My feet had slipped off the stretcher or my oar had missed the water and I was on my back with my feet in the air. 'Nothing to howl about. That's catching a crab. Better men than you have caught them before now ... But not two in one day ... Up you get. Go on now. In! ... Out! ... In! ... Out! Easy all!'

There was no end to the pleasures of Nibthwaite. We made friends with the farm animals, with the charcoal-burners who in those days still dwelt in wigwams carefully watching their smok-ing mounds, with the postman, several gamekeepers, several poachers and various fishermen. We took part in the haymaking, turned the butter-churn for Annie Swainson, picked mushrooms and blackberries, tickled trout under the little bridge, went for rare educative walks with my father who, like my grandfather, was a first-rate ornithologist and naturalist (though neither he nor my mother was good on the names of wild flowers). That road along the east side of Coniston lake, now dangerous with motor traffic, was then very little used. I came once upon a red squirrel, rolled up in a ball, fast asleep on a sunny patch in the middle of the road, picked it up to put it in safety and was well bitten for my pains. I also came upon a wounded heron and, knowing no better, took it in my arms and carried it back to Nibthwaite, looking for first aid. I was lucky not to lose an eye. The heron kept stabbing with its long bill, and I suppose I escaped only because I was hold-

ing my patient so tight in my arms that with its head at my
shoulder it could not reach my face.

We used to catch minnows in the little cut where the Swainsons
kept their boat, and we were taken perch-fishing, each of us
watching a float of a different colour. This, of course, was very
different from merely watching someone else catch fish. Then too,
sometimes, when my father was fishing the lake for trout he
would row his whole family up to Peel Island where we landed in
the lovely little harbour at the south end (that some who have
read my books as children may recognise borrowed for the sake of
secrecy to improve an island in another lake). We spent the day as
savages. My mother would settle down to make a sketch in
water-colours. My father, forgetting to eat his sandwiches, would
drift far along the lake-shores, casting his flies and coming back in
the evening with trout in the bottom of the boat for Mrs
Swainson to cook for next day's breakfast.

We had strange visitors at Nibthwaite. There was my father's
pupil Tsau-Chee, the nephew of Theebaw, who had been at the
dinner when Theebaw the King of Burma suspected a plot,
offered his plate to a dog, and, the dog dropping to the ground,
took pistols and shot one after another thirteen (I am not sure of
the number) of his relations who were dining with him, leaving
alive Tsau-Chee alone. I remember Tsau-Chee for his extreme
skill in making paper boats and for his horror when at night he
found one of my furry fox-moth caterpillars crawling across his
cheek. He did not excite the local inhabitants as did my French
nurse, Victorine. She was the daughter of a fishing family from
Boulogne. I had ceased to have a nurse, and Victorine had long
been back in France when a telegram reached my mother at
Nibthwaite from some friends outside Leeds to say that Victorine
had turned up at their door with her six brothers. She had been
devoted to my mother and to her charges and had thought to give
us a joyful surprise. Finding our house in Headingley closed and
shuttered she had remembered our friends at Adel and, undaunted, led the six brothers, all stalwart fishermen, to ask what
she should do. Our friends put them all up for the night and sent
their telegram in the morning. My mother telegraphed back. My
father rowed across the lake to the Gondola Pier and went up to
the Lake Bank Inn to see what could be done. Victorine and her
family were very tall Normans and there was much stir next day
when they arrived, and still more on Sunday when, in Blawith

Church, they greatly interested the congregation. There was an old man in the village who could remember at least the tradition of the boats at Boulogne and Napoleon's threatened invasion and he, after looking at Victorine and her brothers for some time, remarked, 'It'd have been a gey bad job for us if Bonaparte had brought that lot along.' They lived uproariously at Lake Bank and I think my very hard-up parents must have been relieved when they decided it was time to go back to Boulogne and their fishing.

We all knew that though, at Nibthwaite, we were on holiday, my father was hard at work. On wet days this was difficult for him with his children (in the end there were four of us) busy at the table with saucers of water, sheets of paper and transfers. He consequently had to work on many days when he should have been out of doors. His rod stood ready, leaning against the porch and, on likely days, it was our business, playing by the boat-landing (well out of hearing from the house), to watch for the time of the rise. Close to that landing is the place where the river Crake leaves the lake and here in the shallowish water on a calm day, the first signs were to be seen. The water would be as still as glass and then, suddenly, one of us would see rings spreading where a trout had come up and dimpled the surface in taking a fly. One such rise meant nothing. We waited, watching, and if the first was followed by another and then another, we would race off with the news, burst breathless but welcome into the farmhouse parlour where my father sat at work, and he, knowing that if the fish were rising there they would be rising in the river, would leave his papers, take his rod and hurry across the fields to the Crake. Hard worker as he was, he did not waste good fishing-weather on writing history-books. It was on the windless days when the lake was useless that we had to watch for rises while he stayed in the farm to write.

He enjoyed Nibthwaite as much as any of us. He used to shoot grouse and blackcock on the high fells and we used, as beaters, to struggle through the heather and come down through a big larch wood to the lake-shore where, fifty years later, I was to have a cottage. He used to get sea-trout from the Crake, and I can still hear the sudden scream of his reel when, wading in the pool below the bobbin-mill, he hooked a big mort while my mother was sketching on the bank and I was looking at the seething, squirming mass of eels in the eel-coop by the mill.

He enjoyed spinning for pike in Allan Tarn and on the lake and used to put a spaniel ashore, and whistling to it as he drifted along would bring it splashing through the reeds to drive the pike out of their fastnesses into the open water, where they could see his artificial baits, made by himself and painted realistically by my mother. I remember being with him in the boat and rowing when he hooked a very big pike, some twenty pounds, just off the point by Brown How (where there was a kingfisher's nest in a hole in the rock, with a pile of little fish-bones below it). The pike went off at a great pace, pulling the boat after it, so that my father had no chance of making sure it was properly hooked. 'Back-water, you little idiot!' I can hear my father exclaim as, violently rowing, I pulled after the pike instead of holding water, back-watering and making the boat go the other way. However, in spite of my inefficiency, he got that pike and a very good one it was.

With the end of each Long Vacation we had to leave Nibth-waite and go back to Leeds. We stayed to the last possible day in deepening melancholy. The Gondola did not run during the winter and old Captain Hamill (who let me, as a very small boy, steer his noble vessel, standing behind me at the wheel on the top of the long cabin) performed a rite of his own. When for the last time in the year the Gondola left the pier that we could see from the farmhouse windows, he used to sound his whistle, a long last wail of farewell until he was out of sight. It always rained on that day, both indoors and out of doors. The rain would stream down the window outside, and we with our noses pressed against the glass were blinded by our tears. Then came the packing up, a renewed struggle with the bath, and invariably the discovery that somehow we had more luggage than when we came. Friends among lambs and calves, of course, we left behind us. But there were caterpillars, woolly bears, fox-moths, loopers and cinnamons, with their special foods of heather, oak-leaves and groundsel. There would be a minnow or two to join the aquarium on the study bookcase. There would be a lizard caught on the fell behind the farm, and plenty of agile and evasive newts.

People were really very good to us. I remember one year I had packed all my creatures for the journey into a large cardboard box with partitions and smaller boxes within it. At Greenodd station we had to cross the line, and, just as we crossed it, the train from Lakeside already in sight, I slipped and fell, the box opened and all my livestock scattered in the path of the approaching train. 'Oh, my family! My family!' I cried and began desperately collecting them. As fast as I picked up one newt another made off. Caterpillars were crawling in all directions. That noble stationmaster, earning thereby more than sixty years of humble gratitude, instead of ordering a small boy off the line, himself reversed the signals, held up the train on the bridge a few yards away, came back and on all fours helped with the rescue of my menagerie.

# CHAPTER III
## *Various Educators*

Memory picks and chooses. When I think of childhood, Nibth-waite, the lake and the river come first into my mind. But much of my childhood was spent in other places. I remember Clynnog, the Welsh women in their steeple hats, the guillemots on the cliffs, the dragon-tooth shape of the Rivals, the wild Welsh cattle that stampeded on the shore and the silent clegs that made fishing a test of endurance for my father and sent me stampeding like the cattle. I saw the sea (other than Morecambe Bay) for the first time at Filey, and on seeing it, snatched my hand from that of the accompanying aunt, rushed into the water and sat down. But these places were but poor substitutes for the farm and the lake. Days spent at Nibthwaite were days of holiday. Term-time lasted longer. I have written the Nibthwaite chapter first but this chapter should properly be parallel with it. I have written of holidays. Now for education.

My father was a natural educator and a good one. My mother used to tell how on the day after they had became engaged he came to see her and brought with him a volume of Walter Bagehot's essays (her political education having been much neglected in favour of painting in water-colour) and a volume of Wordsworth with certain poems marked, and told her that he looked forward to examining her on both a week later. They spent their honeymoon on the banks of the Eamont, and though my father was fishing and my mother painting ( I have a charming portrait she painted of one of the trout he caught) he brought a box of books with him and any weather bad for fishing was held to be good for study.

He was full of original theories of education, and I as the eldest of his children was a natural subject for experiment. Knowing that in some countries children grow up bilingual, he thought it might be possible to improve on this. I was to learn English,

French and Latin all at the same time. Hence my French nurse, the redoubtable Victorine. I was learning Latin from my father almost as soon as I could speak (I forgot what I had learnt almost at once and it was never any use to me at school). Observing that men and frogs swim in the same way and that tadpoles do not have swimming lessons, it occurred to him that the young human finding itself in water and out of its depth would probably swim by nature. So one day, my mother not being present, he dropped me naked over the side of the boat. The water was not very deep but more than deep enough for me. I went under at once in an agony of terror. He pulled me out with some difficulty and much disappointment. Some time afterwards, back in Leeds, he took me to the swimming baths where, with that horrible experience in my mind, I panicked disgracefully, refused to learn, was taken home in shame and told that next year, at Nibthwaite, I should not be allowed in the boat. I was myself ashamed and, though I would not put myself at the mercy of the all-powerful swimming-instructor, I brooded over my disgrace and secretly spent money given me by an aunt on visits to the swimming baths by myself. Alone, in the shallow end, and with nobody urging me to take my feet off the bottom, I was soon gingerly lifting them, copying the motions of the little frogs I had grown from spawn, and at the end of three visits was able to announce at the dinner-table, 'I can swim.' 'Don't tell lies,' said my father. 'But I really can,' I said and was grimly taken off to the baths to prove the truth. I do not think I ever saw my father more pleased with me than he was that day. (Much later I taught my young brother to swim by the same easy method that I had used in teaching myself. It is, to stand in the water up to the neck, and to lean back till your ears are under water, when miraculously your feet lift from the bottom, and you make your first strokes swimming on your back. Once you have acquired this small pinch of confidence in the supporting power of water, it is easy to take the next step by leaning forward and swimming the other way.)

I cannot remember learning to read, but my father gave me on my fourth birthday a copy of *Robinson Crusoe* as a reward for having myself read it from end to end. Thereafter I read voraciously and very fast, though I have always been able to forget what I have read, retaining, however, a sort of geographical memory that would send me quickly to the right page in the

right book to find something I had half-forgotten but wished to
remember. My father had the same power of rapid reading, with
a much more accurate memory. Thus, when he was at Merton,
studying for a mathematical degree, it occurred to him to sit for
the history examination without other preparation than the
reading he had done in his spare time. He passed with honours
and, thus accidentally, history became his career. He would
otherwise have been a mathematician.

But for his experiments, from which the rest of his family were
exempt, on account of their notable failure when tried on me, I
think he was a very good educator. I always remember the
occasion when one of us, coming to the end of some activity or
other, was heard by him to ask, 'What shall we do now?' His
reply was immediate and final. 'Go to bed. If you have nothing to
do, go to bed and stay there till you have. You will then be the
better able to do it.' After that I cannot remember any of us
asking somebody else to suggest employment or amusement. We
always had more to do than we could find time for. No one tried
to 'amuse the children' except by handing out the transfers that
made us tolerant of wet lake-country days. Our toys were few
and simple and would be despised by the unfortunate children of
today who cannot play without equipment and even uniform. I
remember a 'kid' doll, made of leather with a vapid, blue-eyed,
china face, and a rough wooden railway locomotive with solid
wheels. I could put the doll in the tender and sit myself astride the
yellow, blue-striped boiler and propel myself along the garden
path by the use of my fat legs.

Whenever we were not out of doors we were reading or listening to my mother reading aloud. Fortunately for us my mother
enjoyed this and read extremely well. For one thing, she would
never read aloud to us a book that she did not enjoy reading to
herself. This simple rule, which should be observed by all mothers
who read aloud (and I am sorry for the children of mothers who
do not), saved us from a deal of rubbish. Any book worth reading
by children is also worth reading by grown-up persons. But
children begin by being omnivorous. To them the miracle of
being able to read makes any book miraculous. A course of
second-rate books can blunt that new-found faculty of reading. It
is the more important to protect a child from the overwhelming
flood of imitation books that are poured out each Christmas.
These 'books' cost their authors nothing to produce and can be

turned out at high speed. They do not, as a real book does, become part of a reader's inmost life. They look like books but are not. And grown-up persons who try to read them aloud find that they lose interest in them, cannot read them well, and are never tempted to go on reading longer than they had intended. My mother and her children shared their books together. She was as impatient as we were for the next chapter. We, of course, were always asking her to tell us what was going to happen. She would no more do so than she would allow us to over-eat ourselves on Christmas pudding. Today I have heard a B.B.C. official say that they cannot read a book aloud because children will not wait to hear the story read. They must have so-called 'dramatised versions' which compress thirty chapters into five 'scenes', and offer no more than skeleton plots. People say that a child must have 'free choice'. But how is a child to know the difference between good and bad, if all look alike and he has not by experience of the good so trained his palate as to reject the bad? We were never conscious that the bad was being withheld from us, but in fact it was. I think our parents' principles in this matter were those of Tennyson's Northern Farmer who told his son 'Doänt thou marry for money, but goä wheer money is.' We did not know that we were forbidden to read rubbish but we were given every opportunity of reading the best.

*Holiday House* by Catherine Sinclair, the first of modern 'children's books', we knew at second hand from the story-telling of a favourite aunt. We knew *The Rose and the Ring* very nearly by heart, some of Lear, the two *Alice* books, *Sylvie and Bruno* and *The Hunting of the Snark*. We knew four Kingsleys, several Charlotte Mary Yonges, Mrs Ewing's *A Flat-Iron for a Farthing* and *Jackanapes*, and the whole spectrum of Andrew Lang's fairy books, which I collected one by one at Christmas and on birthdays. *Robinson Crusoe* I have mentioned already, and the three Ballantynes given me by my grandmother. *Treasure Island* we knew and loved, but I remember my father's shocked astonishment when I did not realise that *The Black Arrow* was in comparison a poor machine-made thing. We were lucky in having the *Jungle Books* hot from the press. Henty was never a favourite; his heroes were flat and colourless beside Blackmore's John Ridd and Carver Doone and the lively three-dimensional characters I met in the pages of Scott. My mother read much of Scott aloud to us, and at the same time I was racing through him

for myself at a speed that my father tried to check by cross-
examining me on the book I had been reading before letting me
take the next from that magic shelf. Then, of course, we knew
Andersen, Grimm and *As Pretty as Seven* and Collingwood's
*Thorstein of the Mere*. I remember only one 'comic' and only one
copy of that coming into our house, and that was during a
seaside visit, when a grotesque figure labelled Ally Sloper, on long
stilts, stalked down the street and (I suppose as an advertisement)
handed a copy of the 'comic' of that name through the window of
our upstairs lodgings. We hoped much from the manner of its
arrival, but there was nothing to read in it beside the silly pictures
and we never saw it or wanted to see it again.

I do not think that there was anything in my childhood for
which I have more reason to be grateful than my mother's regular
reading aloud, and the habit of eager reading to myself that her
reading encouraged. In those days it was thought risky to borrow
children's books from a library, because they might have been
read in bed by children suffering from one or other of the usual
maladies and so have become omnibuses for the passage of
microbes from one house to another. The effect of this was good.
We did not have many books, but those we owned we read
again and again, and they improved at each re-reading.

I never attended a kindergarten, though I was an occasional
visitor to one that was regularly attended by my sister and brother
and so learned how to make clay cotton-reels, bird's nests and eggs.
Instead I enjoyed a succession of educators whom I shared with
the son of one of my father's friends. This was Ric, Eric Rucker
Eddison. His father was Octavius Eddison, a Leeds solicitor,
whose saddle-horse I have seen, in those leisurely days, tied up
outside his office in the middle of Leeds. His uncle, Dr John
Eddison, was a friend of Andrew Lang's. Both lived at Adel, a
few miles further out of Leeds than Headingley. Ric was about my
own age. He and I shared first a governess, a kindly, comfortable
Miss Glendinning, who lived by the Shire Oak. The Eddisons'
dog-cart used to take her to Adel, picking up me on the way.
Charles, their coachman, was a stout Yorkshireman. Miss
Glendinning was not thin and I was so solid that there was
scarcely room to wedge me in between them. Charles always
asked me if I had had ham for breakfast, looked grave on the
days when I had not, but said he did not suppose it mattered if I
had put away plenty of bacon. He attributed his own rich growth

to ham and bacon and said there was no need to eat anything else. It was always a sorrow to Charles that Ric in spite of unlimited bacon never properly filled out.

Miss Glendinning was presently succeeded by a long series of unlucky tutors. My friendship with Ric, thus begun in the nursery, lasted until he died during the last war, after a long career in the Board of Trade, and the writing of some very unusual books, *The Worm Ouroboros*, *Styrbiorn the Strong*, other romances and a very fine translation of *Egil's Saga*. *The Worm Ouroboros* was a book of strange power, a story of fantastic heroes in a fantastic world, written in a consistent, fastidious prose that seemed devised for that purpose. The language, the place-names and the names of the heroes were for me an echo of those ancient days when Ric and I produced plays in a toy theatre with card-board actors carrying just such names and eloquent with just such rhetoric. Gorice, Lord Goldry Bluszco, Corinius, Brandoch Daha seemed old friends when I met them nearly forty years later. Ric throughout his life had a foot in each of two worlds, and the staid official of the Board of Trade was for ever turning from his statistics to look out from the towers of Koshtra Belorn. Of us two Ric was always the leader, and throughout our lives the tone of our relationship was exactly what it had been when he was Ric (short not for Eric but for Fredericius) and I was Bony (short for Bonifacius), enacting terrifying scenes in the Adel nursery.

Ric's favourite motto, often quoted in crises of our long war with our tutors, was 'Discretion is the better part of Valour', but he knew how to temper discretion with daring and sometimes showed an ingenuity and a power of assessing the behaviour of grown-up persons that, as a small boy, I looked upon with awe. Consider for example, the sad case of Mr A., one of the long series of tutors who endured for a while and disappeared. Our tutors were of all kinds and Ric dealt with them differently. One or two we really liked, notably a Mr Pegg, who took us to Knaresborough to see the castle and the well whose dripping turned everything to stone. Mr A. we disliked extremely and Ric decided to get rid of him. His plan depended on accurate timing and a knowledge of his mother's views on education. We knew at what time Mrs Eddison would be going upstairs to dress for a tea-party. That was enough, if she would be punctual, and she usually was. Ric and I sat down to arithmetic, one on each side of the table in the nursery with the victim-tutor sitting between us at the head of the table. Ric became more and more annoying, with a long series of stupidities, echoed by me, until we could feel that the tutor was at the point of explosion. A glance at the clock. The time had come. We simultaneously bombarded the poor tutor with idiocies until at last, outraged beyond bearing, he rose in wrath, smote right and left and brought both his pupils toppling, chairs and all, to the nursery floor. There was no need for us to raise the piteous wail we had in readiness. Steps were running up the stairs. The door opened and there was Mrs Eddison looking at the field of battle. Mr A. left that afternoon.

Then there was the defeat of Mr B. He, in contrast with the departed disciplinarian, believed in being a boy among boys. In advance of his time, he tried to give work the character of play. Thus after breakfast we ran out into the garden, whence with appropriate noises he 'hunted' us in to our lessons. Ric bided his time. There came a day when Ric's parents and mine were to go away for some short visit to friends, I was to sleep at Adel and the tutor was to be in sole charge. Ric made his preparations beforehand. The parents departed. Next morning the usual 'hunt' began but this time instead of allowing ourselves to be driven in to work, we slipped out of the garden, through a coppice and made for the road. 'Gone away!' shouted the young man, hiding his annoyance when at last he saw us in the distance. We were moving at a steady trot, and the tutor soon gave up all pretence of play and roared at us to come back. By that time we had crossed a wall, were out of sight and were making for a famous rock on Adel Moor. There was one way only of climbing the perpendicular side of this rock. We reached the top just in time, rapped the tutor's knuckles when he tried to follow us, and spent the day there in comfort. The tutor waited below, telling us we would come down soon enough when we wanted our dinner. In the middle of the day we opened a tin box and ate sandwiches, cake and lemonade. Ric politely offered a sandwich to the tutor. Late that night as it was growing dark, and we had had a second meal, the unfortunate Mr B. said that if we would come down and go home with him he would refrain from telling our parents what we had done. Ric's moment had come. 'Not so, O Paleface,' he observed. 'We will come down, but there shall be no seeking of revenge. Else, O Paleface, we ourselves shall tell our elders when they return. If, on the other hand, all is Peace between us, Peace it shall be and none shall ever know of our victory. Think well,

O Paleface.' There was a long silence. Ric had calculated with diabolical cunning. The tutor could not disclose our villainy without exposing his own incompetence, which would also be exposed if we were to confess. His face reddened. He capitulated and with spirit. 'So be it, you disgusting little brutes.'

'No insults between honourable foes,' said Ric.

'Peace, O Braves,' said the young man with a laugh.

'Honest Injun?' said Ric, doubting his own success.

'Honest Injun!' said the tutor. 'But for goodness' sake hurry up.'

We came down from the rock, gave the tutor a last bottle of lemonade from our store, which he drank gladly, having had nothing since breakfast. We walked home together in silence, except that the tutor asked, 'Tell me one thing. How long had you been planning all this?'

'Many moons,' said Ric.

'I see,' said the tutor. 'It is wrong to treat you as children. I shall treat you as men. No more hunting to lessons. I shall expect to find you in the schoolroom at nine each day and no nonsense about it.'

That night we decided that the Paleface had behaved well. He had no more trouble with us, but I think that Mrs Eddison, observing our now notable regularity at lessons, suspected that we had been treated brutally during her absence.

It should not be supposed that I was any better than Ric. There were those who had reason to think that I was, if possible, worse. I had a vindictive dislike of grown-up persons, however kindly, who tried to be witty at my expense (by asking, for example, 'Who was the father of Zebedee's children?'). There was in Leeds a lecturer on agriculture called Archibald, the kindliest of men, whom we knew both in the lakes and at home. He was remarkable for the gleaming baldness of his head. He rashly, coming on me feeding my guinea-pigs, asked 'Do you know that if you pick a guinea-pig up by its tail, its eyes will drop out?' I had been asked that question before. I looked up at him innocently. 'Mr Archibald,' I said, 'if anyone were to lift you up by your hair, would *your* eyes drop out?' and the next moment was fleeing for my life. I think any unprejudiced observer would have said that Ric and I were a pair of horrid little boys, and that it was high time we were sent to school.

# CHAPTER IV

## *First Schooldays*

My first school was a day-school, half way between Headingley and what was then the Yorkshire College. I reached it by tram but could sometimes, by running, save my penny fare. I remember little of it except a kindly, intelligent master, a hymn-tune, and that, until I left, it had never occurred to me that learning was an unpleasant form of toil. The school was not interested in games. We assembled there in order to learn. When lessons were over we returned to our homes. Each day began with morning prayers and the singing of a hymn to the accompaniment of a loud but wheezy harmonium. 'Rock of Ages' was the hymn I liked. The word 'rock' was enough to bring me a picture of Brockbarrow and the crags and rocky slopes I knew behind the farm at Nibthwaite. No doubt for some quite different reason it was a favourite hymn of the headmaster's. We sang it often and the day was made for me when the headmaster announced its number in the hymn-book, read the first line and stood silent while the harmonium wheezed out the tune alone before beginning again when we joined it with our voices. I remember too some sort of a celebration at the end of a term, when, after the elder boys had let their parents see Macbeth slaughtered (with a rattling affair at single-stick between him and Macduff), the very small boys had their chance and, as the Mad Hatter, I helped to put the Dormouse (now an admiral) into the tea-pot (a well-disguised bath) at the Mad Hatter's famous party.

But I was not at that school for long. My father, still anxious to give me as much as possible of a lake-country background to make up for being born in a town, sent me to a boarding school at Windermere. Another reason for choosing this particular school was that an aunt of his lived at Windermere, and a third reason may have been that when he met the headmaster they were able to forget less interesting topics and talk about the river Bela which they both fished.

The school was the Old College at Windermere to which, in preparation for the great public schools, went many of the young sons of the lake country families. There were Machells and a Gandy and some Staverts from Kendal, the lake country leaven of a mixed lot of boys from Carlisle and the manufacturing districts of South Lancashire. Some were the sons of rich men. Others, such as myself, were not. A few of the sons of the rich, who went fishing in Norway with the headmaster in their holidays, were naturally on a different footing from the rest of us. I was the only small boy with an academic father whose books were beginning to find their way through the schools and universities. Much was expected of me, and expected in vain. It may have been a good school for some boys. It was not so for me. Work here was not learning but merely the anxious avoidance of punishment. I do not suppose I really knew less when I left that school than when I first went there. A worse thing had happened. I had lost the power of eager learning for its own sake, and was not to recover it until, many years later, with school behind me and earning my own living, I set about educating myself. All I got from that school was a reading, spread over several years, of the second book of Virgil's *Aeneid*, passages of which I still remember, like that of the serpents coming over the waves to wrestle with Laocoön and his sons, or that of the breathless moment when Laocoön has hurled his spear against the hollow, reverberating belly of the wooden horse,

> 'stetit illa tremens, uteroque recusso
> Insonuere cavae gemitumque dedere cavernae'.

Another line from that passage was to serve me in good stead at Rugby when a master, enraged by some enormity of forgetfulness or absent-mindedness, said, 'You will come round to my house at two o'clock when I will give you something to remember.'

'Quicquid id est timeo,' I muttered to myself, 'Danaos et dona ferentes.'

'What?' he exclaimed. 'Say that again.'

I repeated it and he burst into a roar of laughter.

'All right,' he said. 'I see the classics are not wholly wasted on you. I'll let you off for that.' Thenceforward he looked on me with an indulgent eye.

At the Old College, as at the school on Headingley Hill, the headmaster had a favourite hymn, 'Sun of my soul, thou saviour dear'. We sang it often and when his father, who was Vicar of Milnthorpe by the river Bela, died and the whole school was taken by train to Milnthorpe to see him buried, the headmaster, with tears on his cheeks, told us it had been his father's favourite hymn also, made us practise it the night before and, next day, much moved, we sang it at his father's funeral. In those days there was a Bible Reading Society, joined by the whole school, and its members were given printed cards showing a passage to be read for each day of the year. These I enjoyed, and came to know the fine prose of the Authorised Version very well.

Apart from the Bible, the school took no interest in our reading, except by setting us a holiday task, chosen, I suspect, chiefly to impress our parents. I made up for lack of books at school by reading voraciously in the holidays everything except the book set for holiday reading which, except once, was always left for the last few desperate, melancholy days. The exception was Carlyle's *French Revolution*, set as a holiday task when I was eleven or twelve, perhaps because my father had edited Carlyle's *Frederick the Great*. For some reason I dipped into this early and, having dipped, went in head over ears, read and re-read, and, when set to write an essay on it after coming back to school, stopped only when the headmaster said I had written ten times more than I should and cut off the supply of paper. I was thankful to Carlyle thirty years later when, with no knowledge or experience of politics, I found myself in the middle of the Russian Revolution and had not only to observe but also to explain, at least to myself, what was going on under my eyes. The only book that I read for pleasure in term-time was Rolf Boldrewood's *Robbery under Arms*, brought to school by one of the other boys and of particular interest to me because my maternal grandfather, though, unfortunately, not a bushranger, had spent much of his life on the very ranges where Starlight and the Morgans did their desperate deeds and I, alone in the school, had seen a blackfellow's boomerang and even thrown one.

I was extremely miserable at that school. I had no such friend there as Ric, and was so lonely that on the one occasion when I heard a kind word there, as the headmaster's wife, passing me on the stairs, patted my head and said 'Cheer up, old man,' I was speechless with surprise and had to run to the water-closet to hide the tears I knew to be ridiculous. My parents had no suspicion

that all was not well. Once a week we were given time to write a
letter home. For this we sat at our desk, with a master sitting at his
or walking round to see that we were writing legibly. My letters,
whether read or not, were in danger of inspection. They nearly
always echoed the approved sentence, 'I am very happy', and
usually went on with gossip about white mice or with news of
walks to vantage-points on Orrest Head or on the road to Troutbeck from which I had been able to see, in the distance, the hills
that I had seen from Nibthwaite. Small boys are reticent and
resilient and, not knowing the world, are ready to make the best
of it. When parents receive letters from their sons beginning 'I am
very happy' they must not be too sure that their sons are living in
Elysium.

I was fortunate in many ways. The first of these was that the
hills were there, so that I could always remind myself that the
much-loved Coniston valley was not so very far away. The
second piece of good fortune was the presence in Windermere of
my great-aunt Susan. There had been two of these great-aunts,
Aunt Susan and Aunt Mary, and sometimes we had gone from
Leeds to Harrogate to visit them when they were taking the
waters. I saw my first Punch and Judy Show on the Stray at
Harrogate, and at Christmas time there as the cover was lifted
from the turkey I asked what that large bird was and was told by
Aunt Mary 'a Harrogate sparrow'. Now Aunt Mary had died and
Aunt Susan lived in one of three small houses known as the
Terrace, above the railway station, on the Windermere-Kendal
road. Some people would not have chosen to live within such
close reach of the sound and smoke of the trains. But my great-
aunt, daughter of the Manchester surgeon, was living on railway
dividends (it seems odd today to think that her shares in the
London and North Western Railway were once upon a time most
profitable) and, as she said, she liked the smoke and the noise
because out of that smoke and noise came her bread and butter.
So she lived there with her ancient maid, Mary Jane Robinson,
and kept a proprietary eye on the railway just below her garden.

Across the road from the Terrace was Rigg's Hotel, from
which, daily, the coaches drove off with their four horses, horns
blowing, and drivers and guards in scarlet, a splendid sight. And
one of the drivers was a relation of Mary Jane's, 'Red Coat
Robinson', and he sometimes was to be seen and even to be
spoken to, great man as he was, sitting over a cup of something

warm in Mary Jane's kitchen, where she used to make toffee for me. There was also a tortoise in the backyard and at one time a hedgehog. I was allowed to go up to the Terrace for Sunday dinner after going to church at St Mary's where, sitting in the school pews with the others, I could see Aunt Susan and tell myself throughout the service that I should presently be walking with her up to the Terrace, miraculously for a few hours *not at school*. Sometimes on special occasions she obtained leave for me to come to see her during the week. She was a spirited old lady. I remember coming in one day when she was playing hymn-tunes on the piano. Suddenly she struck a wrong note and the next moment with resounding crashes she brought down all ten fingers on the keys, again and again, with repeated volleys of sound, all the way down the keyboard from the treble to the bass, when with a final thunder of the lowest notes she looked up, saw my startled face in the doorway and sat there laughing at herself.

As long as she could scramble on the fells she could never resist the call of a fox-hunt. She was a great toxophilite and in dark green uniform with tabs and tassels, quiver and longbow, used to take part in the archery meetings on Belle Isle, the long island that stretches across the mouth of Bowness Bay. She had an old Tompion chiming clock in an ornate case of gilt and turtle-shell which she told me was one day to be mine (it is chiming as I write this) and no one was allowed to wind it except the clock-maker from Kendal, who used to come once a week for that purpose, when he was refreshed after his labours by being given a glass of sherry, carried into the dining-room by Mary Jane and set beside him on a small tray. School was wiped clean off the slate of my mind when I was with Aunt Susan, and, friends as she and I always were, I said not a word to her of the unhappiness that began again as soon as I left her gate and went, usually late and on the run, as if I were eager to be back, down the hill to the Old College.

Even from that grim time at school there are things that I like to remember. Windermere was a village in those days and from the Old College down to the lake-shore were wild coppice-woods where now are innumerable houses. In those woods, even on an official 'walk', it was possible for a moment or two to be alone, invisible among the undergrowth. I used to listen for the music of a beck that wound its way down these woods with many little waterfalls. Lingering dangerously I used to listen for it again to see if I could still hear it and then run hastily after the others. Even at school I was still able to collect caterpillars and food for them and to watch them until they turned into chrysalises and, long afterwards, to hear a fluttering in the cardboard box in which they slept and opening the box to see the new-born butterflies and moths almost as if I were at home. I remember tickling trout in a beck that ran through a field beside the road between Windermere and Staveley. I learned to play, not too well, upon the penny whistle and this came in useful long afterwards. I am still glad to have known the old drill sergeant who came once a week to teach us elementary gymnastics. He used to reward favoured pupils by throwing open his shirt to show the scar left by an assegai in the Zulu war, and, when urging us to hold our heads up and put our shoulders back, he always referred to Sir Garnet Wolseley. 'As Sir Garnet says to me, a British soldier should always walk as if one side of the street belonged to him and he expected the other shortly.'

Best of all I had the great good fortune to be at school at Windermere in February 1895 at the time of the Great Frost, when for week after week the lake was frozen from end to end. Then indeed we were lucky in our headmaster, who liked skating and wisely decided that as we were not likely to have such an experience again (the lake freezes over only about once in every thirty-five years), we had better make the most of it. Lessons became perfunctory. After breakfast, day after day, provisions were piled on a big toboggan and we ran it from the Old College to the steep hill down into Bowness when we tallied on to ropes astern of it to hold it back and prevent it from crashing into the hotel at the bottom. During those happy weeks we spent the whole day on the ice, leaving the steely lake only at dusk when fires were already burning and torches lit and our elders carried lanterns as they skated and shot about like fire-flies. I saw a coach and four drive across the ice, and the roasting of an ox (I think) on Bowness Bay. I saw perch frozen in the ice, preserved as if in glass beneath my feet. Further, here was one activity in which I was not markedly worse than any of the other boys. On a frozen lake in the grounds of the three Miss Fords at Adel, a kindly foreigner, Prince Kropotkin, had guided my infant footsteps. I had learnt to move on skates and was thus better off than most of the boys who had never skated at all. Those weeks of clear ice with that background of snow-covered, sunlit, blue-shadowed hills were, forty years after, to give me a book called *Winter Holiday* for which I have a sort of tenderness.

In later life I have had many friends but I had none at the Old College. One reason for this was that I cut a contemptible figure at all games. I have never been very good at games, though I have enormously enjoyed them. But until my first terms at Rugby had been made miserable in the same way it was not discovered that I was so short-sighted as to be almost blind to detail unless very near. I have never been able without spectacles to see the eyes of a man talking to me except as vague blurs. Such eyesight is no hindrance to the enjoyment of landscape, nor yet to reading and the detailed examination of things near by. But, to take one example, to be unable to see your opponent's eye in a fight is to be absolutely at his mercy. Our headmaster was a muscular Christian. He had been a good boxer himself and loved nothing better than to pick a brace of small boys, fit them with boxing gloves and teach them the elements of self-defence. When I was thus set to battle, it meant merely that I was continually battered in the face, blow after blow coming which I could not foresee or counter in any way. I could do nothing but stand up to be battered. No great damage can be done by a small boy wearing boxing gloves but there is something dreadful in not being able even to try to parry blows of which you know nothing until they land one after another on your eyes and nose. I saw no worse when my eyes were bunged up and used to welcome the bleeding of my nose because as the blood poured down, my turn at fighting came to an end, so that I could use a handkerchief and save my clothes. The headmaster called me a coward. The other boys jeered at me and knowing my utter inability to retaliate used to attack me at any odd moment just for fun. It was the same at football, when I seldom saw the ball until it landed in my face. It was worst of all at cricket, a game which, once these early horrors were forgotten, has given me a great deal of pleasure. Obviously, if a boy cannot see a ball, he cannot hit it. He cannot catch it, nor is he likely even to stop it unless by painful accident. The headmaster, disgusted at my fielding failures, set himself to cure me. He made me stand while he threw a cricket ball at me again and again, other boys laughing at my frantic efforts, jeering when the ball hit me, fielding it themselves and throwing it back to my tormentor to try me with it again. He meant well, I have no doubt,

and did not for a moment suspect that he was throwing cricket
balls at a blind boy. I nearly went off my head and next day ran
away from school.

It was not a very good example of running away. I did not run
away romantically, to join a ship and go to sea. I did not run to
seek a refuge among friends, for I had none within reach. I did
not try to go home, or even to my dear great-aunt for, much as I
loved her, I knew very well that in the matter of running away
not even she would be on my side. I merely ran away, without
any thought of destination. I ran away over the Kirkstone Pass,
taking the turn to the right off the Windermere–Ambleside road,
trudging blindly through the Troutbeck valley, climbing up and
up the steep, winding road and at last, very tired, passing at the
summit of the pass the Traveller's Rest, no rest for me, the old inn
that claims to be the highest in England, and so on and down the
other side between the enormous hills into country I had never
seen. My only idea was to keep going. Tired right out, I was still
trudging like a machine when my running away was brought to
an end by the sight of a coach climbing up towards the pass from
Ullswater. Hitherto, at sight or sound of other people, I had
slipped off the road and hidden till they went by. Here there was
no bracken in which to hide, no trees, and I was too tired to do
anything but keep on walking. The coach moving slowly up the
steep came to meet me. A shout came from the red-coated driver
on the box-seat. It was my friend Red Coat Robinson. He asked
me where I was away to and I could not tell him because I did not
know. 'Tha'd better climb oop here, lad,' he said, making room
for me beside him, and I had not the strength to refuse. My
running away was over and I came back to Windermere on the
box-seat of the Ullswater coach. I cannot remember my coming
back to the Old College. I do remember, however, that I suffered
no punishment. Nothing was said to me. No questions were
asked. Neither my parents nor my aunt were ever informed of
what had happened. It was almost as if, without Ric's conscious
strategy, I had in blind misery done something that if reported
might be double-edged and cut both ways. For a long time I
expected a terrible vengeance. It never came.

During my first years at the Old College, my father, fishing or
writing his history-books according to the weather, still took us
all to Nibthwaite for the summer holidays. It was fishing that
brought those lake-country holidays to an end and cost my father

his life. Late one night, after fishing for sea-trout in the dark, he climbed, with a heavy basket, from a pool by the bobbin-mill, caught his foot under an old grindstone and fell forward over it. From what I heard afterwards I think he must have fainted. On coming to, he felt sure from the extreme pain that he had sprained his ankle and that he had better force himself to use it lest it should so stiffen as to spoil the rest of his holiday. He fished on and then, in an agony of pain, walked back to Nibthwaite with his catch. Next day the foot was badly swollen. It never grew better. For a long time he walked with crutches, the foot monstrously bandaged. The doctors were slow in finding what had happened, probably because my father was so sure himself. In the end they found that he had damaged a bone and that some form of tuberculosis had attacked the damaged place. His foot was cut off. Things grew no better and his leg was cut off at the knee. Even that was not enough and it was cut off at the thigh.

For some years after the accident Father refused to be defeated. He could no longer walk ploughed fields after partridges so he bought an old tricycle, rigged it with a gun-rest on the handlebars and driving it along with one foot still shot an occasional bird. He gave up grouse-shooting except from a butt, whereas in old days he most enjoyed walking the birds up, alone with his dog. He went on fishing, but wading, even after he had his cork leg, was difficult for him. He was very hard to stop. He went on going to Nibthwaite and I well remember lying in the boat off a bank of reeds to retrieve wild duck after which my father was wading from the shore. I heard a shout and a sudden splashing and saw an artificial leg waving above the reed-tops. It had come off and my father was standing on one leg in the water, with his gun in one hand and his leg in the other, calling me to bring the boat into the reeds for him. That must have been in his last summer at Nibthwaite and I never went there again until I was earning my own living and went there by myself.

I suppose my father must have written to the Old College asking about my prospects of a scholarship. He can never have suspected how absolutely those years at school had been wasted. The headmaster picked another boy and me from among the rest and did his best to prepare us for examination. He was a good classical scholar himself and, as I said before, I am still grateful to him for the second book of the *Aeneid*. This other boy and I laboured over paper after paper from previous examinations. We were told of likely questions the examiner might ask, but unluckily of none so simple as the one that floored me. We were taken to Shrewsbury to sit for the examination and when I saw the boys rowing on the river I badly wanted to do well and win a scholarship to a school where boys could row instead of playing cricket. Rowing I knew something about. Alas, after we came out from the examination-room with the papers of questions, the headmaster glanced hurriedly through them. 'Not too bad. Not too bad. You'll have done all right with this. Superlative of parvus?' My heart sank. 'Parvus, minor, minimus.' I knew it perfectly well, but in my anxiety I had trusted to general principles and knew that in my answer to that question I had written 'Parvissimus'. 'No scholarship for you here,' said the headmaster, and of course he was right.

My next and last attempt to win a scholarship was at Rugby, where there were particular reasons why I wished to do well. My father's old schoolfellow, Robert Whitelaw, was a housemaster there and, partly on his advice, my father had resigned from his chair at Leeds so as to be nearer London and free for political work. He was only forty-six, was making a considerable income from his history-books which were used in schools all over the world, was writing political articles, was to have been temporarily a sixth-form tutor at Rugby and was eagerly looking forward to a political career. He refused to recognise that even the amputation of his leg had failed to save him. He had already moved to Rugby when his illness suddenly grew much worse and when I came there to sit for the scholarship he was laying in bed desperately ill. I went into his room to see him and knew how much he hoped that I would win it.

There were a hundred and two competitors for the nine or ten scholarships and we sat for the examination in New Big School. I stayed not with my father and mother but in Whitelaw's house, where I met for the first time Ted Scott and his elder brother John, who was very kind to both Ted and me. More than twenty years later we three were to be closely associated on the *Manchester Guardian*. Next day a list of the first hundred competitors was pinned up on the door of the school, the scholarship winners at the top of the list. Having a modest (and rightly so) estimate of my learning and having learnt by this time that no matter how well I might know a subject I always did badly under examination, I began reading that list at the bottom, where I expected to see my name. It was not there. By the time I had come half way up the list and had not found it, an incredulous hope began to dawn. Could I, after all have done better than I feared? I read on, higher and higher, name after name, until, in growing excitement, I had reached those names beside which were printed the scholarships that had been awarded to their owners. Hardly able to breathe I read on until I came to the very top of the list and knew the dreadful truth. I had not won a scholarship. I was not even in the first hundred but was either No. 101 or No. 102, one of the pair protected by a merciful anonymity from knowing who was last of all.

I went miserably back to Windermere and there, a few weeks later, the headmaster's wife came to me in the dormitory over the gateway in the old square tower that used to rock in high winds. She sat down on my bed and told me that I should not see my father again. He was dead and I lay and wept with my head under the bedclothes. I have been learning ever since how much I lost in him. He had been disappointed in me, but I have often thought what friends we could have been had he not died so young. There were years after his death during which I took no interest in sport of any kind and indeed had not a day to spare from reading and writing and the walking that served both, but later my ancestors began to have their way with me, and by the time I was thirty fishing had become what it has remained, one of the passions of my life. It has been a delight to me to fish the waters he fished, because he fished them.

# CHAPTER V

# *Rugby*

Next day I was given a black tie and a packet of sandwiches and put in the train to go to Rugby where my father had died. My mother and he had already moved into the house in which he had meant to live during the new life that had been opening before him. It was a pleasant little house on the outskirts of the town, on the Clifton Road, not far from the cemetery. My mother was in no state to attend the funeral. My brother and sisters were thought too young. I walked alone behind my father's coffin which, carried by six of his friends of unequal height, lurched horribly on its way. As the earth rattled on the lid of the coffin I stood horrified at myself, knowing that with my very real sorrow, because I had liked and admired my father, was mixed a feeling of relief. This did not last. After the funeral more than one of my father's friends thought it well to remind me that I was now the head of the family with a heavy responsibility towards my mother and the younger ones. And my mother, feeling that she had to fill my father's place and determining to carry out his wishes now as when he was alive, told me (though I knew only too well already) of my father's fears for my character and her hopes that from now on I should remember to set a good example to my brother and sisters.

My greatest piece of good fortune in coming to Rugby was that I passed so low into the school (Lower Middle II) that I came at once into the hands of a most remarkable man whom I might otherwise never have met. This was Dr W. H. D. Rouse, who, on leaving Rugby, became headmaster of the Perse School at Cambridge. He had a background different from that of most Rugby masters. Born in India, besides being a great classical scholar, he was a translator from the Sanskrit, a collector of Eastern folklore, who amused himself in his spare moments by putting English songs and shanties into Latin and Greek, spent his holidays

52

practising modern Greek with the fishermen of the Aegean in
whose boats he sailed, and was not content to tug the young
dolts of Lower Middle II through the elements of Greek and Latin
grammar but took every opportunity to give them an interest in
the language that was their own. Every now and then he would
read us a poem or a passage from a book and then set us to write
something of the kind.

On one of these occasions he read us the ballad of King John
and the Abbot of Canterbury and gave us a week in which to
write a version of the story for ourselves. My father had read me
that ballad more than once and I knew it nearly by heart, so, with
great enjoyment, I produced a pretty accurate imitation of it and
even of its metre. Rouse read it, called me up to his desk and
asked if I had copied it from a book. I told him I had not, but that
I had known it for a long time. How had I come to know it? I
told him my father had read it to me out of an old book. Had I
got the book still? I told him No, but I thought my mother
would know where it was. He asked to see it, and, after a long
search at home, the book was found, a brown leather collection
of such things, not Percy's. He was much interested in the book
and from that time had a special eye for me. Then one day he read
us a chapter from Sir John Mandeville and set us to write what we
thought Sir John might have written if in the course of his travels
he had skipped a few centuries and come to Rugby on a half-
holiday and seen a game of football in the Close. He made me
unpopular in Lower Middle II by reading aloud my account of the
battle with 'ye pumpkin', chuckling from time to time as he read.
He made himself unpopular with my mother when, happening to
meet her, he told her that he thought she had a son who was going
to be a writer. He invited me to his house for tea and talked about
books. He forgave my incapacity for Latin grammar and Latin
prose because I justified him by doing reasonably well whenever
my task was not to turn English into Latin but to turn Latin into
English. When I was ill in bed he brought me armfuls of books.
He saw nothing wrong in my determination some day to write
books myself, and to the dismay of my mother did everything he
could to help me.

I spent a term or two as a day-boy before Robert Whitelaw,
my father's old friend, found room for me in his house. This gave
Rouse opportunities of helping me that he would not otherwise
have had. There was some incompatibility between Rouse and

Whitelaw, both great schoolmasters, great classical scholars and great lovers of English literature. Rouse, I think, was a Tory, Whitelaw a Liberal. This may or may not have affected their mutual relations. In one way or another they were out of sympathy, and when Rouse rashly urged that I should be given every chance of becoming a writer, my horrified mother appealed to Whitelaw who, knowing something of my father's fears, would probably have agreed with her even if he had not been predisposed to disagree with Rouse. After I became a boarder in Whitelaw's house, and had moved into another form, I naturally did not see Rouse so often, but our friendship lasted for over half a century.

I owe it to Rouse, and to a mathematical master who remarked to him that I seemed unable to read a figure on the blackboard without coming to peer at it, that at long last it was discovered something was seriously wrong with my eyesight. I do not know when it began to go bad. My eyes, judging from a crayon portrait of a bulbous baby, and from a photograph showing Ric and myself and one of our unfortunate tutors, looked like the eyes of normal folk. There was nothing to suggest that there was anything wrong. I had no difficulty in reading (it was not until I was nearing fifty that, as I came to need stronger glasses for seeing my dry fly at a distance, I came to need quite other glasses while knotting that same fly to my cast). I could see hills far away and could usually tell a blackbird from a thrush. My mother was very young and came from a long-sighted family where spectacles were unknown. I was her first child and she was so soon occupied with new babies and with my father's illness that it naturally never occurred to her that I might be short-sighted. My father wore spectacles only for reading and frequently forgot them. I remember them not on his nose but as an object that lay about on his table. I could not complain for I had no means of knowing that my eyesight was not the same as other people's. Anyhow my blindness brought with me to Rugby the same unhappiness that it had made for me at Windermere. My schoolfellows soon discovered that if attacked I put up only a ridiculous and ineffective defence and I suffered accordingly. Cricket was a misery even after I had been given spectacles, because I was slow in focussing and was, besides, nervous of having them broken. Oddly enough, though useless as a bat, I came to like fielding and became a fair catch particularly in the deep field, where I had time to see and to judge the course of the ball. Bad player though I was, I came to take great pleasure in squash, rackets and fives, learnt to juggle with three balls at once, and even now, though I have only once made a break of over thirty and call that a Red Letter Day on which, with the help of lucky accidents, I make a break of twenty, I will go a long way for the pleasure of a game of billiards. At Rugby football my eyes hampered me much less than at association, the game we played at Windermere. A moving boy is an easier thing for a blind boy to intercept than a moving ball. I loved the game, played in the scrum, and did in the end scrape into my House Fifteen. I mention these things by way of showing that it was not a dislike of games but actual blindness that gave me a reputation for general muffishness from which it took me long to recover. I remember when I came into Big School, wearing my new glasses for the first time, my tormentors gathered round and one of them said, 'You think that we'll stop ragging you because you are wearing those things. You're jolly well mistaken.' My glasses were broken times without number, often by myself. I had to take them off for swimming, and then was so blind that unless I had been able to put them in a very safe place I had to beg somebody to find them for me, and more than once trod on them while looking for them. My blindness, when discovered and reported by Rouse, did a good turn to the rest of the family, who were from that day taken regularly to the oculist.

Whitelaw's House is still called after him who was one of the most notable teachers of his generation. The boys who spent their time at Rugby in that house were very fortunate. A house depends to an extraordinary degree on its elder boys, and they cannot but reflect something of the man in whose care they have grown to their estate. There were houses at Rugby, as at other schools, where the housemaster was no more than a hostile power of which the boys were wary, houses in which, if only for this reason, he was a mere jailor completely out of touch with his prisoners. This was not so at Bob's. His nickname itself was affectionate and extended to include his family. There was Bob and there was Ma Bob (kind but not very efficient) and his two daughters, known as the Dolls. We had nothing to do with Ma Bob and the Dolls, except when we were invited to take a meal with them in Bob's part of the house, but we liked and laughed at them just as we liked and laughed (affectionately always but by no means openly) at dear old Bob with his Bantam bicycle and his long-drawn-out emphasis on the 'Who' when, on Sunday evenings, he read aloud to us '*Who* is the happy warrior, *who* is he?' I missed much by never reaching 'the Twenty' that was his special form, next below the Sixth, but it is something to have been in his house.

Our part of the house was joined by a passage to the quarters of the Bobs. We were a self-contained community, living in studies round a quadrangle, sleeping in large dormitories, feeding in a great refectory on the walls of which in black lettering on the panelling were the names of those of our precursors and contemporaries who had distinguished themselves in the school. My own name, I may say, was never in the slightest proximity to such honour. There was a changing-room downstairs where we put on our football clothes and shed them muddy on coming in from the playing fields. There were some bathrooms upstairs but here, downstairs by the changing-room, was a row of cubicles with loose tin tubs in them, where we washed off the dirt after our games and took cold baths daily, emptying each his tub with a pleasing splash after use. High above the quadrangle there was a 'pupil-room' where members of the sixth form administered rough justice with a cane. In the pupil-room, thanks to Bob, there was a very tolerable library which we were allowed to use freely, in addition to the splendid school library which was housed in a building of its own with a statue before it (unveiled while I was there) of the author of *Tom Brown's Schooldays*, a work of which it was fashionable to hold a low opinion on account of its obvious inaccuracies. There was a buttery with a serving-hatch through which a butler served mugs of beer when I first went there, though shandygaff was already the more popular drink.

The system of fagging, now I think modified, was then in full swing. It was not really oppressive, though a small boy might be unlucky in his fag-master who, however, was restrained from serious tyranny by the public opinion of his peers. Boys in the lower forms were all liable to fagging, and were severally allotted to individual members of the sixth form. I was extremely lucky in being the slave of R. H. Tawney, then Head of the House, who afterwards became an economist, author of *The Acquisitive Society* and one of the leading theoreticians of the Labour Party. I dusted his study with a feather brush, blacked his boots, made the toast for his tea and lit his fire for him, this last an accomplishment that has been of the greatest use to me in many parts of the world. I must say that I found him an admirable employer of labour. The worst point about fagging was that any member of the sixth form could at any moment lean from the high balcony or put his head out of his study window and yell 'Faaag!' whereupon all we underlings in our studies on the ground floor had to leave whatever we were doing and dash out into the quadrangle. The last one out had to run on whatever errand the great man chose to send him. It seemed to me that I was nearly always last, in spite of arranging my study with all the furniture on one side so that my partner and I had a clear fairway to the door.

I think Bob himself chose the partners who were to share a study, though if we had a choice of our own he usually agreed to it. For the most part there were two of us to a study. I never rose high enough in the school to have a study of my own. My first companion was a dull boy of whom I remember little but a visit, rather unwilling on his part, to the Lilbourne Steeplechases. There we saw and were seen by the school marshal who with a curiously doubtful eye watched us being helped by a bevy of bookmakers to start home on a tandem bicycle which we were unable to mount alone. He did not speak to us, nor did he report us afterwards, and I have since thought that his presence at the races would have displeased the authorities as much as our own. Later I shared a study with H. R. Ricardo, now Sir Harry and a Fellow of the Royal Society, whose name is on the Kelvin-Ricardo engine. Even in those days he was dreaming of and drawing designs for dirigible torpedoes. He and I used the school workshops together, he being the leading spirit. We made a small gas-engine, an electric motor and a very minute triple-expansion steam-engine. Geoffrey Scott, another boy of my age in White-law's house, intended to be a writer and became one, but he went quickly up the school and was rightly contemptuous of my early experiments. There was also Geoffrey Scott's cousin, E. T. Scott, the son of C. P. Scott of the *Manchester Guardian*. I was friendly with Ted Scott at Rugby though he moved quickly up the school and I did not. His elder brother John won the famous Crick Run. This was a very long run, of some eleven miles, for which no boy was allowed to enter without medical examination. Ted and I, privately and consulting no doctors, did on one occasion do the run by ourselves. I remember this every time I pass through the Crick Tunnel on the way to or from the north, because, having come so far, we added to the interest of our run by going down the side of the railway cutting and into the tunnel itself. Years afterwards, when I wrote for the *Manchester Guardian*, Ted Scott became one of the best and closest friends I ever had.

Another scientist in the house beside the ingenious Ricardo was Lester, a quiet, aloof fellow who, though no higher in the school, had been lucky enough to be given a study to himself. Chemistry was his passion, and his study stank like a laboratory. I shared, as a spectator, in one of his experiments when, following the instructions of a book, he made nitro-glycerine in a test-tube and, having made it, did not know how to get rid of it. We dared not put the test-tube down, for fear a slight jar might detonate it and destroy Bob's house and all in it. We took turns in holding it until the time came to go down to school. We waited till all the others had left the house and then, expecting every moment to be blown up, poured the stuff gingerly down a drain in the Hillmorton Road and ran for our lives to take our places in form. It was a sultry day of summer and about half way through that lesson the windows of the room were shaken by a single, sudden clap of thunder. Lester and I glanced at each other with white faces. I well remember our relief when, on coming out of school and looking anxiously up the road, we saw people going quietly about their business, no crowd, no hurrying sightseers, no volcanic crater anywhere and Bob's house standing where we had left it. I have often wondered what Lester did in after life. He may, like so many others, have been killed in France. I have not found his name among those of the scientists who, in exactly the spirit in which he, dreading the results, made nitro-glycerine, are busily engaged in playing atomic tricks that may in the end destroy the world and shake the balance of the universe.

After I had lived down the memory of the time that was made miserable for me by my undetected blindness, I had what I can best describe as tolerable years at Rugby. I moved very slowly through the lower school, perhaps because while always deeply interested in something I so seldom happened to be interested in the work I was supposed to do. I joined the Natural History Society and, as one of the 'bug-hunters', was sometimes excused from cricket, going on botanical expeditions with 'Puff' Cummings, the senior science master, and searching for fossils in the new cuttings that were then being made for the Great Central Railway. In the school Natural History Museum there are (or were) enormous ammonites dug up there and laboriously brought back by one who might perhaps have been better employed.

Bicycle expeditions took me more than once to Lutterworth Church to see the wonderful fresco of the Judgment Day on the wall behind the altar. Visiting ancient buildings I used to note happily those on which I found the bear and ragged staff, the insignia of Warwick the Kingmaker. Memories of Walter Scott took me to the rather disappointing ruins of Kenilworth Castle. And the intense delight in visible things (that was never impaired by my short-sightedness), the delight that had given me the best-remembered moments of my childhood, was still mine as a schoolboy. The long evening shadows of the great elms in the Close, a blue butterfly seen one summer holiday on the top of Roundaway Down above that enormous Wiltshire landscape, a glade in a wood at Brinklow, joined the crowding snowflakes outside the nursery window at Leeds and scene after scene at Nibthwaite, like things kept as it were in store that I could and did take out of my memory to look at instead of the lesson-book on my desk. This bad habit of absorption in anything other than the work that was my immediate duty has persisted all my life, and I have been most unjustly rewarded for it. I have been allowed, for example, to put into my books my pleasure in the sailing and fishing that have taken so many of the hours that should have been spent in other ways, and so have been able both to enjoy my cake and to keep it.

At school, forgetful, absent-minded though not exactly idle because though I neglected my work it was always because I was busy with something else, I progressed so slowly and showed so little promise that it was small wonder my unwavering conviction that I was going to be a writer seemed as absurd to my masters (with the exception of Rouse) as to my contemporaries who were, one and all, my betters, even, now that I was no longer in Rouse's form, in English composition. The thing was ridiculous and I remember a junior master coming to my study and asking, 'What is all this about you wanting to write? What are you doing about it?' 'Reading the classics,' said I in self-defence. He looked at the book lying open on my table. It happened to be *Pickwick Papers*. 'Classics! Faugh!' said he in disgust and went out. It was perhaps an unlucky choice. But no matter. I had been reading since I was four years old and for my age I had read a very great deal. One term we had worked, slab by slab, so many lines to a lesson, through a book of *The Faerie Queene* and I had gone plunging on by myself to the neglect of other things. I had read a good deal of Shakespeare, a good deal of Carlyle, a lot of Stevenson, and every book of folk tales I had been able to get hold of. My Greek grammar was hopeless but I was taking great delight in the limpid Greek of the New Testament. In the school library I rushed eagerly through one book of exploration after another. At home I had my father's library on which to draw and joined my brother and sisters to listen to my mother's reading aloud. I suppose I was learning something all the time but I had nothing to show for it and had not the sense to keep my ambitions to myself. When asked what I was going to be I always gave the same answer, and always it raised a laugh from those who knew my position in the school and cost me endless ragging, besides discomfort at home.

My mother had inherited my father's fears lest I should turn out as irresponsible as my grandfather, and thought writing a profession likely to bring out the worst in me. Further, my father had written many educational books, but he had managed to do this in what time he could spare from his regular work as a professor or from shooting and fishing. My mother was horrified at the idea of my thinking of writing as a sole means of making a living. One of her sisters had written several novels, and this Aunt Helen, who towards the end of her life was my great friend and valued critic of my children's books, was brought in to make me see sense. 'Knowing how to write will be useful to you whatever you do,' she told me, 'but you are the eldest son and your first aim must be as soon as possible to be earning your own living. Choose any work you will and make a living by it, but do not dream of writing except in your spare time.' My mother thought it was wicked of Rouse to encourage my mistaken ambitions and appealed from him to Bob Whitelaw. Bob's weight was added to that of everybody else. Any small signs of intelligence I had shown were in science and in my engineering with the young Ricardo. A boy who was going to write would at my age be near the top of the school. And again, I must remember that it was my duty to begin to earn as soon as I could. Rouse's offer to make a special effort to prepare me for Oxford was not accepted. There was no smallest likelihood of my winning a scholarship. Life at Oxford was costly. My mother could not be asked to keep me there while I prepared for what? for a profession that guaranteed no regular income. In the face of all this I weakened and agreed, as a second best, to become a scientist.

The result of this was that in my last year at Rugby, after struggling into the Lower Fifth, I joined a small group of so-called 'specialists' and began to make some progress in mathematics. If Latin and Greek grammar, at which I was bad, were essential to a writer, mathematics, at which I was equally bad, were essential to a scientist. Now at Rugby, on the classical side, mathematics were taught in 'sets' which did not correspond to the 'forms' where our places depended on our Latin and Greek. I was in the bottom set but one. A. E. Donkin was consulted, a really fine mathematical teacher, and he saw a chance of showing a spectacular example of what could be done. I was as keen as he, worked as I had never worked before and, running always ahead of our programme, was translated in two terms from the depths to the heights, from the dull valleys of elementary arithmetic to the

in air of differential calculus and the binomial
ow which of us was the more delighted. This
cience seem more reasonable, although in my
ing a magazine mostly written by myself and
ith the proceeds of which I bought a copy of
oems and (hedging) a good little book on
also made a humiliating first appearance in
ia died. I had, from my earliest years, had a
because our copy of Jules Verne's *Journey to
h* (of which I shared her high opinion) had
my father and inscribed in her own hand. I
e of earnest doggerel at the suggestion of the
rked it into the local newspaper and paid me
lay, working in my study, I heard a noise of
ngle, and recognised the tune of 'We'll all
it was some minutes before with hot cheeks
that the words that were being sung to that
se of my funereal verses. That was early in
ch forward in history that jerked us from the
the Duke of Wellington into the modern
e by the death of the Queen, the Jameson
t and the sight of two Rugby masters stand-
e school gateway and looking together at an
*ly Mail.*

the Lower Fifth. We spent the summer

holidays that year at Scarborough. I worked very hard to make ready for matriculation at Leeds and to everybody's astonishment, my own most of all, I passed in the first division, thanks I believe to doing well in precisely those subjects that had least importance for one who was supposed to be setting out on a scientific career.

# CHAPTER VI

## *Leeds Revisited*

Going to the Yorkshire College at Leeds (it did not become an independent university till after I had left) meant that for the first time in my life I was not conscious of a surrounding atmosphere of doubt or disapproval. This emancipation was immediate. For some weeks I stayed in the house of Miss Baines who was an old friend of my family, and also a relation of Talbot Baines Reed, who saw nothing wrong in my wanting to write books. She and her sister had a good library, and I had a free run of it. Later I shared lodgings with a worthy young cousin who was to be an engineer and regarded all books other than technical ones as so much waste of time. But to offset this there was Mrs Bruce at Meanwood, who had been very kind to me as a small boy, and was no less of a friend to me as a young man. Her husband had been a bibliophile and she gave me books on book-collecting and never thought of reminding me that I had come to Leeds for any other purpose than that of reading for its own sake. Presently I was in lodgings alone, with pictures of Tennyson, Browning and Carlyle on the walls, reading and writing until late at night and working in the College laboratory or attending lectures during the day.

At Leeds there were two notable professors; Smithells who had become famous for his ingenious method of analysing the different parts of a candle-flame, and Stroud, Professor of Physics, who presently left his chair to develop, as a partner in the firm of Barr and Stroud, his inventions of range-finding telescopes, to which gunnery and photography are alike indebted. I sat under these famous men and enjoyed their lectures but found the mathematical teaching less interesting than that of A. E. Donkin at Rugby. I enjoyed working in the chemical laboratory with blowpipes, bunsen-burners, test-tubes and retorts. Outside the College buildings, however, my determination to accept the second best and become some sort of scientist rapidly weakened.

My old affection for the dirty, smoky town of my birth awoke in all its strength. I was free to enjoy the fog, the busy streets and the open country so near by. I was free in a new sense. There were good bookshops in Leeds and my allowance of pocket money, that would have been ridiculously inadequate at Oxford, allowed me, who had no expensive tastes, to buy books, cheap ones, without disapproval from anyone. And in those days books were indeed cheap. At the secondhand booksellers treasure was waiting to be trove at a penny or twopence a volume. New editions of famous books were to be bought at one-and-six a volume in the Scott Library, a shilling in Morley's Universal. A shilling a week spent on books soon meant a respectable collection.

I was free in other ways also. Thomas Arnold's spirit was still strong at Rugby in my day and we were made to go to chapel far too often. My father had made a regular practice of taking his family to church on Sunday, partly, as my mother told me much later, because he thought it good for the cook and the housemaid, but, in spite of one or two parson-uncles for whom he had great respect and the horde of parson-cousins for whom he had very little, he had not been in any sense a bigoted Anglican, and I remembered being taken by him once to the Unitarian chapel near Leeds Town Hall and hearing from him of Joseph Priestley. Seeing that building made me visit it again, when it came into my head that there were more forms of religion than the one I had known at Rugby. I set myself to make a pilgrimage, going every Sunday to a different place of worship, Unitarian, Wesleyan, Congregationalist, Church of England, Baptist and, in deference to my Quaker ancestors, to a meeting place of the Friends. Here I had an unfortunate experience. I liked the decent quiet of the meeting until one of the Friends thought he was inspired to speak. I think he was mistaken. He stood up and grasping the back of a pew and shaking it so that it rattled, he shouted 'God the Father! God the Father!' again and again and very fast until he suddenly collapsed, choking for breath, with a froth of white foam about his lips. I suppose I might attend a thousand Quaker meetings without witnessing anything so horrifying or so unseemly.

Free from the tyranny of the Arnold tradition in the matter of church-going, I was also free from that of organised games. Instead I indulged a delight in walking which lasted until over-exertion with a heavy pack in 1912 brought long-distance walking to an end for me.

The decisive moment found me in the College library. I had gone there from the laboratory to consult a book on mensuration or magnetism, and happening on some shelves where the books were classified not by their subjects but by the names of their authors I saw two tall brown volumes with richly gilt lettering and decoration on their backs: J. W. Mackail's *Life of William Morris*. I began dipping into one of them, sat down with it and never went back to the laboratory that day. I read entranced of the lives of the young Morris and his friends, of lives in which nothing seemed to matter except the making of lovely things and the making of a world to match them. I took the books home with me, walking on air, across Woodhouse Moor, in a thick Leeds fog, and had read them through before I went to bed. No second-best choice would satisfy me now. Nothing would change my mind. Nothing should stop me. From that moment, I suppose, my fate was decided, and any chance I had ever had of a smooth career in academic or applied science was gone for ever. For days after that I moved in a dream, reading that book again and again.

But I did not at first know what to do. I was no rich man's son who could live the life Morris had lived. Nothing could excuse me from the need as soon as possible to earn my own living. But I no longer thought of science as a means to that end. I had to find a way of earning a living that would allow me at the same time somehow or other to learn to write. I knew very well that I had everything to learn. It did not occur to me to brave the criticism that would have greeted a proposal that in default of Oxford I should move over from the faculty of Science at Leeds to that of Arts. I could excuse the collapse of my resolve to please my mother by becoming a scientist only by showing that, by going some other way, I should even sooner cease to be a burden on my family.

For the better part of two terms things dragged on so. I was working as hard as I have ever worked, but not at science. I was writing and reading, reading and writing, and my landlady exclaimed at the frequency with which she had to empty my waste-paper basket. With extreme lack of practical sense my choice of form was that least likely to bring a financial reward. I had a passion for William Hazlitt and, to balance my admiration for his athletic discursive prose, had never lost my childhood's passion for fairy stories. I wanted to write essays. I wanted to write tales for children. There was no great demand for either in

3

Leeds in 1901. And in any case I still had to learn how to write them. Thinking of writing plays, I went once or twice to the sixpenny seats at the Leeds theatres, and to the pantomime to see how that was made and whether it would not be possible to write one that should not be so rough with the story. But it seemed to me that with so little money to spend it was better to buy books which outlasted an evening, and I began at Leeds the practice of saving money on food in order to spend it on books which, while I was still a young man, gave me a good library and a damaged stomach. A Leeds weekly magazine the very name of which I forget printed some small rubbish that I wrote, and I did at last bring myself to ask for an interview with Mr Phillips, the editor of the *Yorkshire Post*, for which my father had written occasional articles. The Phillipses had at one time been our next-door neighbours in Headingley. Mr Phillips received me at the editorial office in a pungent atmosphere of raw apples. He was in the habit of eating them while at work. He opened a drawer in his desk, took one himself, and offered one to me, and we sat there eating apples while he warned me wisely against attempting journalism until I was a great deal older, with a university degree. He suggested that I should come to see him again in five years' time. Meanwhile he offered me another apple, showed me that his drawer was full of them, and solemnly advised them, raw, as an aid to composition.

Mackail's *Life of Morris* had sent me not only to *The Defence of Guenevere* and the *Volsunga Saga* but also to *News from Nowhere* which brought about an odd tea-party that might have altered my life but did not. The girl-students at the College were mostly training as school-teachers. Among them were two chemistry students, Zelda Kahn and Sophie Cardoza. I had never spoken to them, but one day they stopped me in the corridor, said they had seen the book on my bench in the laboratory and supposed that I too was a socialist. Had I read Robert Blatchford? They lent me *Britain for the British* and for a week or two I bought a copy of the weekly *Clarion*. They asked me to tea with them. I went to their lodgings and their grim landlady brought in the tea and TWO boiled eggs. Of course I said I did not eat eggs, whereupon they said that they did not either and we solemnly ate bread and butter while the eggs cooled. I hope they were eaten after I had gone. Both parties to this encounter were very shy and except at a distance I saw no more of the two young socialist propagandists.

If it had not been for those unlucky eggs we might have become friends and I might, as early as 1901, have met some of the revolutionary leaders I was to meet for the first time in Russia in 1917. In those old days when she was a student at Leeds, Zelda Kahn was in close touch with the group of Russian revolutionaries who were living in exile in London. But for those eggs I might have met them then, and gone to Russia with a mind politically less blank. But in 1901 and for many years after that I should have been astounded to learn that I should ever have to take part in politics. In those days in England it was still possible for a young writer to regard contemporary politics as a matter for the politicians.

The problem of my immediate future was solved in an unexpected manner. It became clear to me that I was going to do badly in the Intermediate Examinations. I did not want to disgrace my father's name in Leeds where it was so rightly respected. Something had to be done at once. I must immediately produce an alternative to a scientific training that would both offer a livelihood and at least indirectly lead towards writing. Mr Phillips had wisely told me not to go into a newspaper office. In any case daily journalism seemed to have no sort of common ground with the life of William Morris, even if it had with the life of William Hazlitt. Books had, and, surprised that I had not thought of this before, I went one day to a bookseller's in Briggate and asked him who were the best of the new publishers. He mentioned two or three, of whom one, Grant Richards, was publishing the World's Classics. For months one volume in that series, Hazlitt's *Table Talk*, had never been out of my pocket except when I was reading it, or at night when, as a sort of magic rite, I kept it by my bedside and, after reading, put my spectacles on it to keep watch over it and, in a sense, to go on reading it while I slept. That afternoon in the College library I wrote, rewrote, copied and copied again a careful letter to Mr Grant Richards, telling him my age, my interests, what education I had had, and asking if he would employ me among books in any capacity whatsoever. I dropped that letter in the pillar box outside, not daring to put off posting it lest it should not get posted at all. I felt I had burnt my boats. I was extremely frightened, but thought it might not be answered, in which case I could think things over again. But Mr Richards answered my letter and said that I had better come to see him. This brought about an immediate crisis. I had to tell my mother. She took it much better than I had expected. For this there were a number of reasons, the most influential of which was that publishing was not mere writing but a very respectable business. My father's and mother's oldest friends were the Maurice Macmillans. My mother also knew Septimus Rivington and the Longmans. All three firms, Macmillan, Rivington and Longmans, had published some of the educational books that were now the main source of my mother's income. All that she had seen of publishers predisposed her in their favour. Further, if I were to be employed in a publisher's office, the risk of an unsatisfactory university career would be at an end. Again, if I wanted to be among books I could, as a publisher, be among them without having to live by writing them. Finally, the lease of the house at Rugby was shortly coming to an end. My brother had gone into Whitelaw's where, starting in the school at the point at which I had left, he was doing very well. There was nothing to keep her at Rugby. My elder sister, then at finishing school in Paris, wished to be an artist and could attend a studio in London. From all points of view London would be a better centre, and if I were to work there as a clerk in a publisher's office I should be able to live at home. My mother sent me the money for a return ticket to London and urged me to put on my best suit of clothes.

Mr Richards, a young man of twenty-nine, was established in highly ornamental offices in Leicester Square, accurately described in Arnold Bennett's *A Great Man* as the offices of Onions Winter. It was on the side of Leicester Square opposite the Alhambra and from it one had a good view of the statue of Shakespeare pensively surveying the Empire Music Hall. A green tiled arch crossed the front of it, with a door on the left and a lattice window where Mr Richards's latest books were displayed filling the rest of the arch. He had begun young as a publisher and had already scored some considerable successes. He was an extremely well-dressed and elegant creature. His business was expanding fast and he had a use for some cheap young men. He lolled back in his chair and, fingering my letter, asked why, among all the publishers in London, I had chosen to write to him. I produced from my pocket my copy of Hazlitt's *Table Talk*. He asked a few questions about what other books I had been reading, considered a moment and then said, 'In my office you will have a chance of learning the whole business of publishing. That may be worth something to you. I cannot tell what you may be worth to me, but if you like to come here and begin at the bottom I shall pay you eight shillings a week.' I was for accepting there and then, but he said that I must first consult my mother. I went back to Leeds in a whirl of enthusiasm. The critical step had been taken. My mother went to town to stay with friends. She called on Mr Richards and was charmed by him. His offer was accepted and, within a year of leaving Rugby, I had become a London office-boy with a salary of eight shillings a week. After all, it is a great deal better to be paid to learn publishing than to pay to learn to be a scientist when you want to be something else. My mother was quite pleased and I had been intoxicated by the smell of the books fresh from the binders, and of the great stacks of printed sheets fresh from the printers that seemed to fill every floor of Mr Richards's offices. My university career was over, not to reopen for more than half a century.

# CHAPTER VII

## *Office-boy in London*

When I first came to London I lived for some time in a house in Clapham together with half a dozen young men who, slightly my seniors, did not have to leave Clapham so early as I on their way to work. I was often at Leicester Square by half past eight or very little later. I enjoyed that time. After an early breakfast I put on my new bowler hat, the symbol of my calling (my top hat I had danced on, the day I left Rugby) and set out on a delightful slow journey by horse-drawn omnibus, from Clapham down to Chelsea Bridge, and so, changing sometimes to a green Piccadilly omnibus, sometimes to a yellow Camden Town one, came at last, usually at a run, to Leicester Square. Let it not be thought that I was a privileged apprentice. Far from it. I was at first put under Mr Bailey, the chief clerk, and was set to writing invoices and told to improve my handwriting. But I was ship's boy and had to lend a hand wherever wanted. When new books were going out in bulk I worked as a packer and learned to make a parcel with the proper knack, write labels by the thousand, check books against invoices and finally stagger to the post under those smaller parcels that were not taken away by Carter Paterson. Mine also was the job of saving postage by delivering parcels by hand to booksellers between the Monument and Knightsbridge. I welcomed these journeys and came to know the city very well. It was marked for me by bookshops as the sea is marked by buoys. At the lunch-hour on days when the others were too busy to go out, it was my job to go to a public house round the corner and bring back two plates of 'meat and two veg' and two pints of beer for the two chief clerks. I found a way of carrying all this at once in my two hands and took great pride in never having dropped a tankard or broken a plate. Then, about six o'clock (sometimes much later), I would be driving home again, sitting whenever I could beside the driver with whom I was usually on most friendly terms. I used to plan on the omnibus what I would write that night. All the time I was writing, writing, and throwing away the rubbish that I wrote.

Office-boy and errand-boy alike, I soon knew quite a number of authors by sight. I was sometimes sent to collect a manuscript. It was thus that I met M. P. Shiel for the first time, in a lodging in Guilford Street, where he was sitting on a chair in the middle of a bedroom, writing on a pad and throwing down the sheets as he wrote them to be picked up and put into order by a young woman who was sitting on the floor keeping a baby quiet. I joined her on the floor and waited, watching Shiel and thinking of Balzac. Shiel stopped at last and gave me the bundle of manuscript for which the printers were waiting. Incredibly he said, 'No time to talk now (I had not said a word), but you can come and see me again.' In this way began an odd acquaintanceship that lasted many years, not without its surprises, as when he invited me to supper on a prosperous day when he had about a dozen guests and was living in a handsome flat. Without preamble of any kind he said, 'I want to introduce you to my sister.' I turned to see beside me a smiling negress. I sat next to her at the supper-table and while Shiel was, as usual, discoursing on philosophy, she painted for me a delightful picture of Shiel and herself, small children sitting on an island under a palm-tree, hidden among the leaves of which, in a tin box, he kept his precious manuscripts. I do not to this day know the truth about Shiel's ancestry, but he had in him something of the flamboyant turbulence of the elder Dumas and, like Dumas, he may have owed something to Africa. At the time I met him he had outgrown the period when he had been one of John Lane's young men writing stories in elaborate prose such as *Prince Zaleski* or *Shapes in the Fire*; he was writing serial stories at great length for *Pearson's*, *Tit-Bits* and such magazines, each chapter ending with a crisis 'to be continued in our next', so that when he prepared them for publication as books he had to disguise as best he could the concessions he had made to please his editors. The best of his books have a queer, flickering light in them, occasional volcanic power and an originality that lifts them high out of the morass of popular melodrama. *The Purple Cloud*, in which all mankind is destroyed except a prisoner in a dungeon in Stamboul and a girl drifting alone in a ship — something like that — is a good example. Gollancz was printing a complete edition before Shiel died, but it came to an abrupt end when Gollancz found that Shiel had signed his agreements with complete disregard of other agreements whereby the copyrights belonged to somebody else.

The family with whom I lodged at Clapham were the Comptons and were, I believe, in some way related both to me and to the famous Comptons of the Compton Comedy Company, the parents of Compton Mackenzie. But I did not meet him until much later. While I was working as packer, clerk, porter, errand-boy and juggler with the clerks' meals, he was beginning his more glorious career at Magdalen. The other lodgers in the house at Clapham were young men of serious purpose, and their chief care was to do nothing that was not 'good form'. Some of them looked oddly down their noses when I told joyfully of my mid-day errands to the tavern by Leicester Square. There were in that house occasional tickets for free seats when the Compton Company were playing in a suburban theatre, and I think it was one of those tickets that let me see *The School for Scandal* for the first time. But such occasions were rare. I read on my way to and from Leicester Square. I read until my eyes closed at night, and very few evenings passed without my trying to write something, even if it was no more than a description of driving up Piccadilly into a sunset over Hyde Park Corner. One day, one of the young men, a clerk in a shipping office, asked to see what I was writing. He read it and looked at me with pity. 'I say,' he said, 'if you think anybody is ever going to *pay* you for stuff like this, you're mis-taken. You'd much better chuck it. Why not do fretwork instead? Then you'd have something to show for all the time you're wasting.'

He spoke in vain, though he was right about the rubbish I was writing. But William Hazlitt was much more real to me than any of those young men. And by that time I had with great daring been to see a cousin, a living poet, Laurence Binyon, whose *London Visions* I had bought for myself. Binyon had been extremely kind to the dumb young animal I was. He had given me dinner and afterwards had taken me to the Westminster Hotel and given me my first lesson in billiards. It seems odd, now, to think of Binyon teaching anybody billiards. I suspect that, baffled by his tongue-tied young cousin, he took me to the billiard-room in desperation. A slight difference in age lessens as one grows older but seems enormous at seventeen. We became friendly a few years later, but after that first kindly billiard-

lesson the shyness that was an impediment to me in many other
ways would not allow me to call on him again until I had a
clearer reason for doing so than my admiration for his poetry.
It was long before he knew that walking out of town (as I
sometimes did) I used to make a detour through the little streets
of that island of quiet that lies behind the Abbey, to see the light
in his window and to think of him in there at work.

My book-buying went on, mainly from the penny and two-
penny boxes in the Charing Cross Road. Also, as an office-boy
employed by the firm, I was able to buy for next to nothing shop-
soiled or damaged copies of books returned by the booksellers
and, of course, had my early pick of any books that were
'remaindered'. Mr Richards had many good books on his list that
came to be sold in this way. I remember buying *The Wallet of
Kai Lung*, *Erewhon* and a lovely edition of Sir Thomas Browne.
In the office I paid eightpence apiece for the World's Classics,
whereas they were published at a shilling. I was given breakfast
and supper in my lodgings but had to provide my own mid-
day meal. I did not succeed in doing without it altogether in order
to buy books but came near it. After bringing in the two pints and
the plates of 'meat and two veg' for the clerks I used to buy myself a chicken croquette, which cost twopence, or two bananas
from a barrow in Great Pulteney Street which sold them at a
penny-halfpenny the two. My drink, when I was not content
with water, was coffee from a stall at a penny the cup. My life
was certainly very different from that of Rugby. My contemporaries there were going on to Oxford and Cambridge
while I was working in London and earning perhaps as much as
what they would have thought impossibly meagre pocket-
money. Now and then, as a bowler-hatted office-boy laden with
parcels, or sitting on the backboard of a van delivering books on
publication day (which I much enjoyed), I used to see one or
other of them on the London pavements, wearing school or
college ties, going to Lord's, perhaps, for the Rugby-Marlborough
match. None ever recognised me and I should not have known
what to say to any who had.

Hours were long even in normal times. The office was under-
staffed and prosperous. On the busiest days I used to stay there
invoicing and packing till as late as eight or even nine o'clock.
There was no payment for overtime, which, since I was determined to show I had been right in coming to London, I looked

upon almost as a privilege, though I do remember once in the Christmas rush when we were working very late indeed, being given a shilling by the chief clerk and told to go and get myself some food and not dawdle about it. I think I can claim to have been a good office-boy, for within a few months of my arrival in Leicester Square I was being given my share of much more responsible work. My lately acquired mathematics were found useful and it was discovered that I could make the necessary calculations in ordering paper. I became familiar with a new vocabulary — 'laid' and 'wove', 'deckle-edged', 'octavo', 'quarto', 'crown', 'duodecimo' and 'foolscap' — and was presently hurrying through Long Acre to Spalding & Hodge's to discuss the paper for a new book, or being sent to Bain's to explain just what we wanted to see in the way of samples for bindings. I could 'cast off' a manuscript and say how many pages it would fill if set up from one fount of type and how many if set up from another.

At this point I suggested to Mr Richards's manager that as I was now doing a clerk's work, and more than that of a clerk, it might be thought that I deserved a higher salary than that of an errand-boy. But by that time two other young men had been put into Mr Richards's office to learn the business and the manager pointed out that I was fortunate in learning so much more than they and that I ought not to expect a rise in salary until I had been there at least a year. I cannot remember whether or not he did in the end raise my pay to ten shillings a week. He certainly raised it no higher and I, ungratefully conscious that I was already doing a man's work and giving to it much more time than I was paid for, was slightly disappointed.

In Cecil Court, St Martin's Lane, there were several shops with new and secondhand books in the windows and, after eating my mid-day croquette, I often had a look at them instead of those in the Charing Cross Road, on my way back to Leicester Square. One of these shops was devoted to theosophy, philosophy, spiritualism and kindred subjects, and it was here that I bought a very well printed and edited American edition of Hume's *Essay on the Human Understanding* which delighted me and continued to delight me for many years. There were at least three publishers in the Court. On one side of it was a firm called Greening, whose main stock-in-trade was novels, some of which were described as 'sensational'. On the other side was a firm that published popular technical and scientific periodicals. A few doors along was the

Unicorn Press which displayed in its window several volumes of poetry and books illustrating the work of famous painters and engravers. This firm had published my cousin Binyon's *Odes*. One day I saw in the window a notice saying that 'An Assistant' was wanted. There could be no harm in asking about it, so I went in and met for the first time Mr Ernest Oldmeadow, a short, stout, beady-eyed little man with an odd air of lay-brotherhood. I learned afterwards that he had been a Nonconformist minister. He later became a wine-merchant, a writer of popular novels, a music-critic, a restaurant proprietor and, after conversion to Roman Catholicism, a successful and respected editor of the *Tablet*, almost the official journal of that Church in England.

At the time I saw that notice in his window he had had none of these successes and was finding it more difficult than I at first realised to keep the Unicorn Press from crashing through the very thin financial ice that was supporting it. Even so, he had in a very high degree the manner of success. Handicapped from the start by lack of money, the Unicorn Press had had very good intentions. It had published, under Oldmeadow's editorship, a number of volumes of the *Dome*, in the tradition of the *Yellow Book*, the *Savoy* and the *Pageant*. It had published books of verse by Oldmeadow himself, Wilfrid Wilson Gibson, Gordon Bottomley, Sturge Moore and others. It was publishing critical well-illustrated books on the brothers Van Eyck, Hokusai, Leonardo da Vinci and the engravings of Altdorfer. It seemed that I was just the assistant he had been looking for, and he offered me a pound a week. I tried to disguise my astonishment. He did not ask for an immediate decision. I had not yet spoken, or until that day even thought, of leaving Grant Richards and I wanted also to ask the advice of Binyon who, since the Unicorn Press had published a book of his, could probably tell me something about the firm. I saw Binyon, who said that he thought very well of them as publishers. I then saw the manager at Grant Richards's, who said that I was a fool to think of leaving but wrote me out a testimonial which I still keep as a proof that I was an efficient office-boy. I gave formal notice and so, after some six months as office-boy in Leicester Square, found myself earning a more than doubled salary as general factotum in Cecil Court.

Mr Richards's manager was, of course, right. If I had indeed been hoping to be a publisher, I had made a bad mistake. In the office of the Unicorn Press was none of the eager rush and bustle of a busy firm pouring out books of all kinds. I had slipped out of the tide into a quiet, almost stagnant backwater, of no use whatever to a future publisher but of very great use to me. Its overhead expenses were small but, even so, it was not publishing enough books to build up the turnover needed by even the smallest of such firms. The permanent staff consisted of Oldmeadow, myself and a small Cockney errand-boy. When Oldmeadow wanted to make a great show of activity, Mrs Oldmeadow used to come down from their flat in St Martin's Lane and spend a few hours at the opposite side of my table. There was a small inner office with room for a table and two chairs, where Oldmeadow used to interview authors and write the music-criticisms that were, I feel sure, more profitable than the publishing. In front of that was the main office, no more than the front part of a small shop. Out of that had been cut a minute lobby (standing-room for two), with a frosted glass door and at one side a sliding ticket-window through which we issued books to the rare buyers and could inspect visitors and decide whether or not to let them in. Visitors who came with manuscripts and a wish to talk about their possible publication were always admitted with ceremony and dealt with by Oldmeadow himself. The admission of visitors whose work the Press had already published depended on circumstances. Poets are oddly eager to be printed and some, I learned, pay hopefully for the publication of their books, their payments to come back to them as a share of the profits, if profits there are. I knew little of accounting but my natural interest in what was going on was balked at every turn by the entries or the lack of them in the large red ledger that was supposed to record the costs of every book. The other ledger, that showed the daily sales, if any, was kept by me and did accurately tell what money was coming in, but I do not think that Oldmeadow himself knew the cost of production of any of the books he published. However, he had not that manner of success for nothing. I have known a visitor come storming through the outer door and rage so powerfully through the *guichet* that some knowledge of a pending crisis reached the inner office without help from me. I have seen Oldmeadow come out and, like a practised doctor dealing with a mental patient, shepherd the raging one into the inner room and close the door behind them. I have heard the tones of rage soften and turn at last to quiet talk. And then I have seen the door open and Oldmeadow and the visitor come out, chatting like old friends, and been a little startled at hearing Oldmeadow say, pointing to the vast red ledgers, 'You need have no worry at all about the accounts; Mr Ransome is in charge of them,' and seen the visitor, who had come in like a lion, go out the mildest and happiest of lambs. I did not realise at first, as I did later, that the firm lived under an almost continual threat of disaster. All I knew was that though some of the books seemed to have no sale at all, some of the others, that had very small sales, were books that I was proud to think we published. I did my best to sell them and sometimes surprised Oldmeadow by persuading booksellers to order 'seven as six and a half' or even 'thirteen as twelve' of books of which he had hardly expected them to take more than one or two. But these propagandist excursions were few and for the most part I had little to do beyond being visible in the office and acting as it were as a first line of defence. I had ample time for reading and writing and made all the use of it I could.

By this time my mother had left Rugby and taken temporarily a small house in Balham, one of a long, uniform, red-brick row, and I left my Clapham lodging and joined her. I had breakfast and supper at home and a season-ticket between Balham and Victoria Station. My mother had been shocked at my leaving Grant Richards but had been reassured by the approval of Laurence Binyon who, though a writer, had a regular and respectable job in the British Museum. Also, instead of being an expensive undergraduate, I was earning a pound a week at the age of eighteen and was paying half of it towards the cost of my keep. The rest I retained to cover my bus-fares and the buying of books, which, as hitherto, left me very little for my lunches. I read during my daily train journeys. I read at the Unicorn Press. And most nights I wrote and read till I could not keep awake. Sometimes I took a short walk on Tooting Common, and lamplight among green leaves joined other visible things that I liked to remember. Sometimes I came late from town when I had been given a free ticket to a theatre or a concert. There seemed to be more such tickets in those days. Oldmeadow, who was writing music criticism for the *Outlook*, often had two tickets for the same night at different theatres or concert-halls, and when this happened I profited. Some of our visitors, such as J. F. Runciman of the *Saturday Review*, would occasionally, when passing through the outer office, ask me if I could use a ticket, and in this way I saw and heard much for which I could not have afforded to pay. After these evenings I used to come home in high excitement, walking from the station through lamplit streets (always a pleasure), to find dear Miss Sidgmore, my sisters' governess (who had come to us many years earlier from my parents' great friends the Hart Jacksons at Ulverston and loved as I did the valley of the Crake) sitting up for me with a small saucepan and some nutmegs to mull and share with me a glass or two of claret if there was any left in the decanter that lived on the sideboard. My brother used to come home from Rugby for the holidays (his career there was in marked contrast with my own but we were always close friends and he watched what I was doing with a mixture of amusement, horror and understanding). I remember going with him to the local theatre where we saw a magnificent melodrama, *The Great Millionaire*. The millionaire villain, his wealth and his villainy proved by his possession of a motor-car, ended with a satisfying crash in the middle of the stage. There was a cliff above a sea-shore. In the distance we could see the headlights of the car, moving rapidly. They were coming nearer and nearer. The roar of the engine was heard. The car was heading straight for the edge of the cliff and so for the audience trembling in their seats. There was no deception. The car did indeed shoot over the edge and landed on the shore below. A dramatic climax that left us helpless with laughter and tears. I should like to see that play again.

During this time at the Unicorn Press, when I was hard at work learning the elements of my craft, I early discovered that the difference between narrative and discursive prose is much more than a superficial difference of form. It is a difference between two incompatible gaits of mind. In narrative it is as if the mind moves forward with the story. In essay or article the mind remains as it were tethered and makes sallies in this direction or that, returning towards the tethering-post before sallying out once more. This is a very crude statement of the case but is an explanation of something that has bothered me all my writing life and, I suspect, must bother others unless my own mind is peculiarly stiff. I could not turn suddenly from writing stories to the writing of an article or the other way about. The change, whichever way I made it, seemed to put my sentences out of tune. The quality of what I was writing was quite immaterial. It was bad anyhow, but it was much worse if after getting into the habit of spider-like darting out first one way and then another in writing essays I tried instead as a storyteller to move snail-like towards some distant goal. This has always been so, and even now, towards the end of a long life of writing, if I have to write a review it means the loss of many days before I have got rid of it and can get back to the writing of a story. Perhaps I should put it otherwise and say that I could never write anything unless I had persuaded myself that I never meant to write anything else. Perhaps I am still the small boy who when he made paper spills horrified his father by thinking of spill-making as the occupation of a lifetime. This difficulty I had in changing from one gait of mind to another made my progress extremely erratic. For months on end, with Hazlitt as tutelary deity, I wrote essays, whole books of them and could then write articles, similarly discursive, for which I began to find buyers. Then there would come a revulsion and, trying to write stories and battling with a mind accustomed to writing articles, I would almost revengefully burn the essays and for months would write nothing but stories which, worse than the essays and without saleable by-products, would similarly be burnt when I turned essayist again. Both made good blazes. I think the stories made the better, when burning sheets flying up the chimney set it on fire to the horror alike of my unfortunate mother and her indignant neighbours.

I was an essayist at the time of King Edward the Seventh's coronation and, with a week's holiday and Winterslow Hut in my mind, went down to Dorking and lodged very cheaply in an old inn in the main street, the pride of which was its doorstep worn very nearly through by the feet of Dorking beer-drinkers. To this visit I owe a meeting that has delighted me for all these years. This was with the barmaid of the inn. I noticed first that she was always reading, and next that she had her own bookshelf behind the bar and that it held all or nearly all the works of the very popular Marie Corelli. I said something to the barmaid about her fondness for books and she spoke with enthusiasm of *The Mighty Atom* and, I think, *The Sorrows of Satan*. 'And you know, sir,' she went on, 'the author—he isn't a woman. She's a man and he lives near here and on my afternoons off I walk over to see him sitting in his garden under Box Hill. Her real name's George Meredith.'

# CHAPTER VIII

## *Keeping Afloat*

In 1903, while I was employed to do nothing by the Unicorn Press, I began to earn small sums for stories and articles from the daily and weekly newspapers which (with plenty of paper) were more hospitable than they can afford to be today. In the summer of that year I had my first holiday, other than Bank Holidays and the free week at the time of the Coronation, that I had had since leaving Rugby. There was never a doubt in my mind as to what I was to do with it. I hurried north to Coniston (by the night-train so as not to lose a single minute) with Hazlitt in one pocket, Keats in the other, J. B. Mayor's *English Prosody* in my knapsack together with a notebook, and in my mind a determination to try experiments and fill the notebook with poetry. I was then nineteen. Some of my contemporaries were still at school, others in their first year at Oxford or Cambridge. Thanks to the Unicorn Press and to my evening writing I was already self-supporting. I have never walked into a railway station and bought a ticket with greater satisfaction.

The foolishness of trying to write poetry when I could not made possible one of the greatest pieces of good fortune that ever came to me. I had taken lodgings (one pound for the week, all found) at Bank House in Coniston village. On the day I came there I hurried to the shore to dip a hand in the lake as in childhood, and then walked up by the side of the Copper Mines Beck, found a large flat rock between the torrents, jumped across to it and settled down on it with my notebook. It so happened that on that day Mr W. G. Collingwood, Ruskin's biographer, had been painting a picture higher up the Old Man. Towards evening he was walking home and on coming to the bridge over the beck saw what he thought was a corpse washed up on that flat rock. He called out and was relieved when the corpse lifted its head. I got up and jumped ashore, because the noise of the rushing water

was such that I could not hear what he was saying. He asked me
what I was doing and I told him I had been trying to write poetry.
Instead of laughing, he seemed to think it a reasonable occupation,
and we walked down to the village together. Before we parted he
asked me to come round the head of the lake to see him and told
me his name and I then remembered that he had written *Thorstein
of the Mere*, the best-loved book of my boyhood and, further, that
in 1896 my father and mother with all of us had shared a picnic on
Peel Island with him and his wife. Long afterwards Mrs Collingwood told me that she remembered that meeting on the island
and her surprise that my mother, who was a very pretty young
woman, could have had a family of such very ugly children. She
did not tell me this until I had long been adopted almost as one of
her own.

I very nearly let my good fortune slip. Day after day of my
holiday went by and I was too shy to call at the house. My last
day came. I had my meat tea at Bank House and then walked
round the head of the lake, up the hill past Tent Lodge and came
to Lanehead. I turned back from the gate but turned again, went
up to the door and rang the bell. I could hardly have come at a
less suitable time. Mr Collingwood, napkin in hand, came to the
door and took me at once into the dining-room where he, Mrs
Collingwood, a formidable Miss Harrison and William Canton
were sitting at dinner. I was extremely scared, little suspecting
that William Canton was to become Uncle Will alike to me and
to the Collingwood children, and that Mr and Mrs Collingwood
were to become touchstones by whom to judge all other people
that I met.

I went back to London with an all-but-empty notebook (except
for a few pages of indescribably bad verse) knowing that I should
never be afraid to come to that door again and looking forward to
the next year when, I had been told, I was not to leave my calling
till the last day of my holiday but was to come round the head of
the lake as soon as I reached Coniston.

That same year I decided that I was making enough as a freelance to do without the Unicorn Press which, moreover, was
showing clear signs of mortality. I resigned just in time, as it
turned out, for a few weeks later, passing Cecil Court, I saw a
small crowd outside the office and, from afar, saw the Cockney
office-boy and his mother violently shaking the railings that
guarded the windows and haranguing the crowd on their wrongs.

The Unicorn Press, it seemed, had come suddenly to an end. Peace to its ashes. It had paid me a pound a week and left me free, when not dealing with the rare customers, or delightfully voyaging round London with parcels on the top of omnibuses, to sit in front of the fat ledgers with nothing to enter in them and to read undisturbed.

At about this time I joined the London Library, my first subscription having been paid by my kind godparents, the Aclands, and in my lunch-hour I used to hurry round to St James's Square to return books and take out others. In the office of the Unicorn Press I had read clean through Balzac in the English translation published by Dent with introductions by George Saintsbury. I had entered Henry James with *The Sacred Fount* and gone on with *Daisy Miller* and *What Maisie Knew*. I had read Mrs Meynell's slim books of essays, Kenneth Grahame's early books, and great quantities of plays. I was also pounding through Carveth Read's *Logic* and from Hume had moved on to Bishop Berkeley.

At the Unicorn Press I had also made some friends. The Unicorn had published Gordon Bottomley's first book and when he came up to town from the lake country he brought with him *The Crier by Night*, which I much admired. Yone Noguchi, a Japanese poet, had published from his lodgings a brown paper pamphlet of poems. I read a review of it, went to the lodgings in Brixton to buy the pamphlet and there met both Noguchi and another Japanese, the water-colour painter, Yoshio Markino. Just round the corner from Cecil Court, in St Martin's Lane, was St George's coffee-house where, two floors up, was a smoking-room where chess was played and twopence bought a good cup of coffee. Here, over the chessboard, I met two brothers called Clayton. I never learned what they did for a living, but one day, while we were playing chess, a man with a fine-cut, sad face, looking very unlike a townsman, stopped beside our table. We came to talking and, when we left the coffee-house, walked away together. This was Edward Thomas, come up from Kent with a bag full of books he had reviewed. I went with him to Thorp's across the way, where he emptied his bag and sold the books and then walked along the Strand to Fleet Street and so to the office of the *Daily Chronicle* where he refilled his bag with new books to take home with him and review in the country. He was some five years my senior and I became his devoted partisan.

One evening one of the Claytons took Thomas and me to a fifth-storey flat in the Gray's Inn Road, where a civil servant and his wife Peggy were 'at home' once a week. He was a compact little Welshman with a fine voice, she a large handsome Scottish peasant lass who had educated herself and made her way in the Post Office. I had seen M. P. Shiel writing like a man possessed, throwing the pages on the floor for his wife to gather. This was a different kind of Bohemia. Peggy wore long green dresses with big beads about her columnar throat. Her husband, like Shiel, wore a velvet jacket but, unlike Shiel, was content to be without doing. He was kind, quiet and watchful and he sang 'A King there was in the North Countree' better than I have ever heard it sung by anybody else. One of the Claytons said of him, 'Why should he do anything? His philosophy fits him like a glove.' They valued acquaintanceship with Edward Thomas and, I suppose, tolerated me for his sake. Later in that year, after I had resigned from the Unicorn, I used to bicycle in on Fridays from Balham to the Gray's Inn Road, and then run up the stairs, all those five storeys, run, I say, carrying my bicycle shoulder-high. No wonder I am not much good at running now. Later Peggy visited Paris and there met a sculptor as remarkable as herself. The life in the Gray's Inn Road broke up. Jacob Epstein and his Peggy began their lasting partnership on a quite different plane of reality.

Some of these friends I took proudly home, where they produced an effect which I had not expected. My mother, who had not yet lost hope of seeing me a solidly established business man wearing a top hat instead of a bowler, regarded them as dangerous Bohemians, whose influence was entirely in the wrong direction. She said that nobody had ever heard of them nor ever would, and told me that I should some day learn that all my swans were geese. Not that she disliked them. She could not but admit that as human beings they were very pleasant, but she blamed them for not warning me off the dangerous ground that they habitually trod. Not one of them was earning a respectable living in a respectable way. My brother and sisters laughed at them and only the other day Sir John Squire reminded me that in my family (though not by me) Edward Thomas had been habitually known as 'Teddy Tommy'. Further they dressed in a manner shocking to a London suburb in those days, Markino threadbare and with frayed cuffs, Thomas in rough country tweeds most unsuitable for wear in London. And as for hats, far from aspiring to the top

hats then fashionable, they did not even wear bowlers. Gordon
Bottomley produced the best impression. He too wore a soft felt
hat, but wore it in a way entirely his own, with no cleft in the
crown, so that it rose like a chimney above its very wide brim.
His slow speech and elaborate manners were impressive, even
though my mother did wish he would refrain from addressing
her as 'gracious lady'.

It needed no great courage to leave the Unicorn Press once I had
recognised that it was not a dependable raft and might soon leave
me to sink or to swim. But, once I had left it, I was sometimes put
to strange shifts to keep afloat. I knew that I had learnt enough
about publishing to be sure of work in a publisher's office if and
when I should recognise that I could not make a living by writing
alone. But that recognition, though it would have pleased my
mother, would have meant defeat for me. What seems odd to me
now is that it never occurred to me to try to get work in a newspaper office. But if I had done so I should have been unable to do
the enormous amount of unpaid reading and writing that was
made possible by my haphazard way of earning money. My
reasons against going into a newspaper office were in no way due
to any prejudice against newspaper work, but by this time I knew
two or three reporters and had the liveliest fear of being irrevoc-
ably drawn into the spinning maelstrom that newspaper life
seemed to be. At all costs I wanted to be free to go on with my
own education, which had almost nothing to do with the writing
for which I was paid. I did not mind what I wrote and, whatever
it was, regarded the writing of it as a technical problem, thought
it good practice and wrote it as well as I could. Even such scientific
training as I had came in useful. I wrote articles on new inventions
for trade journals, travel-articles to fit sets of photographs of
countries I had never seen, articles on the dead to chime with their
centenaries, anything in fact for which I could find a market.

The strangest of these shifts was due to an accident. I had fallen
on a very lean patch and did not want to confess it at home. I
determined to sell my old bicycle. Riding it down the Brixton
Road in search of a suitable knacker for such crocks, I happened
to see a poster of that day's *Daily News*. It advertised an article by
G. K. Chesterton, for whose *Twelve Types* I had a deep admiration. I had one penny left in my pocket. I turned my bicycle,
jumped off, went into the shop and bought a copy. I looked at the
paper standing by my bicycle and my eye was caught by a small

advertisement that asked for an experienced journalist with a thorough knowledge of athletics. Enquirers were bidden to call between three and four at an address in Brixton Road. I could hardly claim to be an experienced journalist, but I had suffered enough from athletics at school to justify my saying that I knew something about them. The hour was three. The address was close by. I gave my bicycle a last-minute reprieve and rode on down the Brixton Road until I came to a narrow, grimy house with a strip of trodden grass in front and a waiting crowd of anxious candidates. A blowzy lady was letting us in two at a time, and two at a time, after an interview that seemed to last no more than two seconds, the rejected were passing out. My turn came. I was asked about athletics and mentioned Rugby. Instead of being immediately flung out I was put into a dining-room that smelt of cats, given some paper, told to write something about football, and given an hour in which to do it. Before the hour was up the man who had interviewed me came in, looked through what I had written, told me that I was to be paid thirty shillings a week, and that I would be expected at nine o'clock on the following day. In the passage, on the way out, I met a thin, red-nosed, seedy-looking man who had also been engaged. Next morning I was told that my colleague had arrived drunk and been sacked, so that I could congratulate myself on having his opportunities as well as my own.

I settled down to be an industrious ghost. My ingenious and plausible employer made a business of hawking round ideas for popular books about games. These were commissioned by various publishers, some of whom bore great names and should have known better. It was then my employer's business to provide two things, first an adequate book, and secondly a name well enough known to sell it. Some sterling, illiterate footballer, cricketer or swimmer would pocket a windfall of five pounds for the use of his name. And I, in that catty dining-room, and later at home when I proved that I could write faster there, poured out the books. I wrote from two to six thousand words a day and my employer generously raised my salary to thirty-five shillings a week. He must have thought he had found a gold-mine, for he was buying for two and three pounds apiece books the copyright of which was his to sell in a much more generous market. Twenty and thirty years later I have been amused to see on bookstalls, still bought by would-be athletes, some of the books of practical instruction, still masquerading under once-famous names, that I produced during my six weeks of ghostly and breathless activity. Six weeks, at such a salary, were enough to set my finances right again. My employer parted from me with what I can well believe was genuine regret and I returned to the study of Berkeley's *Theory of Vision* that had been thus temporarily interrupted.

I was slowly finding my way to work of a different kind. This was regular weekly reviewing, and I owed my first opportunity for it to a benevolent little weekly called the *Week's Survey*. I had sent to this paper (enclosing, as so often, a stamped addressed envelope for its return) a short essay that for some reason or other sufficiently pleased B. Paul Neumann, the editor, to move him to ask me to call. I called, was told to send in other things of the same sort, was sent off with a parcel of books for review and, the following Saturday, on coming to the office again, beheld a miracle. On a board outside was a printed bill of the contents of that week's issue and there, in fine large type, I read my own name. Reviewing was a great help because I was paid twice over. I was paid for writing the reviews and soon found myself, like Edward Thomas, selling the books at one-third of the published price to Thomas Thorp in St Martin's Lane. What with freelance journalism and reviewing I presently felt myself so much of a capitalist as to be able to disregard my family's prophecies of disaster and to move to the neighbourhood of friends in Chelsea, so escaping from the disapproval of which I was never able to be unconscious, though I well knew it was mainly caused by my mother's affectionate fears for the future of her unsatisfactory son.

I found a large empty room over a grocer's shop at a rent of a few shillings a week. It was a hot day and I had persuaded a boy with a small van to take me from Balham to Chelsea. I had practically no furniture but a great many books. I piled all my books into the van and, lest any should escape on the way, sat myself on the tail-board, a van-boy once again. Of this I am now ashamed. I should have thought of my mother's feelings and not mounted the tail-board of that van in full view of all our neighbours who were watching from behind their lace curtains and their aspidistras. At the time no such thought came into my head. My driver was not in a hurry and neither was I. After a delightful, slow rumbling journey to the river and over Battersea Bridge, we stopped at the World's End public-house, where, while my driver loitered over his beer, I read the admirable scene in *Love for Love* where Mrs Frail and Mrs Foresight banter each other over a visit to that one-time scandalous place. We then went on and unloaded my library, I bought apples, cheese, bread and beer for my supper and some packing cases by way of temporary furniture, had a brief skirmish with my landlord who mistrusted a lodger with only books as distrainable chattels, sat exultantly at the open window, fell asleep and woke with a cold in my head.

In Chelsea I fell among friends and was extremely happy. Edward Thomas used to visit me there and I sometimes went down to his cottage in Kent, when he and I and his dog Rags used to walk ourselves tired, eat bread and cheese and onions in a country inn and come home to smoke long clay pipes which we lit with spills twisted from the leaves of the books of would-be poets he had reviewed and knew to be unsaleable even to our almost omnivorous benefactor Mr Thorp. Thomas had a home-made bookshelf by his fireside and kept it stocked with verse meet for the burning. That bookshelf perhaps had its part in saving me from further attempts to be any kind of poet.

I owed a great deal to Yoshio Markino, for taking me to the house of Miss Pamela Colman Smith in the Boltons. She was an artist who had been discovered in Jamaica (or perhaps on a visit to America) by Ellen Terry who had brought her to England. She had a weekly 'evening' in her studio and I was soon one of the fortunate ones with a permanent invitation. There were always actors and actresses at these evenings, and sometimes Ellen Terry herself would illumine the whole room just by being there. Here I met for the first time W. B. Yeats whose poems Pixie (as our hostess was called by everybody) used to read aloud so well that even now, fifty years later, I cannot read them to myself without hearing her read them to me. A strange mixture of people came to those evenings. Ellen Terry brought the Craigs and my cousin Christabel Marshall who, as Christopher St John, translated Sudermann's play *The Good Hope* that was staged by Ellen Terry, when the whole party at her invitation went to Hammersmith to see it. Yeats used to bring Irish players from the Abbey Theatre, and he had given the name of 'opal hush' to the innocuous blend of claret and fizzy lemonade that we used to drink. Poets came there and read their poetry, but none as well as Pixie herself read 'The Happy Townland' or 'I went out to the hazel wood'. I took Gordon Bottomley there and, though Pixie was afterwards wicked enough to mimic the grave solemnity of his slow speech, she knew him for a poet and invited him to come again. Miss Nona Stewart, sitting at an eighteenth-century instrument that may have been a spinet or a harpischord, used to sing the song of 'Spanish Ladies' to music that had been written down in that very room, when Masefield brought a shy old sailor, and Pixie put screens round him to save his shyness, and the old sailor, who had been dumb in the light of all those candles and with so many strangers waiting to hear him, sat invisible and whistled the delicate old tune, slightly different from the version more generally known.

Sooner or later would come the turn of the Anansi stories. These were the Negro tales that Pixie had heard as a child in Jamaica. She told them in the dialect in which she had heard them. Each story began in the same way: 'In a long before time before Queen Victoria came to reign over we ... ' Then would come the story. 'Der lib in de bush one black fat shiny spider call Anansi ... ' or 'Der lib in de bush one king an' dis king he was de mos' beautiful king dat eber was, but dis king him hab one BEARD!' Pixie used to squat down on the floor to tell these stories, playing while she told them with small wooden figures she had made and painted to represent the characters. The stories were very easy to remember, being real folk-tales handed down by word of mouth. Everything forgettable had been filtered from them through the years. Trying one day to tell someone what they were like, I began with 'In a long before time before ... ' etc. and found that the rest followed without any effort on my part. For many years in many places I used to tell these stories that I first heard in Pixie's studio in the Boltons, and again and again have come back to find the children to whom I had told them telling them for themselves, and more than once I have heard the children of the children to whom I had told them telling the stories they had heard from their mothers and telling them, they too with some echo of Pixie's Jamaican accents, though they had never heard Pixie nor even heard me repeating them at second hand. I think I learned more of the art of narrative from those simple folk-tales than ever from any book.

Among the pleasantest of the people who used to come to those weekly evenings were an American artist and his English wife, Alphaeus and Peggotty Cole, who had a studio between Edith Grove and Gunter Grove on the south side of the Fulham Road. He was a son of Timothy Cole who will be remembered for his wood-engravings of old masters that were published month by month in the American *Century Magazine*. Alphaeus had had a strange childhood, dragged hither and thither about Italy from one gallery to another by his father's choice of pictures to engrave. He went back to America in the end and there became, I believe, a most successful portrait painter.* In those young days in Chelsea his taste was all for cardinals with a fine play of sunlight from a window over their scarlet robes. He painted with great technical skill and immense industry and the peak of his year was varnishing day at the Royal Academy, where he was a frequent exhibitor. His wife was from the north of England and was a modeller in clay. They were nearly as poor as I and all through my time in Chelsea we used to celebrate together the sale of a picture or a story. Close by the World's End there was a small wine-shop where, on great days, we would buy for one shilling and three-pence a large flagon of Australian burgundy to enliven a supper of macaroni cheese, and on still greater days we would go sailing into town, all three of us, on the top of a horse-drawn omnibus, and have one-and-sixpenny *table d'hote* dinners at Roche's or the Maison Brice in Old Compton Street, Soho. They had small justification for their faith in me, but it was a great help to me to know they had it and when Peggotty, who was strong on the social side of a painter's life, gave an 'at home' in their studio for the benefit of some American visitor who was likely to buy a picture from Timothy Cole's son, I used to go round and do my part in making the buyer feel that he was lucky to get it.

I have sometimes regretted that I could not have had a few years without having to write for a living. Most writers have but a limited number of productive years and it was perhaps unlucky that I had to begin spending mine so young. It was certainly the unhealthy, irregular meals I ate, my steady buying of books instead of food, that brought about the internal troubles that have been a nuisance through most of my life. At the same time I doubt if any young man at a university living in comparative comfort can ever know the happiness that was mine at nineteen, depend-ent solely on what I was able to earn and living in a room of my own with the books I had myself collected.

* Alphaeus and Peggotty Cole wrote to me from New York in 1957, he then aged eighty and a National Academician, and still busy painting portraits.

# CHAPTER IX

## *The Collingwoods*

The collapse of the Unicorn Press gave me, some months later, an unexpected excuse for going back to the lake country. Gordon Bottomley lived in the Cartmel valley within easy reach of Ulverston, where Mr William Holmes had a small commercial printing press and wished to do more with it than print a local paper and the posters of the neighbouring races, sheepdog-trials, hound-trails and agricultural shows. Titus Wilson of Kendal had been publishing books for some time, and Holmes, with that example before him, may have thought of publishing as a means of keeping his machines busy when not occupied in other ways. Bottomley was then devoted to Rossetti and Morris and still more so to their successors, the writers and draughtsmen of the *Yellow Book*, the *Pageant* and the *Savoy*. Holmes, plain Ulverston business man, can hardly have divined into what strange bypaths he was to be led when Bottomley's father, a business man of Keighley, came to terms with him for the printing of a book by his son Gordon. The book was to be published in London by the Unicorn Press, but Gordon Bottomley was to have a free hand in its production by William Holmes's Ulverston works. This book, *The Gate of Smaragdus*, was of full foolscap size, printed in green ink entirely in small capitals on specially chosen, slightly tinted paper and bound in two shades of green. The Unicorn Press collapsed and Holmes, who had looked forward to long collaboration with them, asked Gordon Bottomley what he should do. Bottomley suggested that he should talk with me. I, no doubt wearing in Holmes's eye the halo of experience with two London publishers, hurried to Cartmel where I had a pack of cousins, spent an afternoon with Bottomley and went on to see Holmes. He set forth his plans, which included the publication of a quarterly that should carry on the tradition that Bottomley admired (this project faded away), a series of small books of prose and verse by new authors and some larger books of more general appeal. My part was to keep a look-out for young authors and to arrange with a firm in London to act as distributing agents for the Lanthorn Press, which took its name from that chosen by Bottomley for the quarterly which never appeared. Naturally the first young authors who came into my mind were Edward Thomas, Cecil Chesterton and myself, and I went back to London exulting in the knowledge that I had found a publisher for my first book of essays. True the book was to be 'a very little one', but it was to be something very different from the vamped-up rubbish about athletics that I had produced as an industrious ghost. I reported my good news to Neumann, the editor of the *Week's Survey* and he, swivelling gaily in his editorial chair, was delighted, said he would print anything I sent him, was as good as his word and paid me by the measured inch, so that I sometimes got as much as a guinea for an essay that, if I had had the money, I should gladly have paid to be allowed to write. In Chelsea Cecil Chesterton, whose *Gladstonian Ghosts* was similarly printed in Ulverston, the Coles and I celebrated over a sardine supper with which we found Australian burgundy went extremely well.

By the time the leaves were opening on the trees along the Embankment I had a fair amount of printed writing from which to choose the papers for my own little book. I also had some money in hand. I arranged with my landlady (I had changed my first lodgings for one where I did not have to cook my breakfast) to keep on my bed-sitting room at a small retaining rent and, with a knapsack full of books for review and a portable typewriter, went once more through the big grey archway at Euston that was the gate to the enchanted North. I went to Coniston, found lodgings again close by the bridge in Coniston village, dipped my hand in the lake as usual, looked at the Gondola that I had been allowed to steer when eight years old, had supper and, after reading a little Hazlitt, slept to the sound of the Copper Mines Beck pouring down from the Old Man.

Next day I walked round the head of the lake and up past Tent Lodge to Lanehead, to renew the acquaintance of that one shy visit of the year before and of the meeting on Peel Island in 1896. Nothing that I can write can adequately express what I owe to W. G. Collingwood and his wife, my very dear 'aunt'. Mr Collingwood had been one of Ruskin's roadmaking under-graduates at Oxford. He had come to Brantwood to make a

translation of Xenophon and from that moment until Ruskin's
death (and after it) had sunk his own ambitions entirely in his
devotion to that great man. When he married, he settled on
Ruskin's account in a cottage at Gillhead by Windermere, moving
afterwards, so as to be nearer Ruskin, to Lanehead, a mile along
the road from Brantwood to Coniston village. He was an admirable landscape and portrait painter. He was a geologist, an
archaeologist, and an authority on the Scandinavian sagas. He had
translated Kormak and written a book, illustrated by his own
water-colours, on *The Sagasteads of Iceland*. He had written
*Thorstein of the Mere*, a book about the coming of the Norsemen to
Coniston (for long called Thurstonwater) and the valley of the
Crake where I had spent the happiest days of my childhood, a
book that had delighted my father as well as his children. He had
written a book on the philosophy of ornament and another as a
guide to the Lake Counties. In *Coniston Tales* he had collected his
contributions to a family magazine edited by his son Robin who
was later to be the chief authority on Roman Britain and Wayne-
flete Professor of Philosophy at Oxford. In that little book there is
a short story which I still think is one of the best ever written.
Whatever he wrote was first-rate of its kind. And all that he
wrote was written with complete disregard of its possible market
value. *Thorstein* was published by Arnold, and his *Life of John
Ruskin* by Methuen, but for the most part, living at Coniston, he
did not trouble to seek London publishers. Book after book was
published locally, some by Titus Wilson in Kendal, some by the
same William Holmes in Ulverston who was now to publish my
own dear (then, not now) bantling. Once he had finished a book,
he was content to see it printed and was entirely indifferent to its
subsequent fate. There never was a man who did so much unpaid
work for other people. The devotion of the whole of his youth to
Ruskin was matched by the infinite labour that in later years he
used to put into the editing of ill-written manuscripts by earnest
local archaeologists. Mrs Collingwood was perhaps the better
painter of the two, though more limited in range. They kept their
house going mainly by the sale of pictures at annual exhibitions.
When the time for an exhibition drew near there would be a
flurry to collect pictures to send to it, but during the rest of the
year the future did not trouble them. He wrote and they both
painted with complete disregard of possible sales.

That first day Mr Collingwood, though he was at work when

I came, took me into his study. I can see it now, the books from floor to ceiling, the enormous long table piled with books and manuscripts, the unfinished canvas on an easel, the small table at which he was writing and, over the fireplace, his lovely portrait of his wife, in a small boat with two of the children. He put me in one arm-chair, shifted his own from the table and asked about what I was doing. The miracle for me was his assumption that what I was trying to do was worth doing. Later in the morning-room I met Mrs Collingwood who was soon, when he spoke of her to me, to become 'your aunt', the Dorrie to whom on one of her birthdays Ruskin had lifted his glass with the toast, 'To Dorrie—and all angels!' The two elder girls (the youngest was away at school) came in with their painting things from the garden, and with them an Austrian cousin, very voluble in an English entirely her own. Dora was a year and Barbara two years younger than myself, Hilde, the cousin, about the same age. In the afternoon we went down to their boathouse and out in the *Swallow*, a one-time fishing-boat, monstrously heavy to row but not bad under sail, the first of a long dynasty of *Swallows* in my sailing life. I came back with them to supper and walked round the head of the lake to my lodgings with my head in a whirl, now and then skipping in the happy privacy of the dark. A new life had begun for me that day. From that day Mr and Mrs Colling-wood treated me as a son of their own. From that day I had behind me a family who did not assume that I was heading for some disastrous failure and were not convinced that whatever I was doing I should be better employed doing something else. Those two gave me something I had not missed because I had not till then known that it could be. The whole of the rest of my life has been happier because of them.

Next day I was on the lake again with the three girls. We rowed to Lands Point where, while I lay on the shore and wrote, they made sketches of the old Hall of the le Flemings and its boat-house, and I remember that as we rowed away Hilde made us turn back. There was a white lifebelt hanging on the wall of the boathouse and Hilde noticed it only as we were rowing out of the bay. 'Quick!' she cried. 'One other minute! I have forgot the safety circle.' I was bidden to come early next morning and 'my aunt' packed us off with a bun-loaf, a pot of marmalade and a kettle to go down the lake to Peel Island, the island that had mattered so much to me as a small boy, was in the distant future to play its part in some of my books, and is still, in my old age, a crystallising point for happy memories. Another day Mrs Collingwood was painting in the Lanehead garden and, needing a human figure, planted me with my books in the middle of a bed of lupins. Robin and Ursula, the two younger children, were away at school. Robin was at Podmore's, at Grange, but had already won a scholarship to Rugby, the first of the long series of scholarships and fellowships that marked every stage of his brilliant academic career. At his father's request, one day when I went over to Ulverston to see Mr Holmes I went on to Grange to see Robin. Mr Collingwood did not seem to think that my own dismal failure at Rugby disqualified me from telling Robin something of what he was likely to find there. I suppose Robin must have been about six years my junior. Those six years shrank rapidly as he grew up.

One day Mrs Collingwood asked me for how long I had booked my room in the village and told me that she and Mr Collingwood had been talking things over, that until Robin came home for the holidays I could use his bedroom, that there was a room downstairs, next to the study, which I could make my own for work, and that I should be welcome to both. I gave notice at my lodgings and at the end of the week made two journeys to the pier at the Waterhead Hotel with my typewriter, my knapsack full of books and my travelling bag. Barbara, Dora and Hilde rowed *Swallow* across from the Lanehead boathouse and helped me to carry my things up the steep pathway to Lanehead. From then until my return to London I lived in a golden haze. I suppose it rained sometimes (it usually does) but I remember only continuous sunshine. I remember going to sleep that first night hardly able to believe what had happened and being woken next morning by 'my aunt', always the first downstairs, playing Beethoven on the piano in the morning-room.

Every day began with music. Ever since her marriage Mrs Collingwood had played before breakfast. When I first knew Lanehead the music was Beethoven, Mozart and sometimes Mendelssohn. Bach came later, introduced by Robin. That early-morning music set as it were the tone for the whole day's work. At Lanehead work and not its material rewards was the only thing that mattered. Everybody was working. When we had had breakfast and a run across the garden to look out from below the pine trees to the Old Man towering above the lake, the house was

silent. Mr Collingwood was writing in the study. Mrs Collingwood was painting. The girls, all three, were at work with easels
or with clay in the Mausoleum, a tumble-down conservatory that
was used as a studio. We would all meet again at lunch-time and,
in the afternoon, we younger ones would go forth with bun-loaf
and kettle, to sketch or read in the open air, to make our fire by
the shore of the lake, to talk of all we hoped to do, and to come
home to supper in the Lanehead dining-room (once a kitchen)
with its huge fireplace (the house had been built on the site of an
old inn) with a brass bugle on the mantelshelf.

It was in my aunt's character that on coming into any room she
always looked for a draught, in order to sit in it. There were two
doors in the dining-room, one opening into the hall and one into a
passage which led to the scullery, kitchen and larders. A door in
the passage was open to a flagged yard. The door to the hall was
never shut. 'My aunt' sat at the end of the table in whatever gale
was blowing between the two doors, with a window always open
at her back. We sat at the sides of the table, in shelter. Mr Collingwood did not like sitting at the head of the table, but sat at the
side as if to insist that we were all equals together. My aunt at
her end of the table in her beloved gale had the hard work of
pouring out for all of us and helping us to what was going. After
supper we younger ones used to go out to 'the lair', a grassy bank
below the garden from which to watch the sunset over Walna
Scar, and then, as it grew dark, we would come into the big
morning-room that was always full of flowers. My aunt would
play to us. If there was singing there were one or two songs that
would always bring Mr Collingwood from the study and she
would use them to call him if she thought he had been working
too long. Then there were stories. She used to read aloud to us
from Jacobs's four volumes of *English Fairy Tales* and *Welsh
Fairy Tales* (too little known even today). I can hear still the
eerie threat she used to put into the voices of the Hobyahs ...
'Hobyah! Hobyah! Hobyah! Tear down the hemp-stalks, eat up
the old man and woman, and carry off the little girl.' But little
dog Turpie *barked* so that the Hobyahs ran off; and the old man
said, 'Little dog Turpie *barks* so that I can neither sleep nor
slumber, and if I live till morning, I will cut off one of his legs.'
Then they would make me tell one of the Anansi stories I had
learnt in Chelsea and we used to lie on the floor exchanging old
tales in front of the fire (a fire is a very pleasant thing in a lake

country summer night in a house where doors and windows are kept open) until at last we would each take a candle in a brass candlestick and go upstairs, to lie in bed listening to the owls and dreaming of next day's work, to wake in the morning to the music of a new day.

Collectively, as a family, they adopted me and I was delighted by each small happening that helped to make me feel that I was so adopted. I remember still my extreme pleasure the first time Mrs Collingwood trusted me to go to the village to do an errand for her at Coward's, the grocer. I rowed across the lake and, just after I had left the hotel grounds and come out on the road, I passed a hawthorn tree that had shed its petals all about it, a patch of glittering snow on the dust. During all that time the leaves of the trees seemed more luminous than they are today and the hills had sharper edges. I would stand gaping at this or that as if I feared I should not remember it for ever. I need have had no such fear. On the lake or on the further side of it I used to look for the pale corner of the Lanehead house where it showed through the trees below the fell and tell myself that I could not really be one of that loved family. After meals we all helped in clearing away and I valued my right to share in this. My chair, after a meal was over, had its particular place against the wall, between the door and the sideboard, and many years later, when I came to Lanehead after long absence abroad, my aunt laughed as I got up from the table after dining there and without thinking pushed my chair back into the old place where it had stood in 1904.

Of course I fell in love not only with the Collingwoods in general but with Barbara in particular. It would have been a monstrous freak of nature if I had not fallen in love with one or other of those girls. Barbara, for her part, had the good sense not to fall in love with me and, though it took her a year or two to decide the question, we laid the foundations then of a friendship that, since it has lasted nearly sixty years, seems likely to last for the few more years that may remain. In early youth such friendship is touched with magic. It was in an Arcadian ecstasy that I spent those weeks making my first book ready for the press.

In Ulverston eager, ambitious little Mr Holmes was hard at work. He had Gordon Bottomley's folio on his hands, with Gordon seeing to it that the book should be, as he said, 'fit to put into the hands of Ricketts and of Shannon'. He was also busy with a book by Mr Collingwood, *King William the Wanderer, an old*

*British Saga, from old French versions.* He had Edward Thomas's *Rose Acre Papers* to set up and was indulging me in a practice that should not be encouraged among authors, that of sending a book piecemeal to the printer. Other publishers have let me do this, but no publisher today would allow any author to be such a nuisance, and young authors are taught better manners at the start. About twice a week an envelope used to arrive at Lanehead from Ulverston and set Mr Collingwood in his study and me in the next room reading through our proofs. I have always been bad at noticing typographical errors, 'listening' to my own prose rather than 'seeing' it. Barbara helped in reading those first galleys, and Mr Collingwood finding her busy with them, laughed and said 'You have got the beginnings of an intelligent public already.' Years later, when I was in Russia, Barbara and Mr Collingwood between them read the proofs of *Old Peter's Russian Tales* for me and those of an eighteenth-century story called *The Elixir of Life.* No other books of mine have needed less subsequent correction.

The last proofs went back to Holmes and I went back to London. My aunt, greatly trusting, had asked me to look for a flat for the Collingwood family who were coming to town for the winter, so that Dora and Barbara could attend classes at Cope's studio.

# CHAPTER X

## *London Again*

With such friends behind me and entrusted with such a mission I went almost eagerly back to London. I dumped my typewriter and luggage in my bed-sitting room at 1 Gunter Grove and hurried round the corner to Alphaeus and Peggotty Cole to herald the coming of the Collingwoods and to ask for Peggotty's help in finding a lodging worthy of them at a price they could afford. The shrewd Peggotty heard me to the end. 'Piper,' she said (the name indicates a player upon the penny whistle), 'Piper, you have fallen in love.'

'And a very good thing too,' said Alphaeus, stepping back from his easel and looking at his painting with his head birdlike on one side.

'Much too early,' said Peggotty.

'Can't be too early,' said Alphaeus. 'Why, by the time I was his age ...'

There was a moment's storm in the studio. Alphaeus was suppressed and the three of us went out to sup at a little restaurant in the Fulham Road and to look at advertisements of furnished lodgings on the framed noticeboards of house-agents and tobacconists. We did not find what we wanted that night but we did next day. Alphaeus was left to his painting and Peggotty in the role of exigent housewife put the right questions to agents and landlords while I stood by, thinking that each place we inspected had been chosen until, on the pavement outside, she explained in a very few words how impossible it was. We found in the end a small furnished flat, with a tiny balcony, on the fourth floor of a new block in Edith Grove, the street that runs parallel to Gunter Grove between the Fulham and the Kings Road. Peggotty took care that my letter about it to Mrs Collingwood answered every question that my aunt, who must have been given a very false impression of my efficiency, was likely to ask.

Mrs Collingwood took the place without seeing it and in a very short time the whole family from Lanehead were established there. I could run round to see them in two minutes and took great pleasure in showing off my Chelsea friends to them and them to Chelsea. They too had to hear the Jamaican stories at their source, to go to picnic parties at the Coles's and to think Edward Thomas as wonderful as I thought him. Mr Collingwood presently took a studio in the Boltons, and, waiting until the light was going so as not to interrupt his painting, I used to go round there, sit with him by the glow of the stove and listen to his painstaking comments on whatever story I was trying to write. Barbara, poor dear, had not made up her mind to say Yes or No, but the astonishing thing is that both her father and her mother would have been pleased if she had decided to marry me. Indeed when I took No for an answer and went off into Surrey my dear aunt called me back, which Peggotty Cole thought was rather unfair.

Edward Thomas, wishing to leave his cottage in Kent and be in London for a while, joined me in Gunter Grove and took the other room that my postman and his wife had to let. Looking back now I suppose ours were poor lodgings, but Edward's room caught the morning sun and mine the afternoon, and for me it would have been happiness enough, no matter what the room, to have one of my own, to be earning my living by writing and to have my friends so close about me. Edward was older than I and married with a family, so that for him the poorness of these rooms was not in any way enchanted and he went home again after about a month. 'I run away from home every day,' he once said, 'but I always come back for tea.' Still he was not always melancholy even in town, and it was his Welsh songs that startled the postman, sleeping below, into tumbling out of bed. Many years later, a careless biographer wrote that I had owned the house and had allowed Edward to pay me rent for a 'hateful' room in it. No doubt Edward found the room hateful but he did not rent it from me and, as for owning the house, I owned nothing in the world except a few books and a typewriter. I was just beginning to buy bits of furniture, and years afterwards Mrs Collingwood used to tell how she had laughed, driving up the Fulham Road on the top of a horse-drawn omnibus, at the sight of Edward and me, walking gravely along in the gutter, one behind the other carrying between us a green-varnished deal writing-desk intended for the writing of masterpieces.

Another regular visitor to Gunter Grove was Cecil Chesterton whose kindly, gnarled face I can see now lit up by the match he was holding to his pipe, sitting on the edge of my bed in the dusk, letting his pipe go out and lighting it again to go out once more, but never interrupting his tremendous spate of talk that poured over the heads of Dora, Barbara and myself, who at that time took no interest in politics though much in the Chestertons. He too joined Edward Thomas and me in the first list of books to be published by the Ulverston printer. Later, when he wrote a book about G. K. Chesterton, his brother, and had to preserve his anonymity, it was I who had to sign the contract for that book with the publisher, Alston Rivers. Cecil Chesterton was then still living with his father and mother in Warwick Gardens. I re-member coming in there with him unexpectedly and finding them at some meal in their dining-room, each behind a rampart of books, with food grown cold beside them. He told me that all their meals were like that, and that often, engrossed in their reading, they would forget to eat at all until startled by the arrival of their next meal with the other still waiting on the table. When he and his brother were both at home, there was usually argument instead of reading, with much the same result. I never knew so united a family with such a passion for debate. Gilbert Chesterton had lately married and was living in a flat across the river, by Battersea Park, and here I met E. Nesbit and her husband, the rather florid Hubert Bland, with his monocle dangling from a broad silk ribbon, a confident, blustering creature for whose works both Chestertons had an exaggerated respect and I had none, though I had a great deal for the works of his wife.

A parcel with the Ulverston postmark arrived at Gunter Grove. I opened it with shaking hands, to find half a dozen copies of my first book, bound in pale mottled paper boards, with a brown cloth spine and a label with the title on it. There was a copy for Barbara, one for Dora, one for the older Collingwoods, one for the Coles, and I went home that afternoon with one for my mother who could not disguise her feeling that this was yet one more nail in the coffin of the respectable future she had hoped for me. No matter. I was now an author with a published book and thought of it as a nest-egg almost bound to bring about the miracle of another. I can remember patting its silly little cover much as I have patted a boat when she and I have been alone at sea and struggling along in unkindly weather. I should, however, hate anybody to think that I mention my early books because I suppose them to have any sort of value.

The only excuse for those early books is that they were written (and unfortunately published) at a time when I should have been a university student and saved from myself by the laughter of my fellows. Instead I was keeping myself alive by selling what should have been mere exercises. It surprises me that I was able to sell them. I wanted to write essays or stories, but it never occurred to me to write such essays and such stories as were published in the popular magazines. I was ready to write anything for anybody, but in fact wrote things that could not have been worse designed for making money. Everything was bad about them, and only my worst enemy or most foolish friend would resurrect their corpses now. What was remarkable was the kindness, the hopefulness, the confidence even, with which they were treated by some of my elders, by W. G. Collingwood and William Canton, for example, who never wavered in their belief that all this ceaseless scribbling would some day be justified. Remembering this gratefully now, I can but hope that I have myself in turn been tender to the early efforts of the very young. It is a daring thing to write at all and confidence is something easily lost. I know now how careful Mr Collingwood was lest he should shake mine in those days when I would rush round to Bolton Studios with a new draft of a story, read it to him while the light was going, and he, cleaning his brushes and putting them aside, would sit on by the red glow of the stove, talking of its faults as one craftsman with another, always with the silent assumption that it was worth while so to talk because of something I should some day write.

Bad as that first little book was, it was (perhaps because of its youthfulness) reviewed very kindly when reviewed at all. Neumann of the *Week's Survey* (in which much of it had appeared) did his best for it. It made me a few friends in unexpected places. Mrs Richmond Ritchie saw a copy, liked something in it and invited me to call. I put on my least disreputable clothes and went (very nearly turning back from the doorstep) to her house in a square near the river. I was shown into a very large drawing-room, where Thackeray's daughter was talking to Miss Edith Sichel. She said, 'Well, here we are. I am a well-known novelist, Miss Sichel is a celebrated critic and Mr Ransome has written a book of essays which we both like very much.' They must have thought me a dumb oaf but they gave me tea and were very kind to me and I think I owed to them the good will I found in at least one editorial office to which they advised me to take my wares. The book suggested to the publisher of a small weekly newspaper that I could be useful to him. He asked me to write 'a little paper' for him every week, gave me a column to fill and paid me twelve shillings and sixpence an article. Twelve and sixpence a week was the nucleus of a regular income and, though I thought nothing of his newspaper, I was delighted to have a free hand in a column of my own. But to have a free hand in a column is to be bound to use it each and every week. It is not freedom at all. I should have been better off without that weekly twelve and sixpence. A quarter of a century later, when C. P. Scott asked me to write a weekly essay for the *Manchester Guardian*, I found it was more than I could do. Political leading articles, where the antics of politicians provide the subjects, are easy enough. It is the building of bricks without straw that is so difficult and so damaging. The attempt to do this, combined with the bad influence of some of Richard Le Gallienne's work and with the difficulty of trying to write articles and stories at the same time, partly explains why my second book, made up of some of these articles, is even more distasteful to me than my first. But at the time, aged twenty, I plunged gaily ahead, thinking of Steele and Addison and of Le Gallienne's *Prose Fancies* and was encouraged on my mistaken course by letters from readers in different parts of the world. I had yet to learn that it is impossible to write anything, no matter how bad, that will not, sometimes because of its badness, meet grateful echoes from people who feel that it is written directly to themselves.

Those were wonderful days in that winter of 1904. With the Collingwoods just round the corner, I had the lake country with me even in London, and a whole family who shared the simple view that, so long as it was possible to pay one's way without actually starving, work was what mattered and money of no importance whatever. I never starved but I was always hungry. A solid meal could be made from a haddock and the cooking of it wasted no time. Haddocks could be bought in the Kings Road. I used to buy my haddock and take it home, then boil a kettle of water on the fire, and pour the boiling water over the haddock in a saucepan, put the lid on, read for another ten minutes, when a meal would be ready that would last for twenty-four hours. Eggs were a penny each. Porridge made my saucepan suffer because, reading while I stirred, it so often happened that I burnt it. But I thought myself a goodish cook. No one ever boiled an egg better and I was a good hand at buttering eggs, at least to suit my own taste. When rich I used sometimes, not often, to go to public houses that had their shilling, tenpenny, or even eightpenny 'ordinaries', of beef, Yorkshire pudding, roast potatoes and stringy cabbage. If not quite up to such extravagance, a few pence were enough to buy a massive helping of bread and cheese and pickled onions, and twopence bought a half-pint of beer. In bad times I could always keep going on a diet of cheese and apples: cheese because both cheap and nourishing, and apples to counter-act the constipating effects of the cheese.

Chelsea was always, so to speak, my home village, but I had friends also in Hampstead, which in those days was to Chelsea something of what Montmartre was to the Latin Quarter. The Dryhursts lived in Downshire Hill. Mrs Dryhurst and her two daughters, Norah and Sylvia, were passionately Irish. Robert Lynd lodged close by and he and Sylvia were friends of mine for nearly fifty years, indeed until they died. Mrs Dryhurst had a 'day' (I forget which it was) and on that day her drawing-room was full of young people who, if not Irish, at least had no objection to Home Rule. There were always more of us than there were chairs, and poets used to read their poems aloud while we sat on the floor. At about six o'clock Mr Dryhurst, who had never quite been forgiven for being English, used to come home from the British Museum, open the drawing-room door an inch or two, enough to look in on the Irishry, and disappear again at once. Clifford Bax was one of those young poets. I remember he wrote to me on his birthday, ending the letter with the words, 'Eighteen today and NOTHING done!'

Once or twice a week I used to drive into town on the top of an omnibus, usually meeting Cecil Chesterton at St George's coffee-house or at the offices of the *Week's Survey*. Half a dozen of us, with Neumann himself, were writing practically the whole paper, though we could not persuade ourselves that anybody read what we wrote. About that time J. L. Garvin became editor of the *Outlook*. He gave me a lot of work to do. Cecil Chesterton used to take me to an odd debating club in a court off Fleet Street, at which I think I must have been a welcome member, because I never spoke, whereas the others could hardly wait for their turn. Not that I was by nature silent. In those days London stayed long awake. Cecil used to come back to Gunter Grove with me, arguing until at last he would leave me to walk north to Warwick Gardens and I, too stirred up to sleep, would, if it were a fine night, walk the sixteen miles out to Epsom for breakfast, get a breath of the country, and hurry back by train. The Epsom walk today would be mostly through suburban streets. Then, once I had cleared Clapham Common and Tooting, it was a green walk all the way through Mitcham and its lavender-fields dodging Sutton and so to the open downs.

Some time that winter before the Collingwoods went back to Coniston I went for the first time to Paris. I was, as usual, doing a lot of reading. I was wrestling with Kant's *Critique of Pure Reason* and had been led into the by-paths of Schopenhauer through the accident of meeting at the Collingwoods' flat T. Bailey Saunders, a dry, uncomfortable little man but one of the best of Schopenhauer's translators. The more difficult I found it to write stories, the more interested I became in the technique of storytelling, and I filled notebooks on that subject with ideas for the most part useless. I was beginning to read French for pleasure and re-membering the nursery French I had forgotten at school. It was interest in French storytellers that sent me to Paris. I had a few pounds in hand and told myself that I had better go now, in case I might never have as much again. I put a shirt or two into a portmanteau and was off, taking a third-class return ticket by Newhaven and Dieppe to save money. This was the first of many crossings and the memory of it is lost in a palimpsest of all the others. I know only that I was not seasick, even coming back when, in much worse weather, I travelled in the steerage with a large crowd of Armenian immigrants who squatted in rows, supporting each other, groaned all together in dreadful rhythmic chorus, following but never quite in time with the rolling and pitching of the ship, and were sick without reserve.

I am not myself immune from seasickness but have only twice been sick in steamships, once suffering from lack of blood after an operation and once on account of a kitten. I was crossing the Gulf of Finland in a small steam vessel sorely buffeted by a north-easter bringing sleet and occasional hail with it. I was keeping my foot-ing in a sheltered place behind the funnel when round the corner

of the wheelhouse came a very small kitten, high on its thin legs,
its fur sodden, its balance uncertain as the steamer lurched on its
way with a horrible corkscrew motion. The kitten staggered and
swayed, its feet wide apart. I watched it and suddenly said to
myself, 'That kitten is going to be ill.' A moment later its legs
gave way, it slumped down and, with its chin on the deck, was
dreadfully sick. I rushed for the rail and was sick too. I have never
been sick in any of the small boats I have sailed, perhaps because I
have always been too busy in them. I have sometimes had a
companion who was not immune, and for him I had an instant
cure. He would come up out of the cabin and, the moment I saw
the colour of his face, I would leave the tiller, tell him to take over
and myself go below, leaving him in sole charge. Again and again
I have come up half an hour later to find him cured. It is unfortunate that in cross-channel steamships the captain cannot call
upon his seasick passengers to take a trick at the wheel. But this,
like seasickness itself, is a digression. Back to France.

That first visit was in winter. The rain was pouring from the
brims of the varnished hats of the drivers of cabs and omnibuses.
Coloured lights glittered in the puddles and lit the deep streams
that at the street corners were pouring noisily down into the
drains. In the air was that sharp smell of Caporal tobacco, that I
was soon smoking happily in a clay pipe like a skull with green
glass eyes. That glitter, that smell, the shouting of the newsboys,
'La Presse! La Patrie!', the tremendous cracking of whips, that
other well-remembered smell of roast chestnuts, the glow of the
charcoal fires of the chestnut-sellers, the roar of iron-shod wheels
on cobbles, still make Paris for me, the Paris of Balzac, Zola, the
Commune, the Dreyfus trial, the old Paris of the nineteenth
century of which I was just in time to catch a glimpse before it
was gone for ever. I paid four francs a week for a lodging on the
top floor of the Hôtel de la Haute Loire, where I was so cold that
I used to dance to be warm enough to sleep, until I made it colder
by unluckily putting my foot through one of its flimsy walls. I
spent an hour each day in the Louvre, looking first of all for the
Poussins and Lorraines that had meant so much to William
Hazlitt. I had a return ticket, so that I knew I could safely spend
all I had. I bought my first French books, cheap editions of Dumas,
Hugo and Gautier, at the stalls under the colonnade at the Odéon,
and delightedly found an early Yeats, *The Shadowy Waters*, in a
box at the quayside. With these treasures in my portmanteau,

4*

and two plaster-of-Paris replicas from the Louvre rolled up in my shirts for safe travelling, I came back penniless to Gunter Grove, feeling that the door was ajar into a new world and that I had set my foot there so that it should not close again.

# CHAPTER XI

## *Wall Nook Farm*

The moment there were buds on the trees in London I was in a hurry to get back to the north country. The Collingwoods went back to Coniston at Easter in 1905 but before the end of the winter I was planning a busy summer, far enough from Lanehead to keep me from being too often on the Collingwoods' doorstep, though both the Skald and my aunt had told me I should be welcome there. Gordon Bottomley was living then in an old house called Well Knowe outside Cartmel, and he found a lodging for me at Wall Nook, half a mile up the same side of the valley. For the next three summers I was there whenever I could escape from London. Wall Nook was a farmhouse. The farmer was a tall, kindly man called Newby Towers whose politics were not those of his energetic, bustling wife. In those days women had no votes, but Mrs Towers saw to it that if she could cast no vote on the right side, at least Mr Towers should cast none on the wrong. On the eve of the poll she took away and hid her husband's trousers and Mr Towers had to spend Election Day in bed. They gave me a good bedroom looking out over the fells and a sitting-room with a big round table in it and a high-backed chair, and fed me well for a pound a week. I was there for three happy summers and heard long afterwards that someone had asked Mrs Towers what sort of a lodger I had been. 'Eh!' she said, 'the most contentedest young man that ever was *and* the one that eat the most marmalade.'

Here I worked and walked and sometimes in the summer evenings wrestled (Cumberland and Westmorland style) with the postman and other young men who were practising for the Grasmere Sports. I would rise in the morning to the noise of fowls, sponge down in cold water (there was no bathroom), breakfast magnificently on porridge, eggs and bacon and Mrs Towers's excellent marmalade of which each winter she made many pots to last me through the next summer. Then, after a

sniff of the good air outside I would settle down in an absolute
quiet, work till lunch, walk a little, perhaps going down to Well
Knowe to listen to Gordon Bottomley playing Scarlatti, work
again and then walk down to Cartmel to an old house full of
young cousins, walking back again to find a jug of milk and a
plate of biscuits waiting for me on the table, to read a little and at
last to fall asleep listening to the churring of the nightjar in the
wood.

At Well Knowe, not more than a few minutes' walk by a foot-
path from Wall Nook, Gordon Bottomley, mild of eye, slow of
speech, archiepiscopal in manner, lived with his father, his
mother and his aunt, for all three of whom he was the pivot of
their lives. At that time he was a profound admirer of Rossetti,
Pater, Ricketts and Arthur Symons, whereas his father, who had
been an accountant at Keighley, had a much more athletic taste,
preferring the bracing air of Hazlitt and Landor. I have a photograph of the elder Bottomley standing proudly beside his son. 'I
had always wanted to have a poet for my son,' he once said to me.
'The day he was born I went out to a bookseller's and bought a
complete set of the Canterbury Poets and set the whole row of
them in a bookcase on the wall above his cot.' He was a most
lovable old man and Gordon Bottomley had made all his dreams
come true. Gordon had a weakness of the chest for which he
needed country air. He lived from year to year looking forward
to and remembering his short visits to London and the friends he
met there. 'We can live in the country but yet be of the centre,'
was one of his sayings. When I first knew him there was often
blood on his handkerchief and he was supposed to be dying and
this explained the attitude of his father, his mother, his aunt and,
later, his wife. He survived them all and lived his threescore years
and ten. As he grew older he outlived the affectations of his
youth, wrote many good plays and some lovely poems, such as
'Cartmel Bells', the simplicity of which was in complete contrast
to the orchid-house atmosphere of his early verse.

I wrote and burned a great many stories at Wall Nook. I had
always other work to do there. I read manuscripts for several
publishers and usually had a boxful of them in the corner of my
room. I suppose the publishers thought that I could summarise
plots for them and winnow away the worst of the rubbish as well
as anybody else and at much less cost to themselves. One year I
was much occupied with *Temple Bar*. Maurice Macmillan, the

father of my friend Daniel with whose brilliant progress as a schoolboy my own steady failure had been so often compared, sent for me when I was in town. He had for some time been watching with amusement, horror, but not disapproval, my comic career among publishers and he now did me a very good turn.

When Macmillan's bought Bentley's, they took over, among other properties, *Temple Bar*, a monthly magazine. Maurice Macmillan had taken a personal interest in it, but it was obviously creaking towards a standstill. This he recognised. It was edited by Mrs Gertrude Townshend Mayor, the widow of a former editor, and he did not wish to disturb her. 'But', he said, 'the magazine cannot go on for more than another year, and if you like you can try what you can do with it. Mrs Mayor will remain as editor but you can do whatever you like, so long as you do not make her feel that she is being pushed out of the way. You had better go to see her and come back and tell me how you get on and whether such an arrangement can be made to work.' He consulted a note on his desk and said, 'She tells me she will be at home today and tomorrow and suggests that you should come to tea.'

I have no idea what Mr Macmillan, one of the kindest and most tactful of men, had said to Mrs Mayor, but she was entirely charming to me. I went straight from the Macmillan office to the little house in Ealing where she lived. Mrs Mayor was sitting in her drawing-room, a little old lady in a flowered silk dress with piles of manuscript beside her on tables and on the floor. I had been reading Leigh Hunt's *Imagination and Fancy* on my way to Ealing, and I cannot remember now whether it was Mrs Mayor, or a friend of hers who joined us at tea, who told me that she had sat on Leigh Hunt's knee as a child and put cherries into his mouth. Leigh Hunt had been born in 1784 and had been a friend of Hazlitt. Our acquaintance could hardly have had a better beginning. Mrs Mayor further endeared herself to me by confessing that she never went to town without enjoying 'a potter down the Charing Cross Road' and a look into the boxes of secondhand books.

She made my work with her entirely pleasant by agreeing almost eagerly to anything I proposed. But it was too late to save *Temple Bar*, once to be found on drawing-room tables throughout England, particularly in vicarages and country houses. Its time had passed and it carried visible signs of the approaching end. The supply of paper had been cut down and it carried less print to a page than in its better days. Further, we were handicapped by a great mass of accepted matter, some of it already in type. Still Mrs Mayor was always ready to take my swans for the swans they really were and I was able to bring into that last volume of *Temple Bar* the work of several of my friends. Our editing did not take us long, because we had so little space to fill. When I was in London I used to have tea with Mrs Mayor once or twice a month, share the melancholy business of looking at things we knew we should not last long enough to print, and send several months' material to the printer, so that I could go north and there make up the magazine from galley-proofs, fill odd spaces from a store of poems kept for the purpose, send it to press from Cartmel or from Coniston and be free for other work. Maurice Macmillan paid me a welcome fifty pounds for thus assisting at the deathbed of *Temple Bar*. I should have been happy to do it for nothing.

While I was at Wall Nook I wrote for another publisher three silly little nature books for children ('Not bad for a little town boy,' was Mrs Collingwood's kindly verdict) and, at the suggestion of Ford Madox Hueffer, *Highways and Byways in Fairyland* (a good idea wasted). Hueffer made an appointment for me to meet him outside the House of Commons. What he was doing there I do not know. I kept the appointment and met him, a large blond confident man whom I, ten years younger than he, found most impressive. He had seen some fairy stories of mine and wanted me to write one of five little volumes that were to be published all together in a small cardboard case. For this venture he wrote *Christina's Fairy Book*. Netta Syrett, Anne Pye, Lady Margaret Sackville and I wrote the other four. We were paid ten pounds apiece for them, which seemed a lot of money for very little work. The three bad little 'country' books were unlucky. Their publisher went bankrupt at once and but for a small advance on the three of them I was not paid anything at all – a hard blow indeed.

Edward Thomas came up to Cartmel to walk with me and talk with Gordon Bottomley. Mrs Towers seldom had other guests staying in the farmhouse, but I remember a Liverpool family, headed by a tremendous shaggy old man. On the ground floor, in the room opposite my own, there was a tinkling piano used sometimes for solemn one-finger exercises by Mrs Towers's little daughter. I too used to strum on it, having taught myself to play simple tunes. One day I was hammering through the Marseillaise when I heard thunder on the floor above and down came the old man with flaming eyes. 'Who's playing my tune?' he shouted. 'Play it again.' I played as best I could and he roared the words. It was as if the little room was full of marching men. He was an old Communard of 1870.

At Wall Nook began one of the best friendships of my life. One evening, to my jealous disgust, I saw another young man coming through the garden gate and being welcomed by my own Mrs Towers. He was a lean, eager-faced young man and he walked out next morning with a bulky book under his arm. The book was very like *Hall & Knight's Algebra* and I put him down as a mathematician, no use to me at all. For three days we lived at Wall Nook without meeting. He had decided that I was something equally unwelcome. Then, one afternoon, we set out at the same time, collided in the doorway, and presently were talking. I forget how far we walked that day, along the road over Bigland and beyond. We were very late home that night, talking, I think, of Santayana, to whose *Life of Reason* Bottomley had introduced me. We laid that day the foundation-stone of a friendship that was to last our lives. Mrs Towers was delighted and thenceforward served our meals together.

Lascelles Abercrombie, after that first visit, came often to Cartmel and Wall Nook. He was courting his Catherine at Grange but used to walk with me part of the way when at weekends I walked over to Coniston, to see Barbara, spend the day on the lake and walk back at night. We used to start out from Wall Nook, keep along the high ground on the west side of the Cartmel valley, down the steep hill to Lowwood Bridge and so to a small inn with a delightful name, the Hark to Melody, with a painted signboard that I always believed to be a Morland, showing a pack of hounds in full cry. By the time we reached the Hark to Melody, we used to think we had fairly walked a pint. We then walked on by the road over the flats on the further side of the Leven, crossed Rusland Pool, neglected the Dickson Arms because Lascelles had a poor opinion of its beer, turned right by the Bouth road (unless for old sake's sake I wanted to have another look at Greenodd), came over the hill and down again to Spark Bridge and drank our second pint in the Red Lion at Lowick Bridge.

I had friends here from my Nibthwaite childhood among the charcoal-burners in the coppice-woods, and then and for many years thereafter they used to leave clay pipes for me at the Red Lion. No one will smoke such good pipes nowadays. A new clay pipe is a raw thing, apt to burn the tongue. But the charcoal-burners used always to put their own new pipes on their pitsteads under the skilfully built mound of wood that was to smoulder in its skin of turfs until it turned to charcoal. Then, when at last the mound was opened, they found their pipes glossy and coal-black, ready to give a cool sweet smoke from the first pipeful of tobacco. The right tobacco was Kendal twist. This could be had black or brown. The black, as Edward Thomas complained, was strong enough to knock out the unaccustomed southerner like a blow from a battering ram. The brown was a good deal stronger than the strongest Navy plug. Smoked in a pipe that had been through a charcoal-burner's fire, it was delicious. In those days our beer (better than today's) cost us fourpence a pint and our tobacco threepence-halfpenny an ounce. Pipes were a penny each, though most inns kept a stock of them in the bar and any customer could have one for the asking. One year Lascelles's Catherine and her sister rented a little cottage just round the corner from Bottomley's and I used to visit them there with Lascelles and play with a wild mouse, Percy, who lived in a hole by the cottage door and was on the best of terms with all of us except John Tubbs, a liver-and-white spaniel given me by the Hart Jacksons of Ulverston. It was tactful to leave him behind when calling on Percy.

Back in London, in the winter of 1906, I moved from Gunter Grove to Carlyle Studios in the Kings Road. The studios were presided over by two very kind old ladies, the Misses Gray, and they had a few rooms to spare in the part of the building that was too narrow to suit painters or sculptors. I had two communicating rooms, and was very comfortable there, with my books and a tiny Adam fireplace with a hob that seemed designed for my kind of simple cooking. In one of the studios below lived two Balmer brothers, of whom one, Clinton, had made decorations for some of Gordon Bottomley's poems, and the other had written stories in some of the popular magazines. Both were interested in music, and with cello, piano, violin and flageolet we must have been a nuisance to our neighbours. In Sloane Square there was the Court Theatre and we were regular attendants in the shilling

seats at the early performances of Shaw's plays. There was good
music too in a flat on the Chelsea Embankment, close by the
power station, and here I used to meet Clifford Bax from Hampstead, and play chess with him. One afternoon a famous chess-
player was there and sat in a room taking tea with our hostess and
a friend while Bax and I sat in another room over the chess-
board. We consulted, agreed over a move and called it out.
Laughter and talk went on unceasingly, but the moment we had
called out our move, that chess-player, who had no board to
look at, would instantly call out his answering move, and move
by move, we consulting, he playing blindfold, our defeat came
nearer until at last the voice from the inner room quietly
announced 'Enough! Mate in three moves,' and it was so.

Masefield came to Carlyle Studios and I went down the river
to Greenwich, where he was living at Diamond Terrace, tip-toed
out through the tiny garden to see Judith bubbling, tight-fisted,
in her cot, and walked with Masefield over Greenwich Park to
the river, where we sat in a tavern with a window over the water
and watched a full-rigged ship towing up to the docks after her
long voyage. Then, too, I had 'Uncle Will' to visit, William
Canton, up in Highgate, dismally plodding at his history of the
Bible Society and, like W. G. Collingwood and W. H. D.
Rouse, urging me to take courage and write a long romance,
without wasting any more time on short-breathed experiments.
This was just what I wished some day to write, but I failed, and
failed and failed again.

At the Covent Garden end of Henrietta Street, where the
*Week's Survey* had its office there were several literary agents. My
first friend among them was C. F. Cazenove, and I mentioned his
name to Masefield, whose agent he became. I was not myself
much use to any agent, nor could any agent do much for me, yet
I came to owe to one of them the commissioning of the first book
I wrote that was not altogether a makeshift. In the same block as
Cazenove's offices were those of Curtis Brown. I had friends for
whom they acted and so had become acquainted with a clever
young woman who had recently joined them. This was Stefana
Stevens, who subsequently made two successful careers for herself. In the first, as E. S. Stevens, she became a very popular
novelist. In the second, after she had married Edwin Drower of
the Sudan service, later Sir Edwin and Judicial Adviser in Baghdad,
she became an authority on Middle Asian folklore and religions

and, by making nice clean copies for the priests, was able to bring to England and the Bodleian Library many original texts that would otherwise have remained unknown in the small hill monasteries of Iraq.* When I first met her she was studying Romany and I was head over ears in Borrow and Charles Godfrey Leland. One day, in the winter of 1906 when Cecil Chesterton and I were having tea at the St George's in St Martin's Lane, she came across to our table and said, 'There's a book that ought to be written, and you are the one who ought to write it, a book on Bohemia in London, an essayistical sort of book, putting Bohemia of today against a background of the past. Think it over. I've got a publisher waiting for it.' It did not take much thinking over. By next morning I had sketched a synopsis. Two days later Curtis Brown had a contract ready for me to sign. The publishers were Chapman & Hall, whose offices also were in Henrietta Street and, to my further amazement, Curtis Brown sold the book (still unwritten) to Dodd Mead & Co. in America. In both countries I was to have a respectable royalty, and an advance on account, and was asked to let them have the book in time for publication in the autumn of 1907.

I set to work at once in Chelsea and the London Library, did a great deal of the rough work and found a good artist to make pictures for it. This was Fred Taylor, whose black-and-white poster of a newsboy (used to advertise W. H. Smith & Son) suggested to me that he could do just what we wanted. He thought so too and we worked well together. I had no idea then that I should one day be illustrating my own books, but Taylor, after seeing some of the sketches I had made at Cartmel and Coniston, took me with him to the meetings of the Langham Sketch Club, where a group of draughtsmen used to share a model, putting down a shilling apiece for the evening. In the early spring I went off to Cartmel with a crate full of books, had more books from the London Library sent after me in relays, and settled down at Wall Nook to be Hazlitt, Lamb and Leigh Hunt all rolled into one.

I was twenty-two when I began that book, twenty-three when I finished it, but no one could have guessed that from the book, which is written almost as if from a great distance I were looking back on my own youth. It has much rubbish in it but is not

* In 1955 she was given a doctorate of letters by Oxford University; in 1959 she was made a D.D. of Uppsala in Sweden.

wholly bad, though I should be sorry if it were to be reprinted. I had given myself a free hand by writing in the opening chapter that 'Bohemia … is a tint in the spectacles through which one sees the world in youth. It is not a place but an attitude of mind.' And I told no more than the truth when, in the final chapter, I wrote, 'My life will be the happier, turn out what it may, for these friendships, these pot-house nights, these evenings in the firelight of a studio, and these walks, two or three of us together talking from our hearts, along the Embankment in the Chelsea evening, with the lamps sparkling above us in the leaves of the trees, the river moving with the sweet noise of waters, the wings of youth on our feet, and all the world before us.' In spite of its childishness, the book has an odd infectious quality that made it some surprising friends.

I finished it before the summer ended and went up to London with it, a little worried because in one of its chapters I had written of M. P. Shiel in a manner that, though friendly, I feared he might not approve. I told him what I had done and asked if I might dedicate the book to him. Shiel, not hoodwinked in the least, replied, 'Dedicate the book to me and libel me as much as you please.' I always liked him, even when, after I had presented a letter of introduction from him to a friend of his in Paris, who must have passed the news on, other friends came rattling at the door of my hotel bedroom, asked for him, said how much they would like to wring his neck, and peered eagerly all round my room as if they half-hoped I might have him there, hidden under the bed. The last time I saw him was many years later, in St Martin's Lane. He passed me, panting, a stout elderly man in a velvet jacket, running along the edge of the pavement, in and out of the gutter, elbows well tucked in. 'Wait!' he gasped. 'Back in a minute. I turn at St Martin's Church.' I waited for him and he came back. He had long given up his early belief in sour milk as an elixir of life, at least in English sour milk, but now made a point of running each day from his lodging to St Martin's Church, and strongly advised me to do the same. If a man were to run a mile or two every day, he was sure, there was nothing to prevent his living for ever.

Within a few weeks of my manuscript reaching Henrietta Street the book had been set up and the proofs corrected. It was published before the end of September, a stout grey volume, looking like a real book, of which I was extremely proud. It was praised far beyond its deserts and at great length. Arthur Waugh, son of Edwin Waugh the author of *Lancashire Tales*, and himself the father of two highly successful novelists then in the nursery, the managing director of Chapman & Hall, at once commissioned another book, the subject of which was to be less limited. It was to be a book with the thinnest of threads on which I was to string a series of chapters, essays in the manner of those chapters in *Bohemia* that he thought had particularly touched the hearts of my reviewers. The title, he thought, was a good one, *The Book of a Thousand and One Pipes*. It may have been a good one. It may have been too good for me. I was never able to write it. Not for the first time nor for the last, I was to haul in sheets, put the tiller hard down and go off on a new tack.

# CHAPTER XII
## *Montparnasse*

My mother had moved to Edinburgh to make a home for my brother Geoffrey. With characteristic thoroughness he had made up his mind to be a printer and was going through the whole seven years' apprenticeship that a master-printer needs, working his way from the compositors' bench through all the departments of that intricate business in the works of R. & R. Clark who printed most of the Macmillans' books and were among the half-dozen best printers in the world. My brother liked the Scots and they liked him. He used to say that he never heard better talk in his life than that of his fellow-compositors who, while setting up type by hand (this was before the deafening and deadening lino-type machines had come into general use), were wont from one end of the day to the other to argue the problems of philosophy. Like Hazlitt they could have said that nothing affected them but an abstract idea. Geoffrey was a great player of the bagpipes. When during summer holidays the family stayed at Ulpha in the Duddon valley, my mother who, like many English folk, liked bagpipes best at a distance, forbade them near the house and Geoffrey, undaunted, used to climb Caw and play them on its summit. Here, in Edinburgh, he used to take his pipes to the top of Arthur's Seat. He was, I believe, the only Englishman admitted to membership of the Scottish Pipers' Club. To join it a man must play his way in, judged by the listening experts, and I think a member of the club has the right to have six pipers play at his funeral. None played at his. He fought in France, was wounded three times and went back yet again to be killed early in 1918.

My mother's house was in Dalrymple Crescent, Morningside. My eldest sister was studying art, and my younger, who in some subjects had outgrown the learning of our dear Miss Sidgmore, was a pupil of the very clever nuns of an Edinburgh convent. In a street near by was the office of Messrs T. C. & E. C. Jack with

whom I already had some slight acquaintance. I had always liked
Edinburgh, if only because no matter where a man may stand in
that rock-built, windy city, he has only to look one way or other
to get a glimpse of distant hills. My brother was an admirable
guide to it. With him I walked to Leith and Portobello, to look
out across the Forth with memories of David Balfour and Alan
Breck Stewart. With him I walked in the Pentlands, and on a
New Year's Eve he took me to the Tron Church to see Scotsmen
dancing in rings round a smiling tolerant policeman and to hear
the crash of broken glass as Scotsmen, emptying their whisky-
bottles, saluted the new year by hurling the bottles at the church.
On an earlier visit I had thought of taking a lodging in one of the
crowded wynds of the Canongate as a suitable place in which to
write fairy stories. Now, with *Bohemia in London* off my shoulders,
my mind was full of other things. I was again worrying over the
technique of narrative which I found at once so interesting and so
difficult, and I had, I thought, an excuse for as much reading as I
could persuade a publisher to pay for. One day, on impulse, I
turned into the offices of Messrs Jack to see what Edwin Jack
would say about it. His firm had been publishing several series and
I suggested a new one. I proposed a number of volumes that
should illustrate the art of storytelling, each one to consist of
stories selected by myself and prefaced by a short study of an
individual storyteller. Edwin Jack liked the idea and decided on
'The World's Storytellers' as a general title. I was to be editor,
responsible for finding translations where necessary, and the
introductions were to be so planned that they could eventually be
used as chapters in *A History of Story-Telling*. I was to be paid for
any translations I made myself, and any money I might need
while working on the book was to be advanced on account of
payments and royalties to be earned. I doubt if any English
publisher would have been so rash, though more than one said
afterwards that they would have welcomed the idea.

I went back to London at once, paid my good landladies at
Carlyle Studios to keep my rooms for me and was presently on
my way to Paris to work in the Bibliothèque Nationale and
produce the first volumes for Jack. A life as a writer of critical
essays seemed to stretch invitingly before me into a distant future.
(The spill-maker again, though I was now no longer eight but
twenty-three.)

After those first few days in the winter of 1904 I had made it

almost a rule that when particularly hard up I must take a cheap
return ticket to Paris just in case I could never afford to go there
again. Clive Bell, all unwittingly, had a share in bringing about
this resolve. His mother in Wiltshire was a friend of one of my
aunts, and to please one or both of them he was extremely kind to
me. He was a year or two older than I, mathematically speaking,
but many years further along his own road. He distinguished
sharply, as I did not, between ancients and moderns, and already
dismissed as out of date and uninteresting much that I, still
omnivorous, revered. He had had poems printed and had enjoyed
the exciting comradeship of his contemporaries at Cambridge at
a time when I was thinking myself lucky to be able to keep
myself fed by writing anything that I could find someone to buy.
He must have been terribly bored by his ingenuous companion.
But he hid this and took me with him to Montmartre, where
there was a fair in the Place Clichy and it was possible to ride on a
merry-go-round with painted wooden pigs and ostriches, and
even to one of the big cafés of the Boulevards where he introduced
me to a famous lady straight out of a Manet picture, with whom
we sat at a marble table and drank a queer, pale drink over which
I had a struggle not to choke. Already he knew how, by his way
of looking at pictures, to make other people look at them too, and
when, more than forty years later, I saw a man looking in that
particular way at a picture at one of the exhibitions of the London
School, I knew him at once as the Clive Bell whose certainty in
all matters of art, whose fluent French, whose knowledge of a
wider world than mine, had so impressed me long ago.

His Paris was that of Mallarmé, mine that of Balzac and Gautier,
and these I had read at that time only in English translations. I was
tongue-tied with the natives. Clive Bell was at ease and at home.
When we went down to Tours, where Bell was studying and
living in the house of a commandant at Saint Symphorien, I was
still more out of it, though I did know one universal language in
chess and had some uproarious games with the conductor of an
orchestra in a café of the town. I lodged there in a hotel that can
hardly have changed since the days of the Three Musketeers. It
had a central courtyard, round which, at the height of the first
storey, ran a balcony on which were half-a-dozen or so open
cubicles, each with a hole in the floor. There were no other
sanitary arrangements (indeed at that time, even in Paris, hotel-
keepers used to take prospective guests to the newly installed

water-closets and solemnly pull the plug to show how wonderfully they worked) and while the guests were engaged in the cubicles the waiter would lean at ease against the balustrade and act as focal point of a general conversation. I began to learn French in a hurry, and wished I had learnt a little more at school. I wanted to learn it so as to be able to read it, but envy of Clive Bell was a valuable spur.

I think I should confess that I never did learn French, to talk it as it should be talked, but I learnt to read it as easily as English, and to rattle away in a language the French understood and that later Remy de Gourmont, Paul Fort and even Anatole France used to forgive. But I am no sort of polyglot, and when I learnt Russian my French went to the bad, and if I tried to talk one language after reading or talking the other, words of both met in my throat and almost choked me, and today I should be dismayed if I had to talk either, though I can still read both with the utmost ease and pleasure.

In 1907, on reaching Paris, I went first to the hotel in the Boulevard Raspail where I had once stayed in a galvanised tin box of a room on the roof at a rent of four francs a week. This time I had a better room but presently hunted round for a cheap studio and found one on the sixth or seventh floor of a great block of *ateliers* in the Rue Campagne Première, that had been built from the remains of the Paris Exhibition. Here too the walls were thin, but mostly of wood, with the outer walls almost entirely of glass. In those days the Quarter did its best for hard-up students, and I was able to furnish my studio for next to nothing, with a narrow box-mattress for a bed, a kitchen table on which to work, and a pleasant little iron stove that burned charcoal or *boulets* and more than once came near to closing my career by asphyxiation.

I sent a drawing of my studio to my mother and also a sketch of the whole building and she pointed out at once that if anybody were to upset a stove in any of the studios the whole place would flare up like a match-box. Was there a fire-escape? There was not, but I agreed to calm her fears by making one. I went out to look for a stout rope that would reach from the top of the building to the bottom. After looking at several ropes in a neighbouring shop and rejecting them, I found one that seemed strong enough and threw an end of it over a beam and swung on it to see if it would bear my weight. The *patronne* from behind her desk watched this performance with a face increasingly grave. She left her desk, waved aside the man who was serving me, and spoke seriously in my ear. 'No, no, Monsieur,' she said, 'you are young and life is still sweet.' I reassured her and went out of the shop with the big coil of rope over my shoulder. Back in my studio I had to try it. I fastened one end of it round my box-mattress, wedged so that it could not shift and paid the rope out of the window. I had been a little mean and it did not quite reach the ground. Still, it did not look much too short and I climbed out of the window and began to go down. My fire-escape, meant to save life, very nearly took me to my death. I went slowly down the rope, passing as I went the glass fronts of the lower studios. At that time Paris was suffering from an epidemic of robberies with violence, and the sudden appearance of a man on a rope outside his studio on the fifth floor shocked a French artist at his work. I had reached the floor below his when a window opened above me and he leaned out, voluble and hostile. '*Au secours!*' he yelled. '*Les Apaches! Les Apaches!*' I could do nothing but continue my descent. And then that lunatic, no doubt thinking that he was virtuously defeating a marauder, grabbed my rope and began trying to shake me off it. I became the bob of a pendulum that was beginning to swing. There was a crash of glass and then another. Hand over fist I went down to tinkling music, in a shower of glass. I had six feet to drop at the bottom and a lot of glass to pay for. But my mother, on hearing that I had now an efficient fire-escape, was at peace. I thought it better not to tell her how it had been tested.

Montparnasse in those days was a delightful place. The American invasion had not yet made living there expensive. We were all hard-up together. The rich went elsewhere. I wore ready-made corduroys like most of the other students, and I well remember how, after I had breakfasted at a little *crémerie* four or five times, the *patronne* behind the counter called her husband from the kitchen. He looked at me and nodded and that morning and for the rest of that visit to Paris the bill for my *petit déjeuner* was half what it had been. There was a little restaurant in the Boulevard Raspail where the madame in charge, first Madame Garnier and later Madame Leduc (God bless them both!), allowed us to feed extremely cheaply and to pay when we had the money. I never heard of an English student who went away from Paris without settling up with Madame, who had even been known to lend a little pocket money to students who temporarily had none. In my studio I cooked my own breakfast, making the best coffee

I have ever tasted by means of a nickel percolator that fitted over a glass, and scrambling a couple of eggs in butter to go with the luscious *croissants* that the baker used to deliver, still warm, at the studio door.

After breakfast I used to walk through the Luxembourg Gardens past the statue of Sainte-Beuve who (while I was being a critical essayist) had a niche not far from Hazlitt's in my private Pantheon, and so to the Odéon Theatre and the bookshops under its arches. Some days I would hurry on over the river to the Library; on others I would loiter along the quays where it was possible to pick up astonishing bargains from the boxes clamped to the parapet. I used to lunch wherever I happened to be, going for the most part to the small restaurants patronised by the cab-drivers, whose shiny varnished hats always showed where good food was cheaply to be had. Then back to my studio to work again until it was time to hurry across the Boulevard Raspail to Madame's for dinner. I remember some of her dishes still. Brains in black butter was one of my favourites, but she prided herself rightly on her chateaubriands, her tournedos, and her vol-au-vents. We were a very mixed lot at that restaurant, English, French, Swedes, Hungarians, Americans and Poles. The Poles used to crowd in all together, chatter over the menu, depute one of their number to order a dish, the others not ordering until it had come and he had eaten his first mouthful. Then there would be a chorus of enquiry. '*Dobshe? Dobshe? Dobshe?*' And if he answered '*Dobshe*,' the others, apparently sure that what was liked by one would be liked by all, would order the same dish. After dinner a coffee or a book at the Dôme or the Versailles at the top of the Rue de Rennes, or at the Closerie des Lilas, where Paul Fort held court. Sometimes a party of us would go to the Bal Bullier opposite the Lilas, sometimes to the Gaîté Montparnasse, a most friendly little music hall in the Rue Vercingetorix. Then back again to my studio to read until I could no longer keep awake.

There were many distractions. Some of my friends made a habit of going out to Fontainebleau where it was possible to hire cheap hacks. I used at first to refuse to go with them because I had never learned to ride. My only experience of horses had been as a small fat boy when I shared a governess with E. Eddison. Ric had a globular pony and used to sit on it while Miss Glendinning and I walked alongside. When it was my turn, Miss Glendinning used

to lift Ric off and put me in his place, but was unable to do so
without rousing the pony's suspicions. He always knew that
something was wrong and, after going for a few yards, would put
his head down and stop suddenly, when I used to slide over his
head and find myself on the ground with the pony's nose sniffing
at my face in innocent curiosity. This was obviously not enough
to qualify me for going out with these Parisian horsemen. However, I was persuaded by one of them to go and look at a riding-
school near by. A crowd of young men, badly dressed like myself,
were standing in a group, watching two or three others riding
solemnly round a ring. A stout cavalry sergeant was in charge.
Presently he pointed to one of the young men. The young man
answered with a number. The sergeant roared out the number,
followed by the name of a horse. '*Cinquante-neuf ... Pégase!*' A
groom led Pégase from some inner stable. Pégase had a saddle but
no stirrups. The young man gripped neck and saddle and swung
himself up. Pégase took his place in the circling procession. This
had happened several times when the sergeant suddenly pointed
at me. I said nothing. '*Numéro?*' said he fiercely. '*Soixante-sept,*' I
replied on the spur of the moment. '*Soixante-sept ... Bucéphale!*'
Bucéphale, a monstrous grey, was led forth and, somehow or
other, doing as I had seen others do, I found myself in the saddle.
Round and round we went and I was duly cursed for not holding
the reins right. Finally we trotted and, just as I had made up my
mind that I could not keep on a moment longer, we stopped,
everyone dismounted, we were told when to come again, and the
lesson was over. I had quite unintentionally attached myself to a
class of young men destined for the French Colonial Cavalry. I
had several more lessons before suspicion was aroused and I
thought it better to keep away. I had never been promoted to
stirrups, and when at last I went out riding with my painter
friends, I could not use my stirrups but used to cross them on the
saddle before me.

In Paris I found an artist to make a series of portraits to illustrate
the World's Storytellers. This was Miss Jessie Gavin, who, like
Abercrombie, came from Liverpool. With her I felt that the north
country was not so very far away, and we used once or twice a
month to go by train to Rambouillet and then walk some twenty
kilometres in the forest, ending with a vast dish of scrambled eggs
at a little inn before catching the train back to Paris. She was an
etcher and lived in a flat above the Quai St Michel where she had

her etching press and was looked after by a charming old woman called Victoire who the first time I was there lost the little note-book in which she kept their household accounts, and thereafter, for years, always announced me as '*le monsieur qui a volé notre carnet*,' regularly to be rebuked by Miss Gavin, who pointed out that I had no interest in their *carnet* and that Victoire herself had probably dropped it in the market.

I met the American sculptor Jo Davidson the morning he arrived in Paris with some clay figurines in a wicker basket. He was at once welcomed into the studio of another young sculptor (also Jewish-American) and, meeting this young man in the Rue Vercingetorix I was hauled off at once to meet the new genius he had collected. Jo Davidson nearly starved in Paris but took his chance when it came, just in time, when the famous Madame Steinheil accused him of being the murderer of her husband, and every lady with a *salon* in Paris wanted to exhibit him among her guests. His fortune was made, and later, after triumphs in America, he went to Russia and made portrait-busts of Lenin, Trotsky and other leaders of the Russian Revolution.

I was troubled at that time with violent headaches, for which I found walking the best though a painful cure. I used to set out from my studio half-blind with pain and, stumbling resolutely on, would find the pain lessening and at last gone altogether. One day with one of these headaches I set out from the Rue Campagne Première and walked out by the Lion de Belfort to the fortifications, when, though I found my headache slackening, the fine spring evening made me unwilling to turn back. I slept that night at Longjumeau, bought a toothbrush and, next day's weather being even more inviting, walked on and on, day after day, by Étampes, Angerville, Artenay, and so to Orléans, Blois and the country of the Loire, sleeping for the night in little roadside inns where a bush hung over the door advertised shelter and food 'for men and beasts' as in the distant past. On these roads I learned to drink wine straight from the goatskin. The roadmenders and others on their way to work, with a small handcart carrying their tools, were never in a hurry, and always wished to talk. They would stop when they met anybody and would be much offended if he were unwilling to stop also. Then from the handcart they would lift the goatskin bloated with the red wine of the country, and hold it, pinching the spout at the level of my nose. I had to open my mouth, when they would relax their grip and a powerful jet of

wine would squirt to the back of my throat. The trick of this
drinking is to swallow and keep on swallowing with open mouth.
To close the mouth, if only for a second, is to invite disaster.

Two or three days out from Paris I sent a note to the concierge
at Campagne Première, telling her to stop delivery of my milk
and bread until I should return. I bought a knapsack of sorts in
Orléans, a clean shirt and a cheap six-holed whistle-pipe, as I had
left my own behind. The whistle-pipe was presently useful. I
caught up on the road with a party of travelling showmen, their
wives, their children and three light-coloured bears. We got on
very well together and slept that night, bears and all, in a barn.
They sang, asked me to sing and when I pulled out my whistle-
pipe instead, proposed that we should continue our travels
together. This did not last long, for I could not dawdle at the pace
that suited the bears and their owners. But I was with them long
enough to enjoy methods of dealing with a by-law that forbade
their staging a performance in a village. They seemed to know
beforehand whether such a by-law was in force. If it was, they
would call a halt some little way outside the village. They would
refresh themselves, give the bears a loaf or two of bread, and take
breath before action. Then they would enter the village at high
speed and, immediately, begin their forbidden performance.
Instantly, an indignant shirt-sleeved Frenchman, working in his
garden, would shout to them to get out as quickly as possible.
'Who orders that?' 'I, the Commissaire!' 'That's a fine story. A
beautiful village like this and a little runt like you pretending to
be its commissaire! You don't take us in that way. Where's your
uniform?' The commissaire would soon be screaming with rage,
and the villagers delightedly listening to the bear-leader telling
him things about himself that they would not have dared even to
whisper. The bear-leader would flatly refuse to believe that the
commissaire was anything but an imposter. Finally the commissaire would dash into his cottage, and, a moment later, spitting
with rage, would continue the duel from his bedroom window,
while hauling on his uniform trousers. Then he would come
down. The bear-leader would appear dumbfounded at the sight
of the uniform and would instantly march his troupe out of the
village. The whole population of the village, delighted with what
they had heard, would march out with them. And the bear-
leaders, once outside the commissaire's jurisdiction, would begin
their performance to a crowd of grateful spectators whose

centimes rewarded the cheeking of the village commissaire rather than anything out of the way in the tricks of the bears.

I have never learned to draw, but at this time I always carried a sketch-book in my pocket and, on the long walk that resulted from that fortunate headache, I did a number of drawings of gargoyles. My wanderings in the Loire country ended at the delightful little town of Meung, where lived Jean de Meung of *The Romance of the Rose* who has a place in any history of story-telling. From Meung I went back to Paris, and another steady bout of reading, before sending the texts of the early volumes of the World's Storytellers to Edwin Jack, buying a tent and going once more to Cartmel and to Coniston.

# CHAPTER XIII

## *Owen Mansions and Low Yewdale*

Coming back from Paris in the spring of 1908 I moved ambitiously from Carlyle Studios (my two old landladies were retiring into private life) to a flat in Owen Mansions, Queens' Club Gardens. I had there a good work-room, plenty of bookshelves, the first of the big tables I have always liked, two armchairs, one given me by my mother, a kitchen, airy bedroom, a bathroom and a 'daily woman' who used to come in the mornings to tidy up, though I did most of my own cooking. Now the worst of having such things is that they predispose the owner to marriage, and at the same time seem to make marriage more likely, quite regardless of the presence or absence of the right young woman. Such a flat seems to be wasted on a mere bachelor, and before he knows what is happening nature is at her old business of abhorring vacuums and the bachelor is a bachelor no longer.

Further, now that I was no longer hoping sooner or later to marry Barbara Collingwood, I had acquired the very bad habit of beginning the day's work by writing a love-letter to some real or imaginary person. What was worse, if the letter seemed a good one, I sometimes, to my shame, put it in the pillar-box. I can see no excuse for this. Not all my correspondents were as quick and witty as Sylvia Dryhurst who replied 'Very nice, but you should do it in person. Come along tomorrow afternoon and propose at four, sharp. And then we'll have tea.' Another time, horrified at what I had done, I had to pursue the letter to the banks of the Clyde. Sylvia presently married Robert Lynd and both were good friends of mine until they died. I blush even to think of my stupidities, for it was not that I had fallen in love with anybody, but merely that I wanted some sort of reassurance, and that I wanted to have someone at the other end of the breakfast-table, to walk with, to make a home with and, using Hazlitt's phrase, perfectly expressive of this kind of domesticity, someone with whom 'to gather mushrooms to drop into our hashed mutton at supper'. I was now twenty-four but, as always, a great deal too young for my age, and knowing much less of life than is known by most boys of eighteen.

I wasted as little time as possible in London, went north as usual and soon had an admirable base at Low Yewdale under Raven Crag, at the head of the Coniston valley. I had civilised lodgings in the cottage of a charming old couple, Mr and Mrs Bennett. Mr Bennett lent me an ancient leaden tobacco-box, and himself put slivers of apple in it to keep my tobacco from growing too dry. Mrs Bennett used to dip the water for washing out of Yewdale Beck that sang just under my windows, and more than once I found a minnow swimming in the jug. Here I kept my boxes of books and worked in bad weather. But for good weather I had a second home, in a tent on a small mound close to Yewdale Beck a few hundred yards up the valley. This must have been one of the first tents seen in these valleys which are now thick with campers. In those days there were no great houses doing a brisk trade in 'camping equipment'. Mine was a 'King's Herdsman's tent', of rather heavy canvas with poles that fitted into tubes, crossing each other at the top of the tent like rabbits' ears. I had already been learning what I could of gipsy language from Leland and from Borrow's *Romano Lavo-Lil*, and had made friends with several groups of travelling showmen and tinkers, some of whom (not the tinkers, who had a cant of their own) were still talking Romany. The Bennetts were not very fond of these visitors, and began by suspecting the worst, though my gipsies behaved nobly and nothing was ever missed while they were there. One gipsy in particular, Arthur Stanborough, was a frequent visitor and he had a friend, a Stanley, who had remained loyal to Stanborough when most of the gipsies were cold-shouldering him because he had married a tinker girl instead of a true gipsy. I learnt from them of the gipsy centre at Millom, 'where all the old buck Romans go in the winter' to sit by the fire and talk Romany among themselves. It was these two who showed me the Romany game in which, when a lot of gipsies are together in a tavern or elsewhere, each man shows some small object to the rest, a handkerchief, a coin, a pebble, a pipe, a ring, or what not. All the others have a look at each object whereupon the game begins without a word said. The men will sing, drink

1    Ric Eddison, A.R. and Mr Pegg

2  A.R.'s father

3  A.R.'s mother

4  W. G. Collingwood

5  Mrs Collingwood

6   Barbara Collingwood     7   Dora Collingwood

8   Robin Collingwood

9 and 10   A.R. as war correspondent

and tell stories, moving from one group to another until, when the evening ends and it is time to pay the score, the gipsy who can show the largest collection of the chosen objects stolen from his friends has his evening's drink for nothing, the total score being divided among the less successful pickpockets. This I may say is a much better game than poker and brings into play a greater variety of talents.

I greatly valued these friends, not because of any serious study of their language, but because, like my old friends among the charcoal-burners and the Swainsons at Nibthwaite, the Towerses at Cartmel, they helped to make me feel that I had a countryside I could call my own. I valued them for their own sake and, as I valued the corncrakes in the fields below the bobbin-mill, the heron by the lake-shore and the otters sporting by moonlight in the lake, as proofs to myself that I had again come home.

Then, in a different category, there were the friends with whom I wished to share my home country. I was busy carrying on at Low Yewdale the editing of my storytellers for Edwin Jack, and Miss Gavin, who was doing woodcutty portraits for them and for my pretence at a history of storytelling, brought a portfolio of them over from Paris when she came in the summer to visit her relations on the Mersey. Miss Turner, who married Jan Gordon the art critic, and with him produced some lively illustrated travel books, came to Coniston for a few days, and on a general walk over to Ambleside put us all to shame by her tree-climbing skill when we had stopped for bread and cheese and beer by the Drunken Duck at Barngates. Lascelles Abercrombie was there in that happy summer with his Catherine. They were shortly to be married and in that year he published his first book *Interludes and Poems,* which was welcomed by Masefield and others to the delight of us all. They brought friends, the Rawlinses of Skelgill, and Dixon Scott who, like Lascelles and Miss Gavin, came from Liverpool. We were all young enough to delight in slogans, and it was one day at Low Yewdale that Dixon Scott, in momentary rebellion against the somewhat hothouse atmosphere then admired by Bottomley, proclaimed that what we wanted was 'Roast Beef and Rose-buds!' Dixon Scott was a brilliant talker and, when he came to London, lions of all kinds fed at his hands like lambs. He died of dysentery at the Dardanelles and never wrote the books that Lascelles and I and all his other friends were sure he would one day write. With Stevenson's *Edinburgh* in his mind he wrote a very good little book on Liverpool, and a volume of literary portraits called *Men of Letters*, to which Max Beerhohm wrote an introduction. But his best memorial is the volume of his letters edited by Miss Mary McCrossan, the painter, and published in 1932. That book reflects the intensity with which he tried to make experience his own by finding the right words for it. This determination gave his early letters a preciosity that both Lascelles and I found irritating, but from the first we knew he would grow out of it, and the latter letters show that he was indeed doing so. He had an extraordinary chameleon-like power of fitting himself for his company. He seemed to one after another of his widely differing elders a promise of fulfilling that elder's dream of what he would wish himself to have been. He fell in love with my Yewdale tent and next year bought one for himself and pitched it on Wansfell above Skelgill. There was continual coming and going of the whole lot of us between Yew-dale, Skelgill and Cartmel, and I used also to walk over Walna Scar to Ulpha, to see my mother, brother and sisters, and to bathe in Lang Dub in the Duddon.

My relations with the Collingwoods were the same as ever, in spite of their recognition that there was no longer any likelihood that Barbara and I would marry. I used to take carefully chosen specimens from my Yewdale visitors for exhibition at Lanehead, much to my aunt's amusement. Years after she used to recall how one young man from London trying to make polite conversation told her that he thought it was a pity that people were allowed to eat immature vermicelli instead of letting them grow to macaroni. The younger Collingwoods were beginning to catch us up. Robin was now near the head of the school, and soon to leave Rugby for Oxford. I am not sure which year it was when he brought a friend of his from Rugby, Ernest Altounyan, the son of an Armenian doctor and an Irish nurse, to stay at Lanehead. He shilly-shallied a little between Dora and Barbara, but in the end married Dora and took her away to Aleppo. When he first arrived I was jealous and thought him quite unnecessary. I think it was in this year's summer holidays that Robin Collingwood built a boat out of two packing-cases with a skin of canvas, and suc-ceeded in crossing the lake in it, from the Lanehead boathouse to the Gondola Pier before it sank and left him to wade ashore. We were also sailing *Swallow* and *Toob*, an eight-foot dinghy which Robin fitted with a single leeboard fastened by a rope to the middle thwart, so that it could be put over the side to port or starboard according to the tack on which *Toob* was trying to sail. These two were presently joined by *Jamrach*, a partly-decked sloop belonging to Miss Holt of Tent Lodge (and of Lamport & Holt, the shipping firm of Liverpool) and meant for the use of her cousins, the Rawdon Smiths, one of whom had been at Rugby with me and the other with Robin. These two were not markedly web-footed and I do not remember seeing *Jamrach* sailed by anybody but Robin and me. We had great fun sailing *Jamrach* and *Swallow* against each other, each of us singlehanded.

This account of the summer of 1908 seems to be full of friendships and fooleries, but in fact it was a season of very hard work, reviewing, reading manuscripts for publishers, preparing for press volumes of the World's Storytellers, writing chapters to go into the history, and sometimes turning resolutely from all this to further experiments in narrative. Anderson Graham printed a fairy story of mine in *Country Life*, and asked for more, but instantly what had seemed a promising spring dried up. When at the end of the summer I went back to London, I had no time to spare, working at home and in libraries all day, and in the evening taking hard exercise on roller skates at Earls Court and Olympia.

While I was tidying away poor *Temple Bar* I met Miss Ethel Colburn Mayne, one of the contributors, who was afterwards to write a very good book on Byron. One day, this autumn of 1908, she invited me to a dinner in Soho to meet a young protégé of hers, a schoolmaster at Epsom called Hugh Walpole. Her guests were to meet at the entrance to the Palace Theatre in Cambridge Circus and to dine at *Le Petit Riche* in Old Compton Street. In those days I wore a brown corduroy coat and, on coming to Cambridge Circus a few minutes early, saw with some annoyance another man in a brown corduroy coat of exactly the same colour as my own. I hoped he would go away before Miss Mayne's guests arrived. But he did not go away. On the contrary, just as I was staring at him he began to stare at me and in the end we both spoke at the same moment and asked the same question. 'Who are you, wearing my coat?' He was Charles Marriott, novelist and later art critic, and we agreed, in case of questions, to explain that we had each lent a coat to the other. Then came Miss Mayne with her pink young schoolmaster. I cannot remember the names of all the other guests, though I think there was another novelist, Miss

Winifred James, an artist called Rigby, and a poet who was also the son of a poet, probably Dr Hake.

When the party broke up Walpole came back with me to Owen Mansions and we talked till very late about his plans. He told me that night that he was determined to be a novelist and, further, that he was determined never to marry because he was sure that, to a novelist, marriage was a handicap. He left me to go back to his school at Epsom and within twenty-four hours I had a letter from him in which he spoke of the wonderful friendship we had begun, with the natural result that I shied violently and felt much less friendly than when we had been sitting in my room discussing the risks of giving up schoolmastering and depending on an inkpot for a living. There is a comic reference to that talk in a letter of his printed in Rupert Hart-Davis's wise biography of Walpole, the best account of an inky boy that has ever been written, from which I learned that I was not alone in being put off by his over-enthusiastic manner in welcoming what he was so often ready to proclaim as the foundation of an eternal friendship. On the other hand, wiser persons were not so put off, and he was soon to leave Epsom, to write his best book, *Mr Perrin and Mr Traill*, to become the beloved friend of Henry James and of Arnold Bennett and to proceed from success to success trailing clouds of social glory that did not dismay him in the least.

# CHAPTER XIV

## *Disasters*

Among my acquaintances in London was Ralph Courtney whom I met at the office of Curtis Brown. He later became a disciple of Rudolf Steiner. I never knew him well, but he came to be closely concerned with my marriage and indirectly with my escape from it. He eventually married a clever and beautiful art-student, daughter of the Spanish Consul in St Petersburg, and he took me to the studio where she was working where I met a crowd of art-students other than those I knew in Chelsea. They too were in the habit of roller-skating at Earls Court or Olympia and after a hard day at my typewriter I used to join them and skate furiously in the evening.

One day Courtney and a friend came to my flat in Owen Mansions, bringing with them a young woman, Miss Ivy Walker, who was unlike anyone I had ever known. She announced at once that she was not a barmaid, alluding, I suppose, to the impropriety of coming with young men to a young man's rooms. I should not have thought of it myself, for it had seemed perfectly natural that the Collingwood girls should visit Carlyle Studios or have tea with Cecil Chesterton and me in Gunter Grove. She had an extraordinary power of surrounding the simplest act with an air of conspiratorial secrecy and excitement. I cannot remember exactly how it came about, but I think I must have countered her remarks about the irregularity of her visit by saying that we could put that right by marriage, or something equally silly. Anyhow, what began in jest turned into earnest and I 'fell in love', not happily, as with Barbara Collingwood, but in a horrible puzzled manner. It was as if I had one foot in a nightmare. Presently we became engaged, whereupon she told me that she was already engaged to her cousin who was abroad. Then she told me that she was looking after the cousin's mistress and illegitimate child. She told me of her home life. Of her mother, who was partly Portuguese, she told me that, to keep her happy, she had persuaded her mother that the Sun God was in love with her, and that her mother had allowed herself to be decked with flowers to receive him, when a sudden thunderstorm had frightened mother and daughter alike. Of her father she said that he had a passion for power, and used to tie up her dog and beat it under her bedroom window. From all this fantastic horror I was to rescue her and I could see no other way before me.

I went to Bournemouth to meet her parents and they did little to belie her portraits of them. Each took the opportunity to speak against the other. Her mother told me that in her youth she had been called 'The Pocket Venus'. Her father told me that he was a solicitor but that he had made less money by law than by playing billiards with his friends. He was the son of a squire's daughter who had married the curate and throughout a long life had been able to 'keep him in his place'. Our engagement was never formally recognised. Indeed I made more than one attempt to break it off, which resulted in horrible scenes. The cousin, on returning to England, was brought to see me, as were several of her other suitors, whether to impress me or them I could never make out. Finally early in 1909 she told me that her father had agreed to our marriage, on condition that his agreement should be kept secret, and that, as he did not want a wedding from his house, she should arrange an elopement (for cheapness' sake) after which he would immediately accept the accomplished fact. I think this must have been true because of what did in fact happen. I made a last attempt to elude the inevitable, and then idiotically agreed to a Scottish marriage. This proved impossible and we were married at a registry office on March 13, 1909, and also in a church on April 1.

I was able to sublet my flat, and we set up house at Stoner Hill Top, Petersfield, in a cottage found for us by Edward Thomas. He had a cottage under Butser, and Stoner Hill Top was on the very edge of Stoner Hill looking out over a precipitous drop to the plain of Petersfield and, beyond the plain, to the South Downs. Our two cottages were about half a mile apart, and Edward and I walked together as hitherto. I was already a month or so late with my *History of Story-Telling*, which was due at Jack's on March 31, so that I had little time for anything but work. I had hoped that, once I had removed her by marriage from the fantastic atmosphere of her home life, ordinary life would be possible for her. It never was. We had not been married more than a few weeks when she told me she had learned that her cousin and two other of her former suitors had met and discussed a plan for her abduction and detention in a lighthouse bought for that purpose by the cousin. She asked me to buy a revolver. I noted in my diary that I felt justified in doing so 'in case any of this melodrama should take a practical shape' and that 'in case of any future trouble' I had 'taken the precaution to write down here my only reason for such an action'. To this note I later added another 'Have not yet bought the revolver, 29 Nov. 1909.' I never did buy one. I had by that time become accustomed to a life in which from one day to the next I never knew what new form melodrama would take. Nothing could be too extravagant. Nor could I ever take any plain statement at its face value. I did not think she was to blame for all this. Brought up in a house where her father and mother competed for her affection, and accused each other of every kind of horror and depravity, she had had no chance of growing up a normal human being. Her father said of her mother, 'She is like a blow-fly depositing — is it five million or only five hundred thousand? — poisonous germs wherever she sets her foot.' Her mother was ready to say as much of her father and to go further in horrible particularisation. With this nightmarish family background of mutual hate what could be expected?

It was as if a guillotine had fallen to cut off for ever the life that I had known. For a moment I thought I might recapture it and give to Ivy the life I had loved myself by taking her to the North. We went to Cartmel, where my dear old Mrs Towers welcomed her to Wall Nook; to Coniston, where she was welcomed at Low Yewdale. Three days of the North were enough. She could not see the kindliness of the north country folk because, though they would call a cheerful greeting, it never occurred to them to touch their hats. We went back to Stoner Hill Top, where I hurried on with chapters on storytellers for the overdue book and told myself that with time everything would come right.

By now several of the little books of selections had been published and better reviewed than they deserved. Masefield, alone of my friends, protested that I was wasting time. 'Don't write about Gautier,' he said, 'but bring him and his cats alive in a story.' I had small hope of being a storyteller now, and fate was busy turning me into something else. A young man, Martin Secker, was planning to set up as a publisher. He was still working in another publisher's office and there noticed the rejection of a manuscript he had liked. This was *The Passionate Elopement* by Compton Mackenzie. He had also noticed my introduction in the volume of Poe in the World's Storytellers. He wrote to Mackenzie and to me, offering to publish *The Passionate Elopement* and to commission me to write a book on Edgar Allan Poe. Mackenzie and I were thus Secker's first two authors. Mackenzie tells me that later I sat with Secker to hear him read the first chapters of *Carnival*, that I was sure of its eventual popularity and that ever since he has had a high opinion of my critical judgment. We were presently joined in Secker's list by Walpole, Brett Young, Machen and Ivor Brown. I introduced Abercrombie, and Secker published seven or eight of his books, beginning with his *Speculative Dialogues*.

Much of the winter of 1909–10 we spent in lodgings at Peak's Farm, near Semley in Wiltshire, where besides the reviews and other small things, I worked on Poe, did some translations from Daudet and sent more of the storytellers to press. In March we moved to lodgings in Bournemouth, where my daughter Tabitha was born on May 9. My wife had insisted that I should be in the room while my daughter was being born but, just before the delivery was complete, her doctor had the humanity to send me to his own house for a bottle he pretended to have forgotten. He too, poor man, had been given a place in the general fantasia. It had been explained to me that my mother-in-law had been allowed to suppose that he was in love with her while he was in fact in love with her daughter – and so on, and so on.

My brother was now working with Ballantyne & Hanson, and probably on this account my bad habit of sending books to the printer piecemeal, to be set up in galley and afterwards put into order, was allowed to continue. By August about half the book on Poe was in type, and we moved to lodgings at Milford by Godalming. There I made friends with a postman who persuaded me to try fishing in the Wey and showed me how to set about it. I caught two roach, and thus rediscovered the pleasure I had known as a small boy watching a perch-float. I had not fished since my father's death, but thanks to that postman fishing has been one of the chief delights of the later years of my life.

I sent the last of the Poe book to the printers, and turned to a book that was commissioned but never finished; it was to be a book on roads and walking. I now owned a small light-weight tent that would stow in a knapsack and I planned a pleasant series of chapters on my Yewdale gipsies, my French bear-leaders, French roads, English roads, and so on. At the beginning of September, to fill the interval between the sending off of the last typescript and the arrival of proofs of the rest of the book, I went off to the lake country, living here and there in my little tent, and for the moment shrugging off what, once I was away from it, seemed a bad, incredible dream. Charming things happened. At Coniston I set up my tent in the Lanehead garden. The two elder girls were away, but Robin, now at Oxford, was at home. He and I, talking Benedetto Croce, sailed down to Peel Island in *Toob* and *Jamrach*, and set up our camp at the top of the steep rock on the eastern side of the island. Ursula, the youngest Collingwood, bicycled along the Nibthwaite road by the edge of the lake in the morning and then swam across to the island with my proofs fastened on her head, waited while Robin and I went through them, and then swam back to the mainland with them and caught the afternoon post. Another day Robin and I raced in *Swallow* and *Jamrach* to the foot of the lake and back.

Plans for the winter were still unsettled, when my aunt asked me if I would care to live in Lanehead during the winter term, while Mr Collingwood and she were away. It would be a great deal better for Lanehead to be inhabited than shut up to grow damper than it was already. I felt about my daughter as my father had felt about me, that as she had not been born in the Lake District she should at least be brought there as soon as possible. Ivy wanted at least for a time to be well out of reach of her mother. She was then back in our Bournemouth rooms, and within ten minutes' walk of her parents. I went back to London and Bournemouth, fixed up a good deal of work for the winter, and then returned to Coniston. The Collingwoods left Lanehead on October 7, and Ivy, Tabitha and her black Jamaican nurse arrived the same day.

My book on Edgar Allan Poe was given much better reviews than it deserved. It had at least considered Poe's theories and his self-conscious technique in writing stories instead of talking exclusively about his 'mastery of mystery and horror'. It had also, for the first time, given a detailed account of the strange position, almost that of a French writer, that Poe had won in France. But I knew well that it was not much of a book and was astonished by the reviews and particularly by the letter written to me by G. E.

5*

Woodberry, the American authority on Poe. I was dissatisfied with the book, but still more dissatisfied with my own power of writing stories. Also I was playing about with several notions that then seemed to me to be discoveries, and when Secker urged more books of criticism I was prepared to agree with him. If that was what was wanted, who was I to refuse to supply it?

Secker asked me to choose a subject. Poe had first interested me because of his methods of construction and indeed of invention. I wanted now to write about another man who also knew or thought he knew what he was doing with his words. At that moment 'native wood-notes wild' did not interest me, and I told Secker I wanted to write a book on Robert Louis Stevenson. For a long time I had been planning and making notes for a book on Hazlitt. Secker did not think he could sell a book on Hazlitt but was ready to agree that I should write one on Stevenson. Then, only a few days later, he telegraphed an urgent appeal. Would I write on Wilde instead of Stevenson?

If that telegram had come before the Collingwoods left I feel sure I should have refused. At Lanehead the tradition of Wordsworth (whom Mr Collingwood's father had known) was still alive, and Hazlitt's quarrel with Wordsworth not forgotten. For Mr Collingwood, as for Wordsworth, Hazlitt was a bad disreputable fellow and he thought it would be a mistake if I were to write on him. He would have been still more against my writing a book on Wilde, whom he had met as one of the undergraduate navvies under Ruskin's leadership on the Hinksey Road. I should almost certainly have listened to him on Wilde, though I should never have agreed with him on Hazlitt. Secker asked me to answer at once.

Wilde's prose was artificial enough. His 'Critic as Artist' seemed to promise just such opportunities of discussion as I needed. The Stevenson could follow. If Secker wished to have a Wilde first I did not really mind about the order in which I wrote the books. I told Secker I would do as he wished and he sent off to Coniston Wilde's complete works in the pleasant little green-bound edition published by Methuen. I had not the smallest suspicion of the troubles that this decision would bring. And it is only fair to say that I do not think that Secker when he commissioned the book had any idea that he was inviting me to put my foot in a hornet's nest.

For the rest of our time at Lanehead I was incongruously reading Wilde in Mr Collingwood's study, turning about a dozen proverbs into stories (duly burnt),* putting together some half-dozen other stories into a small volume for Secker (that ought to have been burnt), finishing up the second of two bulky anthologies for Jack, putting together a book of essays (that I did have the sense to burn), sailing on the lake, collecting from the Red Lion at Lowick the clay pipes, blackened in their fires, that my old friends the charcoal-burners had left there for me, and walking to the Duddon, to Windermere, to Cartmel, by the old well-known roads.

It was during this visit to Coniston that I so nearly lost Miss Holt's *Jamrach*. She was a half-decked sloop-rigged boat and very sensible. At the end of October I took her away from her mooring by the Tent Lodge landing-place and, with a light southerly wind and sunshine, tacked down the lake, thinking I should have an easy run back. I was about a quarter of a mile from Peel Island when the wind fell away altogether. Suddenly I heard a shrill hissing and looked over my shoulder to see a black sky, a black lake, and a sharp line of white from shore to shore. I had no steerage way, and could not turn to meet what was coming. Nor had I time. One moment I was drifting in a dead calm. The next the squall was upon us, and before the boat could ease things by moving, the boom had flicked upright and over, there had been a violent jibe, the jaws of the gaff had smashed, the mast and sail had slapped into the water, and poor old *Jammy* was lying on her beam ends. I hauled the sail down by main force, and she righted, when I found myself sitting in water, with the lake splashing round and over the coamings of the well. The violence of the squall had passed, but it was now blowing strongly from the north, driving the wreck towards the rocks at the northern end of the island. I had not come out prepared to do repairs, and there was very little time to spare. Luckily I was wearing boots with stout leather laces. I took them off under water and with the laces roughly fettled up the gaff-jaws until I could hoist a bit of sail, enough to get her moving. She cleared those jagged rocks that would certainly have holed her had we touched by about two yards, and drifted while I baled and got things more or less to rights. It was a slow job, and though the wind dropped after that

---

* In her book, *Edward Thomas: The Last Four Years*, Eleanor Farjeon says that he was doing the same, turning proverbs into stories, but I had no idea that he was doing anything of the sort.

freak of a squall it still held from the north, and it was black night before I could beat back to the head of the lake and put *Jamrach* on her mooring, where little *Toob*, the dinghy, was awaiting us half-full of water.

The Collingwoods were coming home for Christmas and in the middle of December we left Lanehead for London.

# CHAPTER XV

## *Further Calamity*

In no way expecting the trouble the book was to bring me, I went on with preparatory work on Wilde. I had also much else to do. The *Fortnightly Review* had commissioned an article on Remy de Gourmont who for some time had been very kind to me. He was then fifty-three, but I thought of him and wrote of him as a very old man. For several years I had been regularly visiting him in the Rue des Saints-Pères and thinking of him as once I had thought of Sainte-Beuve. He is still not known in England as well as his critical work deserves. Anatole France said of him, 'Remy de Gourmont is the greatest French writer alive. It has happened to all of us to write stupidities: to de Gourmont, never.' Of course, with a book on Wilde to write, I went to tell him about it and to ask advice, and he sent me to Anatole France, Stuart Merrill, Paul Fort and others who had known Wilde. I found Sturge Moore (whom I had known since my days at the Unicorn Press) staying in Paris and he, like Masefield, told me I was wasting my time on criticism. But neither he nor any of my French friends foresaw the trouble I was running into. Anatole France introduced me to Champion, the celebrated bookseller, who gave me the run of his wonderful shop, was content to sell me hardly anything but was tireless in answering, then and long after, every question it occurred to me to put to him. He and Anatole France alike at least pretended to be pleased to find an Englishman interested in Aloysius Bertrand, that characteristic specimen of the French romantic movement.

I came back to London with a mass of notes at the beginning of February 1911, in time to correct the proofs of a book of stories that will happily never be reprinted. I had a long talk with Binyon, who told me that the first thing to be done was to make sure that I had the good will of Wilde's literary executor. He wrote to Robert Ross. Ross asked me to call. I gave him a copy of my book on Edgar Allan Poe by way of showing him what I planned to do. He approved and promised to let me see a great deal of unpublished material. Secker was delighted and on March 26 I sat confidently down to begin the writing of my book, quite unaware of the deadly feud that was being fought over Wilde's grave. I had written a bread-and-butter article on the information given me by Wilde's French friends. This was published by Holbrook Jackson and some of the details in it were immediately questioned by Reginald Turner and Ross. I remember being very much afraid that Ross would on that account lose faith in me and revoke his promise to check my book for accidental errors of fact.

I need not have feared. Ross took no end of trouble. He seemed sure that mine would be a good book, and thought it all to the good that it should be written by one who had never known Wilde and was interested merely in making a critical study of a writer. Through him I met Wilde's two sons and their friend Mrs Ada Leverson, the 'Sphinx', whom I liked, Mr R. H. Sherard, whom I found revolting, and the eccentric Walter Ledger, the bibliographer who had a wonderful collection of Wilde books in a house at Wimbledon where he also kept the gear of a small sea-going sailing boat. He invited me to go sailing with him, but Ross told me that at intervals he suffered from homicidal mania and was accustomed to have himself shut up. I have always regretted that I did not sail with him, for he kept his *Blue Bird* at Pin Mill, and, if I had gone, I should have known that charming anchorage twenty years earlier. Such eccentricity in Ledger as I saw was quite harmless. He used to come to town dressed as an old-fashioned Jack Tar, with open neck and a blue-and-white sailor collar and bell-bottom trousers. He was an extremely efficient seaman, used to make up all his own rigging, was a member of the Royal Cruising Club which I was to join a dozen years later, and in general brought a strange breath of salty air into the somewhat greenhouse atmosphere of the literary Nineties.

Ross himself I found delightful. That he was a friend of Laurence Binyon's meant a lot to me, and I knew how much he had done for Wilde before his death and what an enormous amount, as his literary executor, he had done for his books and for his sons. He was extremely amusing, alert, witty and selflessly devoted not only to Wilde but to any artist whose work he liked. He was at that time much interested in Eric Gill. He showed me one day a beautiful little gilt figurine of a Madonna and Child that he was buying for some gallery or other. He saw that I

admired it. 'Take her home,' he said. 'I don't need her for a week.
You take her home and look at her whenever you can. Let me
have her back by next Saturday.' I did not take the risk of having
the little statue in my care, but Ross's offer was just like him. Later
he entrusted me with the complete typescript of *De Profundis* and
let me take it away to Wiltshire, where we had taken at a very
low rent an old farmhouse at Hatch, by Tisbury.

This was a two-storied grey house with mullioned windows. It
stood on a narrow lane that ran through the hamlet about a
quarter of a mile above the little river Nadder. The farmyard and
its buildings were retained by the farmer who was working two
farms and himself lived in the house belonging to the other. From
the garden there was an open view across the valley to the woods
of Wardour and the high ridge of the Downs. It was in very good
walking country, within easy reach of Salisbury and Hazlitt's
Winterslow and to the west Shaftesbury. To the north were
Salisbury Plain, Warminster and the country I knew and liked
about Devizes. It was not the Lake District, for which no other
country could ever be a substitute, but it was clear of the influence
of London, its centre being Salisbury. There were people living
round about who had never been further.

I camped for the first time at Hatch on May 2. Edward Thomas
joined me next day. Ivy came about a fortnight later, followed
presently by William Canton, with whom I visited Shaftesbury
and Wardour Castle. On the way up the long hill to Shaftesbury
I remember Canton's delight at looking *down* on a kestrel hover-
ing high over the valley below. A fortnight later we were joined
by my small daughter and her black nurse. Soon after that came
the last of my long walks. I was very anxious to find a publisher
for Abercrombie's prose and wanted Secker and Lascelles to meet,
so set out north to talk it over with Lascelles, who was then living
at the Gallows, Ryton, in Gloucestershire. I carried a tent on my
back, went by train to Dauntsey, and found myself on the second
day walking on and on without finding a suitable camping-place.
The result was a walk of something like fifty miles, until finally I
pitched my tent in the dusk by the Stroud and Gloucester canal.
I struggled on to Dymock next day but had done some damage to
my inside and arrived at the Gallows in a very poor way indeed.

With Lascelles and Catherine I was back in the North again, no
matter where we might be, and this was so throughout our lives.
The Gallows was a delightful old cottage and Lascelles did much of

his best work there. In that June of 1911 he read me the first part of *The Sale of St Thomas* that was published like 'Mary and the Bramble' in a little blue-covered pamphlet. That poem was completed in 1930 and the dedication of part and (later) the whole to me has been and to the end of my life will be a source of extreme pleasure. The first part alone appears in the *Collected Works* published by the Oxford University Press in 1930. The completed poem was published by Martin Secker in 1931. Lascelles and I, talking all the way, went as far as Wincanton by train and thence walked to Hatch by way of Mere and Hindon. Secker was to come a few days later, and in the meantime I was doing my best to get together a team to take part in the tug-of-war competition on Coronation Day, then close at hand. Hatch was a very small hamlet, but it had some heavyweights, and I thought that we could make up for our lighter members if we did a little practising, and learnt to apply such weight as we had all at the same moment, and to pull rhythmically as soon as we felt any weakening of our opponents. The meeting between Secker and Abercrombie went off very well, and Secker published not only *Speculative Dialogues* but *Towards a Theory of Art*, *Romanticism*, *Phoenix* and *Four Short Plays*, one of which, 'The Adder', is based on a piece of 'folklore' wickedly invented by myself, though, as Lascelles said, if it was not folklore it ought to be. Lascelles hurried home and the unfortunate Secker remained to watch our efforts in the tug-of-war and to feel himself oddly misplaced in a scene of bucolic festival. There had been laughter when Hatch entered the competition but the other teams, from Tisbury and the larger villages, had done no training, confident in their beef, and one after another we hove and hauled, hove and hauled and pulled them over the line. Until it came to the final, when we suddenly found ourselves pulled by an irresistible force, and learned only afterwards that the inhabitants of the town team, indignant at the success of the smallest village in the neighbourhood, had crowded closely round and, unseen by the umpire, had tallied on to the end of the rope behind their team so that we were pulling against no rival eight but a rival score.

By the middle of July I had written some two hundred pages of the rough draft of the Wilde book. I had also written an article on 'Kinetic and Potential Speech', besides doing some reading for Macmillan and other publishers, and a lot of reviewing. Michael Lykiardopoulos of the Moscow Art Theatre came down to Hatch with an introduction from Ross, to arrange a Russian translation of the Wilde book, that was made by himself for the Scorpion Press of Moscow. This was set up and Lyki had corrected the proofs but its publication was postponed by the war and then by the revolution.

About this time I met a remarkable man whose *nom de guerre* was Charles Granville and whose escapades influenced the fortunes of many besides myself. He set up as a publisher calling himself Stephen Swift, published Katherine Mansfield's first book *In a German Pension*, and a weekly edited by Belloc and Cecil Chesterton called the *Eye-Witness* and later the *New Witness* was distributed and partly edited from his office. When Maurice Baring was away in Russia, Chesterton used to get me to read Baring's proofs, because Baring made frequent quotations from the dead languages and Chesterton grossly overestimated my scholarship. This little paper was a pleasure to all of us and replaced the old *Week's Survey* in our affections. Tuesday was the meeting-day for its contributors, and on that day the page-boy of the Adelphi Hotel in John Street used to stand on the steps of the hotel scanning the hansom-cabs that turned into John Street from the Strand. He knew us all by sight and was nimble in darting down the steps and holding up a hansom with the cry, 'The Editor's in the cellar!' And there in a basement room we would hear them and find them, Belloc talking like his books (I used to listen for a reference to 'a bullet-headed French gunner'), G. K. Chesterton shaken by internal laughter, quivering like a gigantic jelly, and Cecil Chesterton, who could out-argue either of them, though he could not write so well, laughing until his eyes disappeared at things slid into the conversation by the much quieter Maurice Baring. The offices of the paper were a few doors along the street, just beyond No. 5, where Martin Secker was building up his extraordinary list of books. Just as I had not the smallest suspicion of the disasters that threatened from my book on Wilde, so I had no foreknowledge of the attendant disaster that was to come upon myself and others of that party in the cellar from the ingenuities of the paper's publisher.

Charles Granville called himself and wished to be a poet. I think that he became a publisher first of all so as to be able to give his poems their chance. He had a magnificent way with him. He invited me to visit him at Bedford, to meet a much older Arthur Ransom (spelt without the 'e') who held that in the distant past our families must have been related. This modest and kindly old man spoke with enthusiasm of Granville's generosity. Granville had indeed been very kind to him and he had delighted Granville by having a high opinion of his poems. I could not much admire Granville's poetry but was naturally pleased by his anxiety to publish my prose. He even wanted to publish a series of volumes of critical essays, so that I could write on whatever subject I chose and be paid for it while writing. Secker had neither the capital nor the folly for any such scheme. Granville was the publisher or distributor of the *Oxford and Cambridge Review* which published my article on 'Kinetic and Potential Speech', one of the subjects on which Lascelles and I were for ever arguing. Granville then began to expound a grand design whereby he should become the publisher of all my books, past, present and to come, paying me a regular income on account of royalties. This carrot looked very good to the donkey, and I still think it was meant to be good. It is odd to remember that many years later Jonathan Cape began what was to be a very successful publishing of my books with a rather similar plan.

I wrote that year on Kant, Peacock, Paracelsus and Stevenson, mostly short notes and articles hitched to new books, working for the *Oxford and Cambridge Review* and the *Fortnightly* (growing a temporary beard before daring to present myself when invited to call at that august office). In September, with the final draft of my Wilde nearly done, I went north to recover from a desperately worried summer with a few happy days at Coniston.

In December I was busy with a translation of Remy de Gourmont's *Une Nuit au Luxembourg* for Granville. In January 1912 I saw the proofs of *Wilde* and Ross read through them for me, looking for errors of fact and correcting one or two dates. Granville's carrot was still beckoning and I set about the foolish business of bringing all my books under his control. He produced a new edition of *Bohemia in London*, which had been out of print for some time. He took over the sheets of the little book of tales published by Secker. Disaster was now very near.

The first copies of *Oscar Wilde: a critical study* were ready on February 16. On March 8 I agreed that all my books should be published by Granville if I could recover control of the rights. On March 12 Secker agreed to let me buy back my books on Wilde and Poe. On March 13 Lord Alfred Douglas issued a writ for libel against me, against Secker and against the Times Book

Club. This was completely unexpected, at least by me. I had taken the view of Lord Alfred that anybody must take who has read the whole of Wilde's *De Profundis* letter, but I was anxious to avoid giving unnecessary pain, and had gone so far as to avoid (where I could) mentioning him by name. On the 14th Ross, Secker and I saw Sir George Lewis, who said he would do all he could to get the affair finished as soon as he decently could. All this was bad enough, but it was not melodramatic enough for Ivy, who improved on it by telegraphing to my unfortunate mother to say (quite untruly) that there was a warrant out for my arrest and that I 'was in hiding in London'. Fortunately my mother already knew enough of her informant to take these statements with a grain of salt.

Offers of help came from all sides. Robin Collingwood, by now a young Oxford don, asked me to make use of the whole of his savings. This happily was unnecessary but it was heartening to know that I had such friends. I needed all the heartening I was given on finding myself involved in an unexpected law-case and a bitter personal quarrel in which I had no manner of interest at the precise moment of a change of publishing arrangements which had promised a cessation of financial worries. The first hope that Sir George Lewis had encouraged, namely that he might succeed in bringing the case early to an end, faded altogether. I had no choice but to go on and defend myself as well as I could.

There was nothing to be done but to work and, with the quicksands of my marriage under my feet and a most unsavoury law-case ahead of me, I was finding work more and more difficult.

One of my plans for books was for a study of the nature of the grotesque. I had earlier amused myself by making drawings of gargoyles on Notre Dame and at Blois, and that is how it came about that a challenge from Ivar Campbell led to a start with a coster's cart and a donkey from the courtyard of the British Museum (where I was working at grotesques in the Print Room). Five pounds had bought the whole outfit in the Caledonian Market, a fine tilt-cart, green with yellow roses on its sides, and a noble upstanding Jerusalem donkey. We carried a tent and cooking things on the cart and a knapsack full of books for review. After leaving the Museum, we spent the first night at Campbell's family house in Bryanston Square and set out early next morning, only to be held up for a long time at the gate of Hyde Park. In those days private carriages only were allowed into the Park, and the policeman at the gate was unwilling to be persuaded that a coster's cart and donkey could be a private equipage. Nearly fifty years later I still think that a donkey and cart move at the ideal speed for land travel. We did about ten miles a day and it took us ten days to go from London to Tisbury by way of Ashtead, Cobham, Guildford, Godalming, Crooksbury Common, Windmill Hill by Four Marks, Kingsworthy where it rained in the night and we made a very wet start, missed our way skirting round Winchester, and camped that night at Norman Court, moving on next day by Winterslow, and so to Salisbury where we camped in the woods above Wilton and, after a wet week-end, followed the ancient British road along the Downs and so to Hatch.

Half way through June Lascelles Abercrombie came to Hatch on a bicycle. Martin Secker had commissioned from him a critical study of Thomas Hardy for the series of books he was planning of which my *Poe* had been the first. I remember urging him at all costs to be careful lest he should find himself involved in trouble of the kind that had overtaken me. The trouble that he met was quite different. Wilde had been dead a long time before I agreed to write a book on him. Thomas Hardy was still alive. Lascelles and I bicycled from Yeovil to Dorchester. We went up to Hardy's house and I lay on the grass at the side of the road some distance away while Lascelles went to the front door to call on his hero. Presently Lascelles returned, white, shaken, unable to speak. Hardy had taken him for a sensation-seeking reporter, had refused to listen to any explanation, and had roughly slammed the door in the face of the man best qualified in all England to write of Hardy the study that Hardy would least have disliked. Much later Hardy came to realise what he had done and was contrite and ashamed. I wanted to go to the house myself to speak for Lascelles as the modest Lascelles could never speak for himself. But he would have none of it and we rode miserably away. Comfort came later that day from an unexpected source. We had ridden on to Maiden Castle, that wonderful hill-fort of ancient times. There we had met a shepherd with whom Lascelles talked about the old ways round and up that great earthwork. We had then climbed to the top, leaving our bicycles against the wall of a sheepfold at the bottom. When we came down again, refreshed by the great sky and strong, clear air, we found that the shepherd had laid on each of our bicycles a gift of very fine mushrooms. There was hospitality and friendliness in Dorset after all, and, in the ancient

amphitheatre near by, Lascelles, himself once more, determined
to write his book on Hardy in spite of the hostility with which he
had been received, stood in a state of ecstasy, reciting Hardy's
poetry.

The donkey-and-cart expeditions had a sequel in July. Ivy had
said that she wanted to come too, and a second donkey and cart
were hired. This journey had an odd end. On July 31 a visit to
London was debated. I was against it as waste of time, but was
outvoted by the other two, and the three of us went up to London
and spent the night in Bryanston Square in the house of Campbell's parents who were away in Scotland. Next day Campbell
told me that he had to go north to join them and we went back to
Yeovil to collect the donkeys. Two days later, in an inn at
Templecombe, Ivy said that she had something very serious to
tell me. She said, 'I think I ought to tell you that I am Ivar
Campbell's mistress.' I was a little startled but replied, 'I suppose
that means that you will be wanting a divorce. We had better go
back to London to see a lawyer and find out how best to set about
it.' At this she was taken aback, at once withdrew her 'confession'
and said, 'I'd better tell you exactly what happened. When we
went to London I had agreed with Ivar that he was to come to
my bedroom that night. Then, after I had gone to bed, I changed
my mind and locked my door. I never heard him come, but in the
morning there was a bit of paper pushed under the door and on it
Ivar had written "I can't, because of Ransome." You see, it's really
worse than anything because he never tried the door, so he doesn't
know I had locked it.' I do not know how much truth there was
in that story. I think none. It was in tune with so much else that
was certainly fantastic. Hope of escape may have flickered for a
moment but no more.

By the beginning of October the typescript of the first of the
books of essays that I was to write for Stephen Swift had gone to
my brother at Ballantyne & Hanson's in Edinburgh to be set up.
I had now brought all my other books that were worth bringing
into the Stephen Swift list. The arrangement with Granville was
promising a settled future. Suddenly, unexpectedly, a new blow
fell. On October 8 I had a telegram from Cecil Chesterton to say
that Granville had bolted. Just as I had put all my eggs into one
basket, the bottom of that basket had fallen out.

I went up to London and found the office of the company in
chaos. Granville the managing director had fled abroad, but there

was said to be much more than that to the story and no one knew anything for certain. His secretary had gone with him. There was talk of a big cheque from the *Oxford and Cambridge Review* that had somehow gone adrift. There seemed to be nobody in the office with any authority at all. I had none myself but I saw that I was in danger of losing every asset I had, so I sat down at the big table and came daily to the office and sat there again, determined not to stir until I had at least extracted my books on Wilde and Poe and the book being printed in Edinburgh. Forty years later, at the Garrick Club, I heard Ashley Dukes tell the story that for the first time explained the sudden flight of our Maecenas. Granville had been at a dinner-party where one of the guests was a well-known London magistrate who, after the ladies had left the dining-room, called Granville apart and said to him, 'I never forget a face. You came up before me in such and such a year, accused of bigamy. You were given bail and absconded. I shall do nothing tonight because we are fellow-guests in this house, but I shall make it my business first thing in the morning to let the authorities know that I have seen you. And now, shall we join the ladies?' Granville left early that night, and next morning was on his way abroad with his secretary. They were traced, followed to Algiers and thence brought back to England on an embezzlement charge, with which the authorities did not proceed, being content to send poor Granville to prison for bigamy in spite of the willingness of his wives to give him testimonials as a good husband.

The firm of Stephen Swift was put into the hands of liquidators. I appealed to the Authors' Society to help in the rescue of my books, but their secretary replied that there was no way of hastening the process of law. A way was found. I had a considerable claim against the company and an arrangement was made whereby I temporarily lost the copyrights of some of my books but was able at once to control those on Wilde and Poe and the unpublished book that was still at the printers'. Again friends helped nobly. Macmillan's took over the publication of *Portraits and Speculations* (which had an ignominious end as a 'remainder'). John G. Wilson, then of Jones & Evans and later in charge of Bumpus and the most famous bookseller of his day, took over on my behalf the bound copies of the Wilde book and also of the Poe, and Methuen let me know that they would bring out a new edition of *Wilde* and continue the sale of both books as soon as the Douglas case was over.

# CHAPTER XVI

## *The Douglas Case*

That winter of 1912–13 was one of continual nightmare. From day to day I never knew what to expect at home, and these troubles had a background of horror in the Douglas libel action. I envied the equanimity of Cecil Chesterton who seemed to look forward to his battle with Godfrey Isaacs (the 'Marconi Case') which was to come on towards the end of February. On February 25 Lord Alfred Douglas was committed for trial on a charge of criminal libel. For a moment I had a hope that this would mean that he would drop his case against me. I had hardly realised that his case against me was no more than a preliminary skirmish in a personal feud between Douglas and Robert Ross, though Sir George Lewis had explained to me that if Douglas won his case against my book it would greatly strengthen him in any subsequent action against Ross, and that Ross might then suffer indirectly for having allowed me to see the unpublished parts of *De Profundis*, so that I felt I had to go through with the thing, much as I hated it.

Ross introduced me to Bernard Shaw who had been an eye-witness of a scene at the Café Royal which seemed to me to confirm what I had said in my book of the origin of Wilde's public disaster.

I was having tea with Shaw and Mrs Shaw in their flat in Adelphi Terrace a day or so before my case came on. I had asked him what he remembered of the scene in the Café Royal when Douglas was urging Wilde to bring his action against Lord Queensberry. Shaw said, 'I remember the meeting perfectly. It was a *Saturday Review* gathering when Frank Harris was editing it. Wilde and Douglas came in and Wilde asked Harris to come and give evidence that *Dorian Gray* was the most moral book in the world. Harris said, "Look here, Oscar; they are going to prove sodomy against you. Clarke will throw up your case. I am sure of

it, and I advise you to leave the country while you can." Wilde
said, "It is at such moments as these that one sees who are one's
real friends," and stalked out of the Café. Little Douglas stalked
out with him, showing that he too was in a huff.'

Of his own relations with Wilde, Shaw said, 'Wilde and I
never quarrelled but never got on well together. When we met
we were amiable, but we looked at each other as much as to say;
we can't do it. And there it was. After he was sentenced I tried
with Stewart Headlam to get up a petition to have him out but
nobody would sign it except Headlam and myself. And that
would have been worse than useless. Headlam was a crank and
everybody knew it, and everybody knew that I was a crank too.
I was talking to poor feckless Willie Wilde about that and he said,
"You know Oscar is not a bad man. He is a very good man. Any
woman would be safe with him." That was just like Willie.'

Anybody interested in the hearing of the case will find a very
full report (so I am told) in *The Times* of April 16, 19, 22 and 23,
1913. I have not read it myself. The whole affair seemed to me an
irrelevancy. What had I to do with the fierce feud between
Douglas and Ross? It was sheer misfortune that Secker had asked
me to write about Wilde instead of about Stevenson or Hazlitt.

I have learnt from experience (of a long series of surgical
operations) that human beings are happily so constituted that
pain, no matter how agonising, is not remembered when it has
ceased to be felt. I know that I sat through those four miserable
days in the Court of King's Bench, four miserable days for which
I had been waiting for thirteen miserable months, but now, forty
years after, I could not write a consecutive account of what
happened. I remember only isolated moments. Thus, I remember
Douglas's bulky friend T. W. H. Crosland standing immediately
in front of me and trying to intimidate me with a ferocious glare,
not knowing that I could not see him without recalling the rather
endearing story of his first arrival in London from Yorkshire, by
road, pushing a perambulator that was shared by manuscripts and
a baby. I remember sitting as it were in the front row of the stalls,
with Sir George Lewis and Robert Ross on my left, looking up at
the alert Mr Justice Darling. Douglas's counsel, Hayes, contrived
to suggest that Remy de Gourmont's *Une Nuit au Luxembourg*
(which I had translated from the French) was an obscene work
invented by myself, and that its supposed author, Remy de
Gourmont, did not exist. Luckily I had heard some rumour that

this book was to be mentioned and I had brought a copy of the French edition to court with me and, while Hayes was making his ridiculous suggestion, I took the book from my attaché case and laid it on the solicitors' table where it was seen by Mr Justice Darling. This particular effort by Douglas's counsel cannot have done anything but harm to his client, but in the whole case no one did so much harm to Lord Alfred Douglas as was done by Lord Alfred himself in the witness-box.

It was fortunate for me that Douglas had brought his action not against me alone but also against my publisher and the Times Book Club for selling my book and issuing it to their sub-scribers. Secker, the original publisher, had made his separate peace with Douglas (excusably, since he had no further financial interest in my book, having already sold his rights in it). But the Times Book Club were still in the case. My counsel, instructed by Sir George Lewis, was an eminent and much respected Irishman, J. H. Campbell, subsequently Lord Chief Justice of Ireland, whose every word showed that he had not thought it necessary to read my book. My proper defence was the character of my book as a piece of non-sensational literary criticism. Of this Campbell soon showed that he was completely ignorant. I had once or twice looked round in astonishment at what seemed to me the danger-ous irrelevance of Campbell's remarks when I felt a touch on my shoulder. I heard a whisper and not a very quiet one; 'Never mind that old sheep. I'll put your case for you.'

It was F. E. Smith, who was appearing for the Times Book Club and had realised that if I lost my case his clients would lose theirs. He was as good as his word and, saying next to nothing about the Times Book Club, did what Campbell should have done and spoke on behalf of the author, or rather of his book. I was always grateful to Lord Birkenhead for this, but I believe that my case was won for me by Lord Alfred Douglas and the judge. Mr Justice Darling had listened with growing impatience to Douglas's replies to counsel and in the end began to question Douglas himself. Douglas showed up so very badly that, possibly to the judge's disappointment (he was, I thought, interested and would have liked to hear more) but certainly to my relief, though I thought it a risky decision, Council on my side consulted for a moment and then announced that after Douglas's admissions they proposed to call no further evidence and that their case was closed.

The judge then put five questions to the jury, who retired for what seemed to me an unconscionable time. When at last they came back into court, their answers were in my favour and, immediately after my annoyance at being congratulated on the result of a struggle that, win or lose, had meant nothing to me but thirteen months of wretchedness, I hurried off to the East Strand Post Office to telegraph the news to my mother. An American journalist in the crowd sweeping out of the Law Court startled me by asking what I was going to do now. 'You have', he said, 'the ball at your feet.' 'Get rid of it,' I replied, 'as quickly as I can.' If any ball was at my feet, it was a ball from a game I was not playing and did not intend to play. I had made up my mind at all costs to write no more books that could by any conceivable mischance involve me again in such misfortune.

My wife could not understand this view at all. She had enjoyed as much as I had loathed the publicity of the Douglas case, and had resented my refusal to arrange for her to sit at the solicitors' table. Mr Justice Darling, early in the proceedings, had suggested that ladies should leave the court because of the character of the evidence they might otherwise have to hear. Ivy had not done so and I owed much to the tact and resources of Daniel Macmillan who came daily from his office to the Law Courts, spent the luncheon intervals with us and mercifully made argument impossible by his presence.

# BOOK TWO

BOOK TWO

# CHAPTER XVII

## *Journey to the Moon*

I was now twenty-nine and still hankering after the writing of stories. I should still have been so hankering even if the Douglas case had not sickened me of critical work, though for years to come I went on arguing with Lascelles Abercrombie over one new theory after another. But I wanted to write narrative of a particular kind and had made a lot of unsuccessful experiments in writing fairy stories. In the London Library I had come across Ralston's *Russian Folk Tales* and, while disliking what seemed to me the unsuitable 'literary' prose in which they were written, saw what rich material was there, differing from the Scandinavian folklore to which I had been introduced by Collingwood, and also from Grimm and the folklore of Brittany, Wales and the Highlands. I had made up my mind to learn enough Russian to be able to read Russian folklore in the original and to tell those stories in the simple language that they seemed to need. For ten years I had been repeating to the children of my friends (and to grown-up friends) the Jamaican stories that I had heard from Pixie Colman Smith and I believed that in so doing I had learnt a method that could be applied to quite other material.

At this moment, with the Douglas case over, and with Methuen making ready to bring out a new edition of my book on Wilde, now rescued from the shipwreck of Stephen Swift, I saw in Russian folklore not only material for a book of stories of the kind I hoped to write, but also a way out from my personal troubles. Ivy had been persuaded by a mutual friend to talk things over with Sir George Lewis in the hope of devising some sort of amicable separation. I do not know what passed at that interview except that it was highly dramatic and that in the course of it Sir George told Ivy that he now perfectly understood that in the interests of both of us and for fear of worse things our marriage ought to be dissolved. My wife had said that under no circumstances would she divorce me. I did not want to marry anybody else. All I wanted was to bring that marriage to an end. Going to Russia seemed to promise answers to more problems than one.

There is a little-known book by Daniel Defoe, called *The Consolidator*. I have a copy of the first edition, 'Printed and to be Sold by *Benj. Bragg* at the *Blue Ball* in *Ave-mary-lane*, 1705.' It is an account of a journey to the moon, and a beautiful example of Defoe's skill in producing an effect of truth. No one in 1705 would believe the story of a traveller who claimed to have flown directly from Fleet Street to the moon. So Defoe's supposed traveller goes abroad; he goes to Germany and that, in 1705, is already a long way from home: from Germany he goes to Russia where anything may happen; from Russia he goes to China, and by that time the final step from China to the moon seems little more than a crossing of the street. Well, I should have preferred China as being further away, but it did seem to me that Russia would do very well as a first stepping-stone to escape. In those days it was possible to go almost anywhere in Europe without papers, but for Russia a passport was necessary, and that fact alone seemed likely to discourage pursuit.

I began, in the Defoe manner, by taking a very small bite at the cherry and booked a passage to Copenhagen in a cargo-boat. We went round the Skaw and steamed slowly through the Kattegat in fog. It was the last week of May 1913 and a very light wind off the Danish shore brought with it the scent of lilac. As we passed Elsinore the mist stirred for a moment and showed the green copper roofs of the castle. That smell of lilac and that lovely sight on a misty morning of early summer come often to mind forty years later, seeming to mark not so much a beginning as a re-opening of the life I had known at Coniston and Cartmel, the life I had thought ended for ever in 1909. I slept aboard the steamship in Copenhagen harbour, going ashore by day, delighting in the canals, the ships in among the houses, the sailors' taverns with such mottoes as *De gamle Vikinger drak altid et glas*, reminding me of the sagas I had read at Lanehead. Pervading everything, like that scent of lilac over the sea, was the pious memory of Hans Christian Andersen. Some day I might yet learn to write tales that English children might overhear with pleasure, or had those years since 1909 put that kind of writing for ever out of my reach?

From Copenhagen I crossed in the ferry-boat to Malmö in Sweden, arriving there on 'Barnen's Dag', Children's Day, which

I took for a good omen. Then, on a 'hard seat' in a third-class railway-carriage, I went on to Stockholm, another stage towards the impossible moon. I had in my pocket a message for Strindberg's daughter from her mother in London. I found the flat where she lived and rang the bell. The door was opened, one inch, on a chain. Suddenly the young woman who was looking warily out loosed the chain, opened the door, pulled me in, closed the door and bolted it, made me an ally without even asking who I was, and told me she was on the point of running away. As I was running away myself I could but sympathise. I helped with her packing. The bell rang. There was knocking at the door. We froze in silence. Steps sounded going down the stairs. Side by side, leaning out of the window we saw a man, husband, fiancé, friend (I did not ask and was not told) come out on the pavement. The young woman watched to see which way he went, sent me to stop a cab and a few minutes later was hurrying to the railway station. I never met any of the Strindbergs again and do not know what was the story of the fleeing daughter.

From Stockholm half way through June I took steamer for St Petersburg and another world. I do not remember whether it was at Hango in Finland or at Mariehamn in the Aland Islands that I saw my first Russian gendarmes with their gigantic boots, belts and whiskers, and heard from a fellow-passenger that when, in Russia, there is a sudden silence in a room and conversation stops, whereas the English say 'An angel is passing', the Russians say 'A policeman is being born'. Now for the first time I was seeing the beautiful sea-approaches to Stockholm and the thousands of rocky islands along the Finnish coast where in after years I was so much to enjoy sailing in my own small boat. I remember standing on deck while the steamer slid on over a smooth sea, and my first sight of the Kronstadt forts and the gilded domes and spires of St Petersburg rising out of the water as the wooded sides of the gulf approached each other and we came near the mouths of the Neva.

I was received with extraordinary hospitality by the Anglo-Russian family of one of my Chelsea and Paris friends. One of them was waiting on the quay. My passport had been stamped in the steamer by the officials who had come aboard at Kronstadt and I had hardly stepped off the gangplank with my typewriter before I was rattling over the cobbled quay in a *droshky* with the wooden *duga* joining the two shafts together and arched high above the horse's shoulders. That first arrival in Russia was rather like playing snapdragon. I was no sooner in Russia than I was out of it again. I was driven straight from the quay to the Finland Station, and, after an astonished glance at the ikons and candles in the booking-office, was sitting in a suburban train on the way to my friends' *dacha* or country house, some thirty miles on the Finnish side of the frontier.

The *dacha* was a pleasant wooden house among pine-trees, almost on the shore of the gulf. There is little work done in offices during the middle of the northern summer. Schools and universities are closed. I reached Finland in time to know the magical 'white nights' of the nearly Arctic summer. All night long I heard the nightingales. I had been very lucky in my friends. The head of the family was an English (but very Russian) timber-merchant, shipping timber for pit-props from the northern forests. His wife was a Russian who was never without a book. When I was there the book that she was carrying about the house and garden was Herodotus. One of her sons had made a long journey into Central Asia. One of the daughters was a black-and-white artist of great originality. The whole family approved of my wishing to learn the language they habitually spoke and hurried me up the first steps with laughter and determination.

From Terioki I went back to St Petersburg, and on along the southern side of the Gulf of Finland (still not in Russia proper) to Dorpat (Yoriev in Russian and Tartu in Esthonian) in the Baltic Provinces where I stayed in the house of a firm of English flax-merchants. Norman Whishaw was living alone at that time, in sole charge of the office, and presently it was agreed that I should join him, paying a very modest sum for my food while I learned Russian as fast as I could. He had sometimes to make journeys through the flax-growing country and these journeys I delightedly shared. We would travel day and night through the forests, changing horses at the post-stations and would often on waking learn that we had travelled many miles though, as we looked sleepily from our carriage at the trees it seemed to us that we were still exactly where we had been when we fell asleep.

Of all this I remember odd disconnected moments, the bob of a float on the still water of a lake, the glitter of lanterns in the summer night when we were changing horses at a posting-inn, and again that same glitter of lanterns multiplied by their reflections where boys waist-deep were taking crayfish from the

11, 12 and 13   Evgenia

14    On board *Slug* off Riga

15    Baltic picnic

16 and 17    Karl Radek

18    A.R. with William Peters

19   *Racundra*

river Embach. Nor can I forget a noisy students' feast at Dorpat University where our hosts proudly exhibited the ancient urinals, fitted with handholds and padded semi-circular sockets into which the sufferer was to drive his head, and, of course, the Latin motto above each of these contrivances, '*Vivat qui sequitur!*'

I worked now and then at a book on Stevenson that Methuen's were to publish (they subsequently released me from that contract). But first and foremost I was wolfing the elements of Russian. Of this I must say something, lest people should think I am making any claim to be a linguist. I have always been very bad at languages. I never learned to talk Russian as a Russian talks it, though I was soon rattling away in it without stopping for a word, and found no difficulty at all in learning to read it. My method of learning Russian was so simple that I am surprised it is not generally used by people who need to learn a new language in a hurry. I had no compunction about pressing everybody I met into my teaching staff, and with good temper and much laughter everybody turned tutor. But that was not my real secret. I made friends with Russian children and, even more important, I bought and studied the Russian child's first reading books, the equivalents to 'The cat ate the rat' and then, more advanced, 'The blue cat ate the purple rat', and so on. Working through these simple readings, I promoted myself as it were a year each week, so that, starting as a child of five learning to read for the first time, I was, at the end of a month or so, a rather backward child of ten. Building thus a foundation of useful nursery Russian, I could, by attacking the newspapers with a dictionary, widen my vocabulary. It should be remembered that I did not begin by dreaming of becoming a Russian scholar, or even of being a fluent talker. All I needed was to be able to read the Russian collections of folk-tales. For anyone so lacking in ambition, Russian is one of the easiest of languages. For many years teachers of Russian and their pupils have spread the notion that it is a difficult language, thus raising their own commercial value. They have been helped in this by the readiness of foreigners to panic at the sight of the Russian letters of the alphabet, which present no difficulty to those who have struggled through the first two pages of a Greek grammar. Once the hurdle of the alphabet has been cleared the student will discover that the hospitable Russians have done all they can to make his progress easy. Russian nouns are modified at both ends. The verbs have gender as well as tense and number.

6

There are thus plenty of signposts to help the reader, though the very fact that makes reading easy makes it difficult to speak or write the language correctly. For simple one-way traffic, Russian into English, which was all I wanted, these continual pointers make it hard to go wrong. Similarly the absence of such signposts makes it easy for foreigners to make themselves understood in English and difficult for them to translate from English into their own language.

One way or another, bad linguist as I am, I was able at the end of a very few weeks to begin filling notebooks with rough translations of stories from the Russian. The first of these were more or less word-for-word translations into English from a good collection of Caucasian tales that I had found in paper-bound parts in a shop on the Nevsky Prospect. I was to find later that direct translation is not the way to tell Russian stories to English children, and for a reason that should have been obvious from the first. The Russian peasant storytellers, telling stories to each other, could count on a wide range of knowledge that their listeners, no matter how young, shared with them. Young English listeners knew nothing of the world that in Russia listeners and story-tellers alike were able to take for granted. Continual explanation would have been as destructive of the tales as an endless series of asides. The storyteller, if he were to tell the tales as they should be told, had to stand between two worlds and never allow himself to feel that he was showing one world to the other. In the end I used to read as many variants of a folk-story as I could find and then lay them all aside while writing the story for myself.

Towards the end of September I went overland from Dorpat by way of Riga and Berlin to Paris, there to see Vallette of the *Mercure de France,* who was publishing a French translation of my book on Wilde, by Lautrec and Davray. Back in England I put off going to Wiltshire to see my daughter, but, in the end, much against the advice of Lascelles Abercrombie who said that, having once gone away, I should be wiser to make the separation absolute, met Ivy in London, came to a very unsatisfactory agreement and went home at the end of October.

I brought with me Norman Whishaw's translations from Korolenko, but failed to find a publisher for them or, most fortunately, for my own early translations from Russian folk-tales.

That winter I worked hard. I wrote two children's books, one,

*Aladdin,* in rhymed verses with nothing to recommend it but high spirits, and the other a prose allegory of mental processes which I meant to be enjoyed by children who should not notice that there was an allegory at all. It has been enjoyed by a few elderly persons who have not noticed even that it was a story. I stayed with my mother at Headingley, dined with an uncle in the Curfew Club to which my father had belonged, saw a pantomime in the same theatre in which, so long ago, I had seen my first (alas, this time there was no acrobatic cat to climb up by the boxes and run round the dress circle).

On the invitation of Professor Bernard Pares, I went to Liverpool University, where I was much encouraged over my Russian studies, and saw a magnificent sunset from the Mersey landing-stages. I was back in Paris again when an urgent message from Cecil Chesterton and Belloc told me that they had a seat in the Press Boat for the Oxford and Cambridge Boat Race next day and asked if I could get back in time to use it. An hour later I was on the train and duly saw the Boat Race, was soaked through, and made my first experiment in reporting.

# CHAPTER XVIII

## *Russia goes to War*

Douglas Goldring had published some short sketches of mine in a magazine called the *Tramp*. He had become a partner in a publishing firm and most unexpectedly he and his fellow-adventurer wrote to me offering a free hand if I would write for them a descriptive and historical *Guide to St Petersburg*. At the same time Maunsel of Dublin were asking for a book of fairy-tales. I left for Russia at once, reached St Petersburg on May 13, 1914, and in two months and one day had finished my *Guide*. Those two months of hard, delighted work left me knowing the capital of their country a great deal better than it was known by most Russians and made me feel very much at home there. The book was never published because of the war and because by the time the war was over the city had lived through so much concentrated history that the book would have been useless. It was never published but the writing of it had made me free of the city. I knew all kinds of by-ways and could tell Russians where to look for this or that relic of historical interest. I do not think the book had any merit. Many years later I recovered the typescript and destroyed it, but this concentrated wolfing of the city was, though I did not suspect it at the time, the best preparation I could have devised for the strange work of chronicling the day-to-day story of the Revolution which, only three years later, was to turn the place into a palimpsest in which on the city of Peter the Great the city of Lenin was superimposed.

I read everything I could find about the founding and growth of that expression of one man's will-power, this city built in a swamp to be 'a window into Europe'. I wore out the soles of my boots, setting out each day from my room in a little hotel not far from the Nikolai Station. Baedeker and other such works in hand, I took nothing for granted, even making sure at the Alexander Nevsky Monastery that the waiter was telling the truth when he told me that anybody who asked for it was given a free drink of brown *kvass* through a hatch kept open for thirsty pilgrims. Forty years later I have but a rag-bag of memories, Peter's little house, the stuffed horse and the dog which had been with him at the Battle of Poltava, the terrifying glare of the waxwork figure of Peter himself. I remember seeing a vivid pageant of the taking of Azov performed in the open air on a lake in one of the public parks that made an admirable inland sea. I spent much time in the museums and picture-galleries and visited, as far as was possible, the scenes of the many dramatic events in the history of the city. I knew the place where with inexplicable idiocy the young revolutionaries of 1881 had exchanged King Log for King Stork by the assassination of Alexander II, which brought the reactionary Alexander III to the throne. I knew the room in the Winter Palace to which Alexander II, mortally wounded, had been brought to die. I knew the place where the Emperor Paul had met his ignominious end. I visited the fortress of St Peter and St Paul and saw the still grimmer fortress of Schlüsselburg from which, only three years later, hardly credible figures from the past were to stagger out into the light of day.

In that summer of 1914 Englishmen were more than usually popular in St Petersburg. This had a simple political reason. Sides were being picked for the struggle to come, and a visit by vessels of the British fleet gave the Russians a chance of demonstrating their good will. I remember noticing the jaunty cock of Admiral Beatty's hat being shyly copied by young Russian naval officers. The British sailors enjoyed themselves once they had solved their first difficulties and learned that though there were no recognisable 'pubs' there were plenty of beer-shops in the basements below the level of the pavement. This general good will no doubt made things easier for me than they might have been a year or two earlier, but I think I must mention here a document that I found more useful than a passport in opening forbidden doors and smoothing away red tape. Dr Hagberg Wright of the London Library had a very impressive sprawling signature. The paper he used carried the embossed crest of the Library. It so happened that he had written me a very angry letter demanding the instant return of some books I had kept too long. Whenever a policeman or a soldier or minor official tried to bar my way in St Petersburg (and later, on the Russian front or frontier), I found that letter with its crest and that determined signature far more useful than any other 'paper' I possessed. At the sight of it opposition wilted, hands shot up in awed salute, and on one occasion even a messenger was sent before me to warn others that they had better stand to attention. Sometimes, indeed, it did not seem to matter which way up the document was held. Some powerful magic emanated from it, and no one was better pleased to hear that his angry letter had turned into an Open Sesame than Dr Hagberg Wright himself when, years after, he learned of its adventures.

On July 9 I finished my *Guide to St Petersburg*, took two days' holiday with friends in Finland, caught a very few very small fish and set to work again as hard as I could on the Russian folk-tales, though I felt that this work was presently to be interrupted again. There was a feeling of thunder in the air. People in England have already forgotten how unexpected for most of them was the beginning of the 1914 war. The Sarajevo murder had seemed a characteristic bit of Balkan savagery, and few in England guessed that the bell that tolled for the Archduke tolled for the world and rang in a new era of gigantic change. In Russia, with the recent experience of the Russo-Japanese war and the 1905 Revolution, people began at once to talk of the possibility of a conflict in which Russia might become involved. Besides the threat of war there was the threat of violent labour unrest, and this made war seem not less likely but more. I heard early of young officers of the reserve being called to rejoin their regiments. At the same time the May Day strikes had been followed by others. Everybody felt that something was going to happen, but when I asked my literary agent in London to arrange for me to use my Russian as a war correspondent, I had a telegram in reply asking 'What war?'

The disturbances in St Petersburg became more and more serious. Barricades went up. Some of the discontented factories were occupied by Cossacks. There was serious fighting in the streets on the day when the Austrian ultimatum was presented to Serbia, but two days later the strikes had come to an end and, overnight, the now instant threat of war had opened a new channel for popular emotion. Factory-owners breathed freely once more and I heard it said that the Austrian ultimatum had been just in time to save Russia from revolution.

Michael Lykiardopoulos (Lyki to his many English friends), Secretary of the Moscow Art Theatre, who had visited me in Wiltshire, had translated my Wilde book into Russian and had brought about the printing of a few of my short stories and articles in Russian reviews, did me a very good service by introducing me to Harold Williams, who knew more of Russia and the Russians than any other living Englishman. He opened doors for me that I might have been years in finding for myself. He told me once that he knew forty-two languages or dialects spoken in that polyglot country. I have known him talk with a mixed group of Caucasian soldiers on a railway platform and amuse himself and astonish them by telling each man, after listening to him for a few minutes, the race, tribe or district to which he belonged. A New Zealander, he had come to Russia at the time of the first revolution, immediately after the Russo-Japanese war. He had there fallen in love with Ariadna Vladimirovna Tyrkova, a devoted follower of Miliukov, the leader of the Cadet party (Constitutional Democrats). She was a woman of dominating character and tremendous industry, a journalist, a member of the central committee of the party to which she belonged, and, further, a well-known novelist. Her brother, Arkady Tyrkov, was now managing their family estate at Vergezha on the Volkhov river. Williams and Ariadna Vladimirovna used to go down to Vergezha at week-ends and sometimes took me with them and, in 1915 when I had come out of hospital after an operation, that old wooden house on the steep bank of the river gave me many of the happiest of my Russian memories. Now, in July 1914, Williams and I were seeing each other almost daily. He was older than I, and there never was a learned man more generous to the less learned. I owe him more than I can say. It was he who introduced me to Sergei Oldenburg, of the Academy of Sciences, to Rodzianko, to Gutchkov, to Remizov and to countless other Russians whom I might otherwise never have met. He had been the first to suggest that my being able to chatter in and understand Russian was enough to make up for my complete ignorance of daily journalism and that I ought to make myself useful as a correspondent. This he was afterwards to regret but until, during the Revolution, our opposing estimates of the forces at work in Russia divided us, he was one of my best friends. He was a very quiet man, unselfish, extraordinarily kind. I do not think it possible that he can ever have had an enemy.

The Sarajevo murder was on June 28. The Austrian ultimatum was delivered on July 23, and the Austrian declaration of war against Serbia followed on July 28. On August 1 I spent most of the day with Williams. We walked down the Nevsky Prospect to the Hôtel de France where we found Francis MacCullagh, the first of the many professional war-correspondents to reach St Petersburg. Fresh from the Balkan wars, MacCullagh was talking with professional interest of the effect of shrapnel-fire on marching columns. Williams and I listened in silence. We were up very late that night at the great Nikolai, Baltic and Warsaw railway stations, watching the lighting of candles before the ikons by men going off to join their regiments. Already, in the streets of the city, I had seen the beginnings of demonstrations in favour of the war.

Next day, August 2, these demonstrations culminated in an extraordinary scene in the Palace Square. Williams and I, moving with crowds from the Nevsky, found ourselves in the middle of the so-called square, a large open space between the Winter Palace and the Foreign and other Government Offices. Everybody was looking towards the palace. I knew of the last demonstration in that place when, on 'Bloody Sunday' in 1905, troops had fired on the supporters of Father Capon. Away to the left was the statue of Peter the Great on a prancing horse, and the trees in front of the Admiralty into which children had climbed and been shot down for their pains by bullets that had passed over the heads of the demonstrators. Bullets were to fly again in that square, but not yet. Every face in that huge, swaying crowd was turned towards the palace. Suddenly white uniforms appeared on a balcony, perhaps to find out by experiment what would happen. Nothing happened. They retired. Other white uniforms came out in place of them. This time the Tsar was indeed among them, showing himself to the people for the first time in many years, to be greeted with extraordinary emotion and a tremendous singing of the national anthem. The strikes of only a few days before were forgotten. War, as so often before and after, had for the moment welded the nation into one, or had seemed to weld it. There was unreality even then. A rumour, started no one knew where, flew round that the Emperor Franz Josef was dead. On the 3rd he was alive again. On the 4th there were disgraceful attacks against German offices and shops. The German Embassy was sacked (and a helpless caretaker murdered) by a mob unchecked (if not organised) by the police. Less than three years later the Winter Palace had been seized by the revolutionaries, all government buildings surrendered, the prisons opened and the autocracy overthrown.

Not one of my friends of those days could have foreseen that, but, from the very first, there were discussions about possible changes in the map of Europe, in which the grim young officers on their way to the front took no part. It was a civilian, not a soldier, who first said to me 'Germania delenda est'. I heard those words said many times with widely differing intentions when 'War to a Victorious End!' was a slogan that, whether sarcastic or not, meant more in the internal politics of Russia than in her foreign affairs.

More and more correspondents were arriving in St Petersburg and I had a muddle-headed telegram from a literary agent asking whether I could arrange to get news through. I thought I had wasted enough time already, or rather my agent had, and so decided to go home as soon as possible. A young New Zealander, Williams's brother, was also going home. We were warned that we should probably be held up on the way, but in fact were in London seven days later. We left the Finland Station at nine o'clock on a Tuesday morning, slept at Rikhimaki and went on to Rauma next day. Here there were two little steamers supposed to be leaving for Gefle, on the Swedish side of the Gulf of Bothnia. We went aboard one of them but in the evening heard a rumour that the other would be leaving first and hurriedly carried our bags and were amused to see a Russian sentinel examine Hagberg Wright's letter upside down. We sailed late at night and I was told afterwards (perhaps untruly) that the other little steamer had been torpedoed or mined just outside. From Gefle we went to Stockholm and thence to Christiania, whence we had a queer passage in an English steamship.

Instead of going straight across the North Sea we went a very long way north, following the Norwegian coast. We were told that some German destroyers were on their way home round the North Cape and that it was our business to see that no light whatever showed from portholes or windows. We made as good a black-out as we could. I do not know if it was necessary but we were assured that it was, and there did come a moment when, ourselves hardly moving, we became aware of a group of four or five vessels, moving southward very fast, showing no masthead or navigation lights but not as well blacked-out as our own vessel had been by combined amateur and professional efforts. I do not know how far north we went, but we heard, when at last we turned south, that we were well up in the neighbourhood of the Pentland Firth. I did not quite believe that, but when for a very

6*

long time we had been steaming slowly in a thick mist, there was a clang of bells and we heard the anchor-chain roaring out. A few minutes later a little naval vessel appeared alongside out of the mist and a voice asked what we thought we were doing. A voice aboard our own vessel asked where we were, exactly, and the first voice told us angrily that we were on the edge of a minefield or in it, and that if we had not been blown up we ought to have been. We were somewhere off Coquet Island. We were given a course to steer. The anchor came up in a hurry. The little naval vessel shepherded us on our way, told us cheerfully 'All clear now,' and vanished in the mist. We landed at Hull, four days out from Christiania.

# CHAPTER XIX

## *The Elixir of Life*

Francis Acland, the son of my godfather, was then Under-Secretary for Foreign Affairs. He agreed that I had been right to come home, but urged me to waste as little time as possible before returning to Russia. The blindness that had made my schooldays a misery now did me what I think was a service by making me comparatively useless as a soldier. If I mislaid my spectacles or dropped them I dared not move until someone found them for me. I had also other troubles that came to a climax a year later, in a Petrograd hospital, but none that I thought could prevent me from working as a correspondent, and I did not want to throw away unused the good working knowledge of Russian that I had gained with an entirely different object in mind. Harold Williams, Bernard Pares and Francis Acland had all urged the same thing and had thought that I should have no difficulty in finding a newspaper editor who would be glad to print my telegrams. In fact I had a great deal. By the time I reached England all the major newspapers had their correspondents already in Russia and I was too ill to inspire much confidence. Acland did his best for me, even persuading a publisher to offer to commission a *History of Russia* that might serve to explain to the Russians my inquisitive presence in St Petersburg. I did not much like this idea, partly because I thought I could be much more useful as a newspaper correspondent, and partly because the irregular work of a correspondent would allow me to continue the study of Russian folklore that I by no means wished to relinquish unless other work made it absolutely necessary. I wrote articles for half-a-dozen newspapers and magazines in England and America, went on with my translations, fished a little in Wiltshire and Norfolk and finally, after writing rough drafts of three or four stories and selling my *Aladdin* to Nisbet's and other things to the *Century* and the *New York World*, was off once more, with letters of introduction from

Acland, and rather vague commissions for anything I might write. I left Newcastle for Bergen, coming into that beautiful harbour in the very early morning of Christmas Day, sleeping aboard the boat and waking to see the steep-roofed houses round the quays and the white hills behind them.

For the first time I travelled over that wonderful Norwegian railway, climbing up from Bergen and across the snow-covered mountains, looking down into deep valleys at the ice-bound winter rivers, plunging now and again into tunnels, now through rock, now through ice, rattling down at last into Christiania and on across Sweden to the meeting place of frozen lake and frozen sea. The Germans, blockading Russia, were in complete control of the western Baltic and there could be no quick crossing from Gefle to Rauma. Instead there was a train-journey from Stockholm, all the way up the Gulf of Bothnia, to Boden and Karungi and then, far up towards the Arctic Circle, a sledge-journey in the short quarter-light of winter, lying flat on a sledge, kept warm by a Lapp driver who kindly sat on my stomach as we hissed over the snow-track and down a frozen river (smoother than any road) to the Finnish frontier at Tornio. There I felt myself all but home again, climbing into the Russian train that, it used to be said, started unwillingly and often stopped to look back, coming at last to the new-named city of Petrograd late at night on December 30, 1914.

Williams, kindest of men, gave me a cheerful welcome, and told of what had happened, since I left, to the various correspondents. He urged me as soon as possible to go to Moscow, where I would learn much more of Russia than I could in Petrograd.

Ten days later, after sending off more articles to be dealt with by my agents in London and America, I went off to Moscow by the night-train, put up at the Siberian Hotel where I was attacked by armies of bugs and, on complaining to the chambermaid, was enchanted by the arrival of the local bug-doctor, with his little black bag containing magic powders and syringes with which to squirt death-dealing chemicals into the cracks and joints in beds and walls where the bugs lay in ambush. He was a thin, grave little man, looking very much like a country practitioner who had been summoned to attend a midwifery case.

In Moscow I was in a magic world. I saw the Great Bell, the picture of which in that old-fashioned book had inexplicably made me promise myself that I should one day see the bell itself. On January 13 (Russian New Year's Eve) I drove through the Kremlin to the great church and, wedged in a crowd that stirred like a bucket full of maggots, lost my fur hat, which I recovered, and a glove which I did not recover. My *isvostchik* drove at speed over the sparkling snow, shouting '*Beregis! Beregis!*' (Look out for yourselves!) at other people as if sure that they would be grateful for being given a chance to hop out of the way. I was cold (I had not any clothes fit for a Russian winter, except the sheepskin hat that I had bought two years before). The cold prickled in my nose. My moustache had become a block of ice. My eyelashes had frozen to my glasses but, as I caught glimpses of the Kremlin walls, and the fantastic towers and cupolas, I was exulting in the chance I now had of learning this ancient capital of eastern-facing Russia as well as that new capital which Peter had built to face the West.

Next day I met Lykiardopoulos, who told me that the Russian translation of my book on Wilde was complete but that, like much else, it had been held up at the printers' on account of the war. I had last seen Lyki in Wiltshire and it seemed very odd to see him here so entirely at home in the Box Office of the Moscow Art Theatre instead of so entirely out of place on a background of the Wardour woods. With Lyki was Hugh Walpole who, meaning to learn Russian, had come out from England in the middle of September and was very sensibly lodging in a flat the proprietress of which had much experience in preparing young Englishmen to pass examinations in her language. He never did learn to read or talk Russian with any freedom, probably because very wisely he allowed nothing whatsoever to distract him from his novel-writing. I had a great respect for Walpole, for he could not only begin a story but finish it, whereas my stories broke down one after another. I envied him his freedom from the false starts and digressions that had marked my own crab-like progress. I never had any wish to write his kind of book and I am very sure that he never had any wish to write mine, but his example and encouragement were a great help to me then and later when I was trying to write stories.

Until early in February, when Walpole went off to Petrograd, we met nearly every day, and he explained to me how to set about the writing of a novel. He used a loose-leaf book and, beginning a new book on some auspicious day, wrote 'Chapter I' at the top of a page and started, writing straight ahead all the way through until he came to the end. He did very little revision and found it hard to believe me when I told him of writing out chapters of my books on Poe and Wilde three or four times (and some chapters many more times) before I could think of letting them go to the printer. When I next went to England and was able to buy a loose-leaf book I adopted that much of his method and found the detachable leaves most convenient, not because I could write from page one to the end (that skill I never learned) but because the loose-leaf system enabled me to work here, there and everywhere, at all parts of my book at once, inserting individual sheets where I wished. Walpole could from the beginning have written his novels into bound notebooks.

I regret now that I have never kept a proper diary except for the one I used in a hand-to-mouth report on Russia in 1919. I have nothing but staccato notes to stimulate my wretched memory. Thus: 'Walked at night in the Kremlin ... Watched the Blessing of the Waters from a bridge over the Moscow River ... Gorgeous, sunny day ... Gold banners ... Dazzling snow ... Bought warm coat at Tartar shop under outer wall of Kremlin ... Picked up Lyki at his rooms and with Walpole went to the Bat, a cabaret theatre with Punch and Judy war dialogues ... Walpole looked in here for books ... Read *English Review* till 3 a.m., which was silly ... Finished rough draft of *Petersburg and Petrograd* ... Talked with tackle-maker by the river who told me there were six fishing-clubs in Moscow and sold me a fishing-rod for a rouble. Had it jointed for seventy kopecks. Fished through the ice under the Kremlin wall.'

On January 20 I escaped from the Siberian Hotel and moved to a one-storey house in the Donskaya, not far from the Donskoi Monastery. Here I lodged with a very intelligent Russian family of girls and boys, an older half-sister and a kindly mother, not much older than her step-daughter. The father, a senior civil servant, had died not long before, and his family had hardly realised that they were free from him. He must have been a most oppressive character. His portrait dominated the dining-room, and I used to catch the widow glancing at it unhappily, as if to ask forgiveness for the laughter that was resounding round the dinner-table. I rented a small bed-sitting-room and had all my meals with the family, not one of whom, luckily for me, knew any English. I was working rather hard, making rough translations from

Russian folk-tales, writing articles and gulping Moscow as I had gulped St Petersburg. Thanks to Lyki I was often at the Moscow Art Theatre, where, besides others, I saw three plays of Turgenev, Chekhov's *The Cherry Orchard*, Alexei Tolstoy's *Tsar Fedor* and Maeterlinck's *The Blue Bird*.

Then, one day when I was thinking about something quite different, I saw the faint glimmer of a story, somehow growing out of a long dialogue between a philosopher and a homunculus. It was a discussion of the elixir of life, with a few roots still clinging to a book I had read about Paracelsus. This was something very unlike Walpole's novels, and I did not tell him about it in detail in case he should by seeing the weak points of the story make it impossible for me not to see them myself. I did not want to see them. I wanted to write the whole story, if only to prove to myself that I could.

I have always been troubled by a bad conscience, and I had a very bad conscience indeed when, in spite of it, I made up my mind to disregard it and to have a shot at writing *The Elixir of Life*. I spent the morning of February 20 in working out a synopsis in twenty chapters, took a sledge, drove into Moscow and bought a lot of typewriting paper. I had made up my mind to write directly on the typewriter and decided to give myself a fortnight's trial. 'If I can get 40,000 words done in a fortnight, I'll go on with it. The book should be 60,000 words.' I wrote six pages that afternoon, and in the evening tried the effect of my synopsis on the schoolma'am daughter of the family. I did not get 40,000 words done in my trial fortnight, but came near it, writing chapter by chapter during the day, and in the evening reading it aloud in Russian to the Viktorovs. By February 27 I had written 19,500 words. My conscience was bad but I could not stop the thing now. A week later I had written over 34,000 words. My internal troubles were as bad as my conscience and I was daily losing a lot of blood.

Another week took me to 46,800 words and then, just as I began to feel that at last I was going to end a story instead of burning it, I broke my spectacles, playing catch with one of the small boys, and for four days was brought to a standstill. On March 17, with new spectacles, I started again. On March 20 I had 58,500 words in typescript and I had stuck. For two days, with horrible stomach pains, I read *Vanity Fair* and wrote an article on Moscow in winter, and then, clutching my typescript, took the night-train to Petrograd. The Viktorovs had enjoyed and encouraged the Russian reading of my English story, but my conscience would give me no peace. Had I any right to spend more time on it? Was it going to be fit to publish, or was I moving ecstatically in a cloud of self-delusion? Walpole would know and before I made any decision I must have his verdict. In any case I had already stayed in Moscow longer than I had intended.

Walpole, himself fending off influenza with aspirin and hard at work on *The Green Mirror*, was extremely kind. I told him I did not want to waste more time on the book unless I could feel sure of its finding a publisher, and that three at least of its chapters needed pulling to pieces and rebuilding. He read it, laughed at the idea that I should have any difficulty in finding a publisher for it, urged me to do the revision at once, to send the book back to England in time for publication in the autumn, and to go into the country and concentrate on doing nothing else. Next day I missed the train for Dorpat thanks to the idiocy of the hotel porter, but left the day after and reached Dorpat in the morning of April 1.

I do not suppose that anybody who reads this can have failed as often as I had failed in the writing of a story. Nobody, therefore, will be able to understand the happiness of my next few weeks. I was again living as a paying guest (an underpaying guest I always thought) with Norman Whishaw. He used to disappear to work in the office downstairs. I had an upper room to myself in which to write my vampire-philosopher's confessions and the missing vital chapter of the book, 'An Invitation to Eternity'. There was another young Englishman in Dorpat at the time, a young brewer who had been sent out from England to teach a big Russian firm how to brew stout, a drink that had been well thought of in Russia ever since Peter the Great had drunk it at Deptford. If a Russian host wished to do honour to an English guest, 'Imperial Stout' was what he produced, in bottles as impressive as those of champagne. We still drink 'Imperial Stout' in England and have long forgotten that it was first brewed for export to Russia in days when Russia had an Emperor but England had not yet its first Empress. I do not know what they are now brewing at Dorpat, but in those days when Bligh was teaching them the art, he told me that the water of the Embach was as suitable for making good stout as that of the

Trent or the Liffey. He was as full of brewing enthusiasm as I was brimming over with the excitement of (at long last) finishing my first romance.

Whishaw and Bligh were very kind in going for walks with me in the old town and down to the river, looking for early signs of spring, and making generous allowances for my occasional hopeless weakness and inability to do anything at all. I was losing blood, sometimes as often as six days in a week, and that day was one of real triumph when I was able to walk round the town over the river by one bridge and back by the other. Spring was close at hand. The frozen river was breaking its bonds and with the thaw came the floods. On April 17 I had done revising. On the 18th Bligh, Whishaw and I, by way of celebrating, rowed in a boat on the flooded river and smoked in the sunshine, sheltering from the strong current between the big timber-stacks which, though high on the banks, were standing in water deep enough to float us. What had I to celebrate? I do not suppose that I have said anything to suggest to any normal novelist the surprise and ecstasy felt at finishing his first book-length story, by one whose whole life had been littered with the corpses of tales one after another given up in despair.

That night I took a train for Petrograd, more than half-afraid that I was already too late to have my book professionally typed and sent to London, and still doubtful about finding a publisher for it. I could not leave it alone. With the book at the typist's office I read on successive days Sabatini's *The Sea Hawk*, Ivor Brown's *Years of Plenty* and Brett Young's *The Dark Tower* with deep envy of their technical skill, had tea more than once with Walpole and his painter-friend Somoff, discussed 'thickness in narrative', listened to Walpole's reading of the chapter in *The Green Mirror* about Henry and the collar-stud and gave myself a stomach-ache with laughter. I recovered my book from the typist's office in the afternoon of April 29 and sat up correcting it till 2 a.m. I went on correcting from 8 a.m. till 10 p.m. and then, at one in the morning of the first of May, went off with Williams to spend the night at Vergezha. Leaving the train at five in the morning we went slowly up the river Volkhov in a crowded paddle-steamer, slowing down where boats had put off from the shore to inter-cept her. Off Vergezha, where the white-painted pillars of the Tyrkov house showed through the trees above the steep bank, the steamer stopped her engines and drifted on. Williams and I

climbed down into a narrow rowing-boat that was waiting for us.
I was told to get some sleep in a room with a balcony over the
river and kept getting out of bed to look across at the forest and
see upstream the river winding into the distance. My book was
done. I had better not look at it again. I slept at last, and then got
up to walk by the river and play chess with Tyrkov. In the evening we went back to Petrograd to find deep snow, and sledges
running, winter again.

On May 3 I saw Nelidov of the Ministry of Foreign Affairs,
handed over *The Elixir* and dined with Walpole and Williams at
Donon's. The Censor was extremely quick, kept the book only
two days and then gave it back with good wishes. On May 5 I
posted it to Methuen, who had published a new edition of my
Wilde book and had asked for more books of criticism. Then,
taking omens in the usual way, I went out of Petrograd, to
Lachta on the Gulf of Finland, where I had noticed a wide river
flowing into the gulf from the north. I rowed quietly a little way
up a small tributary and, holding to a bush, watched a hare fairly
letting himself go in a private dance. Dropping down to the
big railway bridge, I tied up to one of its piers and began to fish
for pike. I hooked a large one and after a struggle brought him to
the top and saw him bite through the gimp of the trace just as I
had him alongside the boat. I did not know what to make of that
omen unless not to be too sure that having finished one story I
could write another. At the very last moment the gimp might
part.

# CHAPTER XX

## *From Patient to Correspondent*

The moment *The Elixir*, that product of stolen weeks, had gone to England I was again putting in all free hours on the book of Russian folk-stories (*Old Peter's Russian Tales*) for which I had a contract already. Jack's had agreed to publish it. They had, I think, less faith in it than I had, for it was agreed between us that they were to pay me no more than £25 for the first 2,000 copies sold. After that they were to pay me a royalty of 15 per cent on the published price. They did not expect to sell more than the first 2,000, but the book, slowly at first, went on selling. It survived the publishers, who were absorbed by Nelson's, and has been reprinted many times. By 1956 more than 24,000 copies had been sold, besides another 25,000 in cheaper editions. These figures do not include American editions, of which there have been several, piratical and legitimate. I did not dream of any such sales while I was putting the book together. Indeed I should not have thought it unfair if I had had to pay for being allowed to do it. But this is true of all my story-books. It is for me a most fortunate injustice.

Meanwhile I was growing rapidly more and more ill, losing much too much blood and at the same time being unable to throw off a succession of violent headaches that made work all but impossible. This neuritis was not improved by letters from Wiltshire which, until I learned the truth from my mother, led me to think that my daughter was dangerously ill.

At this moment Harold Williams and the Tyrkovs with extreme kindness urged me to come down again to Vergezha, and stay there while I could, going up to Petrograd when necessary. They had shown this same kindness to H. G. Wells. This opened for me, as I think Williams had planned that it should, a window into quite another side of Russian life. Vergezha was the family home of the Tyrkovs. It was an old house with a

portico and a façade of great wooden pillars (in the eighteenth-
century Russo-Italian style), set among trees on a high bank that
fell steeply below it to the river Volkhov. The opposite shore was
flat and low, stretching away to a dark belt of forest. Here was
one of Arakcheev's military colonies, founded with the idea of
breeding soldiers who should spend their whole lives under
military discipline and support themselves by their own labour.
The Tyrkov house had a very different tradition. The head of it
was Williams's brother-in-law, Arkady Vladimirovich Tyrkov
who, as a young student in 1881, had been one of the group of
revolutionaries who planned and carried out the assassination of
Alexander II. He had been imprisoned and sent to Siberia where
he had married a Siberian wife and, when at last amnestied, had
brought her home to a household in which she was an uncomfortable alien. His father, Vladimir Tyrkov, had been a country
landowner, old style, devoted to his land and the beasts and
peasants who lived on it. He would have fitted perfectly into a
story by Turgenev, and rather less well into one by Chekhov. He
had died before I came to know the family. His widow, Sophia
Karlovna, was a most beautiful and saintly old lady. She died at a
great age in England, after the Revolution. Arkady Vladimirovich had long since lost all interest in politics. He cared for and
was loved by the peasants, kept cows and always described himself as a dairy-farmer. It was said that his mind had weakened
while in prison in 1882 and on that account he had escaped the
gallows. He was a moderate chess-player, an admirable player of
*gorodk* (a Russian form of skittles) and a most lovable kindly man.
The family grew and shrank from day to day. There were two
sisters, one unmarried, the other the novelist who married
Harold Williams and swept him with her into the inner circles of
the Cadet party. The grown-up son and daughter of her first
marriage were there occasionally. There was also another brother
with his wife, and besides all these, escaping from the great heat of
the Black Sea, a nephew, young Alexander Tyrkov and his
mother from the Crimea, the widow of an older brother of
Arkady's. Then, too, there were nieces working in Petrograd, and
at any time on any day there might be shouts in the yard, a
tinkling of horse-bells and a large party of cousins and friends
would drive up to be joyfully received and spread all over the
house, to sleep on sofas, mattresses or in the hay-barn.

At Vergezha all traditional feasts were thoroughly kept up. I came there with Williams at seven in the morning of May 22 to find men bringing in birch-branches to decorate the house for Whitsuntide. There were birthdays to be marked by elaborate cakes and ceremonial garlands. With all the continual comings and goings the Tyrkovs were seldom at a loss for somebody's birthday or nameday or other excuse for making it a special occasion. At meals we sat at a long table in the dining-room. There were benches round the walls and during meals the peasants would drift in and sit there, discussing farm affairs with Arkady Vladimirovich and joining naturally in the general talk.

I had a little movable table in the room that I shared with Alexander (Sasha) Tyrkov, and I worked a good many hours each day in that room or on the rickety old balcony outside it, high above the river. Russian schoolboys and schoolgirls had very long summer holidays and there were always plenty of them about, ready to help with my Russian if need be. In the evening I would join the others in their games, or sit with their elders on a bluff above the river, smoking rank *makhorka* tobacco to keep off the mosquitoes and watching the gold sparkles of fires and lanterns on the great rafts of logs, hundreds of yards long with little shelters for the lumbermen at each end, that came drifting down in the blue twilight on their slow way to the great towns and the sea. If work had gone well I would take an hour or so off, to go fishing with some of the younger ones, catching perch, pike, bream, orfes, ruffes and the rarer burbots, all welcomed by the cooks preparing *ukha*, a sort of fish soup not unlike bouillabaisse.

Sometimes it happened that Williams would come down to Vergezha exhausted, and I would go up to Petrograd and send telegrams to the *Daily Chronicle* in his name, as nearly as possible such telegrams as he would have sent himself. My very rough diary notes an odd jumble of events. It tells of daisies being picked for Sophia Karlovna's birthday, and of a wreath hung round her portrait while the peasants crowded in singing songs in her honour. It tells of the floating shop that tied up below the house, hung all over with chairs and pots and pans, brooms and tools, a combined market-stall and caravan towed by a woman. It mentions the finding of a butterfly orchis that I had last seen in a meadow beside the road out of the Cartmel valley to Newby Bridge. It mentions rowing off to one of the lumber-rafts and hearing one raftsman say to another that he did not know what day it was because, floating down the river, he had long lost count. It mentions our going to tea in a convent where we were entertained by a delightful abbess. It talks of the mosquitoes that turned my forehead into a relief map of the Lake District. It tells of my happiness when news came that Methuen had agreed to publish *The Elixir*, and of the disappointment when I came to the end of *Old Peter* only to hear that Jack had decided to postpone its publication.

Happy weeks those seem to have been. Memory is a little like a sundial: '*Horas non numero nisi serenas*'. Hours sparkle as I look back on them, hours at the riverside catching little fish for our supper, the blue and gold hours of summer nights and, above all, the happy hours of work. I forget the almost daily haemorrhages, and the resulting weakness that made the climbing even of a single flight of stairs hard labour, wild headaches one after another, extreme worry, and always the grim accompaniment of the war-news that day by day and week by week grew worse.

The first Russian advance at the beginning of the war, the advance that had done so much to save Paris, had been choked in the mud and blood of the East Prussian marshes. The Russian army was on the defensive and in retreat. Men on leave from the front brought ill news. Men from Petrograd brought news still worse. The sudden, wild enthusiasm that I had seen when the Tsar came out on the balcony of the Winter Palace was as if it had never been. We knew of the failures in supply, of shortages of guns and shells. People were reminding each other of the Russo-Japanese war when ammunition-wagons had been opened at the front and found to hold only cases of champagne that had gone astray. They were talking again of 1905 and of the attempted revolution that had followed the Russian defeat. My brother was fighting in France. The happiness of those summer days at Vergezha was unreal, a thin curtain behind which, close behind it, were the realities of war. The boys with whom I fished knew that if the war lasted their turn would come. I felt, we all felt, that we had no right to enjoy anything. Yet the river and the forest and the white summer nights were there, and every now and then we were happy. And now, forty and more years later, I do not remember that slow, grinding unease so vividly as I remember the smudge-fires to keep off the mosquitoes, the lanterns on the rafts of the lumbermen, the lovely far-off forest, the singing of the nightingales and the endless happiness of work. Fireflies glow brighter in the dark.

My illness was growing rapidly worse. On June 26 there was a fire in the village. With all the others I ran to help and very nearly collapsed altogether. Three times on the way back from the smouldering huts (happily a change of wind prevented the fire from spreading or the whole village might have burnt) I had to lie flat on my back to recover. On July 29 I went up to Petrograd and on August 7, in very high spirits, having just heard from England that Methuen's were to publish *The Elixir* at once, I went into hospital for an operation. 'Very nice little room, very jolly nurses, everything as nice as it could be, just like being in an unusually clean hotel.' I lay there rejoicing and began the writing of another story. Hamilton Fyfe of the *Daily Mail*, fearing the worst, looked in to commiserate with a very cheerful corpse, another letter having arrived from Methuen's to corroborate their earlier telegram. Of the operation I remember only a horrible failure of the anaesthetics. Russia before the war had been largely dependent on Germany for drugs. The surgeon had to stop the operation while I was given a fresh dose so that he could proceed. This does not bear thinking about even after forty years. I did not get my first sleep (one and a half hours) until the fourth day after the operation. It was ten days before with the help of two sturdy nurses I put my feet to the floor, to allow my bed to be made, and instantly fainted. However, Williams had brought me a letter from Methuen's to tell me that Mr Collingwood had said that he would correct my proofs for me, so that there should be no delay.

Everything began to go well. Stucke the surgeon came in to say that he had a present for me in the shape of two nurses who could talk my own language. My first nurses had been a couple of good-hearted peasant girls, kind but almost unbelievably clumsy. My new nurses were two delightful young German women Balts driven from their home by the advancing German armies. They were very well educated and widely read. This, I think was a characteristic kindness of Stucke's, and it made my later days in hospital very pleasant indeed.* These two young women talking of William Morris and Rossetti, visits from Williams and the younger Tyrkovs, the reading of Kostomarov and the making of notes for a story of old Novgorod (never to be

---

* Some years later, after the Revolution, Stucke operated successfully on a girl patient who, however, died through no fault of his. Her brother waited for him outside the hospital and shot dead this kindest of men and one of the greatest surgeons of Russia.

finished) and, finally, by what seems today a miracle when it takes a year to produce a printed book, a complete set of proofs from Methuen's, who had sent the typescript to the printers only in the second week of July. Hobbling down the passage to sit on a chair outside the garden door, I enjoyed that delightful feeling of being new-born into a new world that has been ample compensation for many a painful operation.

This particular operation was pronounced successful, but Stucke and Sokolov, the physician, together and severally gave me solemn warnings that it must be followed by complete rest for a very long time. Sokolov, indeed, rather peremptorily ordered me into a sanatorium and said, 'No brain-work for at least a year,' adding that if I disobeyed the result might well be sclerosis and premature old age. Well, well, I suppose that may be what I am now suffering from at seventy-six, but I think it is more probably laziness. As for resting and going into a sanatorium, that was made impossible in a manner unexpectedly dramatic. Williams took me into his flat when I left the hospital and, the very day that Stucke and Sokolov delivered their ultimatum, he was called to the bedside of the *Daily News* correspondent in Petrograd, who had been taken suddenly ill. He came back too tired to write another telegram after being up all night and I, lying on my back, hammered out my first political telegram which Williams sent off to the *Daily News* on behalf of their ill correspondent. He took it to the Censor's office and when it had gone off to England looked into a secondhand bookshop and came back bringing me (just like him) a delightful reprint of an old fishing book. I had a violent headache that evening and another next day when I wrote my second telegram. For some weeks the headaches and the telegrams seemed inseparable, but gradually I learned to write the one without having to submit to the other. The *Daily News* telegraphed asking me if I could go on sending cables to them. This was the moment when the Tsar appointed himself Commander-in-Chief and the future seemed very uncertain, but, as the tension eased and the *Daily News* correspondent had a secretary most eager to write his telegrams for him, and my good surgeon and doctor complained that it was not fair to them if I did not do as I was told, I agreed to take a month's holiday by way of recovering from the operation and to go home for consultation with the *Daily News* office.

I left Petrograd on September 18, stayed a night at Uleaborg, went on with a very kind sea-captain from one of the ships waiting in the Neva, by Tornio, Haparanda, Stockholm and Christiania, sailed from Bergen on the 23rd, was very seasick, thanks, I suppose, to extreme anaemia, and came to Newcastle on the 25th. I spent a month in England, seeing my mother, my brother, Cecil Chesterton, Francis Acland, the Collingwoods and, miraculous tonic, in a bookshop window a bound copy of *The Elixir of Life*. I did some quiet fishing in Wiltshire and at Coniston, though suffering, in spite of writing only a couple of articles and no telegrams, a further lot of frantic headaches. I was told at the *Daily News* office that their man in Russia had locomotor ataxy and could not recover. They asked if I would care to be their permanent correspondent in Petrograd. I agreed on condition that I might come each year to England and, while in Russia, use my own judgment about staying in Petrograd or moving elsewhere. On October 27, 1915, I was on my way back.

# CHAPTER XXI

## *At the Front*

I was still in a pretty poor way, what with anaemia and those continual headaches, when I sailed from Newcastle. I spent a day in Christiania and another in Stockholm and then, yet again, went by Tornio and Haparanda to the north of the Gulf of Bothnia to arrive in Petrograd at midnight on November 3. I travelled much of the way with Richard Washburn Child and his secretary and they were extremely kind and made things much easier for me than they might otherwise have been. Child was a very successful American writer of short stories and I regarded him with the same respect that I had for Hugh Walpole, as one who could do with ease what I found so difficult. There was workshop talk throughout that journey and much more after we had arrived in Petrograd.

I had left England as Russian correspondent to the *Daily News*, but on arrival in Petrograd found myself in an awkward kettle of fish. I had not had time to unpack before the former correspondent's secretary telephoned to say that I need not trouble because he was much better and would be telegraphing himself. Williams, who knew his doctors, told me that this was quite impossible. I cabled to the news editor of the *Daily News*, to ask what I was to do. Meanwhile, I suspect, the secretary had been busy. The telegraph office in Petrograd announced that telegrams signed by me would not be accepted on the *Daily News*'s account. Two days later I was officially told that the telegraph office had been authorised to accept my telegrams, but this was not confirmed until November 13, after which there were no more difficulties. I heard later that the secretary had wished herself to become *Daily News* correspondent. This may well have been so but, though I was ready to retire at once if the original correspondent should recover, my job in the meantime was to telegraph, and telegraph I did.

There was no trade union jealousy of an outsider practising a trade in which many of the other correspondents were old masters. On the contrary they took much trouble in teaching the new boy the ropes. Guy Berenger of Reuter's, for example, on seeing one of my early telegrams, said 'This will never do. You will bankrupt your paper if you don't learn how to contract.' He explained the use of prefixes and suffixes and original compounds. Thus: 'You must never write DID NOT GO in three words instead of UNWENT in one, and so on. There is a special tribe of disentanglers in every newspaper office who will know how to deal with your cables.' He gave as example a famous telegram sent by a correspondent who had asked for a rise in salary on account of the cost of living and had been refused. He cabled in reply, 'UNCASH UNFED UPFED RESIGN' and had his salary doubled next day. Berenger had been a correspondent for a long time and was full of stories of the past. He liked to explain the advantages of being posted in a place like Russia because if the correspondents needed a holiday they could take it and be sure that the absence of telegrams from them would not be put down to their laziness. He explained that the only thing needed was unanimity, and in the old days this had been easy. He told how one day when all the correspondents had gone to the races he had been delighted when the newspapers arrived from England to find startling headlines: 'What is happening in Russia? No messages from correspondents. Reuter's also silent.' I do not suppose it was a true story, but Berenger with eyebrows lifted to his scalp knew how to make it a good one.

Of other correspondents temporarily in Russia there was Samuel Harper who spoke admirable Russian, and Perceval Gibbon who knew only a little but managed very well with French. Gibbon, like Washburn Child, was a well-known writer of short stories and a close friend of Joseph Conrad. He handed on two good pieces of advice. 'Never, if you can possibly help it, put your story into the mouth of one of your characters.' That was one of them. The other, given him by Conrad, is, I think, the most valuable hint ever given by an old storyteller to a young one who wants to learn how to give his characters reality. It is this: 'Let there be a definite incident in the life of each character which is known only to the author and is never mentioned or even indirectly referred to in the book. If you tell all you know about a character, the reader knows as much as you, and your character will remain in the flat, two-dimensional only. If you keep one of your character's secrets, your reader somehow feels that you know more than he does, and that the character is three-dimensional and stands on his own feet.' This was told me by Perceval Gibbon on November 30, 1915, while he lay ill in bed at his hotel.

There was Harold Williams, of course, back from one of his visits to the Carpathian front, or from Galicia, tired, ill, kindly, alert and knowing more about Russia than all the others put together. There was Hamilton Fyfe, devoted to the *Daily Mail*, proudly cherishing a telegram from Northcliffe, 'WELL DONE HARRY', but with good stories of his chief and his colleagues, like that of Charley Hands who, coming down in the lift with Northcliffe, solemnly took off his hat to the lift-boy. 'Why did you do that, Charley?' asked Northcliffe. 'You never know,' said Hands, 'he may be editor tomorrow.' Northcliffe, who would stand anything from Hands, to whom he was devoted, stared a moment and then broke into laughter. There was an odd little man called Digby, correspondent for a Chicago newspaper who had adventured in Siberia and tried to make a corner in mammoth ivory. There was P. B. Struve, a one-time revolutionary, an economist and editor of a Russian review. There was Bernard Pares, entirely devoted to the Homyakov family who personified for him the cause of Anglo-Russian friendship and Anglo-Russian studies. He spent much time at the front, attaching himself to a Red Cross unit run by the Homyakovs, and used to come to Petrograd brimming over with plans for an Anglo-Russian Institute and for planting out Professors of Russian in every English university. He was a great collector, singer and writer of comic songs. He had one about all the stations on the Portsmouth line for which he could find rhymes. I remember, alas, but a single couplet;

> 'The worthy Lord of Worplesdon
> The houses of the poor pulls down.'

Pares was making a verse-translation of Krylov's *Fables* and always brought with him something to read aloud. Nothing could make him see that it was hardly fair to interrupt Williams in the middle of writing his telegram to the *Daily Chronicle* by insisting on reading aloud to him plans, for example, for the establishment of a chair of Russian in some university not yet so blessed, and when Pares, loudly singing on the stairs of the Hôtel

Continental where Peters and I were living, announced his arrival in Petrograd, we used, by sharing Pares between us, to try and keep him occupied and so give the kinder-hearted Williams the chance of getting through his work.

William Peters was a brilliant young economist, later our Trade Commissioner in Ireland and then for many years in South Africa. In 1915 he held a Carnegie travelling scholarship and was working in the Russian Ministry of Trade and Industry. For a long time, living in the same hotel, we used to dine together and, if neither of us was working late, we used to play a game of billiards at the Hôtel Angleterre, a game which, as we played equally badly, we much enjoyed. After Harold Williams, Peters spoke better Russian than any of us, and he knew far more about the economic background of what was going on.

The war was going very badly for Russia and, for that reason, it was very difficult to win permission to go anywhere near the front. Correspondents were hampered in every way and had to make shift as best they could. I remember an 'eyewitness' account of a battle at Czernowitz in the Carpathians appearing in one of the English newspapers and a suggestion that the other correspondents should club together to buy the binoculars with which it had been possible to observe that battle from Odessa. There was much Russian despondency (well justified) and a willingness among Russian officials to allow it to be thought and said that England and France were not doing enough in the west to lessen German pressure in the east. It seemed to me that a strictly unofficial news agency might do good work by giving the Russian newspapers information about the western front. I went to Moscow and had several talks with Bruce Lockhart (our Consul-General there) who doubted the possibility of an unofficial agency but fully agreed that something of the sort was urgently needed. I felt that the agency should be as unobtrusive as possible (to disguise a little its English origin) and thought of Michael Lykiardopoulos as a possible man to run it. He was already well known among Russian editors and knew the needs of their newspapers. I felt sure that if Lyki were well supplied with information from London the Russian editors would hang round him like hounds about a huntsman, eager for whatever he might deal out to them. Back in Petrograd, I saw Williams who thought well of the idea. On January 22, 1916, I rewrote and typed out the report I had already written and that evening went to the Embassy and showed it to the Ambassador, Sir George Buchanan. He said he thought there was something in it and that he would telegraph to the Foreign Office.

On February I I was at the Embassy and saw Sir George and Colonel Thornhill, the Military Attaché. Thornhill was a little cross and said he could not understand why the Foreign Office had accepted my suggestion when they had taken no notice of similar suggestions by himself. The Ambassador said that my scheme had been approved by the British Government, that he thought an English literary man should be at the head of it and that he had asked for Walpole who would presently be arriving. Walking away from the Embassy afterwards, Williams said he thought that was rather hard on me, but I did not think so. I had never thought of running the thing myself, but had felt that it would be better not to have an obvious Englishman at the head of it, and for that reason had been thinking of Lyki. As things turned out, the Anglo-Russian Bureau that I had planned to be a deliberately unobtrusive source of supply of English news for the Russians, grew under Walpole and Thornhill to be a more and more expensive and obvious propaganda bureau employing a large staff. It was useful as a club for friendly Russians who, naturally, paid no subscription. It organised a certain amount of hospitality and in the end became a joke.

Meanwhile I was having one headache after another and was steadily sending telegrams and articles to the *Daily News*. In odd moments I tried to write another story to follow *The Elixir* but I had not Walpole's enviable power of concentration and of shutting out all interests but one. I used to envy him, sitting at his desk and writing away completely absorbed. I envied but could not emulate. My days were more and more filled by talks with every kind of Russian and I wrote less and less, except for the *Daily News*. I was reading and making daily extracts from half a dozen and sometimes more of the Russian newspapers, though I did in odd moments make rough translations of songs that I heard magnificently sung by Russian soldiers marching through the streets. I had friends among the captains of the British merchant vessels held up in Russia by the war and used to struggle through the snow on the deserted quays to have dinner aboard the S.S. *Ladoga* of Leith and listen to the forcibly expressed views of Captains Reid and Belding, to whom I had been given letters by the Captain Horncastle who had so kindly nursed me all the way to England when I left Russia almost too weak to walk after my operation.

It was March 1916 before I was given my first limited permission to visit the Russian front as a war correspondent. I believe that in the 1939–1945 war correspondents were encouraged and given every opportunity of seeing the war it was their business to describe. In 1916, on the Russian front, they had a struggle to see anything at all. We were fully persuaded that the enemy knew more about the position of the Russian armies than Russia's allies were allowed to know. Further, most of the foreign correspondents knew no Russian, or very little, and so needed interpreters and constant shepherding by some Russian officer detailed for that purpose.

When with another correspondent I got down to Galicia the gratitude of the officer in charge of us on finding that we could sometimes do without him was almost touching. We went to Kiev and thence to the South Western Army Headquarters at Berditchev, where we met for the first time General Brusilov, the smartest-uniformed and most elegant of all Russian generals, later to be famous for his break-through in the west, and for the disasters his armies suffered in retreat. We spent about a month in that strange rolling country that was so unlike Russia. The peasants working on the land were very unwilling to identify themselves as belonging to any one of the warring nations. Again and again, on asking a peasant to what nationality he belonged, Russian, Little-Russian or Polish, I heard the reply 'Orthodox', and when the man was pressed to say to what actual race he belonged I heard him answer safely 'We're local.'

I remember little of what we saw, except the things that no serious reader would think worth remembering, such as an observation post designed by some Russian who had not forgotten the stories told him as a child. It was disguised as a muck-heap in a huge area of ploughed land where there were at least fifty muck-heaps all alike. And of course I remember that other night when, on a quiet sector, I was walking with a Russian officer who mistook his direction and we were suddenly brought up short by hearing German spoken a few yards ahead of us. I still have the little luminous phosphorescent compass by which we found our way back. This was a sector where the enemy forces were Austrian, the trenches were very near together, and a Russian raiding-party, pushing deep into the Austrian lines, found an unguarded waggon of comforts for the troops, mainly musical instruments. These were distributed and I still have the *czakan*, a sort of Hungarian flageolet, that fell undeserved to my share. I remember, too, on one of these expeditions, an Easter Eve service in a tent, with the candle-flames shivering in the wind, and rockets in the sky over No Man's Land to announce that Christ was risen.

I remember interminable driving in vehicles of all kinds along roads that war had widened from narrow cart-tracks to broad highways half a mile wide. Drivers had moved out of the original road to ground on either side of it not yet churned to mud. As each new strip turned to bog the drivers steered just outside it, so that in many places two carts meeting each other and going in opposite directions would be out of shouting distance. I remember Tarnopol and Trembovlya, where the railway staff used to leave the railway-station at five minutes to eight every morning and the hotel staff left it to the Germans to call their guests for them, since station-master and hotel-keeper alike could count on a German aeroplane dropping a bomb on or near the station at eight o'clock precisely. Was it at Tarnopol that I tried to teach Hamilton Fyfe to fish for tench in a horse-pond? Was it here or at Berditchev that he was so angry with me for rousing unjustified ambition in bootblacks? We had an appointment some distance away in local headquarters, and I was slow with my breakfast and came down to find Fyfe outside the hotel with one of his boots already cleaned and a bootboy setting to work on the other. 'You are going to make us both late,' said Fyfe, as another bootboy started on mine. I bent down and told my bootboy he should have a rouble if my boots were cleaned before Fyfe's. The boy's brushes fairly whirled, and I gave him his rouble and set off down the street just as Fyfe's boy was finishing. But my boy could not resist gloating, with the result that Fyfe's boy refused the usual twenty kopecks and demanded a rouble for himself also and with outstretched hand and complaining voice kept pace with the unyielding Fyfe all the way down the street.

But why pile these trivialities together? Looking back now I seem to have seen nothing, but I did in fact see a great deal of that long-drawn-out front and of the men who, ill-armed, ill-supplied, were holding it against an enemy who, even if his anxiety to fight was no greater than the Russian's, was infinitely better equipped. I came back to Petrograd full of admiration for the Russian soldiers who were holding the front without enough weapons to go round. I was much better able to understand the grimness with which those of my friends who knew Russia best were looking into the future. I came back also to find myself telegraphing, sometimes twice and three times in a day. It often happened that the news editor would cable telling me not to send so much. These cables I always disregarded and always, a few days later, he would cable again asking for more.

While working extremely hard for the *Daily News* I was keeping sane by going steadily on with my translations (if only a sentence a day), and sometimes when no telegram needed sending I used to go a few miles out of the city to fish, finding the contemplation of a float a sovereign clearance for such mind as I had left. I was seeing Sergei Feodorovich Oldenburg of the Academy of Science, Valery Carrick and other artists and particularly Dmitri Mitrokhin, who was just finishing the admirable series of pictures (black-and-white and coloured) that he did for *Old Peter's Russian Tales*. Meanwhile the Ambassador told me that he was anxious to keep me in Petrograd and had cabled to London to say so. This was reinforced next day by a peremptory message from the Embassy to say that I was not to leave, and the same afternoon there came a telegram from the *Daily News* to say that I was exempt from military service and was to stay where I was. I had not asked for exemption, but it was perhaps just as well that I had been given it, as things kept going wrong again after any sort of exertion, although there could be no doubt that Stucke's operation had been entirely successful and I was much better able to work than I had been. In June the Ambassador allowed me to send the whole of Mitrokhin's pictures and my final corrections to *Old Peter* safely home in the Embassy bag.

# CHAPTER XXII

## Bombs in Bucharest

After one of my visits to Galicia there occurred a ridiculous incident that I regretted at the time and for long afterwards. I looked in at the Anglo-Russian Bureau and found Walpole busy writing. The moment he looked up I knew that something had gone wrong. Some newspapers had just arrived from England and he had found an article by me in the *Daily News* which he thought ran counter to opinions (in favour of enlarging the Bureau) that Williams and he had recently sent to the Foreign Office. I said that I could not help that. He said that Williams would be very much upset when he saw the article. I said 'Well don't let him see it,' and put the paper in my pocket. Walpole screamed, 'Put that paper down at once.' I was startled into laughing. Walpole screamed again. 'You are not official. I am. That paper is official property.' He had lost his temper completely. I have always been sorry that I did not lose mine. I think that if I had, the quarrel would not have become the lasting thing it did. I saw Williams and told him what had happened and he was indeed upset, not at all on account of my very harmless article, but at there being a quarrel between two of his friends. I told him that so far as I was concerned there was no quarrel. He was sure he would be able to make peace. He tried and failed. He tried again and again. Other people tried also without result. Walpole could not forgive me for losing his temper. It was not until the winter of 1932 (sixteen years later) that peace was made. Walpole wrote in the *Observer* a kindly review of my third Swallows book in which he said that he had also liked the other two. I wrote to him at once, asking 'Is this an olive branch?' He replied, charmingly, 'A twig,' and our old friendship began again as if it had never been broken. Broken on my side it never had been.

In general at this time Harold Williams, William Peters, Bernard Pares and I could very well have written each other's telegrams. Pares was intimate with Gutchkov of the Octobrists. Williams, for the most part, agreed with Miliukov. Will Peters and I had no political affiliations, but so nearly did we all agree in the belief that anything was good that was not likely to disturb Anglo-Russian friendship that, when need was, I could write a telegram for Williams, he could write a telegram for me, and Will Peters could have written telegrams for both of us. We were all firmly on the side of the Russian parliament, the Duma, as against the Autocracy, had rejoiced when the whole country had seemed as one, regretted everything that seemed likely to weaken Russia as an ally and were alike in coming to suspect that the Duma was much more pro-English than the Autocracy. This was entirely natural. The Russian Autocracy could never have felt comfortable fighting at the side of a Constitutional Monarchy against a German Autocracy much closer akin to itself. This became more and more clear, while at the same time it became obvious that Russian parliamentarians hoped that the alliance with England would bring about some modification of the system under which Ministers were responsible solely to the Tsar. In Petrograd one began to hear it said that every Russian retreat brought about concessions from the Autocracy to the Duma, and that every Russian victory encouraged the Autocracy to retract them.

In August, during a visit to the front, Berenger sent a well-meant but silly telegram to England in which he mentioned (most unnecessarily) that the correspondent of the *Daily News* when flying in a Russian aeroplane had come under fire. The truth was that I had indeed flown along the front in one of the old two-seated Voisin machines in which the passenger sat as if in an open canoe with a foot on each side of the pilot, in whose stupidity he had the utmost confidence. It was cold in the air and I well remember beating my hand against the outside of the canoe to get my fingers warm enough to take a photograph. There had been a little shooting over the actual front and the pilot had praised the deafening noise of the engine so very close to our heads, pointing out that even when the puff of smoke flowered quite close to us we could not hear the explosion, and that once we saw that puff we could be sure we had been missed. Our real trouble, such as it was, began when just before dusk we flew back to the place from which we had started. We began to spiral down and instantly there appeared puff after puff of smoke from shells sent up to meet us. The pilot suddenly turned the nose of the machine up, pointing with a grin to a small new tear in one wing. Presently he spiralled down again and again was greeted with shells from below. Once more we sheered off, this time with curses, and on coming back yet again we were, at last, recognised as friends and allowed to land. I dined that night with the battery that had done the shooting, and sat next to the officer in charge. I complained that I did not think he had given me a very hospitable reception. 'Perhaps not,' he replied. 'I'm very sorry, my dear chap, to have kept you waiting on the doorstep, so to speak, but really you ought to count yourself lucky, for usually when we fire at our own machine we hit it.' In case I had not understood, he explained that their aeroplanes had been given to the Russian army because they were not good enough for the French. They were very slow and therefore easy targets.

More and more often I heard, as correspondent for the Liberal *Daily News*, complaints that would not have been made in the presence of correspondents of *The Times* and the *Morning Post*. Long before the end of that summer of 1916 I had heard not merely lieutenants, majors and colonels of the Russian Army, but even generals, saying that Russia had to fight with one hand tied behind her back. There was no outspoken despair among the generals but, even if they said that victory must come first, they were freely telling each other that once the war was over there were things that would have to be put right. Between visits to different sections of the front I was in Petrograd, where I found myself unable to understand the optimism of some of my colleagues. Sazonov, Russian Foreign Minister when the war started, had been replaced by Sturmer, a notorious pro-German. I knew at that time no professed socialists in Russia, but among Octobrists, Constitutional Democrats (Cadets), sober persons of the Right, enthusiasm had given place to doubt, and as each costly Russian advance came to a standstill and then to a retreat, doubt turned to something very near despair and, though there was an endless public chorus of newspapers and statesmen promising 'war to a victorious end', it was becoming more and more clear that if that victorious end were postponed too long Russia might collapse before her victory.

I was in Petrograd at the beginning of August when an official telephoned and asked me to come round to the Ministry of Foreign Affairs. I did so and was asked, 'Would I mind lending them a hand by accompanying to the front a small group of non-Russian-speaking representatives of neutral and other newspapers?' This was a sort of Sunday-school visit. I agreed. I could hardly refuse. We spent a luxurious but uninstructive ten days mainly in railway-trains and then came back to Petrograd. I had already told the *Daily News* that I wanted to come home to report. At this point Roumania surprised us all by coming into the war on the side of the Allies. On the same day I had two telegrams from the *Daily News*. The first agreed that I should come home. The second, ten minutes later, said 'Wait because of Roumania.'

There was the usual struggle with Russian officials who, no doubt, were having their own troubles with other Russian officials about letting foreign correspondents loose in this new and as yet unstabilised theatre of war. Odessa was suggested as a suitable place from which to make a start, but a glance at the map told me that to go to Odessa en route for Bucharest was very much like going to Birmingham by way of Beachy Head. I decided to see how far I could get by a more direct route, even if it meant setting out without waiting for a full outfit of passes and permissions. After all, I still had Hagberg Wright's indignant letter in my pocket. I reached Kiev without difficulty and next day went on to Ungheni, a frontier station immediately in front of the great bridge over the Pruth which was the boundary between Roumania and Russia. The train seemed to be going no further and I had a good sleep in an empty carriage. I was very unwilling to make enquiries, lest I should be sent back or held up for having no right to be there.

At dusk a long munition-train pulled into the station on the line leading to the bridge. A van with an open door caught my eye and with my usually unlucky but occasionally fortunate readiness to act first and think afterwards I grabbed my typewriter and bag, watched till the guards were walking away from me, pushed typewriter and bag into the van and scrambled after them. Presently I heard voices and the clanging of doors and knew that an inspection of the train had begun. I began to think how best to brazen out the obvious fact that I had secreted myself without leave in a munition-train. The inspectors came nearer and nearer, waggon by waggon. They were at the next waggon ahead of mine when there was a violent jolt, curses next door and a rattle and thump as they jumped to the platform. I suppose the engine-driver thought he had been held up long enough. The train moved slowly forward. On the bridge it stopped again and I began to wish I were still in Petrograd waiting for a permit to leave. It moved on. A change in the noise told me we had crossed the river. We were in Roumania. My luck held. On the platform was a French officer and he was so delighted to be able to say what he thought about the inefficiency of Russians and Roumanians alike that he did not think of sending me back. 'You are here now,' he said, 'and my orders are not to let anyone cross. Clear, isn't it? You must stay here. Your passport is enough.' And with that he sent me on to Jassy and told me I should have an uncomfortable journey to Bucharest but that was my affair, not his.

I had a good sleep in Jassy and next morning set out for Bucharest, on a lovely, warm autumn day most of which I spent on the roof of a waggon with a lot of good-natured Roumanian soldiers eating water-melons. There were piles of them, red-fleshed and most refreshing, on the station platforms and a soldier would leap down and throw up one after another with a swinging overhand pass, to be caught like a Rugby football by one of his friends.

I reached Bucharest in the very early hours of Sunday morning and walked amazed through this extraordinary capital, where the most tumble-down of shacks crowded up to the back doors of luxurious modern houses. As early as seemed fitting I called on the British Minister who was very kind and said that if I had anything to send home, a courier would be leaving on Tuesday. I found a room in a hotel in the main square, bought a Roumanian grammar and dictionary and set about learning to read Roumanian as quickly as I could, beginning as usual by buying a book of children's stories. At the same time I was reading the Roumanian newspapers with no pleasure but much determination and finding that, attacked in this way from both ends at once, Roumanian was not too difficult to be read by anybody who knew something of two of the three languages that have contributed most to the Roumanian vocabulary. With Latin and Russian I had a key that turned rustily in the lock, sticking only at the words of Turkish origin.

The Roumanian Minister of Education, Dukas, was extremely friendly to my efforts to learn his language, and found me two young women, from one of whom I took a lesson in the morning and from the other in the afternoon. Again I was most fortunate.

One of these two was Madame Ghetsu, the daughter of the famous Ghetsu who had been the chief compiler of the Roumanian Civil Code. He was living in retirement, a very eloquent old man with the most uncompromising notions of what Roumania would be able to claim after the war. On the wall he had a huge map showing Austro-Hungary and the Balkans and on the map he pointed to the whole of Transylvania as ethnographically Roumanian property.

The Roumanian declaration of war was announced after surprise attacks that took them across the frontier of Hungary in several places, and the Roumanians, misled by the Russian advances in the Carpathians and Galicia, persuaded that they had entered the war only just in time to reap the benefits they hoped for, expected to be celebrating a general victory of the Allies by Christmas, or very soon after. Their initial success filled them with enthusiasm that very soon changed to despair when they found themselves in retreat, when they were themselves attacked in the south, and when the enemy began to bomb a Bucharest that was unprepared for any such experience. It was not bombing comparable with the wholesale destruction to which the advance of civilisation has accustomed us since. It was, however, dismaying to people with no effective means of fighting back. I remember, when the first Zeppelin came over the city, seeing a gallant Roumanian policeman in the main square steadily firing away at it with his revolver.

A flight of half-a-dozen aeroplanes used to come over at eight in the morning, a similar flight at mid-day, a third in the evening, after which a Zeppelin came sailing over and cruised above the city at night, dropping a bomb at intervals, so that I used to imagine its crew up there playing cards and letting a bomb fall at every thirteenth trick. At first there used to be a good deal of anti-aircraft fire, but the dropping shrapnel did no damage to the Germans and much to the Roumanians, and this form of collaboration with the enemy was given up. There was a rigorous black-out and in the corridors of my hotel the only lights were candles, oddly shaded by inverted flower-pots.

The bangs of the exploding bombs made sleep difficult for most of us, but not for J. D. Bourchier of *The Times* who had come here from Bulgaria when that country went to war. He had lived long in Bulgaria, liked the Bulgarians and had left his stud of ponies in their keeping, they giving him an affectionate farewell, and promising to look after his ponies, which I believe they did. He was nearly stone-deaf and when we came down to breakfast, rather sore-eyed after a sleepless night, old Bourchier, very pink and cheerful, used to greet us with the words, 'Well, they left us alone last night.'

Our Military Attaché in Bucharest was Colonel Thomson, who blamed himself a good deal for his share in bringing Roumania into the war. 'They told me at home that I could ask for anything I liked if I brought Roumania in,' he said ruefully when disaster was looming near, 'but I think it would be a little tactless if I asked for anything now.' He was a romantic, handsome, gallant fellow who did not refrain from putting into a political book about peace and war (*Old Europe's Suicide*) a chapter about the house and garden of a lady to whom he was much devoted. I liked him very much and was shocked one morning to hear someone say that one of last night's bombs had fallen on the Military Mission. I went round at once, but before I reached the Mission had heard the story that raised British prestige in Bucharest to almost incredible heights. Thomson and his second-in-command were sleeping in the Mission when they were woken by a bomb dropping very near. 'Roll up in your eiderdown,' called Thomson, 'the next may be nearer.' In the morning they were picking glass splinters out of their eiderdowns and blankets. The next bomb had scored a direct hit on the Mission and blown away half that side of the house. 'And those damned Roumanians never came round to see what had happened to us till this morning.' It was eight o'clock when the Roumanians did come round to look at the ruins, and at eight o'clock Thomson was accustomed to have his bath. The bomb had blown away half the bathroom, which was on the upper floor, but had left the bath itself in the open, projecting over the ruins. The water-supply was still working, so Thomson was having his bath as usual and, hearing voices in the garden below him, voices of Roumanians who assumed that he was dead, put his head over the rim of the bath and told them he would be down in half a minute if they cared to wait. For those times it had been a good bomb, and Thomson and his assistant were lucky to be alive. I had had tea with him in the garden the day before and looking round after the bomb found the gilt leg of the tea-table driven more than half way through a tree-trunk. Later, when it was clear that nothing could prevent a general retreat, Thomson picked me up in his car, and I found my knees lifted to my chin. 'Have a look,' said Thomson and I lifted the carpet to see that the floor of the car was covered with bottles of champagne. Thomson laughed. 'Well,' he said, 'if it has got to be a retreat, I don't see why it should be a dry one.'

Years later, in London, I met Thomson hurrying towards the Strand in civilian clothes and carrying a delicately tinted pair of gloves. He told me he was on his way to address a Trade Union meeting. I suppose I must have smiled and he must have noticed my glance at his gloves. 'Yes,' he said, 'I know I don't look much of a Trade Unionist, but that can't be helped.' He became Lord Thomson, Secretary of State for Air in the first Labour Government, and to the sorrow of all who knew him was killed on the first flight of the airship R.101.

Not even Thomson (though he tried) could persuade the Roumanians to let correspondents go up to the Transylvanian front. Things were already going very badly. I sent a few articles home in the diplomatic bag, thanks to the kindness of Sir George Barclay and, with a party of others, crossed the great bridge over the Pruth at Czernavoda, saw the Russian troops there and soon realised that they were quite indifferent to the fate of Roumania and had no intention of doing more than hold the shortest and most defensible line.

We went down to Constanza, on the Black Sea, but I remember little of it except two mildly comic episodes. I had never seen the Black Sea before and, walking down to the sea-wall with some of the other correspondents, decided that I could not miss my chance of bathing in it. It was late in the evening and dark. The others, while protesting that it was mad in any case to go swimming in October, agreed to guard my clothes, while I climbed down the sea-wall, was nipped by crabs among the rocks below, and had a pleasant swim under a starry sky. I had come ashore again, climbed the wall, dressed and was putting on my shoes, when I heard the noise of an aeroplane approaching from inland. Not very seriously I remarked, 'If that chap is a Bulgarian, the moment he realises that he is leaving the land he will drop anything he has left so as not to waste it on the fish. You had better lie down.'

By now the aeroplane was coming close over our heads. My Roumanian friends did indeed lie down and, willy nilly, so did I. It was a Bulgarian, and he did drop his last bomb, which fell within a few yards of us, luckily on a terrace immediately above

7*

us, so that the blast passed over our heads. My friends, lying down, felt nothing. I had tied my last shoe in the dark and, standing up, was knocked flat, as if by a pillow wielded by a giant. I was quite unhurt except that I did get a bit of a headache. That night we spent in a hotel in Constanza. My room was divided by heavy double doors from the room of an Irishman, Donahue of the *Daily Chronicle*. We sat up talking in his room and when I retired to my own those heavy doors swung to and slammed with a resounding crash. The next moment Donahue and I heard the rush of feet on the floor above. As the crowd hurried down, one gallant fellow stopped, knocked on our door, and warned us, '*Encore un avion! Encore un avion!*' and followed his comrades to the cellar. Donahue called to me, 'Come in here. This is too good to waste.' I joined him and went on listening to his tales of old wars. Some time later we heard footsteps going upstairs, a crowd together, and presently there was a knock and the same voice that we had heard before announced '*Le danger est passé.*'

'So you think,' said the Irishman under his breath, and then, 'Give them time to get their heads under their blankets.' We waited half an hour. All was quiet. 'Now,' said Donahue, 'both together!' The doors swung to with our combined weight to help them. Again there was a stampede from above and we learned next morning that there had been two attempts by aeroplanes to wipe out the Roumanian press, and that our friends had spent the rest of the night in the cellar.

I am reminded of the other childish episode by a much-valued Turkish coffee-mill. Coming out of the hotel in Constanza I met in the street a Turkish pedlar with a load of brass-ware. I asked the price of a coffee-mill. He said, 'A hundred lei,' a monstrous price, obviously the opening gambit of a long haggle that would be enjoyed by both sides. I said, 'Two.' He said that it was a very good coffee-mill. At that moment we heard a bomb drop somewhere in the town. 'Ninety,' he said and reached for the mill which I had in my hand. I said, 'Three,' and held firmly to the mill. Another bomb dropped. 'Eighty,' he said and I rose my bid to 'Four!' The next bomb brought him down with a jump to 'Fifty!' I rose to 'Five!' In the end, the bidding still being punctuated by bombs at a safe distance but usefully loud, he resigned the coffee-mill for twelve lei, its proper price, and was gone. (This was the coffee-mill that was later saved for me together with a fishing-rod as 'the two most important things' by my landlady in

Petrograd when my rooms were sacked by the political police.)
I had been on the point of starting for England when Roumania
came into the war. Having seen what I was allowed to see, I left
Bucharest on October 12, spent a day or two in Kiev, arrived in
Petrograd to find the usual snow and filth of autumn, and a
welcome telegram agreeing to the London visit that I thought was
overdue. I talked things over with Harold Williams, William
Peters and a new friend, Harold Grenfell, who was our Naval
Attaché. The outlook seemed to all three of us extremely grim,
much grimmer I thought than it seemed to most of the officials in
the Embassy. The great Brusilov offensive had petered out.
Roumania, after coming in on the side of the Allies, was largely
occupied by the enemy. After what I had seen and heard on
journeys that had taken me hither and thither on the long
Russian front, after what I had heard of the army's resentful belief
that it was being sent to fight unarmed, I was persuaded that only
a miracle could prevent collapse if the war were to last much
longer. The contradictions, the strains and stresses that with every
month became more obvious promised explosion, and it crossed
my mind that if a conflict was believed inevitable, there might be
those who would provoke it, so as to be able to ensure that it
should take place in circumstances that they supposed would
allow them to suppress it. In any case I did not think it could be
long postponed in Russia while the tension of war continued. On
October 29 I set out yet again from Petrograd on that long
journey through Finland, round the Gulf of Bothnia and so to
Bergen and Newcastle.

# CHAPTER XXIII

## *First Cracks in the Ice*

On November 7 I lunched in London with Francis Acland and Lord Crawford and Balcarres of the Ministry of Agriculture and Fisheries. I told them that I thought we should be considering the possibility that, if we could not bring the war to an end in 1917, we should have to manage without the help of the Russians.

'What do you mean?'

'There will be an explosion of some kind. If the Autocracy becomes afraid of a revolt, its natural reaction will be to provoke a revolt that it can suppress. Such a revolt would give the Autocracy a perfect excuse for saying that it can fight Germany no more.'

Lord Crawford was unbelieving. It was Acland who asked, 'What do you think is the likeliest time for such an explosion?'

I had an answer to that question. I had asked it myself, in Petrograd, and Will Peters had answered it for me.

'The likeliest times will be in March and in October.'

'Why?'

'Because in those months food-shortages in the capitals will be more likely than in any other.'

'But that's rubbish,' said Lord Crawford. 'Russia is one of the greatest food-producing countries in the world, and a food-shortage there is unthinkable.'

Will Peters had foreseen that objection and I, well-briefed, pointed out that Russia was an enormous country, and that there had seldom been a year when there was not a famine somewhere, though the famine was never allowed to interfere with the Russian export of corn. The vital factor was transport, and the war was making such demands on Russian transport that even if there was a tremendous surplus of corn there would not be the waggons and the engines to bring it to the cities where it was wanted.

'So you think there may be riots in March and in October.'

'I said March or October. If they survive March without trouble, they are likely to find it in October.'

This is nothing to boast about, but the fact does remain that Will Peters was right and doubly right, for the two revolutions came exactly when he expected them. There was revolution in Russia *both* in March *and* in October (Russian Old Style), the latter, the Bolshevik Revolution, exactly one year to the day after I had sat talking about it with Francis Acland. There was nothing to be done about it. Events could neither be hurried nor held back.

Anyhow we had done what little we could do, in letting two members of the Government know what we small fry were thinking on the subject it was our business to know. I said as much to A. G. Gardiner, the editor of the *Daily News*, and to one of the Cadburys who owned the paper. I set in train the making of Will Peters's special boots, went to Leeds to see my mother and brother and to talk about Russian studies with Michael Sadler, the Vice-Chancellor of the University; then, once more, to Lanehead for a few days with the Collingwoods, rowing on the lake, walking over Wrynose and the Langdales, and going to tea at Brantwood with the Severns. Back to Leeds again, two days' fishing in Wiltshire, London and off again to Russia. At Newcastle I was met by Will Peters's grand old father, who had made the journey from Aberdeen just to shake the hand of one who was so soon to see the Will of whom he was so proud. I think it was on that crossing to Bergen that we sighted a floating mine and took turns in shooting at it from the bridge until a lucky shot hit the detonator on one of its horns and put an end to it.

I reached Petrograd on December 11, after a journey spoilt by violent headaches, and a few days later left for Pskov and the north-western front. Moving hither and thither on that winter front, where soldiers on both sides were tunnelling in deep snow and where, in the forests, there were forts of pine-logs, like the blockhouses of an Indian tale, and the frost had put an end to the value of the rivers, I met several of the generals who were presently to be lit up in the glare of great events that made now one man, now another, important for a moment. Among them was Radko-Dimitriev, Bulgarian by origin, who had not forgotten that the *Daily News*, in the days of W. T. Stead, had strongly supported the Balkan countries. For that reason, I suspect, he was friendly to me and talked with great freedom

about the mistrust felt at the front about 'the dark forces' at work
in the rear.

Near the end of December I came back to Riga from visiting
trenches west of Kemmern to find a message from Radko-
Dimitriev telling me to come round to his headquarters as there
was something he wanted to tell me. I hurried round, thinking
that this must mean some change of programme. I found the
general stamping up and down his room. He was a short, stocky
little elephant of a man, and the moment the orderly had left the
room and closed the door behind him, Radko-Dimitriev came up
to me, shaking his fist as if it held a dagger. 'Rasputin was killed
last night and I wish this hand had been in it.' He went on to say
that now things would begin to happen ('changes more important than anything you will see here') and that the *Daily News*
correspondent ought to be in Petrograd. I made one more
expedition to the Dvina front and left for Petrograd on New
Year's Day, 1917.

Radko-Dimitriev had been right. Rasputin's death had sharply
changed the atmosphere of Petrograd. It was no longer a question
whether something was going to happen, but simply when?
Petrograd was like a pot of porridge coming slowly to the boil,
with bubbles, now here now there, rising to burst on the surface.
Russian newspapers had become suddenly daring, and were
printing articles that in normal times would have sent the 'sitting
editor' to the fortress. When the censorship was at its worst and
police action frequent, Russian newspapers used to employ,
besides the real editor, one or more 'sitting editors' whose job it
was to take the blame for what their paper printed and to 'sit' in
prison, leaving the real editor free to go on with his work. In the
early months of 1917 there were newspapers in Petrograd that
seemed to go out of their way to invite prosecution, for example
by printing rhymed acrostics in which the first letter and the last
of each line made obvious reference to some forbidden subject.
People used to stop each other at street-corners to call attention to
this or that exploit of the kind in whatever newspaper they
happened to be reading. The murder of Rasputin, carried out by
persons so closely related to the Court that they could not be
brought to trial, showed that the Autocracy was divided against
itself. Even right-wing newspapers published the ambiguous
articles and cryptograms that slipped past the Censor, who pretended not to have seen in them the obvious meanings that were

being discussed in the queues waiting for footholds on the tram-oars. When I got back to the capital from Riga, I began watching events that were moving towards a climax the exact character of which no one could foresee. It was like living on the slopes of a volcano that had begun most remarkably to smoke. It was even more like watching a frozen Russian river, and listening for the first cracks in the ice that would become a chorus, until suddenly, under the spring sun, the motionless river would break up with a continuous grinding roar, when the still calm of the winter would change to violent motion, with huge blocks of ice thrown high in the air and swept away irresistibly to the sea.

I was daily hearing the views of a great variety of people of all political faiths other than socialist. I was meeting Will Peters on most days, and he knew what was being said by the young civil servants in the Ministry in which he worked. I was seeing Harold Williams nearly every day and through him meeting a mixed lot of Russian politicians that did not include any representatives of the socialist parties. Gutchkov, a monarchist, found himself in opposition to the Autocracy because he thought that the Autocracy was inefficient, if not worse, in its conduct of the war. Miliukov, leader of the Cadets, wanted a constitution in which Ministers should be responsible not to the Autocrat but to the Duma. He shared the Autocracy's mistaken belief that he had great personal influence outside the inner circles of his own party. This was perhaps natural because of the way in which this rather dull professor, whose political life had been distinguished by a long series of blunders, was treated by those inner circles. When Miliukov came to the Williamses' flat, court was paid to him with extraordinary solemnity. Harold Williams's own view of Miliukov was a long way the saner side of idolatry. William Peters and I, on the subject of the deified Miliukov, remained silent sceptics.

I had many friends in the Russian army: a few painters, includ-ing Mitrokhin, since famous, then but little known; a few writers and a great number of simple, undistinguished folk, fishing acquaintances and others who, a couple of years earlier, would have been eager to talk of anything but politics. In those grim winter months that followed the murder of Rasputin every one of these people was as if waiting for something, no one knew what.

The word 'defeatism' has come to mean habitual expectation of defeat. In the Russia of those days it meant something quite different. It meant a welcoming of defeat because of a general recognition that disasters on the front were always followed by concessions from the Autocracy. Another common saying in those days was, 'Things have got to be worse before they are better'. The seeming unanimity with which the Russians had gone to war in 1914 was as if it had never been. The Autocracy and 'the politicians', even such politicians as would in England have been thought of as somewhat out-of-date and stiff-brained Conservatives, now regarded each other as hostile forces. They were preoccupied by a struggle of their own and were inclined to consider the war on the long Russian front only as it affected this more intimate struggle. On the front, almost as if in another world, the Russian armies, ill-equipped, suspecting treachery at their backs, were fighting with ever-lessening hope of victory. In the rear all the simple folk who cared nothing about politics but were helplessly conscious that some catastrophe or climax was impending, weighed all news with one question only in their minds. Does it bring nearer the end of the war? I used to try to slip out without being seen by the old porter at the foot of the stairs, in the hope of not hearing that unanswerable question.

Soon after I came back to Petrograd from the northern front, J. L. Garvin telegraphed asking me to become correspondent for the *Observer*. I was delighted and found things much easier. As correspondent for a Conservative newspaper I found doors wide open that would have been scarcely ajar for the correspondent of the Radical *Daily News*, and occasional telegrams to the *Observer* did not seriously disturb persons otherwise well-disposed towards the *Daily News*. I obtained, not without some small preliminary difficulty, a press ticket allowing me to attend meetings of the Duma in the Tauris Palace. Of this I made full use and can see now why the editor and sub-editor must have wondered why I was bombarding them with telegrams at a time when in Russia nothing much seemed to be happening. I could not openly telegraph asking them to expect a revolution, but I could do something to prevent their being caught completely unawares by the events which by now I was expecting tomorrow or the next day.

In telegrams (that had to pass an oddly wavering and capricious censorship), in reports sent by the diplomatic bags, I tried to warn people in England of what was coming, or rather that something was coming whose precise character I could not even pretend to predict. Two things happened. The *Daily News* telegraphed to me to cut down my cables and Milner came to Petrograd to report on the Russian situation. I was not among those invited to meet him because my belief that some form of explosion was imminent was not shared by our official representatives. I knew very well what views on the Russian front were being expressed to the Milner Mission. Meanwhile, waiting for the event, I was every day discussing the news with Will Peters and keeping myself quiet by working on Russian folk-stories or by solving a chess problem before going to sleep at night. On March 2 I received a telegram from the *Daily News* telling me to send despatches only on the most vital matters, and to deal with them in the shortest possible way. A week later the Revolution had begun and I was presently telegraphing two or three times a day and filling column after column. They never asked me to cut down again.

Many things had combined to make me think it possible that the expected explosion in Petrograd would not be a spontaneous revolt but would be deliberately provoked in order that it should be suppressed. I had seen French gendarmes stage-manage a funeral procession so that they should have an excuse for intervening at a time and place most advantageous to themselves. Could I believe that the Russian police were less skilful than the French? I tried a similar experiment. In one of the streets off the Nevsky there was a police-station with, on the opposite side, a small restaurant. I had the good fortune to see a small band of scallywags go into the police-station and presently come out with flags as yet rolled up round sticks. A policeman in the doorway booted the last of the scallywags to the pavement and slammed the door on them. Could this be the nucleus of a patriotic procession? It was. Presently the little group trudged away, a few curious passers-by joined them, presumably to see where they were going and why. I followed. They had not gone far before they were joined by others and by the time they had crossed the Nevsky anybody might have been forgiven for mistaking them for the demonstrative patriots they were pretending to be. I do not know how the starters of these processions were rewarded but they must have been paid enough to make them feel it worth while to trudge through street after street growing in numbers as they trudged, and then to grow fewer and fewer until, at last, a mere handful, they ended up where they had started at the back door of a police-station and handed back their banners.

That was harmless enough, but there were persistent rumours that the police were being trained in the use of machine-guns. Much later it was denied that machine-guns had been planted in attics commanding the streets, but the denials counted for little with those who, like myself, had had very good evidence on the subject. There was one in the roof of my own lodging. It was a strange time. Opposition to the Autocracy was more and more coming into the open. And on the other hand supporters of the Autocracy were doing things that, if not almost hysterical with hatred and fear, they would surely not have done. One morning in the Nevsky Prospect I saw two soldiers carrying a box slung between them. A general in a sledge was coming the other way at great speed. The soldiers, hampered by their burden, made some attempt at saluting. The general, in a towering rage, stopped them, swirled up in his sledge and berated them. They had not put down their burden, stood to attention and given him the full ceremonial salute to which he was entitled. The two men stood respectfully and listened while the general cursed. Then, with the full swing of his arm the general knocked down first one man and then the other, ordered them to their feet and knocked them down again. A horrible story came from Tsarskoe Selo, where a regiment of Guards had protested at their maggoty food. They had no answer to their protest but, at two o'clock of a Russian winter's morning, the alarm was sounded at which the whole regiment had to turn out immediately without waiting to dress themselves. They turned out half-clothed and, some of them without even boots on their feet, were taken for a route-march in the snow. I do not remember how many were said to have died.

# CHAPTER XXIV

## *The Coming of the Soviets*

When at last the revolution began, it came as a surprise even to those of us who had been so long expecting it. We found it almost impossible to believe that the Russian Autocracy, which had seemed an immovable weight, resting on the neck of a people unable to break free, was crumbling and disintegrating under our eyes. At the time I was chiefly disturbed by the arrest of the members of the War Industry Committee, which seemed to me an act as lunatic as would have been in England the arrest of Arthur Henderson. Here was a committee doing its best to speed up the production of the munitions the Russian army lacked. To arrest men who were doing their best to keep the wheels turning was either wicked or ridiculous. A manifesto, telling of their plight, was written by the arrested members, found on the pavement outside the prison, and brought to my door by a youth who, having delivered it, hurried away without explaining who had sent him, asking only that I should show it to the Ambassador. He was probably quite rightly afraid of going to the Embassy himself.

Small disturbances began in the neighbourhood of bread-shops. This was on March 9. There were more disturbances on the following day. I began a peripatetic survey of the city, trying to see whatever there was to be seen. On the 10th I wrote the rough draft of some notes on crowds, and a telegram to the *Daily News* about the disturbances. On that day the dead body of a police officer was brought into the house where I lodged. On the Sunday, March 11, there was serious trouble in the Nikolai Square, by the Moscow Station. I heard at the time that there had been a suspicion that the soldiers would refuse to fire on the crowds, and that the police had disguised themselves in great-coats belonging to the Litovsky Regiment. I have no proof of that, but only the day before I had seen to what lengths the authorities were prepared to go in order to create disorders of a kind they could easily suppress. I had come on a considerable crowd in the Nevsky Prospect close to the Kazan Cathedral, and seen that there were a number of mounted Cossacks among them. It was soon clear that, whereas the crowd asked nothing better than to be allowed to disperse, the Cossacks kept shepherding them away from the side streets to keep them in the Nevsky. I worked my way through the crowd and came upon an orator much excited, yelling, 'Bread! Bread!' He smote on the side of a tramcar and cried, 'Bread! Does the tramcar give us bread? No! Then let us overturn the tramcar!' What, in the end, happened to the tramcar I do not know, becoming more interested in keeping myself the right way up. A line of Cossacks had spread across the road, and, riding on the pavement, had begun to move steadily through the crowd. What interested me was the expression on their faces. It was hard to believe that these were the ferocious Cossacks. Benevolent and cheerful they moved along the pavements and though that night when I undressed I found myself bruised from being squeezed between two of their horses, it was clear that if the Autocracy thought it could count on the Cossacks it was mistaken. 'Go for the police, not us,' shouted a woman. A Cossack shouted back 'Don't be afraid. We shall square accounts with the police later.'

Forty years after the events I find it hard to remember the actual dates of this or that happening at which I was present. But the happenings are more interesting than their dates which, no doubt, are to be found in official and unofficial histories of the time. A memory as bad as mine is a useful sieve, retaining this or that but happily shrugging itself free from a general flux of detail that, as I am not writing a history, there is no need to record.

My room at the time of the March Revolution was on an upper floor at the corner of Glinka Street, where it joined the great square in which stood the Opera House and the Conservatoire. By extraordinary good luck not a single pane of glass was broken in my windows, though the stone all round them looked as if it had had smallpox, so thickly was it pitted with bullet-marks. There was a good deal of shooting in the Opera Square. I was told that machine-guns had been hidden in the roof of the Opera and of the Conservatoire and close by the siege of the prison was increasing the general uncertainty as to the direction from which the bullets were coming. I remember seeing a machine-gun brought up in a hired sledge and planted on the snow. This brought about a certain concentration of fire, and people crossed the square on the run, shielding their heads with their arms as though caught in a thunderstorm. I think that most of the firing was 'jay-firing' aimed above the heads of those who felt themselves to be the targets. Later there was much more serious firing, but in those first stirring days the number of persons shot was extraordinarily small in comparison with the number of cartridges used. Good will was far too general.

The disturbances began to deserve the name of a revolt on March 12. In the morning of that day the streets looked much as usual. *Isvostchiks* were out with their sledges in the morning, but had thought better of it and stabled their horses before night. A regiment marching towards the Nikolai Station found a great crowd pouring into the Nevsky from the Liteini after the capture of the Arsenal. It halted. An officer gave orders to make ready and then to fire, the front ranks lying, and kneeling. I heard a few shots, much shouting and then saw the two crowds turn into one. Soldiers were handing over their rifles to anybody who would take them. I saw small boys and youths shooting with army rifles at pigeons perched on the overhead wires of the trams.

The revolt began to turn into a revolution when fires along the canal proclaimed that part at least of what had been accomplished was irrevocable. Those bonfires were the burning archives of the secret police. The big and grim-looking prison, two blocks from my lodgings, stood a spattering from machine-gun bullets for some hours before surrender. Baron Frederick's house burned well, but I think some personal enemy must have brought about its destruction. Shop-keepers were hurriedly putting up their shutters.

I failed to get into touch with Will Peters and learned the reason only next day when he rejoined me and told me how he had attended a meeting of his committee in the Admiralty and found himself trapped there with some remnants of the Government who, finding a small hand-printing press in the building, had busied themselves with the printing of proclamations urging the people to go home. Later in the day I ran into Major Scales hurrying into the Astoria to encourage the Russians with the news of the capture of Baghdad. The entrance-hall of the Astoria was crowded with Russian officers, and when they saw Scales

fastening his announcement on a pillar they crowded round to
see what was the news that so obviously had pleased him. It was
instructive, if disheartening, to see the impatient disgust with
which they turned away. They were interested in a siege much
nearer home. I think it was not this day but the next when the
sailors from the barracks at the bottom of Glinka Street, after a
persuasive bombardment, came in on the side of the revolution
and, bursting with goodwill and brotherhood, marched to the
Astoria hoping to bring in its inhabitants, which they would have
done if only some silly young officer, wrongly thinking that they
were bent on massacre, had not fired at them, with the result that
a good deal of damage was done.

That night I learned that both sides were alike in not knowing
who were their friends and their enemies. Walking home I had
noticed a young non-commissioned officer with three or four
privates marching along in the same direction as myself. 'Where
are you going?' he had asked. 'Glinka Street,' I had told him.
'Same here,' he said: 'Together,' and I was delighted to be added
to his company. We were marching along the pavement under
the wall of the Commissariat and I suppose the noise of the six of
us suggested a worthy target to somebody on the roof above us,
for there was an explosion some yards ahead that made a hole in
the pavement but did not damage us. 'Nothing to be afraid of,
lads!' said the young non-com. 'Forward!' On we marched,
cheered by his confident voice. I suppose the 'enemy' had no
more hand-made grenades to spare, for he dropped no more on
us, and at the corner of Glinka Street we parted by the door of
my lodgings.

I had another dramatic encounter on the way to the British
Embassy. The wide expanse of the Champ de Mars was deserted
when I saw a cavalryman galloping over the snow towards me.
It did not instantly occur to me that he was concerned with me,
but on he came, pulled up in a flurry of snow and flourished a
revolver in my face.

'For the people or against the people?' he demanded.

'I am English,' I replied.

'Long live England!' said he and was gone.

Incidents like this were happening all over the city. They
resembled those sudden changes of direction which alter the
apparent colour of a flock of starlings. Shop-keepers put up their
shutters, took them down again, and once more barricaded

themselves, trying to make up their minds whether the worst was over. I had the good luck to come on a shop with a mass of unsold halva, a sticky sweetmeat. This I bought, wrapped in a newspaper, and both Peters and I found it nourishing.

On March 14 we made our way to the Duma, arriving at the Tauris Palace just after an officer had been killed in the street outside. We got in without difficulty. Anybody could have got in anywhere in those early days. Hall and corridors were crowded with soldiers, some sleeping on their feet, others, wrapped in their greatcoats, lying on the floor. Rumours flew. The Tsar was on his way from the front to the capital with loyal troops; those regiments were named that had been active in putting down the revolt of 1905. At almost the same moment came the news of the arrest of the Tsar. Prisoners under escort were being brought in, among them the ministers of the Tsar's Government. Already there were signs of the struggle to come. I heard, from the distance of a few feet, on the steps outside the Tauris Palace, Miliukov make the announcement that made civil war inevitable. He had given the names of the new ministers in a speech in the Catherine Hall of the Duma, and been carried out on the shoulders of an enthusiastic crowd. Outside he was often interrupted by questions and asked again and again for his 'programme'. He said, 'I can already tell you the more important points.' (Here I quote from my telegram to the *Daily News*.) A voice: 'Dynasty?' Miliukov: 'You ask about the dynasty. I know beforehand that my answer will not please all of you. But I give it. The old despot who brought Russia to the edge of disaster will voluntarily abdicate, or be deposed.' (Applause.) 'The Government will pass to a regent, the Grand Duke Michael Alexandrovich.' (Continuous hullabaloo.) 'The heir, Alexis, the Tsarevich —' (Angry shouts, 'But that is the old dynasty.') 'Yes, gentlemen, that is the old dynasty, which perhaps you do not like and which, perhaps, I dislike myself.' He explained the need of an immediate decision on the form of government. 'We propose a Parliamentary Constitutional Monarchy. Perhaps others have different views, but if we stop to discuss instead of instantly deciding, Russia will find herself in a state of civil war and the destroyed regime will be reborn.'

Things were moving too fast for any such compromise. At the very moment when Miliukov was hopefully announcing that 'we' on behalf of Russia had made the decision that would be welcomed by the Cadets, another governing body was coming into existence, one that by its very nature was likely to be a more accurate expression of the forces released by the collapse of the old regime. Already, all over Petrograd, soldiers were being invited to choose deputies to represent them, and the workers in every factory were being invited to choose their own.

Thanks to my having done as I was asked to do in showing the Embassy the statement of the arrested War Industry Committee, I found myself most unexpectedly invited to attend the meetings of the 'Soviet' of Workers' and Soldiers' Deputies. I never knew who was responsible for this. I was working in my room when there was a knock at the door. I opened it and was handed an envelope addressed to 'the correspondent of the *Daily News*'. In it was a ticket of admission to the Soviet 'with the right to speak but not to vote'. I never spoke or voted but I thought the right to listen was implied by my ticket and I made full use of it, and so, from the very first days of the revolution, had a better chance of knowing what was happening than most of the foreign correspondents who for a long time took no interest in any Russian politicians Left of the Cadets.

It was my business from day to day at least to try to understand the political kaleidoscope that was being given rude jolts under my eyes. For this I had one advantage in a completely non-political background. I had been so concerned with mere writing that I had no mind to spare for anything else. No political party in Russia had interested me at all. I had done no political journalism, but had written reviews and such for Conservative papers as far right as the *Morning Post* and J. L. Garvin's *Outlook* and for Liberal papers such as the *Week's Survey*, Chesterton's and Belloc's *Eye-witness* and the *Westminster Gazette*. In this I was in a very different position from that of all the journalists I met in Russia, each one of whom had had time enough in which to acquire, unintentionally or on purpose, the political colouring of the newspaper for which he wrote. I am not for a moment suggesting that they did not hold the views they expressed, but merely that the holding of views (any views) made it harder for them to see the facts. Up to the moment of the March Revolution there had been no great difference between us, but the collapse of the Autocracy underlined and exaggerated all political opinions.

There had been differences before. Not all the correspondents were as sure as I that the Russian army was unlikely to go on fighting for ever. There had been plenty who had been able to assure Milner that there was no danger of Russia faltering. In the excitement of the revolution I did for a few days allow myself to think that the army would get, as it were, a second wind and, re-armed with revolutionary fervour, emulate the armies of Napoleon and carry all before it. But I very soon saw that though this might eventually happen it would not happen now, and, all through that summer of 1917 I, like every Russian I knew, was watching for any sign that the war might end before the Russian collapse that seemed to me inevitable.

I saw the revolution against that grim background and could not allow myself to snatch at any of the long series of excuses for illusion that one after another cheered my friends. They looked at events through differently tinted glasses. Chance had brought me into the Soviet of Soldiers' and Workers' Deputies long before other correspondents had thought that body worth observing. From the first day they met it was obvious that the Soviets held what power there was, and that the Duma was an impotent survival. The story of 1917 is the story of the demonstration of that all-important fact.

# CHAPTER XXV

## *The Red Flag Flies*

Already, in the first few days of the March Revolution, small groups of people had begun urging soldiers not to trust the Duma but to obey only the orders of the Soviet of Soldiers' and Workers' Deputies. Others, members of the Cadet party, were loudly calling for all support to be given to the Duma. Two rival Governments were forming side by side, against a background of events that seemed all but incredible. I think that to give an idea of what those days were like, I had better reprint here a few of the telegrams I sent to the *Daily News* as soon as the post-office was willing to let telegrams go out at all.

'Let there be no mistake in England. This was not an organised revolution. It will be impossible to make a statue in memory of its organiser ... unless it be a statue representing a simple Russian peasant soldier. The Russian peasant, educated by nearly three years of war, goaded purposely into action, showed himself stronger than his oppressors had believed, and the few simple soldiers in Petrograd who refused to fire on their fellows struck in two days the fetters from their nation. This is far and away the greatest victory over Prussianism gained in this war.

'Returning from the Duma today I met a steadily marching crowd singing an old peasant song. I thought at first that it was a demonstration but I found that the men were new recruits called to the colours. And what colours? A red flag of revolution is flying over the Winter Palace where the Constituent Assembly will meet. The proud statue of Catherine the Great looks down on the Nevsky Prospect. Today she is holding a red flag in her hand. Since the formation of the new Government until today its members have been day and night in the Duma building, snatching sleep when possible on chairs and uncomfortable sofas. At the British Embassy, after the first day of the new era there was a revolutionary guard. When I passed I saw outside it a motor paying a friendly call, with a red flag fluttering on the bonnet.

'The trams will start again not later than Tuesday, though enormous falls of snow will entail considerable labour in preparing the track ... Food difficulties threatened at first owing to the soldiers not being economists and attempting to solve problems too simply by going into shops and ordering the shop-keepers to sell at pre-war prices. The Supply Commission of the Town Council has now settled maximum prices. Everywhere a tremendous effort is being made to get the railways and other public services working again. The number of railway waggons reaching Petrograd is increasing every day.

'Most of the representatives of the old Government have been arrested. At first they were marched through the streets and lodged in the Duma, afterwards being shifted to the Peter and Paul fortress. They drew up a petition in which, after thanking the Duma for treating them so kindly, they asked to be allowed to remain in the Duma building. This request, however, was not granted. In the Duma yesterday, walking unsteadily, as if unaccustomed to the use of their legs, were old men who have spent, some of them, twenty or thirty years in the Schlüsselburg fortress. Some of their old persecutors will probably take their places.

'A strange sight but not uncommon these last few days is that of a general marching through the streets with a private with a naked sword on each side of him. The swords seem to be of all kinds, many of them being fantastic old weapons taken from the Arsenal. A popular form of address is "Tovarish!" meaning "Comrade!" The Minister of Justice, M. Kerensky, has refused to be called "Your Excellency". He has ordered that all portraits of the Royal Family are to be removed from the Ministry and has invited the officials to stop wearing orders and decorations.

'Prominent among the obituary notices in the newspapers are some like this: "KILLED in the street by the Tsar's police, firing from ambush: Red Cross Sister, Manefa Georgievna Thorchovskaya, who was on leave from the Front."

'A week ago all gatherings were forbidden. Now everywhere there are announcements of gatherings of Mohammedans, Catholics, Poles, printers, watchmakers, to choose representatives for themselves. A week ago processions were forbidden, and unless organised for special purposes by the police usually ended in bloodshed. Now everywhere little bands with their slogans and deputations bearing banners are making their way to the Duma building, so many of them that people hardly turn to look at them as they pass.'

Things rapidly returned to normal, or at least recovered an air of normality. There was no need now to worry much as to what would pass the censor.

It was hard to tell who was responsible for what. A Duma committee seemed to have taken upon itself the appointment of a Council of Ministers, some of whom were not even elected members of the Duma. Meanwhile the self-elected Soviet of Soldiers' and Workers' Deputies was growing rapidly as the eloquent dashed off to factories or barracks to get themselves elected 'by acclamation'.

To understand how certain orators obtained great influence and reputation in Russia immediately after the revolution we have only to remember that the Russians had for a long time been starved of oratory. There was no Hyde Park Corner safety-valve for eloquence. I heard Kerensky speak many times, and observed that though the things he said hardly varied, his command of his audience diminished steadily as time went on. When he began a speech, I used to think that he was on the point of bursting. I did not think any man could keep up for so long so violent a pressure. This had at first a great effect on his listeners. He was releasing for them stores of emotion that they were eager to express. I was in the Soviet on April 11 when the 'Grandmother of the Revolution' spoke to the assembled delegates. Kerensky introduced her and, as usual, seemed to threaten the bursting of blood-vessels in his brain. Madame Breshko-Breshkovskaya, fresh from exile, was far calmer. She too, I think, feared that Kerensky would have a stroke. More and more excitedly he was pounding out his eloquence when the little old lady leaned from the platform beside him and stroked his head as if she were soothing a child. She had come straight from the railway station and was still carrying a bouquet presented to her on arrival. After she had made a speech that was a great contrast to Kerensky's, being very quiet, some flower-petals fell from her bouquet. One of the soldier-delegates picked two or three petals from the floor, smoothed them and laid them reverently in his pocket-book.

After attending many sessions of the Soviet I did quite accidentally attend a much more solemn gathering. I had overheard someone say that it would be a pity not to know what was being decided in the Marie Palace, so I went there and found much of it in darkness. I wandered through the dark corridors without being stopped by anybody. Light was coming through chinks and I was feeling my way along the chinks to find the handle of a door, when the door flew suddenly open before me and I fell head first into the room where the Council of Ministers, sitting in red plush chairs with gilt legs, was being addressed by Miliukov, the newly appointed Foreign Minister. I do not suppose that any other Englishman has attended a Russian Cabinet Meeting, and I can say only that I did not do so on purpose, and that my presence there was as brief as I could well make it.

Newspapers rapidly multiplied. So did political parties, and nobody was content until he had found a trade union to fit him. Even the journalists, even those shameless individualists the foreign correspondents, formed themselves into a union and elected a representative through whom to deal with the new authorities. Our chosen representative was Golden, the local secretary of the Save the Children Fund. Perhaps if he had been a journalist we should have found it harder to agree in our choice. Gradually the events of the revolution turned into historical events. It is curiously difficult to preserve an historical event from turning into a dull event that does not seem to have any claim to be historical. On April 5 there was a procession and the burial of the victims of the revolution, hardly so many as I should have expected. I walked across the river to Golden's flat and slept there. Mrs Golden had been unable to forget one horrible incident she had seen. There had been shooting from the attics of a house on the quay. A party of soldiers had forced their way in and presently came out again, dragging with them the general who had, they evidently thought, been doing the shooting. They hurried him across the road and made him stand with his back to the river. They then shot him. 'They shot off the whole top of his head and the wind carried it away over the river.'

# CHAPTER XXVI

## *The Second Revolution*

Before the end of August it was obvious that there would be a Bolshevik* majority in the Soviets that would be reflected in the composition of the Executive Committee. During the 'July Days' the weakness of the Government had been manifest. A Bolshevik Executive Committee could have seized power without difficulty, but the mainly Menshevik and reformist committee did not want power for itself and preferred to keep in power a 'bourgeois' Government to which they themselves could be in opposition, on the Left. It was this simple fact and not any great strength behind his Government that had allowed Kerensky to remain in power for so long. Since July he had been weakened by the double failure, military and diplomatic, disasters in Galicia and failure to bring the warring powers together in conference at Stockholm. Both these failures had brought new strength to the Bolsheviks, and a swing to the Left was inevitable, though, when I went off to England on October 9, I thought I should have plenty of time to go home and be back again in Petrograd before the façade crumpled and the Soviets took over openly the authority which from the first days of the revolution had, at least in Petrograd, been actually theirs.

My diary of that visit to England is all but blank. After landing at Aberdeen I went to Edinburgh, where I spent the night with my publisher E. C. Jack, went to London, talked till I could talk no more, caught a perch weighing 3lbs. 2oz. in Beckford's lake at Fonthill, saw many old friends, including the Collingwoods, and laid the foundations of two new friendships that have lasted ever since, with Mary Agnes (Molly) Hamilton and Francis Hirst. Mrs Hamilton worked with Hirst on *The Economist* and later on *Common Sense*. Afterwards she was to be Labour M.P. for Black-

* An extreme (literally majority) socialist, as opposed to Menshevik, a moderate (literally minority) socialist.

burn, delegate from Great Britain to the League of Nations, a Governor of the B.B.C. and head of a department in the Foreign Office. I never knew anyone with such eagerness in self-sacrifice. To have the friendship of Molly Hamilton was like having an army at one's back.

Francis Hirst believed in Free Trade, Peace and Retrenchment. He always had believed in these things and always would, and his steadfastness in that belief had perhaps cost him the public success he might otherwise have achieved. He had been at Wadham with John Simon, F. E. Smith and C. B. Fry. He had preceded F. E. Smith as President of the Union. He would have liked to be Chancellor of the Exchequer and to have deserved well of his country by a wholesale reduction of Income Tax and Civil Service Establishments. He never had a chance of being anything of the sort, but, in all kinds of political weather, nailed his flag to the mast of a ship manned and officered largely by ghosts, the ghosts of Cobden, Bright, Cobbett and Gladstone. Cobbett, I think, was always in command and, in any argument, people, no matter what their views, listened to Hirst with respectful interest, as to a voice from the past, but without for a moment allowing themselves to be influenced by that voice in the present. I have told in a book mainly about fishing how after a long afternoon of argument in which I had never been able to say 'Yes' to a single one of his propositions Francis would wind up with a charming smile and the bland statement, 'Well, my dear fellow, I'm very glad to know that you agree with me.' 'But I don't.' 'In essentials, my dear boy, in essentials.' And he would listen to no more.

This, no doubt, explained how it was that Molly and Francis, divided in beliefs as widely as Socialism from mid-nineteenth-century Individualism, had been able to work together. The link between them was that between two widely different kinds of pacifism, Hirst disliking war because it meant great waste of money, and Molly disliking it because it meant great waste of human beings. This is not quite fair to Francis, but it is true that the economic unsoundness and inevitable waste were the sides of war uppermost in his mind. Both had welcomed Lord Lansdowne's Letter and both had seen that there was nothing to be lost by a statement of Allied peace-aims that would make it clear to the Germans that it was the Kaiser's Government and not the Governments of the Allies that was responsible for the continuance of the war.

On November 8 came the news of the downfall of the Kerensky Government in Petrograd. I wrote in the *Daily News* that this had long been expected by those who had observed the growth of the Bolsheviks after every move against them made by the Cadets and their associated parties of the Right. 'It remains to be seen whether Petrograd will be followed as easily by the rest of Russia, but in view of the Bolshevik majority in Moscow this is not unlikely, though the Cossacks of the South will almost certainly hold aloof.' (November 9.) The Bolsheviks 'will probably use their new position to press more insistently than their precursors for definition of Allied War Aims. If, however, we wish to force them into a more hostile attitude, and perhaps into a separate peace, we cannot do better than to follow the example of some of this morning's newspapers in loudly condemning what we do not understand.' (November 10.) 'Neither the Bolshevik Government nor the Kerensky Government represents the majority of Russians, because the majority of Russians do not care one way or the other. The majority would acquiesce in anything that should give them bread, peace and some sort of order.' (November 12.)

The English newspapers were full of the wildest rumours, and lately as I had left Petrograd, I could not trust myself to be sure of the truth in this welter of contradiction. Almost at once, however, some of the events foreseen began to happen. The Bolsheviks, who had been swept into power by the general belief that they alone of the Russian political parties were determined to bring the war to an end, did immediately propose that there should be a discussion of peace-terms by all the belligerents. On November 20 they ordered General Dukhonin to offer an armistice to *all* nations. He refused, was murdered by his own soldiers and replaced as Commander-in-Chief by a young lawyer, Ensign Krylenko.

Before setting out on the return journey to Petrograd I had a long talk with Lord Robert Cecil, who had succeeded Francis Acland as Under-Secretary for Foreign Affairs. He told me that he did not think I should be able to get back into Russia and that, if I did get back, I might find things in a much more fluid state than I supposed. He stood in front of the fireplace, immensely tall, fantastically thin, his hawklike head swinging forward at the end of a long arc formed by his body and legs. 'If you find, as you well may, that things have collapsed in chaos, what do you propose to do?' I told him that I should make no plans until I could

20   A.R. aboard *Racundra*

21   Evgenia aboard *Racundra*

22, 23 and 24    Three homes: Low Ludderburn, Harkstead Hall and Lowick Hall

25   A.R. after Russia

26   Mary Agnes (Molly) Hamilton

see for myself what was happening, and that from London I could make no guess in all that fog of rumour where to look for the main thread of Russian history. He gave me his blessing, and made things easy for me, at least as far as Stockholm, by entrusting the diplomatic bag to me to deliver to the Legation there. On December 4 I had collected such visas as I could for my passport but could get none that would let me pass the Russian frontier. Chicherin, appointed Ambassador by the Soviet Government, was in Brixton prison. That last visa would have to be given me rather nearer Russia and by the representatives of whatever Government might then prove to be in power there.

I left London for Aberdeen on December 5, was in Bergen on the 8th, in Christiania on the 9th, on the 11th delivered the diplomatic bag at the Legation in Stockholm and, in the face of discouragement on all sides, set about the task of getting back into Russia. The official British view was that it was impossible.

The local representative of the Bolsheviks, Vorovsky, began by taking the same view, but as he had spent the war-years in exile in Switzerland he was very ready to talk with one who had been present at some of the events which he had been following as best he could in the fog of conflicting reports. He held out little hope but promised to do his best and came later to be a much valued friend. I do not think that Vorovsky can ever have had a personal enemy and I was not surprised to learn when, some years later, he was assassinated in Switzerland that the murderer had never met his kindly cultured victim until the day when he had, and took, a chance of shooting him.

Vorovsky had said he would do the best he could for me, but communications were extremely bad and neither Vorovsky nor anybody else in Stockholm knew for certain what was happening in Finland. At the same time the Stockholm newspapers were competing with each other in printing the wildest stories about what was happening inside Russia. I pestered Vorovsky until he must have been sick of the sound of my voice. In the intervals I enjoyed this winter Stockholm. I lunched at the British Legation where I had outposts in two young Howards who read my Russian fairy-tales, and I much enjoyed forgetting politics altogether in telling them some of the Jamaican Anansi stories.

Bernard Pares, who had also been to England and was hoping to get back to Russia through Stockholm, gave up and went home, eventually to go round the world and come into Russia

8

from the other side by joining Admiral Kolchak. The history of our own Civil War and that of the French Revolution inclined me to the belief that the history of a country is with its centre rather than with its periphery. The possibility of Russian history making a fresh start somewhere outside Petrograd or Moscow had come up during my talk with Lord Robert Cecil, but the more I thought of it the less likely I found it and, wild as the newspaper reports were of the chaos in Petrograd, I found it very hard to imagine the improvisation in Russia of any power capable of ousting that of the Soviets which had been steadily growing since March. I was prepared to go on being a nuisance to Vorovsky much longer rather than fail to reach Petrograd. In the end Vorovsky said that he could not guarantee my getting through, and that my blood would be on my own head if I landed in trouble on the way, but that he had now got a rubber stamp and would use it on my passport.

Once more, as in 1914, 1915 and 1916, I set off from Stockholm on that long railway-journey up the Gulf of Bothnia. Once again, close to the Arctic Circle where in mid-winter there was but an hour or so of dusk at noon, I crossed that icy frontier. Leaving Stockholm on December 21, I came into Petrograd late on Christmas Day.

# CHAPTER XXVII

## A New Beginning

Heavy snow had fallen repeatedly on snow that had never been cleared away. The tramlines ran between deep walls of snow. In the main streets the sledge that took me from the station to my old room in Glinka Street had to weave a twisting, bumping course among hummocks of snow as hard as icebergs. But the city was quiet. I heard no shooting. Some of the street-lamps were lit. There were armed patrols at the street corners, mainly 'Red Guards', in ordinary workmen's clothes, with leather belts and bandoliers of cartridges and rifles slung on their backs. The old doorkeeper at my lodgings asked his usual question: had I seen anything while I had been away to make me think that peace was any nearer? Everything seemed so little changed that I lamented having accepted Vorovsky's kind offer to take charge of the books I had brought with me and to send them on when there was an opportunity. I had thought it probable that my journey would be interrupted, and that the less luggage I had to carry the more chance I should have of getting through.

The result of this kindness of Vorovsky's was a bit of good fortune that neither he nor I had foreseen. Some days after my return to Glinka Street, a messenger asked me to call at the Foreign Commissariat. I did so and there met Karl Radek and, thanks to him, was presently on tea-drinking terms with a widening circle of Bolsheviks. With complete lack of scruple Radek had opened the parcel of books that Vorovsky had addressed to me and finding in it a Shakespeare, a folding chess-board and chessmen, and a mixed collection of books on elementary navigation, fishing, chess and folklore, had, luckily for me, wanted to see what manner of correspondent this might be who was interested in subjects that seemed incompatible.

Radek had been born in Poland and spoke Polish (badly, his wife used to say, because he had talked too much German in exile), Russian (with a remarkable Polish accent) and French with the greatest difficulty. He always talked Russian with me but loved to drag in sentences from English books, which I sometimes annoyed him by being slow to recognise. 'Marley was as dead as a doornail' was one of his favourites and he loved to apply it to politicians and to political programmes that had been outstripped by events. He continually quoted from Shakespeare. He had an extraordinary memory and an astonishingly detailed knowledge of English politics. Born in 1883, he had been educated in the Universities of Cracow and Berne. He had spent a year in prison during the revolution of 1905, had worked on an illegal newspaper in Poland and had then moved to Germany and worked on a Social-Democratic newspaper. At the beginning of the war he had spent some months illegally in Germany, then crossed the frontier to Switzerland and, with Lenin and Zinoviev, had taken part in the Zimmerwald Conference. In April 1917 he had been with Lenin in the party of revolutionaries who travelled across Germany from Switzerland in a sealed waggon, and had stayed in Stockholm until the Bolshevik Revolution. He was now taking part in the negotiations that were presently to end in the Brest-Litovsk Peace.

That meeting with Radek was the first of many. Talking with him was for me like revisiting the Latin Quarter. We fell easily into the habit of 'putting our cards on the table', inviting contradiction, and this in 1917 and 1918 was a good way of clearing our heads. Further, I owed to him my introduction to many others of the leading Bolsheviks.

Petrograd in those days was for me an endless series of political meetings. I subscribed to a dozen or so newspapers, which invited me daily to as many public meetings. Speech can never have been freer. There were meetings in factories, in barracks, all over the place, and I always felt that if I did not go to listen to what one of these meetings was saying, I might be missing a vital clue to what was happening or would be happening next week.

One day soon after Christmas I had had no time to eat at all, hurrying from meeting to meeting, going through my fourteen newspapers, and finishing a telegram for the *Daily News* so late that I despaired of getting it off that night. My only hope was to by-pass all minor officials (obstructive by nature) and find a censor whose rubber stamp carried enough authority to start my telegram on its way. I went to the Commissariat of Foreign Affairs, in one of the great government buildings that faced the Winter Palace.

Wandering unchallenged through the corridors, I heard voices and came at last to a room with a few people in it. I recognised one of them whom I had seen in the Smolny Institute when I had gone there to interview Trotsky. She recognised me and when I explained that I wanted to find a censor to stamp my despatch, instead of remarking that it was long after office hours, she said she thought he was in the building. This was Evgenia, the tall jolly girl whom later on I was to marry and to whom I owe the happiest years of my life.

'Come along,' she said, 'perhaps he has some potatoes. Potatoes are the only thing we want. Come along.'

We set off through the deserted Foreign Office. After long wanderings we were pulled up by a smell of cooking, or rather the smell of food burning.

'Quick, quick,' she said and knocked on a door, but without waiting for an answer we burst into a room where a little old man sat reading, while on a small table in the corner a primus roared under a coffee-pot; the room was full of a horrid smell. She seized the coffee-pot and tipped three potatoes out of it on to a sheet of official Foreign Office paper.

'Thank goodness! They've only just begun to brown. They're still edible,' said she. 'You must try not to let the water boil right out or there will soon be a hole burned through the bottom of your pot.'

She introduced me to the old man and explained what I needed. He went off rather uncertainly to look for a rubber stamp with which to mark his willingness not to prevent the sending of my telegram, and we went back to wait for him. Her sister was there. The old man came in and stamped my telegram. The two girls asked me to stay and drink a glass of tea. I said that now my telegram had been seen by the censor I had to go to the General Post Office to send it on its way. They told me to hurry up and come back. I did so and on my return found several others had arrived and in this odd accidental manner came to be given a view behind the scenes such as no other foreigner enjoyed.

I met more and more of the Bolsheviks, made friends with some and enemies of a very few. My long-ago life in Chelsea and in the Latin Quarter of Paris, evenings with Paul Fort, '*prince des poètes'*, and such wild men as Marinetti, might have been a well-designed preparation for life in this Pompeian society, Pompeian in that all these people were living as it were on the slopes of a volcano which seemed to threaten to overwhelm them altogether. My old hand-to-mouth life in Paris and London had been precarious in its way, but the life of these people was more precarious by far. Not one of them but remembered the bloody suppression of the revolution in 1905. Not one of them but knew that if this revolution of 1917 were to be suppressed every one of them would be killed, no matter how small a part he had played in it. Theirs had been no 'palace revolution' but the complete overthrow of a long-established and embattled system. If they were to fall now, their fate would be that of the Communards of 1871. And here they were, working fourteen, fifteen and sixteen hours a day trying to improvise a Government, trying to keep moving the machinery into which saboteurs were throwing any spanner that came to hand, while with every day the danger grew that German troops would bring back to power the old regime that had been swept away.

I was seeing these people much as in old days I had seen my painters in Paris, not as a rival painter but as a mere writer who was very much interested in what they were doing. My complete lack of any political past was a help, not a hindrance, and I was soon getting a view of what was happening from much nearer than any regular journalist or politician could approach. Seeing these people every day, drinking their tea, hearing their quarrels, sharing with them such sweets as I had, going now with one and now with another to meetings from which most foreign journalists stayed away (there were few who did not need to use interpreters, whereas my simple Russian made me free to go anywhere and at least understand what was being said). Meeting all these people as human beings I could not believe the rubbishy propaganda that was being poured out by other Russians who, hoping for their destruction no matter by whom, pretended that they were German agents instead of the most dangerous enemies of Imperial Germany.

Already I had seen enough to know that there was no hope for the Russian army except in its complete reconstitution as an army of the revolution, when, like the revolutionary armies of France, it might do miraculous things. I knew that if the Germans believed that the Bolsheviks would play into their hands they would soon find they were mistaken. I knew that the system of the Soviets was all but indestructible, in that any bit of it could function by itself. I could see that so long as the Bolsheviks could control the Soviets they were the only power that could long survive in a defeated Russia, the only power that could accept without humiliation the defeat of the old army, because they were determined to replace it with a new one whose officers would hope not for the undoing of the revolution but for its victory. My telegrams to the *Daily News* were in flat contradiction to those of almost every other correspondent, and when Lockhart arrived from England with a mission that was to keep in touch with whatever Government might rule in Russia after the withdrawal of our Embassy he came at once to tell me, 'It's your fault that we're here.'

I was delighted to see him and told him that he ought to get in touch with Raymond Robins, which he did, and from that time there was regular exchange of views and news between the three of us. Lockhart had been Consul-General in Moscow, and very popular there, a cheerful young man with a taste for gipsies, wine and dancing, that much endeared him to the Moscow society of business men, landed proprietors, and actors of the old regime. He was a very good 'mixer' and, with a red-cloth-bound *History of British Socialism* under his arm, was soon on better terms with Trotsky than I was.

Robins was a sometime American evangelist, a Chicago business man, an Alaskan pioneer, a brother of Elizabeth Robins who won fame both as an Ibsen actress and as a novelist. He was the head of a mission connected with the American Red Cross, but his main interest was the same as my own, to understand what was happening and, if possible, to counteract the stream of tendentious stories sent home by other Americans.

That Christmas of 1917 was the beginning of a wholly new life, though I did not suspect it at the time. I used to see Trotsky in the Smolny Institute up to the day of the Government's move to Moscow. When he went to Brest-Litovsk for the negotiations I went on going to his office to get such bulletins as his secretary thought fit to dole out, and sometimes to walk with her until we were lucky enough to find a tramcar going towards the centre of the city. Once, I remember, still after all these forty years, with a shiver of horror, the tramcar started before she had her foot on the step, and she was dragged, hanging on, along the track, lying

on one of the lines so that if her grip had failed she would inevitably have been cut to pieces by the wheels. Those few
horrible seconds during which she lay almost under an advancing
wheel possibly determined both our lives. But it was not until
long afterwards that we admitted anything of the kind to
each other.

# CHAPTER XXVIII

## *The Vote for Peace*

On February 19, 1918, the Soviet Government sent out a wireless message offering to renew negotiations with Germany. No one knew what would happen. Then came the news that the Germans agreed, but it was soon clear that the German army was still advancing and meeting no resistance. On the 23rd the German terms were published, much worse than those which Trotsky had rhetorically refused to sign with his formula, 'The war is over, but we do not sign the peace.' Only thirty-six hours ago Radek had been eagerly discussing how best to get out of the state of tension in which the party had been placed by the joint circumstances of the German advance and Lenin's and Trotsky's telegram offering renewed negotiations. He and many others were in favour of sending an ultimatum saying that if the German advance continued Russia would take it as a definite answer.

Then had come the news that the Germans were sending fresh terms. Already Lenin, in an article in *Pravda*, had opened an attack on Trotsky, saying that 'all knew who in Russia was suffering from the malady of revolutionary rhetoric'. The immediate purpose of that article was to destroy Trotsky's thesis that the allies had already come to terms with Germany with regard to Russia. The ultimate purpose became clear when, after receiving the German terms which, for their severity, were almost unparalleled in history, Lenin, in a further article, disclosed his main line of argument for their acceptance. This was that the international war was the source of the revolution and that, since the international war would continue, it would continue to feed revolution, and that the Russians must at all costs preserve as much as they could of the Russian Revolution itself until such time as 'the bourgeois power bled to death' and the Russian people were joined by revolting peoples in the West.

Lenin spoke of the view he had always held: 'If we refuse, then

tremendous defeats will force Russia to sign a still more dis-
advantageous peace.' He now pointed to the absolute refusal of
the army to do any more fighting, and came out roundly with an
ultimatum: 'Only unrestrained rhetoric could force Russia to war
in such circumstances as those of the present moment and, of
course, I personally should not remain for one moment either in
the Government or in the central committee of our party if the
policy of rhetoric should prevail.' (He afterwards confessed to
Radek that he would not have carried the ultimatum into effect,
since it would have been too great a shock to the main strength of
the Bolsheviks—their party discipline.)

To realise the full effect of surprise and shock made by this
declaration, you should remember that it appeared in *Pravda*, the
editor of which had not had time to change the heavy-type headlines, all of which, like the whole remaining contents of the paper,
were in favour of fighting. On the very same day *Isvestia* contained a fighting article by Trotsky, and *Pravda* printed an appeal
in English for the formulation of a Foreign Legion of revolutionaries to resist the German advance.

On Sunday, February 24 I went to the Tauris Palace where a
meeting of the Executive Committee of the Soviet was announced
for six o'clock. The main parties were sitting separately, but
afterwards sat together. In the main hall excited, angry groups
were arguing. At first, many believed that Radek's war party
would win a majority among the Bolsheviks, but these became
gradually less hopeful. The giant influence of Lenin was such that
opposition to it had no chance. The Social Revolutionaries, who
were less under the immediate influence of Lenin, reported that
they had a majority against peace. There was a complete change
of attitude in the other parties. Just as the Bolsheviks, who had
hitherto been the war party, were now in favour of peace, so,
now, the old Pacifist leaders were virulently opposed to it.

A group of anti-peace Bolsheviks, including Radek, who met
in the Secretary's room, were less and less hopeful as the night
wore on. The general feeling in the Great Hall was one of profound depression. During the inter-party meeting and discussion
Lenin, after stating his own views, came out and sat with his
back against the wall, one leg crossed over the other, his arms
folded across his chest, so confident in the rightness and com-
pelling force of his opinions that he would not even take the
trouble to hear what his opponents had to say. His was the only

cheerful figure in the hall and to look at his confident face was to know that the war party would be defeated.

The meeting of the Executive Committee opened at five minutes past three in the morning. Sverdlov, the secretary, quickly and perfunctorily read through the German terms. They had been read so many times during the preliminary party meetings that I am convinced that not half the members present realised their full significance. Trotsky was not there. He had sacrificed his position when, over-persuaded by Lenin, he had put his name to the telegram offering peace which was a negation of his whole policy. His authority had been so weakened by that step that even if he had been present he would have been merely a prisoner behind Lenin's chariot wheels, and would have had to vote against himself.

There was silence in the house, such silence as there is in court when a judge is about to pass a death-sentence. Lenin came confidently to the tribune and in a fifteen-minute speech gave a relentless unrhetorical statement of his position. He laid stress on the impossibility of resistance and on the fact that other countries were not yet ready to revolt. Therefore, he said, it was useless to enter upon a hopeless resistance in the hope that such action would bring the German, French, English and American democracies instantly to the rescue. He was applauded by a little more than half the meeting.

Martov made a good speech in opposition but, like all the opposition orators, dwelt more on the disadvantages of a separate peace than on the terrible character of the actual terms. I had the impression throughout that the members of the Executive Committee, in the stress of the party struggle, did not realise what it was they were committing themselves to. A vote by show of hands was taken so as to get a speedy result in view of the urgency of sending a reply to the Germans. 112 votes for peace; 84 against; 22 did not vote. Bonch-Bruevitch went out to inform the Government of the result and to telegraph acceptance of the German terms. Then there was a vote by names, giving, I suppose, a more accurate result. One Bolshevik, Riezanov, disobeyed party discipline and voted against signing, for which he was cheered by the opposition. It was terrible to hear the men who, as I well knew, had up to the last moment before the Committee met, been working against signature of the treaty, now, in dead voices, recording one by one their votes for their party against their conscience. The declarations of the parties were then read from the tribune and the Committee adjourned.

There were no sledges yet on the streets. In a cold winter dawn I walked with three Bolsheviks, of whom one had been for peace and two for war. We were all dead-tired and walked like convicts. I could hardly force myself to realise that not quite a year ago, on just such a winter's dawn, I had walked those same streets sharing the joy and confidence of the awakening revolt.

# CHAPTER XXIX

## *With a Pilot Flag to Vologda*

In Petrograd the diplomatic corps was breaking up like winter ice in a sudden thaw. Very few people knew their own minds. Lindley, then in charge of the British Embassy, left by way of Finland where civil war had begun. He did just succeed in getting through. The American and some of the smaller Embassies were planning to move eastward. I decided to keep in touch with the Russian Government, and to move to Moscow when it moved. Robins was also determined not to lose touch with the Soviet leaders, and promised to find room for me when the time came. Francis, the American Ambassador, was leaving for Vologda, some 260 miles north-east of Moscow. Some of his staff hoped that he would, like the British Embassy, leave this dreadful Russia altogether, but he decided to go no further than Vologda which, on a railway map, looked a good strategic position that would allow a further withdrawal either east or north as events might dictate.

The outlook for the Bolsheviks was extremely grim. They had no troops capable of opposing the Germans. The hope that German soldiers would refuse to move against a country in revolution that had declared for peace and announced that it would not fight had been killed by the news that a new German advance had begun. It had already been decided that, whether or no there was to be peace, the Government would move from Petrograd to lessen the enemy's pressure on it, or perhaps to lessen the temptation to the enemy to continue his advance. To historically minded Bolsheviks the move to Moscow seemed a retreat from the West, a crushing set-back to revolutionaries whose hearts were set on seeing red flags in Berlin. I met more than one in tears, at the thought of what would happen to 'our workmen' who, if Petrograd were to fall, would endure 1905 over again and much worse.

I spent about twenty hours on end (February 26 and 27) helping the historian, Professor Pokrovsky, to pack the Imperial Archives. He had no other helpers except a girl secretary and Madame Radek. It was as if the English Foreign Office were being evacuated to York, and Lord Robert Cecil, left in charge, had nobody to help him stow historical documents in sugar-boxes except the wife of an Irish revolutionary and a Russian folklorist who had happened to look in. I saw and packed a number of strange things, including the Russo-German agreement of 1887 for the curbing of Austria, signed by Bismarck himself. There were large packages of documents relating to England and the East. I should have liked to look at these, and it was also hard to prevent Pokrovsky from looking through papers instead of attending to the immediate business of tying the strings of portfolios and packing them into wooden crates. At the last minute it was found that there were no nails with which to fasten the crates and no rope, and a search had to be made in the shops.

After being up all night I was still half-asleep when Lockhart came to my door with an interesting proposal. Robins was going as far as Vologda, accompanying the American Ambassador and hitching the Red Cross car to the Ambassadorial train. Lockhart had not a man to spare but, while meaning to go to Moscow with Trotsky, wanted to keep an alternative plan possible. He asked if I would go with Robins to Vologda, have a look round, and, if it seemed likely that it could be a useful base from which to keep in touch with the Soviet Government, pick the best building in the town, hoist a British flag on it and in this way make some sort of show of claiming it for his Mission. Robins backed this proposal by repeating his invitation to me to come with him. The only difficulty seemed to be that nobody had a suitable English flag. This difficulty was overcome by sending one of Lockhart's young men down river to the quays along the frozen Neva to borrow a flag from one of the British ships held up there since the beginning of the war. The flag they gave us was a Pilot Jack, a Union Jack with a wide white border. I hid it away in a knapsack with my things for the night, took my typewriter with me and joined the train at the Nikolai Station.

There were a number of 'extra-territorial' coaches on that train, Siamese, Japanese, Chinese, the cars of the American Embassy and the car of the American Red Cross. If I had needed more proof that Russia was in no condition to carry on the war until a new army had been built on a new basis, that journey to Vologda and back would have given more than enough. Every station was like an opened hive of grey-brown bees, peasant soldiers demobilising themselves, swarming over platforms and permanent ways, packing themselves into cattle-trucks, travelling on the buffers when there was no other room, hardly bothering to ask the destination of the train that they would not allow to move without them. Every stopping-place stank like a vast latrine. But even this aimless self-demobilisation was less disastrous than to have these dusty millions driven to sacking, burning and destroying in front of the advancing enemy, as they had been driven in Galicia the year before. There were, too, signs that an heroic few were struggling to keep their feet in the maelstrom. I saw rolling-stock, field-waggons and engineering plant evacuated from the Baltic front. Much of it had just been dumped by the side of the line, and would surely rot, but the fact that it was there at all was proof that an effort was being made to keep it from the Germans.

I was sharing a compartment in the Red Cross car with Robins's secretary, aide-de-camp, courier and translator, Alexander Gumberg, an amusing, alert and highly intelligent Jew who had known Trotsky in New York and was extremely useful to Robins in making it easy for him to meet the Bolshevik leaders. What Gumberg's own politics were, I doubt if he could have said for certain. He exulted in the thought of Trotsky, a Jew, tweaking the noses of the German generals at Brest-Litovsk, but I doubt if he was ever a Bolshevik.

We were some twenty-four hours in coming to Vologda along the line that ran on to the Urals, Siberia and Vladivostok. In Vologda Station there occurred an incident that throws yet another faint glimmer of light on the strange failure of a large group of Americans, led by the Secretary of the Embassy, to stop there as directed by the Ambassador. George Kennan, in his books about Russian-American relations, says that there has been no explanation of this disobedience, which, he says, infuriated the American Ambassador. The Ambassador would, I think, have been still more furious if he himself had woken up not in Vologda but far on the way to Siberia. He might well have been unable to come back, and the diplomatic centre of that summer might well have been some other small provincial town even further from Moscow. This would have happened but for the merest accident.

I was woken in the middle of the night by the train jerking suddenly to a standstill. This had happened often before, but lights outside showed that we must be in a station. For some time I thought no more of it, until I heard the loud 'two bells' which mean that a Russian train is unwillingly thinking about getting on the move. I do not know why it occurred to me to wonder where, exactly, we might be, and then to wonder why, if this station should turn out to be Vologda, there had been no noise of shunting and the uncoupling of coaches. I woke Gumberg. We had not undressed completely and soon climbed down from the train where everybody seemed to be asleep. The station was indeed Vologda, and the station-master was preparing to send the train on its way. We ran along it. No, the diplomatic coaches, including ours, had not been uncoupled. The station-master said that he had no orders and that the train was to go on complete. Gumberg, hissing with excitement, held powerful documents, probably from Trotsky, under the man's nose and demanded that before sending the diplomatic coaches on to the Urals, he should first make sure what instructions he had had.

He went unwillingly to his office and at last, still more unwillingly, uncoupled the extra-territorial part of the train, after which the 'three bells' duly sounded and we watched the red tail-light disappear in the darkness. We went shivering back to our compartment to spend what was left of the night. It did not occur to me at the time that anybody was responsible but a careless or perhaps anti-Bolshevik railwayman. Now, after reading Mr Kennan's book, I am not so sure. Many of the Americans in Petrograd were delighted to be leaving and would have preferred to be leaving altogether rather than merely to be moving to a small town on the road to Siberia. The American party in the first train had disobeyed orders and gone on. I cannot help wondering whether some of them were not surprised to be stopped on their way east by a telegram ordering them back to Vologda instead of finding that the Ambassador had, as it were, condoned their disobedience by following them in his sleep and going east himself.

I found Vologda a little, simple country town, white with snow. There was hardly a brick building in the place, but little log-houses of one or two storeys, broad untidy squares and street-markets, with churches in every open space, white churches against the blue winter sky, churches capped with towers of every kind of intricate design, showing the great bronze bells hanging in their airy belfries beside domes of gold or green, of plain grey lead and of violent deep blue, thickly sown with golden stars. Driving from the station in a little sledge with a fat, eager, hurrying pony who did not seem to know care, a little horse of magic in comparison with the lugubrious skeletons that dragged their sledges at a foot's pace through the unswept streets of Petrograd, I noticed the many birch trees in the gardens of the houses and, in those delicate trees, the huge unwieldy nests of the hoodie-crows, which were as numerous in Vologda as pigeons in Petrograd or sparrows in London.

Gumberg had gone off to see to the establishment of his Americans. I drove to the headquarters of the Vologda Soviet, which was in the old house of the Governor. It was a white house behind white walls, with a big porch where a Red Guard was lounging on a table, chewing sunflower-seeds and somewhat rudely demanding people's business. He let me pass without difficulty. I never did have difficulty of that kind, probably because I never expected any. There was a heavy smell of bad tobacco. A crowd of peasants were hanging about the corridors. Two machine-guns in a room on the upper floor were circumstantial evidence of the Revolution which, in spite of the presence of two or three keen little sailors from the Baltic Fleet (who were here recruiting volunteers for the new Red Army), did not seem to have shaken Vologda very deeply after that first, easy overthrow of the old regime a year before.

On that day in February 1918 the first arrest of a member of the Cadet party had taken place in Vologda. The revolution in Vologda, that is to say, was four months in arrears. Even so, the President of the Soviet and the Mayor of Vologda were much disturbed. 'This is the beginning of Civil War,' they said, and were anxiously telephoning and debating what best to do about it. When they learned that the American Embassy was to establish itself in Vologda and was at that moment breakfasting in a train in Vologda Station, with the Siamese, Japanese, Chinese, Brazilian and other diplomats, and that a British Mission might presently join them, they were still more perturbed. At the bare suggestion that the Soviet Government itself might come here if Petrograd had to be evacuated, they were filled not with enthusiasm but with horror.

The more I saw of Vologda the more I liked it, and the more ridiculous I thought the idea of diplomats of any nation settling in this little backwater while trying to keep in touch with a Russian Government whether in Petrograd or Moscow. Clear on that point, my fingers no longer itching to play with the pilot flag, I was more or less free and glad to drive round with Robins, who could not spend all his time arguing with the American Ambassador (as, later, I was to argue with Lindley when he too came to Vologda after leaving Russia by way of Helsingfors and coming back by way of Murmansk). We were both much taken with a little ancient monastery that, most unexpectedly, I was to see again. I heard nothing of the mutual squabbles of the Americans but was in a hurry to get back to Petrograd.

Then a long telegram from the Commissariat of Foreign Affairs was brought to me in the train. It was made up of two rather contradictory messages from the very friendly Karakhan, one suggesting that the Soviet delegates had already signed a peace treaty with the Germans, the other asking urgently for a train to be sent to 'Toroshino(?) ... with a sufficient guard' suggesting that no peace had been signed. This was accompanied by a private telegram from Evgenia to me. She had known that the American Embassy had left Petrograd and that Robins and I were with it, and assumed that we should have to do whatever the American Ambassador decided. Her telegram read, 'As this means war and accordingly your immediate departure further I send my best wishes for a pleasant journey.' This telegram, or rather its first four words, read, I have no doubt, by many to whom it was not addressed, stirred Vologda to its depths. If some girl banging her typewriter in the Commissariat of Foreign Affairs could write 'This means war,' then war it must most certainly mean. I do not remember whether Robins managed to get in touch with Trotsky, through Gumberg, or whether the documents he had and his own persuasive personality were enough. Anyhow the Red Cross car was presently bumping back to Petrograd, attached to a train loaded with rifles for the use of the army of Red Guards that was being desperately gathered for the defence of what was still the capital. At every stop a guard of workmen in rough sheepskins and felt boots tumbled out and patrolled the train with more keenness and discipline than I had seen since the first Revolution. But there were a tremendous lot of stoppages. As for the Pilot Jack that was never flown in Vologda, it stayed at the bottom of my bag until long afterwards when, sailing in my own little boat and needing a pilot, I put it to the use for which it had been originally intended.

# CHAPTER XXX

## *Murder of an Ambassador*

The Fifth Congress of Soviets met in the Bolshoi Theatre in Moscow. Somebody got me a very good seat, near the middle of the stalls, from which I had a first-rate view of the stage on which the Praesidium sat, the tribune from which the orators spoke, and the boxes on the right in one of which were various Allied officials, one of whom was presently to contribute a touch of comedy to an extraordinary scene. It was clear from the beginning of the session that the Social Revolutionaries were purposely working up to a climax. Maria Spiridonova, looking like a nursery governess rapt into uncontrollable frenzy, poured out a rhythmic screaming denunciation of the Brest-Litovsk Treaty, which had been signed on March 3. The Bolsheviks, by making peace with the Germans, had sacrificed the revolution. Better by far to have signed no treaty, to have let the Germans occupy all Russia and so discover for themselves that they could not hold it against an entire population determined to destroy them. There was real danger in this speech, because she was saying what many of the Bolsheviks had themselves been saying up to the moment when Lenin swung the majority into voting for the signing of the treaty. At the same time the reality of the danger was obvious enough to unite all shades of Bolshevik opinion in defence of their party.

Spiridonova herself must have known this. She would hardly have made such a speech unless she was expecting her arguments to be instantly reinforced by events. At one moment I wondered whether something had already happened, the news of which had not yet been released. She went on to denounce the Bolsheviks as agents of Germany, obedient servants to Mirbach, the German Ambassador in Moscow. '*We*, Social Revolutionaries, will *not* recognise the German peace.' There a storm of shouting, booing and cheering, and, though Spiridonova had made it

amply clear that she and her Social Revolutionaries regarded the
Allies as Counter-Revolutionaries no less evil than the Germans,
and were prepared to challenge both enemies at once, a French
representative rose from his seat in the diplomatic box and
solemnly bowed his gratitude for the hullabaloo that he must have
mistaken for a tribute to France. There was a moment's silent
gasp of astonishment throughout the theatre.

We had not long to wait before we knew what was the event
that Spiridonova had been expecting.

It was made possible by the composite nature of the Government, which was still a coalition, a joint affair of Bolsheviks,
Mensheviks and Social Revolutionaries. So genuine was its
composite nature that even the Extraordinary Commission,
whose work it was to keep order, to suppress counter-revolutionary action, and to carry out many of the functions of a secret
police, included members of all parties. This day's work put an
end to that. The Social Revolutionaries' plan had been a dangerous
one, but, as always, they had exaggerated the popular support on
which they could count, and had mistaken the Russian readiness
to applaud emotional oratory for a willingness to cut short a
breathing-space and plunge once more into a state of war. They
planned to make war inevitable by the murder of the German
Ambassador. They believed that they had enough support among
the soldiers to surround the Bolshoi Theatre and arrest all the
Bolshevik leaders in a body, sitting together on the stage. They
further believed that the Germans would have to advance to
avenge their murdered Ambassador, and that the entire population
of Russia would find itself willy-nilly engaged in guerrilla warfare,
which, the sympathies of the working classes being with them,
would spread to every country in the world and bring about the
final triumph of the revolution.

What happened showed that, as in the past, the Social Revolutionaries were well able to organise assassination but quite unable
to estimate or induce any mass support for their plans. The
assassination was easy. Blumkin, an official of the Extraordinary
Commission (which was charged with the safety of the German
Ambassador and other diplomats) called at the German Embassy,
was received by Ritzler, the Embassy Counsellor, and said that he
had an urgent message for the Ambassador. Naturally the
Ambassador received him, whereupon Blumkin fired several
shots into him, leapt through the window, which was on the

ground floor, checked any pursuit by throwing a powerful hand-grenade behind him into the room where it exploded with a bang that I heard several streets away, and himself escaped, leaving the Ambassador dying.

Meanwhile Government reaction to the event was somewhat delayed by the success of some of the Social Revolutionaries in arresting their Bolshevik colleagues in the Extraordinary Commission. There was thus a short delay during which the Social Revolutionaries alone knew what had happened, and even they did not know how far their plans had succeeded. Thus, when news spread that a bomb had exploded near the German Embassy, just as the French diplomat had stood up in his box in the belief that Spiridonova's denunciation of the Brest Treaty was a demonstration in favour of France and her Allies, so now there were plenty of people to believe that the bomb-throwing was the work of the Allies and intended to force Germany to take action of a kind that would make continuance of the peace (such as it was) impossible.

I had left the theatre to get some food during the first interval and was on my way back when I heard first the bang and then, some minutes later, the news. The bang had meant nothing to me except that it was very loud and very near. I merely wondered who it could be who had been so careless with explosives. The news reached the theatre sooner than I did. I found troops on guard at every entrance and, unable to argue my way in, went off to look for Radek in the hope that his eloquence would be more effective than mine on what I thought were a more than usually stupid lot of soldiers.

Before I had crossed the Theatre Square, I heard the rumour that the German Ambassador had been killed, and, as I came towards the front door of the Hôtel Metropole, I saw Vorovsky coming out. He and I had become very friendly, and he soon let me know his view of what had happened. He waved his hand and came towards me whistling loudly a tune, to which he presently put the words, 'Rule Britannia; Britannia rules the waves.' He was quite sure that the Allies were behind the assassination, and was philosophically considering its possible results in a retreat to the Volga and perhaps to the Urals. We both knew that there had not been time to make a new Russian army capable of stopping the Germans if they should decide to advance.

I told him Britannia had nothing to do with it, and that an

attempt was being made by the Social Revolutionaries to repeat against the Bolsheviks in Moscow and elsewhere a seizure of power of the same kind as that which had succeeded against Kerensky in Petrograd.

The plot was masterly except in its complete misjudgment of the masses on whose support its success depended. The Social Revolutionaries could plan the murder of an individual and carry it out with the efficiency and daring that they had shown in the past. They were right in thinking that nobody in Russia liked the conditions of the Brest Peace. They were wrong in thinking that anybody but themselves would prefer a German occupation of Moscow, and in thinking that the murder would be a signal which would make a nation that had asked for peace follow them unwillingly to war.

The plot, however, had been more nearly successful than Vorovsky and I had dreamed, but the timing went wrong, and it was the Social Revolutionaries and not the Bolsheviks who found themselves trapped and unable to leave the theatre. But their supporters had been able to seize strategic positions in many parts of the town and, with Police Headquarters in the hands of the insurgents, it was some time before the revolt was crushed. The civilian populace, however, took things with astonishing calm. I saw mothers sunning themselves and their children in the gardens under the Kremlin wall and showing no sign of interest when a shell fired from somewhere in the town screamed high overhead to land in the ancient citadel. Wandering round at night I found large sections of the town still in insurgent hands, but those hands were oddly inert. They did not know what to do next.

The murder of an Ambassador, even a German, inevitably set up a flutter among the considerable congregation of diplomats who were enjoying a quiet country life at Vologda. The colony of diplomats there were invited to come to Moscow, but it became clear that they were more likely to move to Vladivostok than to the Russian capital. Lenin decided to send somebody to talk to them. Radek was chosen, and when I went round to the Metropole he had interrupted his packing to have a word with Lenin on the telephone. As I came into his room I was shocked to hear him say, 'If they won't come to Moscow of their own accord, I'll put them into cattle-trucks and bring them!'

I said at once, 'If you do anything of the sort you will have only yourselves to blame if everybody assumes that you must be acting under German orders. As you know, I have throughout been working for Anglo-Russian friendship. What you have just said is the first thing I have heard from you to suggest that I have been mistaken, and if you mean to talk to the Ambassadors in that tone you will be making hostilities inevitable.' Radek was for a moment startled. He laughed and said, 'Just wait a minute.' He had put down the telephone but now rang through again to Lenin and told him what I had said, and then, with the instrument in his hand, turned to me and said, 'Well, you Jingo Imperialist, will you come too and see for yourself that there is no hostility about it?' I said, 'How can I do that?' 'Come as my interpreter.' I agreed but hardly thought that the expedition would really come off. However, some days later, I was in the British Mission's room in the Hôtel Elite when a Red Army soldier came to the door, asked for me, and said he had been to my room and left a note there for me from Radek, but that, as the matter was urgent, he had thought it best to hunt through the hotel for me. I ran upstairs and found a note on a scrap of paper: Could I be ready to start in an hour? I hurried round to the Commissariat for Foreign Affairs, learnt that we were indeed off to Vologda, arranged to meet Radek, bolted back to the Mission, told Lockhart what I was doing, got from him a note to Lindley explaining my position, and a packet to give to Captain Cromie, the British Naval Attaché in Petrograd, stuck Plato and Sir Thomas Browne (counter-irritants to politics) in my bag, commandeered a very fine plum cake that was rashly exposed on the table in the Mission, and was off back to the Metropole to join Radek, who meanwhile had been arming himself with all kinds of peremptory documents to ease our journey.

A number of things happened on that journey and at Vologda that illustrate very well the turmoil and the excitement of those lively times. I am the more tempted to record them because, thanks to the time spent in the train, I have detailed notes by which to check my memory.

# CHAPTER XXXI

## *Diplomacy at Vologda*

Radek was waiting at the door of the Metropole with a young
Lettish rifleman, a greedy, lazy fellow, with a face like a frog's,
who was not, it seemed to me, very devoted to the Bolsheviks,
and a shy young man, Nourin, who wore grey cloth-sided boots,
looked as if he had just stepped off the Boulevard St Michel, and
was supposed to have some knowledge of French, a language that
might be necessary on what was supposed to be a diplomatic
mission.

The arrangements for our journey to Vologda had been left to
Chicherin, who had made a mistake in the times, so that we
reached the station at the moment when the train that included
the coupé reserved for us was already leaving. There was a
hurried discussion. We had with us papers that gave us the right
to a coupé on that train, or to have a special waggon attached to
any train that suited us, or, in case of need, to order a special train
for ourselves. Armed with these we went to see the station-master
who, like most of the higher railway officials, was inclined, even
eager, to put spokes in the wheels of the Government, to the fall of
which he was no doubt looking forward. Radek became extremely
angry, but was appeased on hearing that another train was leaving
for Petrograd from the Kursk Station in twenty minutes' time.
We had to go by way of Petrograd because the direct line from
Moscow to Vologda had been cut by an anti-Bolshevik revolt.
Our luggage had not yet been taken from the car and Comrade
Zlobin the chauffeur (a good friend and servant to Radek whom
he loved, as, he once said to me, he disapproved of Bolsheviks in
general while strongly upholding the Soviets) told us that he
thought he could just get us to the Kursk Station in time if we
were not held up on the way. We got there at the precise moment
when the train was due to leave.

We went directly to the office of the station-master but found him a very official person who refused to be impressed by our papers, at which indeed he was very unwilling to look. Radek asked him quite politely, would he give orders to hold the train and find a coupé for us. He refused to do anything of the sort.

Radek: 'I hold you responsible if our journey is delayed.'

Station-master: 'Delighted.'

Radek: 'I will have you arrested if you pay no attention to the order of the Central Authority.'

Station-master, seizing the telephone instrument, ringing violently and glaring at us while talking into the mouth-piece: 'An individual in my office threatens to arrest me if I do not hold the 9.20. He says he comes from the Commissariat of Foreign Affairs. His name is Radom or something like that ... '

'RADEK.' (Shouted across the table.)

'Radek,' repeated the station-master.

There was a long pause after which the station-master in a slightly different tone said, 'The President of the Station Committee is in a room on the other side of the road and will discuss the matter with you.'

'I repeat,' said Radek, 'that if the train leaves without us, you will be held responsible.'

'The train will be held until you have seen the President of the Committee.'

We went out and crossed the square outside the station, Radek by this time white with anger. Upstairs in a house we found, after some difficulty, an intelligent, important-looking railwayman in a soldier's tunic, sitting at a table, talking to the respectfully listening members of his committee. Radek laid his papers before him, and stated his case. The railwayman looked slowly through the papers and then said, with a magnificent gesture: 'Comrade! I appeal to you, as an intelligent man, who has had all the advantages of education. Have you read these papers? If so, you will surely perceive the impropriety of holding a train at the Kursk Station when you have a paper authorising you to use a coupé in a train starting from a station which here in Moscow we call the Nikolaievsky ... '

'Devil and son of a devil,' screamed Radek.

'Comrade, I shall be obliged to close this conversation if you use words unworthy of a socialistic state.'

'There are no words strong enough in any state whatsoever to express my opinion of a man who does not understand that we have come to the Kursk Station only because through an error of the Commissariat we have missed the train from the Niko-laievsky Station, which would have saved valuable time besides sparing me this conversation.'

I forbear to record the succeeding stages of the argument which ended in great-hearted capitulation on the part of the President of Committee, who then, begging us to be seated, himself stood up, took the telephone in one hand and, gesticulating with the other, delivered a speech through the instrument in his best platform style. 'Comrade Station-master, although in the ordinary course of events such procedure is impermissible, disorganising as it does the transport on Russia's already hardly taxed railways, and increasing the labour of citizens and railwaymen, yet on this occasion, convinced as I am (here he bowed towards us) that Comrade Radek and his companions are engaged in work of high importance to the Republic, I hereby, in the name of the advance-ment of the common cause, command that the train which should have left at 9.20 shall be held and a coupé on it be provided for the use of Comrade Radek and his companions.'

I expected him to end with 'Long Live the Republic!' but he merely sat down and seemed disposed to begin a further con-versation on general subjects. It was then 10.15, the train having been kept waiting almost an hour, whereas three minutes would have been enough to get our luggage into it and we could have been already far on our way. Radek, however, well accustomed to dealing with public meetings, cut him short. We all shook hands in a most cordial manner, recrossed the square, went back into the station and about ten minutes later were in our coupé and engaged in a violent squabble of the same kind with another orator, the train guard, who also refused to recognise the validity of our papers and demanded the tickets which we had not got.

By the time we reached Petrograd, the telegraph had been at work and, a miracle of organisation, an engine and a special carriage were waiting for us in a siding, ready to start at once. I told Radek I wanted an hour in the town and he agreed to wait so long for me while I took a cab from the station to the British Embassy and back. The cab-horse was nearly dead and walked as though it were pulling its own hearse. At the Embassy I met Cromie on the stairs and he drove with me some of the way back to the station to hear as much as I could tell him of the situation in Moscow.

I had a particular respect and liking for Cromie, who always seemed prepared to form his own opinion and to act upon it regardless of what opinion the authorities at home would have liked him to form. He was one of the most heroic, simplest, straightest-thinking men I have ever met. Even lazy Russian submarine-commanders, if they did not love him, respected him. No one more than he would have resented the misuse of his death by propagandists urging war against the revolution (he was shot down defending the Petrograd Embassy against the secret police). In the days when I used often to see him in Petrograd, we talked of many things, but it so happened that we never spoke of Coniston, and not until years later did I learn that he, too, had known Lanehead and the Collingwood family who had meant so much in my own life.

There had been great changes on the railway from Petrograd to Vologda since I had made that journey four months earlier. Then every station was like an old blanket from the Russian trenches crawling with lice. Every station was at once a latrine and a caravanserai, alive not only with soldiers but with peasants, old men, women and children escaping from parts of the country newly occupied by the Germans or migrating on account of private alliances formed with the Russian soldiery at the front. Now the worst of that disorder had gone. The stations were much cleaner and not over-crowded, and such soldiers as were about were moving with their detachments and not behaving as a family content to board trains at random, to go anywhere, often not bothering to find out whither or whence, on the general principle that all the world was on the move and that it was best to agree with it and be moving too.

At Zvanka, the junction for the Murmansk Railway, we were held up and the Commandant of the station came to our carriage and asked Radek if we would mind saving the Soviet Government the unnecessary use of an engine by allowing another special car, which was on its way, to be coupled to ours when it arrived. Radek, after a few moments' parley, agreed, on the understanding that we were not to be delayed for more than two hours. He, Nourin, the Lettish rifleman and I went for a walk outside the station, thinking that we might get hold of something to eat. We found three shops which, by their painted signs, professed to sell food. Not one of them but was as bare as Mother Hubbard's cupboard.

An obviously 'bourgeois' Russian in a carriage driven by a coachman passed us on the road, looking askance at us, who were a rather ragamuffin crew. Radek at the moment was reciting *Hamlet*, declaiming 'To be or not to be' for the benefit of our rifleman, who was showing indecision as to whether or not to go straight back to the station. He broke off to stare after the carriage and the billowing purple silk sleeves of the coachman. 'They do not realise even as near Petrograd as this that there has been a revolution.' I laughed and told him that I had only to walk for twenty minutes into the country outside Moscow to find an estate on which no single thing had been changed in the last eighteen months.

Radek became suddenly impatient and wished to get on at once. 'In twenty-four hours', he said, 'we should be on our way back with the Ambassadors.' We hurried to the station where, in a moment, even the Ambassadors were put out of his head by the news that in the car that was to be attached to our own was Smilga, a very old friend of his, now a Commissar with the Army, and on his way to Ekaterinburg on the Czecho-Slovak front.

At about seven in the evening Smilga's car reached Zvanka and was coupled to ours. Smilga, whose joy at seeing Radek was as great as Radek's at seeing him, invited us all into his carriage for tea. There followed a hilarious and hospitable evening. The drink was weak tea, the food sections of a very hard sausage and some formerly white bread, produced with pride but rather marred by extreme old age and green mould. These details seem unimportant now, but I was so hungry that I noted them in my diary with real gratitude. There were candles too, lighting up the observation car in which we sat round the table at our feast, to which I was happy to be able to add the cake I had commandeered from Lockhart's table. There was Smilga, tall, blond with pale blue eyes, thin, pale hair, a straw-like man, weak, ill, enthusiastic; his companion, a solid, stocky Russian, whose name I forget; Radek with dangling pipe and bulging forehead; the frog-faced Lett rifleman; little Nourin much like a Latin Quarter journalist; and myself. I happened to say something about the weapons scattered about the car. That brought Smilga to his feet. He showed me his revolvers, one after another, like a child with his toys, and then fetched his favourite, a shotgun, throwing open the breech and, in the approved fashion, inviting me to look through it. I looked down one of the dirtiest barrels I have ever seen, a barrel so dirty indeed that for a moment I thought I was being called upon to remark on its filthy condition, until, just in time, I saw urgent meaning in the eye of Smilga's companion, and praised the gun and in praising it was eagerly seconded by Smilga himself. I asked him if he got much shooting, thinking of other exiles I had known whose banishment had been their opportunity. 'No,' he said regretfully, 'not much.'

Long afterwards I learned that this warlike fellow, this lover of firearms, was nearly stone-blind, I believe from long confinement, and had hardly fired a gun in his life. Many of the revolutionary intellectuals were like that. Prohibited for so long from having weapons, they were now exulting in the possession of them, like children with forbidden fruit, or boys leaving school and not to be seen without their pipes. This was certainly so with Radek himself, whose revolver during the next few days was to be given a quite undeserved significance. I met Smilga again much later, changed completely, a jovial, hearty, solid person, like a general of the old regime, his red, sunburnt neck bursting from his military collar.

The Vologda Soviet, much perturbed by the importance of its visitors, put a big American car at Radek's disposal, and after making an appointment we drove (our Lettish escort sitting in front and rather shyly parading his carbine) directly from a railway-siding to the temporary American Embassy, a varnished log-house standing a few yards back from a little tree-lined road. While we were still in the hall Noulens, the French Ambassador, came in and was shown at once into some room other than the front parlour into which we were taken to wait for Mr Francis. Several members of the American Embassy whom I had known in Petrograd shook hands with me a little doubtfully, wondering perhaps what excuse I had for being there. Then they left us alone.

The room into which we had been shown was big and light with portraits on the walls of Gogol, Dostoievsky and Chekhov. The books in the bookcases were also such as to show that the original inhabitants had belonged to the intelligentsia. Besides the Russian classics there were long rows of bound volumes of the more liberal Russian reviews.

After a very long wait Radek was seized with an urgent desire to urinate and, after prowling round, opened a door into another room where he found an enormous bed. He decided that it was probably the American Ambassador's bedroom and held a formal debate with himself as to whether diplomatic and extra-territorial rights would be infringed if he were to make use of the Ambassador's chamber-pot.

When at last Mr Francis came in, he shook hands with me (I had met him in Petrograd) and I introduced Radek. The Ambassador preserved every inch of the several thousand miles that separated him and his countrymen from all that was embodied in the room in which we sat. An elderly, uncomprehending man, anxious to make no mistake, perplexed between his sense of his own dignity as Dean of the Diplomatic Corps and his over-humble submission to the stronger will of the Frenchman whom he had left in conclave with other foreign diplomats in another room while he, alone, faced the representative of the Soviet Republic, he made me remember Robins's description of him as 'a stuffed shirt'. Later on I came to realise that 'glove puppet' would be a more accurate description, as it contained a suggestion that such simulation of life as there was in the stuffed shirt was provided by a hand and active fingers within it, and that hand and those fingers belonged to Monsieur Noulens, who had no scruples at all as to the use he made of them.

The conversation began with an argument as to whether the telegram which Chicherin had sent to Francis about the return of the diplomatic corps from Vologda to Moscow was an invitation or a command (as evidently Noulens had tried to make Francis believe). Radek insisted that it was an invitation and protested against the publication of Chicherin's telegram and the answer to it (we had found both printed in an evening news-sheet in Vologda) before the arrival of the envoy whose coming was announced in it.

Radek then outlined the official reasons for which the Soviet Government thought the removal of the Ambassadors from Vologda was advisable. He pointed out that Mirbach had been assassinated by Social Revolutionaries, that they had been accused of being the tools of the Allies, and that as they were actually opposed both to Germany and to the Allies it was likely that they would make an attempt to demonstrate their impartiality by murdering an Allied Ambassador. The Social Revolutionaries had been suppressed in Moscow, which was now comparatively safe, but some of them had managed to get away, and the Government could not guarantee that they would not reach Vologda, where it was very difficult to guard against such things. Further, there was a danger lest there should be at Vologda a rising against the Soviets, in which case the ensuing fighting would be as impartial as the Social Revolutionaries, and it would be impossible to guarantee the immunity of the Allied Missions and Embassies scattered about the town. Finally he referred to the presence of about five thousand German and Austrian prisoners of war who had probably been stirred by the news of Mirbach's death and might seek to avenge the murder of a German Ambassador by murdering an Ambassador of some Allied nation.

These arguments seemed to be having some effect on Mr Francis, but every now and then he could not keep his eyes from straying towards the door by which he had come into the room, and at last he excused himself and went off through that door, no doubt to report his dealings with us to his fellow-diplomats, who all this time were waiting in the wings. At this point we were not without hope that the incident would be smoothly settled and that we should return to Moscow with a full cargo of diplomats. However, when Mr Francis came back into the room his tone was entirely different. He had left the room a more or less normal, if rather disturbed American gentleman. He came back with all his hackles up, as if he had been stirred to battle by someone else. He gave reasons why he considered Moscow less safe than Vologda, which were, one by one, answered by Radek, but we left with the definite impression that the diplomats had no intention of leaving Vologda.

As we drove off through the little wooden town, with its log-huts and its white churches beside the almost impossibly irregular roads, with our Lett, carbine in hand, sitting beside the chauffeur, Radek, much incensed, was once more talking of ultimatums and of packing the diplomats forcibly into their train and bringing 'the whole menagerie' under convoy to Moscow. This was an almost exact repetition of the remarks I had heard him make in Moscow, my objection to which had made Lenin tell him to take me with him. Well, I had come. I had heard his talk with Francis and knew that there was no chance whatever of persuading Mr Francis to do anything of which M. Noulens would disapprove. We might as well have gone back to Moscow at once, but I was so certain that to quarrel with the Bolsheviks was to help the Germans to win the war that, in spite of Radek's failure with Francis, I set about arranging a private, non-official meeting between Lindley, our

27   Writer

28   Fisherman

29   Sailor

30 and 31    Rewards of authorship: above, Carnegie Medallist, 1937; below,
Doctor of Letters, 1952 (right back, next to Wyndham Lewis)

32 and 33    Last years: at Newby Bridge, 1954 (above), and with
Rupert Hart-Davis at Hill Top, 1961

Chargé d'Affaires at Vologda, and Radek. They agreed to meet that same evening.

Lindley's British Mission, which had arrived only a few days before, had established itself in a single-storey unpainted wooden house at a cross-roads. There was a rough, untended strip of grass in front of it, a yellow door shielded by a porch on one side, and a rough verandah where there was usually a table with a cloth over it and a few members of the Mission sitting round it, an easy mark for any Social Revolutionary who might feel inclined to put his party in the right by demonstrating its impartiality in the assassination of foreigners.

Lindley received us in the room beyond the porch where an ostentatiously ill-mannered little vice-consul had draped a table with a Union Jack, as if to make England responsible for his personal offensiveness. In a corner of the room was another small table and behind it a semi-circular sofa. Lindley sat on the sofa, Radek and I on chairs on either side of the table. The general tone of the conversation was friendly and easy and must have surprised the little vice-consul. Radek smoked his pipe, drank tea, and was soon talking to Lindley with greater freedom than I had heard him use with any foreigner except myself.

In this talk there was no mention of any danger that might be threatening the Ambassadors in Vologda, and unfortunately this fact was used afterwards as a proof that there were no such dangers. Radek estimated Lindley pretty highly, assumed that for Lindley, as for himself, personal danger was not a thing of great interest, and preferred to put the matter on an entirely different footing, discussing, not the immediate reasons for a move to Moscow, but the practical advantages that would result from such a move. He pointed out the disadvantages of having half-a-dozen separate, irresponsible and uncoordinated Missions, the voice of none of which could be taken to be that of the British Government. He spoke of the offers of economic concessions made to the Germans and the Americans and said that similar proposals had been prepared for submission to the English, but that there had been no responsible person to whom such proposals could be made. We parted on terms of considerable cordiality, but as we walked away Radek said that though, if he had only to talk with Lindley and Francis, he was confident that good might result, yet on the whole the conversation had convinced him that there was nothing to be hoped.

9

That evening at the Golden Anchor we feasted on eggs while looking through a big bundle of telegrams despatched by the various Embassies and Missions, all of which, with the exception of Lindley's, Radek decided to retain pending instructions from Moscow, and a few telegrams from correspondents, one of which, from the French Havas agency, vividly illustrated the character of Noulens's policy. After mentioning the arrival of Radek, this telegram went on to say that Radek wore a revolver when he came to see Francis, 'et garda son arme pendant toute la durée de la visite'. This was obviously calculated to give the impression that Radek had deliberately tried to frighten the American Ambassador by an ostentatious display of his revolver. Nothing could be further from the truth. Radek's revolver was as much a part of him as his fountain-pen, and it would have been as surprising to see him without it as it would have been to see him with all the buttons of his coat properly fastened, or with a pocket not distorted by a bulging mass of papers. He had just bought a new chocolate-coloured suit of more or less military pattern with breeches which he wore with black gaiters and boots. He was inordinately proud of these clothes, although they did not fit him, and the revolver was an essential part of the costume.

Within a week, on July 16, the Tsar and his family were murdered at Ekaterinburg, and a few days later the Allied Embassies retreated north to Archangel.

# CHAPTER XXXII

# *Through the Blockade to Stockholm*

Directly the Brest-Litovsk Peace was concluded, Russia and Germany were juridically no longer at war. Things were possible that during the long years of the war had never seemed likely to be possible again. In the fluid post-revolutionary Russia I had been certain that the right policy for England was to recognise that Russia was not yet in a condition to fight Germany, and that joining the Germans to fight Russia was not the best way of helping the Russians to defend what of Russia the Brest-Litovsk Peace had left them.

These views, which seemed to me simple common sense, seemed to the White Russians rank treachery, and they assumed, rightly in some cases, that the attitude of British officials would be the same as their own. Hardly a day passed on which I did not hear from Lockhart the latest secret-service report on my activities as a 'Bolshevik agent'. Lockhart knew very well what my own interests were, and it was not without private amusement that he brought to my table a secret-service agent, Reilly, who subsequently became notorious by committing Lockhart to the support of Savinkov and his Social Revolutionary friends, with the natural result of Lockhart's arrest, imprisonment and expulsion from Russia. At the time I had no idea who the man was, but he began at once by saying 'I think I had better tell you that I am a socialist myself. Are you?' I replied, 'I'm not.' The conversation withered after that and I should be amused to know what he put into his report.

I was not always able to play such tricks so easily, and sometimes it seemed better to leave the secret service to nurse its false impressions. Not one of my Bolshevik friends (and I had many) ever tried to convert me to Bolshevism. It was enough for them to know that I hoped to write a history of the revolution and was collecting material with that purpose. There was no pretence on either side. I did indeed want to write such a history. I felt that it was almost a miracle that I should without effort have found myself so placed. And I should indeed have settled down to write such a history if the Bolshevik secret police in Petrograd had not been as ignorant as our own and taken the heart out of me by destroying the immense store of material I had collected. I could not really blame them for this, because during my various visits to the Russian front I had acquired a lot of Staff maps and had used them as dust-sheets to protect the piles of newspapers, leaflets and proclamations that covered the floor of my room.

The Jaroslavl revolt and the seizure by Czecho-Slovak troops of strategic points on the Siberian Railway changed everything. British soldiers were fighting Russian, Allied Intervention against the Bolsheviks was in full swing, and my views made my own position untenable. I still believed that the Russian Revolution was a fact to be welcomed by the Allies. I had made that very clear in my telegrams to the *Daily News* and the *Observer*. Further, I thought that nothing could be more helpful to the Germans than to bring about hostilities between the Russians and ourselves. Everything that happened seemed a promise of this unwanted war.

I was well aware of the extreme personal hostility that my telegrams had raised in those representatives of the English colony who had remained in Moscow. Lockhart knew of this hostility and agreed with me that should Moscow be occupied by the Whites Evgenia would be in the gravest danger. He agreed that this would be grossly unfair and suggested that she should be put on my English passport to make it easier for me to get her out of Russia. In fact she never had occasion to make use of this passport. Until I got my divorce and we were able to get married she stuck to her Russian citizenship, her Russian passport and her maiden name.

Once again I had reason to be grateful to Vorovsky. He was collecting secretaries for the Russian Legation in Stockholm, of which he was to be the head, and offered to take her with him as a member of his staff. This I gladly, and Evgenia with indifference, agreed to, and on July 27 Evgenia left for Berlin on her way to join Vorovsky's Legation.

On July 28 I had a telegram from Lindley, saying that I had not answered his telegram (which I had never received). I no longer had the slightest confidence that telegrams sent off by me from

Moscow would ever reach Fleet Street. If that were so now, while our Mission (Lockhart's) was still outwardly on good terms with the Soviet Foreign Office, how was it likely to be in the event, the now obviously probable event, of rupture? I had to think of arranging a channel for Russian news to England in case of war. The Russians hoped to keep such a channel open and to get news through Sweden to England even if the worst should happen and England and Soviet Russia find themselves at war.

On August 2 Lockhart and his Mission were turned out of the Hôtel Elite, where I for so many months had lived and fed and laughed with them. If it were to come to an open break between England and Russia I should be faced with an impossible choice, and I valued above everything my freedom from having to make a choice, which, once made, would turn me into a propagandist instead of a recorder.

Civil war in Finland closed that way to Sweden. Radek solved the problem for me and I got through the Baltic as a Russian courier, on the understanding that if the Germans stopped me the Russians would stop a German courier until I was freed. I carried an immense despatch case and was accompanied by a Lettish interpreter to translate from my Russian into, of all languages, English for the benefit of the German controls. There was cholera in Petrograd and that, I think, was helpful. The Finnish fear of cholera greatly lessened the anxiety of the Helsingfors officials to detain the ship for a minute longer than was necessary. We were presently moving again and at Mariehamn in the Aland Islands the examination was perfunctory, so much so that in the harbour I was able to photograph Germans in *Pickelhaubes* through the porthole of my cabin. This was rather silly and quite useless as I made a mistake in adjusting the aperture and even if they had come out well the photographs would have been of no interest.

I reached Stockholm on August 5, only to learn that Evgenia was still in Berlin. There was some delay in arranging for my telegrams to the *Daily News* to be sent from Stockholm. Today, looking back on the well-known history of the last weeks of the European War, it is hard to realise how ignorant we were of the imminent collapse of the German war-machine. On August 14 I was able to begin telegraphing to the *Daily News*. A Moscow cable announced the departure in panic of the German Embassy from Moscow, and was followed by news of a collapse of the

Soviet Government. I found both hard to believe. On the 17th came news that the Soviet troops had had some success against the Czechs. And of a Japanese advance against them. There was also news of a new army being drilled in Moscow. On August 28 Evgenia arrived. On August 30 I had one almost happy afternoon. I had lunched with Leighton, a young naval man attached to the British Legation, and in the afternoon he and I went down to Saltsjobaden and sailed in a small oak-built cutter.

On September 5 came the news, which I did not at first believe (though I should by then have realised that any idiocy was possible to our Foreign Office so long as our officials welcomed the entirely unscrupulous persons who needed no credentials other than hostility to the Bolsheviks), of an Allied plot in Moscow and other centres. I had known that Lockhart, without the backing of Robins, had wavered more than once, but I simply could not believe that knowing the parties of the Right as he did, knowing that they had completely lost all popular backing, he could have committed England to their support. I immediately telegraphed to Moscow pointing out that what the Bolsheviks had been reported as doing, namely arresting Lockhart and the whole of his Mission, would in England be taken as proof that those had been right who had said that Soviet Government was pro-German. I had a reassuring message back from Radek.

On October 8 Lockhart and the other members of his Mission arrived in Stockholm. I met them at the station and the first words I heard from Lockhart were 'You know, in spite of everything I am still against Intervention.' They all left for England on October 13.

Evgenia and I had found rooms in a pleasant little house by the water on the sea-approach to Stockholm where I fished for pike and we were visited by a long series of friends, some of whom turned out years afterwards to have been less friendly than they pretended. Among the truly friendly was Paul Dukes, later knighted for his exploits in bringing across the frontiers various members of the Russian Royal Family. (He was a brother of Ashley Dukes with whom for many years I had a series of games of chess and a similar series of games of billiards in the beautiful billiard-room at the Garrick Club to which we used to climb until I could climb no more.) Paul planned to visit Russia in secret and I told him that it would be easy but unwise, as, travelling clandestinely and in disguise, he would get much the same sort of view of Russia as a hunted fox gets of a fox-hunt. After his Russian adventures he went to the Himalayas and studied yoga. His brother Ashley much disapproved of his romantic view of Russia, but it was impossible to take Paul Dukes seriously enough to dislike him, and I liked him as a link with the old days in Petrograd.

Suddenly the war with Germany ended. There was revolution in Germany. German and Austrian armies in the East were turning into rabbles. For a moment I was fool enough to think that intervention would come to an end. I forgot Lenin's belief that English, French and Germans would combine against the Bolsheviks. I forgot Lindley's remark to me about Bolsheviks: 'You don't seem to realise that these people are our enemies.' It soon became clear that Lenin had not been far wrong and that Lindley had accurately set forth the Foreign Office view. The war with Germany was over. The Intervention was to go on. Within a very short time we were allowing German generals to keep their forces intact and to go looting and destroying through the Baltic Provinces on the excuse that they were 'fighting the Reds'.

A few years later, sailing my little boat up the Aa River past the shells of burnt-out factories with storks nesting on the tops of the few remaining factory chimneys, I happened to remark to a local man on the damage done by the war. 'Nothing to do with the war,' said the man angrily. 'This was done after the war by Mr Churchill's Germans.'

Meanwhile there was now a vital change in my position. I had been given leave to bring Evgenia to England. At the same time Sweden had broken off diplomatic relations with Soviet Russia, and Vorovsky's Legation was going to be turned out. I had to make an immediate choice between going to England, taking Evgenia with me, thereby closing the gates of Russia behind me for a very long time, and going back to Russia with Vorovsky. It seemed obvious to me that by going to England I should be sacrificing the extraordinary position I had built up for myself in personal relations with the Bolsheviks. At the same time if England were to be at war with Russia, if Intervention was to go on, my position would be impossible and useless. I put the onus of decision on the Foreign Office.

I saw Clifford Sharp of the *New Statesman*, who was the head of our information service in Sweden, and asked him to find out definitely whether the Foreign Office wanted me to go back into

Russia or not. If they did, I felt I had no right to refuse. The answer was that they thought it would be worth while for me to go. Then, comically enough, there was opposition from some of the Bolsheviks. I had asked for leave to go into Russia to gather more material for my history of the revolution. There was opposition and it seemed likely that I should be refused permission in spite of my friendship with Vorovsky. Fortunately however a copy of the *Morning Post* reached Stockholm with a report in it of a lecture by Lockhart in which he said that as I had been out of Russia for six months I had no right to speak of conditions there. I heard afterwards that a lady in the audience had protested strongly and the meeting had broken up. The protester was Mrs Macmillan, the mother of my old friend Daniel and Harold, the future Prime Minister. I had no further difficulties, had indeed a firm ally in Maxim Litvinov, who had been dependent on my *Daily News* telegrams to keep him (in London) informed of what was happening in Russia, until with the beginning of Intervention they had ceased to appear.

# CHAPTER XXXIII

## *Scotland Yard to the Rescue*

On January 30, 1919, I and three Scandinavian journalists left Stockholm with Vorovsky's party. Of this journey and of what I saw in Russia I wrote in a small book, *Six Weeks in Russia in 1919*, in which is the whole material of a report I made to very unwilling ears at the Foreign Office in London. I had kept a full diary and did my best to give a fair picture of what things were like. The revolution eats its children, and almost all the revolutionary leaders of that time have since been removed by execution or other violent means. My friend Vorovsky was murdered in Switzerland. My friend Bukharin, the most interesting talker of them all, after Lenin, was shot in 1937. Rykov: shot; Krestinsky: shot; Zinoviev: shot; Kamenev: shot; Trotsky: murdered in Mexico. I do not know whether Radek is alive or dead. (I do not think he ever came back from banishment to Tobolsk.*) Litvinov alone survived, and his survival may point the moral of the deaths of all the others. Litvinov was not in Russia at the time of the October Revolution. The others were, and, as revolution is for ever engaged in rewriting its own history, each one of these others was an awkward bit of history too difficult to be explained away by the rewriters. Another point perhaps worth making is that all these men were old exiles and cosmopolitans, like Lenin himself. I had argued with all of them, disliked some of them and been disliked by them, but had liked some of them very much, even in the midst of argument. To look back on that journey now is, for me, to fill the room with ghosts. But I am glad I wrote that little book and I think it will remain of interest, as would, if we had it, the book of any Englishman who in 1789 had been able to meet and talk of what they were doing, with Robespierre, Danton, Marat, and Desmoulins. In the eyes of history the names

* He is believed to have died in an Arctic labour camp in 1939.

of Lenin, Bukharin, Trotsky and Radek will surely rank with these.

On March 11, when my notebook was nearly full, I heard on the telephone that some Americans had come to Moscow on behalf of Colonel House and with the full knowledge of Lloyd George. I was told they were looking for me. I presently found them in a sumptuous little house in Maly Kharitonovsky Pereulok. They were Lincoln Steffens, an eloquent and eager left-wing journalist and William C. Bullitt, afterwards Ambassador in Moscow. Bullitt believed that their mission meant the likelihood of an immediate end to Intervention, and we both thought that I might, knowing the Bolsheviks as no one else had had a chance of knowing them, be found useful in London. I therefore agreed to leave Evgenia with her mother and sister in Moscow while I went to London with Bullitt. I had no difficulties over that journey and did not learn till twenty years later, when Bullitt was American Ambassador in France, how very nearly I was stopped on the way to England and at what strange cross-purposes were some of our own officials. This is the story that Bullitt told me as we watched the big carp in the lake at Chantilly.

He and Lincoln Steffens had come into Russia through Finland in company with a third American who had stayed a few days in Helsingfors. The British officials there, wishing to prevent my taking to England information that they knew would be unwelcome to the Interventionists, had gone so far as to warn the Finnish police to arrest me at the frontier, to keep me in prison, and on no account to report the arrest to the British Consulate, which would, if it knew of the arrest, have been bound to take steps for my release. This delightful plot miscarried. Bullitt, Steffens and I crossed the frontier together, the Finns assuming that I was the third member of the Bullitt party. A few days later a member of the British Secret Service presented himself at the frontier. The Finns assumed that he was I, arrested him instantly, put him in gaol and, when he demanded that they should take him to the British Consul, were all the more convinced that he was I, and blandly refused to do anything of the sort. The more he protested the more sure they were that he was the man they had been told to stop, and the more determined they were not to embarrass the Consul by mentioning the arrest. There he was, safe in gaol, and there, fuming, he had to remain. To all his protests they replied, 'Oh, yes, we know all about that.' At last the third American arrived at the frontier. The Finns, astounded, told him that he had crossed it already with Bullitt and Steffens. Enquiries were made, the mistake discovered, the Secret Service man released. But by that time, Bullitt, Steffens and I, knowing nothing of this miscarriage of injustice, were already crossing the North Sea.

But in 1919 I did not know, as I passed comfortably through Finland, how narrowly I had missed being gaoled, but I did learn on coming to London how ignorant of each other's doings officialdom's right and left hands could be.

As Bullitt, Steffens and I stepped out of the train at King's Cross, a tall man in dark clothes and a bowler hat stepped up to me and said, 'Mr Ransome?' 'Yes.' 'I must ask you to come with me to Scotland Yard at once.' Bullitt raised astonished eyebrows. I asked, 'Is this an arrest?' Bowler Hat said, 'No, but I think you had better come.' I laughed and said, 'Very well. Do you mind taking these bags?' Bowler Hat took a portmanteau in each hand and off we went most amicably. Bowler Hat talked a little in the cab and said that I was to see Sir Basil Thomson, the head of the Yard. 'What about?' I asked. 'He wants to see you,' said Bowler Hat.

I was shown into Sir Basil Thomson's room and asked to sit down in the famous chair where so many criminals had sat before me. Sir Basil, extremely grim, looked hard at me. After a moment's silence, he said, 'Now, I want to know just what your politics are.'

'Fishing,' I replied.

He stared. 'Just what do you mean by that?'

I told him the exact truth, that in England I had never had any political views whatever, that in Russia I believed that this very fact had let me get a clearer view of the revolution than I could otherwise have got, that I now had one clear political opinion, which was that Intervention was a disastrous mistake, and that I hoped it would come to an end and so release me to turn to my ordinary interests.

'Fishing?' he said.

'We are very near the beginning of the season,' I replied.

We talked for some time, in a manner more and more friendly. I told him just why I thought that, win or lose, the effect of Intervention must be bad for our future relations with Russia under any government whatsoever.

Suddenly the telephone rang. He lifted the receiver, smiled, said 'Yes ... yes ... yes ... ' and put it down again.

He looked across at me and laughed. 'Do you know what that was?' he asked. 'That was the Foreign Office, warning me that you are going to land at Newcastle *tomorrow!!*'

What the Foreign Office expected him to do, neither he nor I could understand, but I was grateful for the hint that I might not be so welcome there as in the past. Time went on and he said he would like to continue our talk next day. I said I proposed to report to the Foreign Office. He said, 'Well, you see when they are expecting you.' I agreed to call next day and did so, and he then let me set out more of my reasons for regarding Intervention as a mistake.

'You certainly make out a pretty good case,' he said, 'and I agree with you that the more it's known the better.' My arrest thus ended in mutual good will, and later that year Sir Basil joined C. P. Scott and Lloyd George in helping me when certain Foreign Office officials were trying, this time, to prevent my going back to Russia.

On earlier visits to the Foreign Office my dealings had been with Francis Acland, and later with Lord Robert Cecil. Intervention and my opposition to it had put me into a very different category of visitors. I was allowed to see no one but a temporary clerk. I was less surprised than I might have been, thanks to the hint given me by Sir Basil the day before. All the same, it did seem odd that the only Englishman who knew the Bolshevik leaders with any intimacy, and had just come back from Moscow, was quite obviously regarded as a danger. I told the young man that I had brought with me the material for a detailed report. He said that he would like to see it. Then, perhaps by mistake, he let fall an illuminating sentence. He said, 'Perhaps you do not realise that we could damn you with the Left if we let it be known that you have been working with us.'

I suppose he imagined that I was some sort of politician, to whom such a threat would be serious. I did not care in the least about Lefts or Rights, but was solely interested in doing what I could to counteract the misinformation which seemed to me to have launched us on a course that must end in disaster. I left the Foreign Office and sought out George Lansbury, whom I had met only once before, and told him what had happened and what I proposed to do. I then saw Stanley Unwin and arranged with him to publish the diary on which I was basing my report to the Foreign Office.

My mother was staying at Malling in Kent, but still had a house at Leeds. I went there, found an excellent shorthand-typist and, working sixteen hours a day, produced simultaneously *Six Weeks in Russia in 1919* and my report to the Foreign Office. I ended my report with a sentence to the effect that I knew I was speaking to a hostile audience, but that if there was any point on which they wanted further information I should be delighted to give it if it were in my power. Later the Foreign Office prepared a paper of excerpts from various sources tending to justify Intervention. They asked if I would allow them to use some passages from my report. Knowing what impression could be made by quotations out of context, I replied that I had no objection, on one condition, that among the passages quoted should be this last sentence. They refrained.

Unwin published *Six Weeks in Russia in 1919* and sold enormous quantities of it at the lowest possible price. No one could read the plain statements of fact in that book without feeling that the Russian war could not be justified, if only because the people in the book, from Lenin downwards, were quite obviously human beings and not the fantastic bogies that the Interventionists pretended. The little book makes no claim to knowledge of politics or economics, but it does give a fair picture of what Moscow was like in those days of starvation, high hope and unwanted war. I have just read it through and though I could perhaps revise it to advantage, I am glad I wrote it there and then before the taste, colour and smell of those strange days had faded.

I had known when I published it that the Interventionists at the Foreign Office were hardly likely to thank me. They did, in fact, give me the most miserable summer of my life. Believing that Intervention was on the point of ending, I had left Evgenia in Russia with her mother and sisters in the belief that I should be able to return for her almost at once. I now found that Intervention, far from ending, was to expand, that we were to finance and equip the Whites for civil war on a vast scale, and that there was not the smallest likelihood of my being allowed to return to Moscow. Long before the summer was over, Soviet Russia was shrinking day by day. Siberia was gone, the Ukraine was gone, the Baltic republics were bases for the White forces. I had the horrible knowledge that if Moscow should fall the hatred I had earned from the Whites would be wreaked upon the innocent Evgenia. All through the summer this nightmare was upon me, with the news darkening every day.

I spent many week-ends fishing the delightful little Meon with Francis Hirst. I caught rainbow trout in Neil Green's lakes at Horncastle, and pike in the Medway and in Norfolk. I played a lot of chess, and even tried to get on with another collection of fairy stories. But every day the dangers I feared seemed to grow. I saw a lot of Molly Hamilton, always a strong ally to her friends. I went to Coniston and W. G. Collingwood did not allow his disapproval of all revolutions to cloud for a moment his friendship for me. At Mrs Hamilton's I met Ramsay MacDonald and other leaders of the Labour Party. At Francis Hirst's I met Sir John Simon, Lord Parmoor and the Liberals. But all the time hostile armies were coming nearer and nearer to Moscow. The first ray of hope came from General Sir Hubert Gough who, in the intervals of playing cricket with his daughters, told me that, shocked by the horrors he had seen at Denikin's headquarters, he had come to the conclusion that the Whites did not deserve to be helped.

Thinking that if I could not go to Moscow myself, and knowing that if I did go the Whites would stick at nothing to discredit my reports, I thought that the best I could do would be to persuade somebody else to go, if possible a Conservative, the independence of whose evidence was not likely to be doubted. I looked round for a possible eyewitness whose report, if he were an honest man, I was sure would corroborate my own. I could not find a willing Conservative but did find, as I thought, the next best thing in a Coalition Liberal Member of Parliament with a highly distinguished record in the war. This was Lt.-Col. Lestrange Malone. I gave him letters of introduction and off he went and succeeded in getting to Moscow. But the effect of what he saw was too much for him, and instead of coming back as a Right wing Anti-Interventionist, he swung very far to the Left and was soon on the Left wing of the Labour Party, thus lessening the effect of his evidence. He did, however, take a letter from me to Evgenia, and might even have brought her back with him if she herself had not thought it wiser to stay.

Help came from an unexpected quarter. C. P. Scott of the *Manchester Guardian* read *Six Weeks in Russia* and asked me to visit him in Manchester. I went there, stayed with him at the Firs, learned that he agreed with me that Intervention was a mistake and that he was prepared to do all he could in bringing it to an end. I laid my own private difficulties before him. He asked if I would go to Russia for the *Manchester Guardian* if he gave me a perfectly free hand. I agreed, but told him that I was sure that the Interventionist Foreign Office would prevent my leaving England. He was indignant and said that if that should prove to be so, he would himself go up to London and appeal to Lloyd George. This was the beginning of my long and very happy association with the *Manchester Guardian*. The difficulties in the way of my going back to Russia were more serious than C. P. Scott had thought possible. However, he was not the man to give up. More than once it seemed that all was clear, and more than once we found ourselves faced by a seemingly undinted wall of official hostility.

Meanwhile the anti-Bolshevik forces were closing in. Denikin had reached Orel, Judenitch was advancing from Reval, Kolchak from Siberia, and our own withdrawal from Archangel was still delayed, new forces being sent there even while it had been announced that those already there were to leave. Every day the newspapers told of events that promised an early collapse of Soviet Russia. While I was inside Russia I had not thought that likely. Outside, in the general din of Interventionist newspaper reports, I came to think it all but inevitable, and, though I was still sure that a collapse of the Soviets would not bring the end that the Interventionists hoped, I began to be afraid that I might reach Russia too late.

C. P. Scott saw Lloyd George, he saw Lord Hardinge. I saw Lloyd George and Sir Basil Thomson, who was by now wholeheartedly on my side in this ridiculous scuffle. My Liberal friends were doing their best. But week followed week. White Russian victories were trumpeted almost daily and it was kindly suggested that I might just as well give up as, by the time I reached the frontier, there would be no Soviet Government in Moscow.

At last the Foreign Office yielded, or rather pretended to yield. I was given my passport for Russia, only to find that Norway and Sweden, two countries through which I had to pass, would not give me a transit-visa. I went to Sir Basil Thomson at Scotland Yard, showed him my passport and told him what had happened. He was as disgusted as I was at what he evidently thought was a deliberate tactical trick. 'Leave it to me,' he said. 'They have given you your passport. What happens next is no concern of theirs.'

The next thing I heard from him was that I had better try again for those two visas and, having got them, move as quickly as I could. Sir Basil was something of a sportsman. I was given my two visas and was free to start.

And at this moment the Coal Strike began. There were no trains leaving London for Newcastle, whence a boat was soon to leave for Bergen. There are, however, other ways of getting to Newcastle than overland. Frantic enquiries brought me the news that a coasting steamer was that day leaving London. I raced to the docks with a portmanteau and a typewriter. As I paid the taxi I heard the steamer whistle. I reached the quayside just as the ropes had been cast off and a gap was slowly widening between the steamer and the quay. I threw my portmanteau on board and, with my typewriter, jumped, caught the rail and was helped over it by a smiling sailor. I was off, and for the first time for months knew that there was nothing more that I could do. I could not make the ship move faster. So I settled down to the pleasure of that slow voyage out of the Estuary and up the East Coast, past Harwich and Orfordness and Lowestoft, that in later years I was to enjoy so much in a little ship of my own.

We reached Newcastle. The Norwegian ship was still in port, unable to sail because of the strike. The strikers on the quayside had refused to allow the filling of her bunkers. I was told that there was no hope of her leaving. I went aboard and found a captain as anxious to sail as I was that he should. We sat in his stateroom and drank some sort of Scandinavian vodka and damned the strikers. The man was angrier than I could at first understand. But suddenly he tapped my knee. 'It is this way,' he said. 'My wife did not want me to go on this trip for fear I should not be home for our wedding anniversary. And our wedding anniversary is on Thursday and these devils of strikers ... ! What have I to do with their strike? What will my wife think of me?' And then he called for the Chief Engineer. There was coming and going and calculations on bits of paper. The Engineer laughed. The Captain did not smile. At last he said, 'If they will not give me coal, we sail without! We have coal ballast, mostly dust and rubbish, but we will see.'

And we did. Luck turned my way at last. I do not suppose that such black smoke has ever affronted Newcastle. All the way across the North Sea we steamed leaving an inky trail across the sky. The decks were black. The rails were black. We had the faces of chimney-sweeps. We slowed sometimes almost to a standstill, but we did in the end come steaming into Bergen in our own black fog in time for the Captain's anniversary. I caught the train from Bergen to Christiania and so to Stockholm, and there found a dirty little steamer, the *Kalevipoeg*, now Esthonian, on the point of sailing for Reval. Most of the woodwork in her had been torn out. She was in sore need of paint. She had no heating. Her decks leaked. But she moved, and brought me at last into the harbour of Reval, with the old castle on its rock, looking out over the bay. The news I heard there was grim. General Judenitch had advanced and his forward troops were already within sight of the gilded dome of St Isaac's Cathedral in Petrograd.

# CHAPTER XXXIV
## *A Vital Message*

I found in Reval a very unstable political situation. The Esthonians not long ago had been a subject race under the German Baltic Barons who, in the time of Peter the Great, had transferred their allegiance from Sweden to Russia, largely because Russia was the less Liberal of the two, or the less efficient, and so left them a freer hand in dealing with the tillers of the soil. At the time of the abortive Russian Revolution of 1905 there had been revolts in the Baltic Provinces, bloodily suppressed. With the collapse of the Russian army, the Germans had swept through the Provinces and for a short time the Baltic landlords had been in control. With the collapse of Germany, things had changed again. Esthonia became an independent republic, but at the same time there was a White Russian army based on Reval, and the Russians of Judenitch's army were not hiding their determination to come back and make an end of 'the potato republic' once they had settled accounts with the Bolsheviks.

The Esthonians knew very well what this meant, and were determined that this time their independence should not be buried under mounds of executed peasants as it had been after 1905. They had had all they wanted of war and of civil war, and knew that the economy of their little country depended on the vast hinterland of Russia, which normally kept the port of Reval busy. Without agreement with Russia they were dependent on help from England and France, and the French had made it clear that help was given only on condition that they took part in the Interventionist war. A conference of Baltic states had, rather pathetically, expressed a wish to come to terms with Soviet Russia, but the possibility of peace had receded with the new flare-up of hostilities. When I landed at Reval the Esthonians were almost desperate. Judenitch's army, with its spearhead of tanks manned by British officers, had swept forward almost to Petrograd, but had come to a standstill when the Judenitch Russians were asked to man the tanks themselves. The next section of the long, multicoloured front was held by the Esthonians, and the next by the Letts, between whom and the Esthonians was bitter dispute over territory claimed by both. They could not wish for a White victory in Russia. At the same time they dreaded a White defeat. Meanwhile the war was going on.

On landing in Reval I went to see Mr Piip, the Esthonian Foreign Minister, and told him that I wanted to cross the front in order to go to Moscow. I told him exactly why I wanted to go. He said that the front was fluid and that it would be impossible to arrange any sort of formal crossing. Piip and I got on very well and presently he agreed to send out a wireless message on my behalf to Litvinov at the Foreign Commissariat in Moscow, asking for permission to cross. He asked me to leave him till he had talked with the Esthonian President, and then to return for a further meeting.

When I saw him again he laid all the Esthonian cards on the table. They could fight no longer, he said, for an aim that was to their own disadvantage, a victory by Judenitch. They would like to propose an armistice but dared not do so over the wireless without being assured that the Bolsheviks would immediately agree, because they had been threatened by the French (who were still full of hope in Judenitch) that any weakening on their part would be followed by the abrupt withdrawal of all support by the French and by ourselves. (We were responsible for no such threat.) They could not use the wireless. They dared not put anything in writing, lest some accident should bring it into the wrong hands. Would I take it upon myself to let the Soviet Government know that any suggestion for an armistice would be accepted, and that Esthonia was ready to begin peace negotiations at once?

I agreed. Peace with Esthonia would mean peace on the Lettish front also. It would be the first clear step towards the ending of a state of war that was damaging to both sides and a mad postponement of the recovery of Europe. I did not see how I could take any other decision than to carry the Esthonians' message.

And then came the answer from Moscow to my wireless message asking for permission to cross the front. It was an absolute refusal.

Piip was as disappointed as I. 'No good trying to cross in the face of that,' he said.

I wrote a telegram on a scrap of paper. 'RANSOME ALREADY LEFT FOR MOSCOW.' I passed it to Piip. 'Give me two days start and then send this.'

Piip read it doubtfully. 'You can get through our lines,' he said, 'but after that?'

I told him that once through the White front I thought I could look after myself. No more time was lost. Twelve hours later I was sitting in a hut with some Esthonian officers waiting for the arrival of a man from a farm in the country between the two front lines. He came bringing some farm produce in a little cart. They told him that I was going back with him, across to the other side. He was very unwilling but we presently set off together. We passed what must have been the last of the Esthonian outposts. Suddenly he said, 'I have come far enough. They are there.' He pointed to something that looked like a low earthwork, some three hundred yards away. He gave me my typewriter and small bag and was gone, away towards his farm which was hidden in a dip of the ground some way behind us.

I filled a pipe, lit it, and, with typewriter in one hand and bag in the other, walked over the hummock behind which we had stopped and set out across the open country towards that line that might or might not be the trenches of the Russians. I puffed pretty hard at my pipe, burning my tongue but producing lots of smoke. Nobody, I reasoned, was going to shoot at a man walking slowly across and obviously enjoying his tobacco. Certainly no Russian, whose natural curiosity was sure to be greater than any wish to let off a rifle.

For what seemed a long time nothing happened and I began to think that the farmer, merely anxious not to get into trouble with either side, had just set me to walk in a direction that would take me away from himself. Then I thought I saw something move, as it might be a rabbit. Suddenly the line of that earth parapet was broken by several such rabbits, and I caught a glint of light on a rifle-barrel. I puffed harder than ever. With my hands full I could not wave a greeting and knew that any stoppage to put down my baggage might cause a regrettable misunderstanding. So I walked on, and presently saw half-a-dozen men with their elbows on the parapet, and their rifles pointing in a direction I deplored. I do not like being pointed at, even with unloaded guns. There was nothing to be done about it but to walk on. So I did walk on, and reached the parapet, to be bustled down behind it by some men who had climbed out as I came near, and to be greeted by a puzzled-looking young platoon-commander waving a revolver.

'Who are you,' he demanded, 'and where do you think you are going?'

'English correspondent,' I replied. 'Going to Moscow.'

'You are not going so far,' said he. 'Too many spies crossing the front. We have strict orders that anyone trying to cross the front is to be shot at once. Better get ready.'

'You might at least give me a glass of tea,' said I. There was a kettle steaming away on the bottom of the trench and several glasses that I supposed had been put down when they had seen me making my way across.

'We'll give you that,' said he.

One of the men gave me a glass, and another, disregarding his officer (he may have had some political position), asked what news there was across the front. I told him Judenitch was at Gatchina.

'If he takes Petrograd that means another three months to the war before we turn him out,' said the officer, and the doubts I had felt in England were gone. If that was how these people were feeling they were not going to be defeated.

'Why did you want to go to Moscow?' the officer asked.

'Going to see Lenin,' I said.

'A likely story!'

'A true one.'

'Drink up your tea. I've been given my orders and we'd better get this business over.'

'Look here,' I said. 'I can promise you that Lenin will be very angry when he learns that I have been shot.'

'He won't be angry with me for obeying orders,' said the young man.

'I dare say not. But here I am. I have crossed the front already, and told you I am going to Moscow. If you shoot me and find out afterwards that it was a mistake, you won't be able to put me together again. If, on the other hand, you don't shoot me and find out afterwards that you should have shot me, that is a mistake that you will easily be able to put right.'

'*Pravda*,' said one of the soldiers. '*Pravda*. This is true.'

The young officer looked at the soldier and then at me. I took a drink of tea.

'I'll take you to battalion headquarters,' he said. 'They can settle it.'

'I ask no more,' said I.

With that the affair became an ordinary tea-party, and I knew that my troubles were over. The young man became a charming host, and apologised for the quality of the tea, which, he said, was only cherry-leaves but the best they could get. They all wanted to know how soon people outside expected the war to be over. They were very much interested in my portable typewriter. They tried to make themselves cigarettes with my pipe-tobacco. They asked where I had learnt Russian. They became the friendly, simple people that Russians usually are.

There was one moment of awkwardness at battalion head-quarters, when the battalion commander suddenly stormed at my young officer for bringing me in instead of obeying orders and shooting me on the spot. But the same argument, the comparison between a mistake that could not be put right and one that could be corrected at any moment, worked here also. The decision was to be referred to a higher authority. Presently, here also, we were chattering away about international politics.

I will not describe in detail all the stages of that journey, my night at battalion headquarters, in the house of a schoolmaster who had a portrait of Gladstone on his wall, my dreadful bone-shaking drive in a springless cart in charge of a young commissar whose brother had been killed in the civil war, a repetition of the same old argument at army headquarters, and the final decision to send me to Moscow under arrest; the excellence of my armed guard as a batman, who showed great ingenuity in getting food for us both, the good terms we were on long before we reached Moscow, how he became at last convinced that I was what I pretended to be, and sure that my execution would have been a grave mistake, and how when we came to Moscow he agreed to let me call at the Commissariat for Foreign Affairs on our way to the War Commissariat at which he had orders to deliver me, and how I walked into Litvinov's office to find him reading the delayed telegram that Piip had sent on my behalf to say that I had already started for Moscow.

# CHAPTER XXXV
## *The Luck of a Chess-player*

Litvinov rang up the Commissariat for War and my difficulties were over. I delivered Piip's message. There was telephoning to me from the Kremlin. There were the same difficulties here as on the Esthonian side of the front. The Bolsheviks feared that if they were the first to offer an armistice it would be taken as a sign of weakness and refused. I explained that, for the reasons given me by Piip, the Esthonians were unable to take the first step. I left Litvinov busy at the telephone and went off to find Evgenia and her mother and sisters, with whom I was presently celebrating at a feast of potato-cakes, eked out with a bottle of Horlick's Malted Milk Tablets, which they treated as sweets and ate one after another. I told Evgenia she must make ready to start back with me, and went off to see our old friend Professor Pokrovsky, with whom she was working in the Commissariat of Education, to tell him he was going to lose the most efficient of his assistants.

I had a talk with Lenin, who told me that he had been inclined to disapprove of my *Six Weeks* until he had heard from Radek, who was in the Moabit Prison in Berlin and had praised it for just the personalities that Lenin had thought unnecessary, saying that it was the first thing written that had shown the Bolsheviks as human beings, and that it had brought them alive and talking into his cell. None the less, though that little book was translated into a dozen different languages it was not until 1924 that it was translated into Russian and published with an introduction by Radek himself. We had no copyright convention with Russia, but the State Publishing House presented me with the *Complete Works of Lenin* in lieu of royalties. (This was not quite so funny, nor so practical, as the state payment of Chaliapin for singing in opera. They gave him a sack of flour.) I hurried round Moscow and saw as many of my friends as I could, all hungry and all cold, but all convinced that they had got through the worst.

Then came bad news. There had been a new flare-up of fighting on the Esthonian front, which had been comparatively quiet. The fighting was spreading southwards, and the crossing of the front looked like being more difficult than it had been. At the same time I had come to extract Evgenia and felt sure that the thing could be done. The Russians said they would give us papers that would pass us through their own lines, but that it would be impossible to count on getting any further. Such danger as there was seemed to be from White Russian troops on the other side, not from Esthonians or Letts. Litvinov said that there was such a medley of troops on the other side that we could never be sure into whose hands we might fall.

Anyhow he was as anxious as I that I should get back to Reval to let Mr Piip know how they had received his message. And presently we were leaving Moscow, assured that we should find no difficulties until we had left the Russian lines. We spent the night in Rejitsa railway-station, where I had two very good games of chess with the local police chief. We then went on towards the front and finally were given directions for the village of Marien-hausen which was said to be in the hands of the Reds.

I hired a cart with a horse and a boy, and we piled into the cart such luggage as we had. The Red police chief at the village from which we began the final stage of the Russian part of our journey gave us an escort of a very melancholy militiaman, who sat in another, similar cart, with his rifle, and thought it hard that he should be sent with us on an expedition from which he was sure that none of us would return alive. Away we went on a goodish road, winding up and down over wide, rolling country with here and there patches of forest. We spent the next night in the half-ruined house of a country doctor, camped in the midst of an extraordinary collection of ferns and aspidistras. We could hear rifle-fire and occasional gunfire. In the morning we went on. The noise of the guns made our militiaman more and more uneasy. 'The devil only knows what is happening,' he said, 'but I have orders to take you to Marienhausen and so ... ' He drove on in melancholy silence. Every now and then we heard a burst of firing, and when some of it came from one side, some from another and then some from astern, it was clear that the front had ceased to be static. As the firing sounded now here, now there, he would glance at me and mutter to himself.

We could see no signs of any definite front. Whatever fighting was going on was hidden in the woods. For a long time there were no soldiers to be seen. Then we saw a handful of men, carrying rifles, bending low, and running in the direction from which we had come. They took no notice of us. We went on. The road stretched far ahead. About a quarter of a mile away there was a farmhouse at the roadside. As we came near it, we saw a small group of people, men and a woman, standing in the middle of the road.

We came up to them and asked where the front was. They stared at us and pointed back along the road by which we had come. Our militiaman swung his little cart round and drove off hell for leather for home. Our sturdy boy stood at his horse's head, twisting a straw from one side of his mouth to the other, looking at me and wondering what next. But he showed no sign of bolting. The farm people, who had seen us arrive with the Red militiaman, were looking at us with obvious mistrust. Civil war is civil war, and if they were to be found sheltering Reds ... I said, 'We are on our way to Marienhausen. How far is it? And can you let us have some boiling water to make tea?'

The woman led the way into the farmhouse kitchen. Here was a big stove, and while the water was boiling and Evgenia was preparing to make tea, I set about burning our Moscow safe-conducts and every scrap of paper that might be misunderstood by the Whites. I did not know what troops we might meet next, Russian Whites, Letts or Esthonians, but I did not wish to invite the mistakes that cannot afterwards be put right. The men stood watching. They began to talk among themselves, in Lettish, I think. I did not know the language, but I could see that the burning of those papers had made them fear for themselves. Their attitude became more and more hostile, and I guessed that they were thinking of putting themselves right with the Whites by holding these dangerous characters and handing them over. Then Evgenia had a flash of real genius. We were travelling, as usual in Russia, with our own small tea-kettle, and she had noticed the eyes of the farm-woman enviously upon it. She said, 'We are going on to England where we shall not need this. Would you like us to leave it with you?' A broad smile spread over the woman's face. She talked urgently and fiercely with the men. The argument was still going on when we had drunk our tea, and grew fiercer as we got up to go. The men were clearly unwilling to lose us as possible hostages. One of them made a motion to

detain us at the last moment, but was dissuaded by the woman.
We pretended to notice none of this by-play, thanked them
warmly for their hospitality and set out once more.

I did not want us to be left standing with our luggage in the
road, but also felt doubtful about the fate of our boy. I explained
to him that we were now on the White side of the front and asked
if he would prefer to go back. He grinned, twisted his straw, and
said, 'I have brothers on both sides. It is all one to me.'

We must have looked an odd party. Evgenia was sitting on our
luggage in the cart. The boy, stolidly twisting his straw, walked
beside the horse, and I walked alongside, a sort of nondescript, in
my old officer's greatcoat that I had worn before the revolution,
and a grey fur hat. I had, of course, no military insignia, but might
well have been a disreputable adherent of either side in the civil
war.

Towards evening the road dropped over a low hill and disappeared into forest. At the entrance to the forest a single horseman was on guard, with a carbine slung on his back. On seeing
us, he unslung his carbine and sat there, motionless on his horse,
with his carbine pointing at us. It might have been an incident
from medieval warfare. We were alone, our comic party coming
wearily down the road towards the forest, and this silent sentinel
watching our approach. The boy hesitated.

'Don't stop,' I said to him and he walked stolidly on, his eyes,
like ours, on the horseman, whose uniform I was trying to
identify. It was Esthonian. On that fluid front it might have been
anything.

The horseman kept us covered until we were within a few
yards of him. Then he asked, in Russian (a tribute, probably, to
my long coat and fur hat), 'Where are you going?'

'London,' I replied.

This must have startled him slightly. There was a moment's
silence.

'By what route?' he asked.

'By Marienhausen.'

I expected further questions but, after another pause, he merely
nodded to us to go on. We went on out of the daylight into the
shadows of the forest. There could be no question now as to
whether or no we were within the lines of the Whites. But why
had this sentinel at the gates of the forest been ready so easily to
let us pass?

We very soon knew. The thunder of hoofs sounded behind us. I looked back and saw a small body of cavalry coming after us at a gallop. The solitary horseman must have known that the responsibility of a decision need not be his.

'Keep moving,' I told my imperturbable boy. Then, just as the foremost horseman reached us, I turned round and fairly roared at them, 'Have you got an officer with you?'

They reined up smartly and said they had not.

'Are you going to Marienhausen?'

'Exactly so, Excellency.' Good, I thought, for my old grey coat.

'On with you and tell them I am coming.'

They saluted, and the whole troop galloped past us and disappeared. The thunder of the hoofs died away. We were alone again. Our boy stared moon-faced at me, wondering what sort of an employer he had got. I was wondering myself.

That was another stile crossed, but I could not be sure that the method of crossing it would not raise still greater difficulties ahead. It did not. I do not know what sort of authoritative monster the cavalrymen reported on the road behind them. But they must have reported somebody very different from poor Evgenia, sitting on the luggage, the straw-sucking bumpkin and my very much worried self, only too conscious that, having got rid of my White papers lest they should be found by the Reds, and got rid of my Red papers lest they should be found by the Whites, I should find it extremely difficult to meet serious examination of any kind.

But our luck held. The Whites had indeed captured Marienhausen, but by the time we reached that straggling village, their regular troops had already gone far beyond it and the place was held by irregulars, who, luckily for us, were under the command of a non-commissioned officer of the old regime with a strong sense of what was due to his superiors. After we had left the forest and come within sight of the village, we saw a disorderly crowd in the road and, as we came near, heard loud parade-ground commands. The crowd divided and lined both sides of the road. They were an extraordinary collection of Lettish irregulars, Robinson Crusoes, some with fowling-pieces, a few with rifles, some with pitchforks, all turned into soldiers by having belts round their middles, to hold together their ragged sheepskins. The stout corporal was walking up and down the ranks, doing his best to make them dress by the right and look a little bit more like what he had been accustomed to on parade. My boy looked at me with some misgiving; and, indeed, the idea of being arrested, plundered and possibly finished off by these savages was not a pleasant one. We need not have worried. As we reached the village, a word of command rang out in a good parade-ground voice. All the Robinson Crusoes presented arms, fowling-pieces, pitchforks and all, and then, with a crash, grounded their weapons, as the corporal, with a magnificent, spacious salute, stood before me awaiting orders.

'Have you arranged lodgings for the night?'

'At once. At once, your Honour.'

He went off towards a near-by one-storey wooden house, went into it, came out, went into another, and, coming out again, invited me to inspect it. In the main room a Jewish family were sitting. He disregarded them and led me to another room behind it, almost without furniture. He gave loud orders to the Jews, who hurried to turn the place into a possible camping-place and then brought us a share of their supper. He stood in the doorway and asked if there was anything else I wanted. I asked for our luggage to be brought in, and said that I should like my horse, cart and driver to be ready outside at six-thirty next morning, and that he was to see to it that horse and driver were properly lodged and fed. All, he said, would be as I wished.

We ate a little bread and some soup, and settled down in our clothes, wondering what we should find in the morning. I did not wish to show either eagerness or the slightest suspicion that my orders would not be obeyed. They were. At six-thirty in the morning there was the cart, the horse and a very cheerful boy. There were the Robinson Crusoes and their corporal to give us a spectacular send-off. Our luggage was piled in. Evgenia took her seat on the top of it and we were on our way again.

Thanks to a loud voice and a long grey coat we had been able to deal with Lettish irregulars and a corporal, but I knew that the real danger would come when we met regular troops, who would want explanations and would view with suspicion anybody who had been able to come through the Red front. There were plenty of trees about, we were still in the battle area, and I did not much like the idea that the first embittered officers we met on the White side might, without asking questions, do the natural thing and string us up at once as spies. We had nothing whatever to show that we had any right to be there. However, there was only one thing to do, and that was to keep going and to enjoy the morning sunshine. We marched on and on, very slowly.

At last, coming to meet us on the road, we saw a long column of cavalry, with a small group of officers riding at the head of it. No audacious shout would be any use here. We marched on ... We marched on ... and then there occurred a fantastic miracle, such a miracle as had not been among any of the possibilities I had foreseen. I was walking along, smoking my pipe, and hoping that the moment of meeting would somehow bring the right words into my mouth, when it seemed to me that there was something familiar in the look of the young officer in command. I stared at him. He stared at me. He suddenly shot forward, pulled up his horse, and exclaimed, 'What luck! Now we can have that other game of chess! We were on the point of stopping anyhow.'

I had last met that young officer at Tarnopol in Galicia, when we had played a really memorable game of chess, in which, at a moment when he had obviously been winning, I had been fortunate enough to bring off a smothered mate. Nothing is more galling than such an ending to a game that has seemed won, and he had at once demanded his revenge. We had been interrupted even while we were setting up the pieces and had never met again until now. It never for a moment occurred to him that I had not as much right as himself to be where we were.

He halted his men. Field-kitchens became busy and while soup was being made ready, he and I sat at the side of the road and had our game. He trounced me handsomely. I told him we were on our way to Reval. 'I'll give you a chit to our General,' he said, wrote one, gave it to me and told me where I should find the staff. The rest of our journey was pure comic opera. We found the general in a railway-siding. He was charming, said his own railway-car was at our disposal, apologised to Evgenia for the cockroaches in it and sent us on to Reval in what, in spite of the cockroaches, seemed to us luxury.

In Reval I saw Mr Piip. All went as planned. An armistice was proposed and instantly accepted, and a few weeks later Russians and Esthonians were sitting together in Dorpat to conclude a peace-treaty that was the first sign of the ending of the Interventionist wars, and gave Esthonia the twenty years of independence that lasted until the second period of chaos that began with the Russo-German pact of 1939, the manœuvring that followed and the marching and counter-marching of Russian and German armies that turned the whole of the Baltic Provinces into hell. Some years later, when these horrors were still veiled from us, Mr Piip stopped me in the street and said, 'I have been going through our archives of 1919–1920 and I should like to tell you that you have a very honourable place in Esthonian history.' I think that is the only time that anybody has ever said 'Thank you' for any of my amateur meddling in public affairs.

Once in Reval, with Evgenia safely on the same side of the front as myself, I collapsed with the usual stomach troubles and a sharp attack of something like brain-fever. But Evgenia and a good Esthonian doctor pulled me through, and I bobbed up into a happy convalescence in a fantastic room of the Golden Lion, the mural decorations of which commemorated the stay in it of the Tsar Alexander III. The long-drawn-out worry of 1919 was at an end.

# BOOK THREE

# CHAPTER XXXVI

## *Sailing on the Baltic*

The doctor who looked after me when I was ill in Reval told us of a family with a house in the woods at Lodenzee where I might well find a quiet room in which to write. This was soon arranged and, after going down to Dorpat to see what I could of the Russian-Esthonian Peace Conference, in the little town that both Evgenia and I had severally known as long ago as 1913, we made this house in the forest our headquarters. At long intervals I made a journey into Russia and then, at Lodenzee, untroubled by any censorship, wrote a series of articles for the *Manchester Guardian*. These the Russians sometimes resented, but by now I was not the only correspondent in Russia. Professional journalists were pouring in, and I had only to wait a few months before the Russians had forgotten my sins in their indignation at the greater sins of others, and were glad to let me come in again to have another look round. I do not propose to chronicle every such visit. C. P. Scott of the *Manchester Guardian* gave me a very free hand. I kept an eye on what was happening and went into Russia whenever I thought it necessary. Apart from this work for the *Guardian*, I was doing what I could to pick up the threads of my own work that had come to a ragged end on the day when, on coming out of hospital in Petrograd in 1915, I had written my first telegram to the *Daily News*, my first, indeed, to any newspaper. I had never stopped feeling like a man picked haphazard out of the crowd to act as substitute and field in a Test Match. Sooner or later, I knew, I should be relieved and able to hand over to people far better equipped than myself.

There was still snow on the ground when we first went to Lodenzee, to the wooden house in the forest at the head of Lahepe Bay. But spring came in with a rush, as it does in the Baltic. The little streams unfroze and in a room on the upper floor, with a balcony from which I could get a glimpse of the sea,

I was again enjoying myself mightily, digging into ancient Baltic history, learning a little Esthonian, and once more making endless experiments in the art of narrative, almost all of which ended rightly in the stove. Mr Piip and others at the Esthonian Foreign Office helped me with Russian books that told of the far-away days when Esthonia was strong enough to send an expedition to Sweden and carry away the gates of Sigtuna. I refrain from giving a list of the romances that were never more than begun. But to think of them was a delight to me and, far away in England, Mr Collingwood rejoiced that I was interested in Storkatter as well as in Lenin, and wrote to Professor Ekwall of Lund to find out if there was Swedish confirmation of the Esthonian legend. Their letters helped to make me feel that I was not going to be head over ears in politics for ever. Politicians, I suppose, will not understand how anybody should wish to be quit of politics. But I was not a politician. I have a certain mulishness of character but no ambition of the kind that politicians need. As a small boy I had wanted to write books. I still wanted to write them, just as I wanted to fish and to sail small boats.

Our hostess, at that house in the woods, did not, happily for me, approve of political discussion. War and civil war were still too near. Her guests were so mixed that political talk would have been dangerous to the peace. There were business men. There were officers of the Esthonian army. There were Russians of the old regime. There were Esthonians in a hurry to trade with the new. But there were no quarrels. It was only a short run to Reval and we soon had many friends there. The Wyatts at the Consulate were simple and kind. They were succeeded by Leslie who brought a library with him and had a passion for Henry James.

Not far away, in the woods, to be reached only after a walk along difficult tracks, and the crossing of a small river by walking along a doubtfully balanced tree-trunk, and the careful circumnavigation of a marsh loud with frogs, we found a little lake where we caught perch and pike that were joyfully received by our hostess. There we made a regular camp, keeping up a good smoky fire to win us a rest from the mosquitoes. Walking home in the northern dusk we enjoyed the green lanterns of the glowworms gleaming in the grass at the side of the path. Our hostess, hearing that I was interested in snakes, brought me the not very welcome present of an adder caught by herself. We also had a tame hedgehog that ate ants and woodlice, bread-and-milk and scraps of meat.

Reval, our metropolis and shopping-centre, was built as a fortress on a rock, and from that rock one looks out over a wide bay, with the green wooded island of Nargon on one side of it, a long promontory on the other, and far out beyond the bay a horizon of open sea. I do not believe that a man can look out from that rock and ever be wholly happy until he has got a boat of his own. I could not, and on each of my visits to Reval I walked round the harbour looking for something that would float and had a mast and a sail. I pestered the fishermen, the masters of the little schooners and cutters, the masters of the British steamships that with the coming of peace began to arrive at Reval harbour with goods for the Esthonians to sell to the Russians. More than once I found the quays covered with things under green tarpaulins with my own name blazoned in very large letters, agricultural machinery from Ransome's of Ipswich. Trade was looking up and the masters of the Baltic Corporation steamers and others smuggled English tobacco for me and gave advice about boats, plenty of advice, and promised to bring me an old ship's lifeboat from England, but always forgot.

In the end, walking one day along the beach, I came upon a man putting a lick of green paint on a long, shallow boat with a squarely cut-off transom that had once carried an outboard motor. She had a mast. She was for sale. On the beach beside her were large round boulders. I prodded her here and there and asked her price. The man named a sum that sounded enormous in Esthonian marks but when translated into English money came to something under ten pounds. The price included the boulders on the beach. I hurried off to the harbour, collected a friend from an English steamship, a sea-captain whose kindness makes me ashamed that I have forgotten his name, and brought him to look at her.

'She'll do to sail in the bay,' he said.

'But I want to take her to Lahepe.' This was some forty miles away along the coast.

'Pick your weather,' he said, and added, 'Have you got a compass?'

I had only the little dry pocket-compass that had once brought me back to the Russian lines.

'That's no good,' he said, 'but I saw one that would do this morning when I was in the town.'

I bought that boat, on condition that next day she should be ready for sea, and went off with my sea-captain to a little watch-maker's shop, where we bought two compasses at ten shillings each and he, saying that my need was greater than his, let me have my choice of them. Mine was a small pocket prismatic compass by Negretti & Zambra. It was full of bubbles but, back in his ship, my friend cured that and I hurried off, master if not of a ship, at least of an open boat and of a compass much better than my vessel. I have used that compass since in all sorts of small vessels in the Baltic and the North Sea. It has been with me to China and to the Sudan, and at this moment, still as good as ever, it is lying on the table beside my typewriter. I found Evgenia, told her what I had done and said I would sail the boat from Reval to Lahepe next day. Evgenia, full of quite unjustified faith in me as a mariner, said that she was coming too.

Next day there was an almost dead calm. We were in a hurry to try the boat. The owner had brought down to the beach an ancient, patched gaff-mainsail and a staysail. The boulders had vanished from the beach and were now in the boat. 'Big sail,' said the owner. 'You want plenty stone for ballast.' We climbed in and were pushed off. There were a pair of abominable heavy sweeps with which I pulled offshore, determining never to use them again. I hoisted the sails. There came a breath of wind and slowly, slowly, so slowly that we there and then christened her *Slug*, she moved out into the middle of the bay and we were looking at the rock of Reval from the sea as I had so often promised that we should.

We were in the middle of the bay when the wind died to nothing. *Slug* lay with drooping sails on glassy water. It was very hot. I jumped overboard to get cool and to look at my lovely command. I lay in the water admiring her and did not notice a light ripple that crept across the bay. The sails filled and *Slug* began to move. She moved slowly but I should have liked her to move slower. Evgenia shouted to me to come back to the ship. I swam after her as hard as I could, caught hold of her gunwale, which now seemed a long way above me, and found that I could not get into her. I tried again and again, and began to think that I should have to hang there until she found her way to shallow water. But the wind was getting up and *Slug* was heading as if for Finland. I pulled myself hand over hand along her gunwale to her bows. She had a short iron bowsprit, and with the help of this unsympathetic bit of iron I scrambled back aboard, to be received, very properly, with curses. Afterwards, in shallow water, I tried many times to climb aboard in that way. I could not do it. I suppose the knowledge that there was no other way was the only thing that had made it possible. Once I was aboard, the wind dropped again and we slowly drifted to the eastern side of the bay, landed, took the anchor up the beach, made a fire, and camped. It is astonishing that this experience did not deprive me of my crew.

Next day, with a light wind, we pushed off again. I am ashamed to say that I had only a very small-scale map of the coast. We sailed to the island of Nargon and landed there for a meal. We sailed again and suddenly, after more drifting, found the boat thrown over by a squall, water pouring over the gunwale and some of the boulders shifting. She righted and for about half an hour we moved at a good speed and were pleased with *Slug* for keeping on a fairly even keel, whereas a large trading-cutter that rushed past us heading for Reval had her lee-scuppers under. The wind dropped as suddenly as it had risen, and we crawled slowly westward. Night fell, and a very dark one. Surop lighthouse blinked at us from the mainland. It took us a long time to pass it. Pakerort lighthouse, on the further side of the entrance to Lahepe Bay, told us where the mouth of the bay must be. But we could see nothing. At last, as the Pakerort light rose above us on its cliff, I headed *Slug* southwards by the luminous card of the pocket-compass. Luckily she was moving very slowly. We stared into the darkness, trying to see the line of the land and the sky. Both were black. There were no lights on shore. It must have been about two in the morning and wise folk on land were asleep. Suddenly, close by, we heard a loud barking. Next moment, I thought, our keel must grind ashore. I dropped the anchor over and found bottom with it in two fathoms. I brought the sails down. Tired right out, far too tired to talk, we fell instantly asleep, on the boulders in the bottom of the boat.

We were woken by more barking, so loud and near that I thought we must have drifted ashore while we slept. The dawn had come. I looked sleepily over the gunwale into the eyes of a large seal who, with shining head and dripping whiskers, might have been an elderly business man, bathing at Margate. He blew through his whiskers, barked again, dived, and was gone. What for a moment I had thought were other seals, all round us, were the tops of rocks. I still do not understand how we had come to where we were without hitting any of them. All round us they dotted the water that we must have come through in the dark. We paddled carefully clear of the rocks, hoisted sail to a light westerly wind and an hour later anchored in about four feet of water off the shore at the head of Lahepe Bay, where our friends from the house in the forest were accustomed to bathe. We had no dinghy, so waded triumphantly ashore with our baggage on our heads.

It was a ridiculous beginning, to take an open boat for sixty miles of sailing, mostly tacking, along a coast we did not know, but it was not more ridiculous than some of our later experiments. Evgenia had never been in a sailing boat before, and I owe it alike to her ignorance and her courage that this first voyage did not in any way deter her from other adventures. We have never since been without some sort of boat, and for a number of years worked very hard to make ourselves reasonably efficient, taking every chance of sailing in vessels of every kind as well as in our own.

I will say no more of *Slug*, ill-fated boat. Lahepe Bay was not a very good place in which to keep her afloat. We could reach her only by swimming, and get ashore only by deep wading after bringing her in. We used a raft as a dinghy and it had a bad habit of tipping us sideways into the water. *Slug* twice sank at her moorings. Once we left her snugly at anchor and came down to the shore again to find that her mainsail had been stolen. The Esthonian Admiralty was persuaded to release the few yards of canvas needed for the making of a new one, with which she sailed a good deal better. The thieves were never caught, but one day there arrived a captain, a sergeant and a lesser policeman with a paper they asked me to sign, to say that, in my opinion, 'the Esthonian Police had done their best'. I signed it. Those were wild times, and what more could they have done? The captain of a British merchant ship whom I met looking grimmer than usual told me, 'You are not the only one. Last night, in Reval harbour, with armed guards on the quay, I had the compass stolen out of the binnacle.' We had a lot of fun with *Slug* and the raft, but knew that she was only a makeshift. Our walls were covered with Baltic charts and the plans of boats, and I was able to sweep the worries of writing about Russia out of my head by teaching myself the elements of navigation.

# CHAPTER XXXVII

## *A Brigadier and a Funeral*

One of my excursions to Russia during 1920 was in February. On the evening of the 3rd, after wasting much of the afternoon in bothering the Foreign Commissariat about my passport, I went to the Kremlin to call on Madame Radek and to play with Radek's baby. Radek was away in the Caucasus. The baby, little Sonia, whom I had seen when she was three days old, was now nearly two, and she made friends at once, blowing out matches with great gusto, saying *Dai-ka Spichki,* 'Give matches,' telling me her name, running up to her father's portrait, a very poor pastel drawing, and telling me that was 'papa'. I was talking with Mrs Radek of old times at the beginning of the revolution, when we heard a heavy tread in the next room. She smiled and said, 'Here is someone you know,' and in walked a girl wearing a military cap, a skin coat with the fur outside, a leather coat underneath it, and enormous cavalry boots. She took off her cap, releasing a mop of curly hair, and I knew her for Mira, Radek's secretary of 1918, turned somehow into a different woman. Then she had had a very bad time and was constantly in tears over her bad typing and worse memory, and at being told by Radek (not without cause) to wash her face. Now she had grown broader, her pale face had filled out and become rosy, and she was shy at taking off her leather coat. Underneath it was a very neat, perfectly ordinary girl's dress of blue serge. I could not imagine what the shyness was about. 'It's because I can't get accustomed to being in girls' clothes.' Mrs Radek laughed. 'Let me present you,' she said, 'to a brigade commander of Budenny's famous cavalry army.' And that, indeed, is what this shy and rather tearful young lady had become.

Here is her story. On leaving school she joined one of the voluntary committees for looking after the children of the refugees who poured eastward over Russia at the time of

295

the German invasion. She became a Socialist and took part in the revolution of March 1917, after which she worked with the Bolsheviks, took part in the October Revolution and went out with the workmen who fought against the German advance. Then came the time when she worked as a secretary. In the spring of 1918 she went off to the front to do Red Cross work. She was on the Volga and afterwards in the Ukraine. Then in 1919 she was made Political Commissar of a company, and rose to be Political Commissar of a brigade. She was then with the infantry. She was in Kiev when that town had to be evacuated in a hurry and she organised the removal of all the wounded, for which she was presented with an inscribed gold watch. During the civil war against Denikin, she and some others were isolated and, though she had never been on a horse before, she had either to ride or be captured. She rode eighty miles in a day and a night and thereafter was attached to the cavalry. She fought in one skirmish after another and was given military command of a squadron, rising swiftly to command a brigade, taking part in Budenny's dash through Galicia, fighting all through the Polish campaign, riding from Poland to the Crimea (Budenny's cavalry never used a train), taking part in the defeat of Wrangel when she rode with her men to the rear of Wrangel's army and captured a base, including an American Relief Officer doing accounts in his special waggon and believing that the front was miles away. She was one of the first three of the Red Army to ride into Simferopol. And, after all this, here she was, feeling funny in a girl's dress, drinking tea and eating potatoes in the Radeks' flat, very shy and very unhappy that the war was over, so that she had to come back to typewriters again and their accompanying tears.

She told me of Budenny's Cossacks, who brought away with them their wives and children, for fear the Whites should cut them to pieces. They brought with them, each man, as many horses as he could, his carts and most precious belongings. Each man was his own commissariat and had his own camp-followers. In the Polish war the women and children were left behind, but the carts and spare horses were taken on. If a man was wounded he lay in his own cart, taking to his horse again as soon as he could, rather than be left behind. The baggage-train was a thing to see, cart after cart, with three horses to pull it, and two or three more tied behind. Then there were the camels, which provided endless amusement for the infantrymen of Central Russia, who had never seen such things. Mira described the joy of the soldiers of an infantry division which happened to halt near them on finding that the camels spat in your face if you touched their noses. Every soldier in the division insisted on being spat at in his turn.

She told of the break-up of Wrangel's army, the portmanteaux, rifles, machine-guns, some spoilt but most of them in good condition, left by the flying Whites. She told how Cossacks who had served with Wrangel threw themselves on the mercy of the Reds, explaining that they had run away rather than be put aboard ships to be taken off to Constantinople. Many even of the White officers hid themselves, and in Simferopol she had seen a queue of White officers along a whole street, awaiting registration. The Whites had made a pogrom in the town before leaving it, and buildings were still smoking when the Reds came in. Rifles were lying everywhere about the streets. They found undamaged tanks, undamaged aeroplanes, uniforms for an army. 'We owe all that to you,' she said; 'both on the Polish front and in the Crimea we clothed all our men in English uniforms which you had sent the Whites. The result was a bit funny, for you could not tell White from Red soldiers. All had English uniforms and the towns in the Crimea were crowded with Wrangel's men who had put a scrap of red round their arms.

'What did you do with the Cossacks who joined you and asked to be allowed to fight? How could you tell whom to trust?' 'Simple,' said Mira. 'We asked each man where he came from, and then called for one of our men who came from that place. Then we asked him how he came to be with the Whites. If he told a lie, the Cossack from his village would know, and that was the end of him. If he told the truth, and his fellow-countryman said, "All right," then up with him on one of the spare horses, and on to show what he was worth in the next fight.'

Early in this book I told how Prince Kropotkin guided my infant steps when I first went on the ice at Adel outside Leeds. I had met him again in Russia in 1917. He died in Moscow in 1920, and on February 13 at about half-past eleven I walked out with Jonas Lied, over the Kamenny Bridge, to the Church of the Saviour, hoping to meet the Kropotkin funeral procession there, on its way to the cemetery of the Dyevitchii Monastery. The bier should have left the Hall of the Trade Unions at eleven. It was a cold, windy day, but with clear blue sky and bright sun. We asked a

10*

passing soldier whether the procession had already passed. 'Oh no,' he said, 'it is delayed because they are letting the imprisoned anarchists out of gaol to take part in it, and they have not yet arrived.'

We walked along towards the centre of the town, thinking we should meet the procession and stopping at corners that seemed to offer positions of vantage until the cold drove us to move on. In this way we came slowly to the Okhotnia Ryadi, opposite the old National Hotel, now the First House of the Soviets. From here we could see red flags over a considerable crowd in front of the Hall of the Unions. Again we halted, but, finding that the flags remained stationary, we moved on, making up our minds to wait opposite the white church, the high steps of which were crowded. The little wooden booths, which in the autumn of 1918 had been covered with Futurist decorations, had been removed, but we noticed a small group of people standing by the walls of the disreputable-looking houses. We found that they were selling loaves of white bread and simple cakes. The loaves (very small ones) were four thousand roubles apiece. The cakes, which were really no more than whitish bread lightly touched over with sugar, were fifteen hundred roubles. The sellers were of all classes. There was an old peasant woman, a young man of twenty demobilised from the army, or having demobilised himself from more useful work, and a girl in what had once been a rich cloak of blue velvet. Each had loaves or cakes hidden in a bit of rag or newspaper and, as we came nearer, remarked without emphasis, opening their packages, 'Real white loaves!' 'I too have white loaves.' 'My cakes are very tasty.' The cake-seller was the girl in blue velvet. Her hands were badly frost-bitten. We asked the prices. The two loaf-sellers did not mention the thousands, but replied, as the sledge-drivers reply, 'Four.' 'Thousand' was understood. The girl in blue, with curious precision, said, 'One thousand, five hundred.' We bought two and ate them while we waited. (Very soon the street-sellers were counting not in thousands but in millions.)

It was nearly one o'clock before the procession started. A company of small boys in grey military coats and girls in big white fur hats with flaps that hung down to their shoulders, covering the whole head and neck, formed a line down the middle of the road. Then a company of military students (young proletarians about to become officers) took up their positions and began marking time to keep warm. The crowd was largely made up of young women with their friends, laughing, talking, linking arms and stamping on the snow or even dancing because of the extreme cold. Here and there were more picturesque figures. There was an old peasant clad in skins from head to foot, the fur inside and the untanned leather out. Close to him stood a Cossack with a high black sheep-skin hat, and a great black *burka*, a loose cloak of black very thick shaggy woollen cloth hanging from the shoulders to below the knees.

At last the procession began to move forward from the House of the Unions, once the Club of the Nobility. First came some wreaths, then, on men's shoulders, the elaborately carved and painted coffin-lid, and then, again on men's shoulders, the shallow, open coffin. Kropotkin lay with one very thin hand across his breast. But for the thinness of that hand one would hardly have known that he was dead. The sunshine poured down on his face. I had last seen him talking with Sir George Buchanan, in the elaborately futile British propaganda office on the Fontanka in Petrograd, some three years before. Then, as now, my attention was caught by his nose, so finely cut, so proud, the very index of the old fighter's character. Close behind the coffin came half-a-dozen of the chief mourners and then a mass of his Anarchist disciples. There were some who had imitated his hair, some who had grown beards like his, but not one had a nose worth looking at. Kropotkin was greater than his theories, but these little showy creatures were nothing in themselves, raised as it were spuriously, clinging to his theories like sparrows to telegraph wires. That mob of noseless disciples was an ironic comment on the proud old man being carried before them through the Moscow sunshine to his grave in the cemetery by the river opposite the Sparrow Hills. They carried banners inscribed 'Anarchists demand liberation from the prison of Socialism' and 'Where there is Authority there is no Freedom' but they reminded me of an old cartoon of the funeral of Peter the Great, representing the burial of the cat by the mice. Kropotkin and his disciples belonged to two different worlds.

After the Anarchists with their black flags came the red banners of non-Anarchist mourners, expressing their respect for the old veteran who, by being so much greater than his theories, had taken his place above the programmes and become one of the great revolutionary figures of his century. Last of all came half-a-dozen horsemen, police troopers, symbols of the very authority of whose passing Kropotkin had dreamed. They were led by a fat man in a red fur coat, worrying with his spurs a very fine horse. Lied told me that he was one of the chiefs of the Extraordinary Commission. His presence was as unnecessary as his spurs. There was no disturbance, nor any idea of disturbance. The Anarchist movement will not deserve such respect until among its disciples it can show men with such noses as that of the dead leader.

# CHAPTER XXXVIII

## *From* Kittiwake *to* Racundra

In 1921, after a brief visit to Russia, where I noted in my diary, 'Temperature in hotel reduced to three degrees above freezing because of the fuel shortage,' I was back in Reval in March, writing articles for the *Manchester Guardian*.

The *Slug* had whetted our appetite for a better boat, one with a cabin. Wandering round the harbour we saw one which we decided would take us as far as the little harbour of Baltic Port where we planned to spend the summer. With a timely windfall from an American paper we bought her and called her *Kittiwake* because we liked the picture of that gull in Coward's bird-book and imagined we were the first to think of it. Later we found that a great many other people had the same idea and that there were flocks of *Kittiwakes* in English waters. She was a bit of a joke really, sixteen foot long over all with a beam of six foot and a draught of five—her normal keel having been deepened by a rather flimsy addition. With such a deep draught we needed a dinghy for getting ashore, but there was no boatbuilder in Reval to make one. Eventually I found a firm of undertakers and pointed out to them that if they could make coffins they could make dinghies. They agreed to try and a few days later produced a triangular box looking like the bows of a boat sawn off square by the first thwart. There never was such a boat for capsizing. If I shifted my pipe from one side of my mouth to the other I never knew what might happen. However, there it was, a dinghy, better than nothing. We fitted out *Kittiwake* with mattresses for her two horribly narrow bunks, orange curtains for her miniature portholes, a primus, a kettle, a saucepan, a frying pan, a couple of plates, a couple of mugs, knives, forks, spoons, and were ready for sea.

For practice we started taking her out of harbour every day. She was top-heavy and heeled over to her cabin-top even with two reefs down and we had to steady her with scrap-iron ballast, hoping wishfully that she would learn good manners. But we lost faith rapidly, and this made us more and more determined to have a really good boat, big and comfortable to live on board for months on end and fit to be sailed to England if and when we wanted to do so.

At about that time we met Otto Eggers and both fell in love with him. Before the war he was a very well known boat-designer and boat-builder with a big boatyard in Reval. The war, the revolution, and Esthonia's new nationalism (he was a German) left him without his boatyard and with no hope of recovering all he had lost. Soon we were talking of boats and infecting each other with dreams of perfect ones. It ended in our asking him to design our dream boat and he agreed to do it. This resulted in *Racundra* and my book, *Racundra's First Cruise*.

On the 11th of May we sailed from Reval to Baltic Port. It was a very slow passage as we first became becalmed between Reval and Nargon and then, a strong wind rising suddenly, we had a rough time between Surop and Pakerort, and while we were rounding the last headland the coffin dinghy flung itself bodily up on the counter, hitting me in the back. With the wind astern we came into the bay and turning into the wind to get through the narrow entrance we found that more than half the harbour was filled by a British steamer, the *Cato*, commanded by a friend. A rope was flung from her and presently we were moored in the harbour. I went ashore to book rooms in the little hotel kept by the harbourmaster, and being very tired after twenty-five hours at the tiller fell asleep with my head on his table. It was impossible to live on board *Kittiwake*, but the harbourmaster and his wife were extremely kind and made us very comfortable in their hotel.

We sailed in *Kittiwake*, in *Cato*'s whaleboats and in the harbour-master's little skiff. I fished in the little river Joesuu at the head of the bay. And all the time I was working on a series of articles on Russia's relations with the East.

This happy summer based on Baltic Port ended half way through August when we moved our headquarters to Latvia. We rented rooms in a small house in Kaiserwald, outside Riga, on the shores of Stint See, a pleasant lake beside the forest. A Lettish boat-builder made me, in a few days, a small boat for fishing and sailing with a fishbox built round the centreboard case and a small leg-of-mutton sail.

I had several meetings with Nansen, a hero since my childhood. I spent an afternoon sitting with him on the shore of the Gulf of Riga being smilingly scolded for swimming much too far out to sea. He was then and for years afterwards doing more than any other man to mitigate for thousands upon thousands the miseries caused by the political upheavals of those times. I shall always see him as I saw him that day, the great, blond Norseman sitting under the tall pines which grow to the very edge of that glittering tideless sea, the most civilised person of his generation, unmoved by party bitterness of any kind, imperturbably doing what he knew was right in spite of the vicious attacks that came at him from all sides. Nansen knew the Collingwoods (through the Viking Club) so we also talked of the Skald and my dear aunt.

I now got (not without difficulty) permission to visit the Volga regions, which were suffering from the worst famine in years. I took with me an American cinematograph man who hoped to show America how badly help was needed. We went to Moscow, from there to Samara, and then some distance up and down the river by steamer. Typhus was raging among the starving people, who had no energy and often no means of keeping themselves clean. The dead and the quick were all crawling with lice — the carriers of typhus. I think I owe my immunity to Madame Radek, who made me take a large bottle of turpentine which I rubbed on my neck, wrists and ankles to discourage the loathsome insects. At night I used to sweep clean a bit of the iron deck, trickle a line of turpentine round it and lie down to sleep as it were inside a moat. When we returned to Riga my cinemato-graphing friend, who seemed to think it a miracle to have gone into Russia and come out alive, attributed extraordinary powers to me, so that when a little later another cinematographer had gone into Russia and somehow got himself arrested, I received a telegram from his firm in America which has been a pleasure to me ever since for its frank recognition of comparative values. It ran: PLEASE RESCUE OUR APPARATUS AND IF POSSIBLE OUR OPERATOR. I showed this telegram to the Russians, who were very much amused and said it was a perfect example of capitalist mentality. The operator was released. I am not sure what happened to the apparatus. Back in Riga I settled down to write my account of the famine.

I liked the little fishing dinghy well enough to think it possible that the Riga boat-builder could translate my dream ship (on whose design Eggers had been working while I was in Russia) from paper into fact. The man had built an eight-tonner and was confident that he could build my boat. I went to Reval, talked it over with Eggers, came back with the preliminary drawings, showed them to the builder, and before leaving for England, took a deep breath and signed the contract, determined one way or another to do enough writing to pay for it. This was among the few wise things I have done in my life, for, more than anything else, this boat helped me to get back to my proper trade of writing.

In England I saw a good deal of Ted Scott, renewing our schoolboy acquaintance and laying the foundation of that friendship that lasted till his death. I stayed with him in Manchester and at his cottage at Bosley where, later on, I induced his elder boy to take to fishing. Dick, now middle-aged and a responsible official in the Foreign Office, has probably forgotten a charming episode of his early youth. He was still a small boy when I came to Bosley one summer day and found them all at lunch. I put my car in the yard, and noticed a fishing rod leaning against the wall. From the rod a long line hung and trailed along the ground. Thinking him a careless little brute to leave the line without winding it on his reel, I followed it and found that the end of it was buried in a tin of earth. In the earth, still on the hook, was a worm. Dick had kindly and thoughtfully made his worm comfortable while he ate his lunch.

I saw my mother, Molly Hamilton and, of course, the Collingwoods. In London I was delighted by Fred Ranalow singing Macheath in *The Beggars' Opera*. I did not know then that he had married a girl I used to play with as a child in Leeds, nor did I foresee that many years later he and I would be regular opponents in the billiard-room of the Garrick Club.

1922 began with a very cold January and February during which I was in Riga, Reval, Helsingfors and Moscow. There was a great deal of ice and I had many opportunities of watching ice-breakers and the relentless way of ice with boats. Once I saw a small steamer which had been pushed by moving ice against a rock, overturned, and as she was lying on her beam ends an ice-field went over the top of her. I was able to look in under the canopy of ice to see the vertical decks of the unlucky vessel like a wooden wall inside a huge cave of glass. I saw a steamer limping into Helsingfors after taking a month to get there from Petrograd instead of the normal twenty-four hours. There were reports of ice-breakers losing touch with the convoys they were leading, as the moving ice blocked the channels they made. When ships are in ice, and the more so if the ice has been broken around them, it is the ice that takes command. To watch the edge of a field of ice perhaps two or three feet thick and a mile or so across, creeping irresistibly over another such field, is to know how weak a thing man is.

In March I was in England, mostly in Manchester, but snatching a few happy days with the Collingwoods, enjoying once more paddling across to the village in the old dinghy to bring back bread and a packet of tea, being laughed at by my aunt as in the old days, and sitting talking by the study fire with the Skald himself, who never lost a chance of reminding me that all this scurrying about, while possibly interesting, was irrelevant to my proper work of writing books. I knew that too, but was not as sure as he was that I should some day escape from scurrying.

Meanwhile *Racundra* was being built in a wooden shed on an island near the mouth of the Dvina river. My joy in the process was mitigated by all the delays and frustrations. We much enjoyed being members of the Riga Yacht Club, which was friendly, homely, cosy, and as active in winter as in summer, a popular meeting-place for sailors, ice-yachters and skaters. The only food was pork chops, sometimes apple tart to follow, and always coffee. Monotonous plain food but well cooked and satisfying after a strenuous sail on a really cold winter day. The kind motherly woman who managed the club was equally ready to cook the chops, look after babies too young to be taken sailing, or dry members' wet clothes.

There was another boat beside *Racundra* being built in Riga at that time. Her owner, a Lett, had been to England and seen Thames barges and lighters. It had struck this ingenious chap that if he fitted a lighter with leeboards and rigged her as a cutter he would be able to stow far more cargo in her than in any ordinary boat, and that with her shallow draught he would be able to bring her closer to the shore for loading or unloading and to take her further upstream than an ordinary boat of her size could go. She was built and looked like a large fishing punt, some forty foot long with slightly overhanging ends, square as a barn door, and the same fore and aft. His countrymen jeered, and jeered still more when he added a clumsy leeboard on either side. He

appealed to me as an Englishman to say that in England such
boats were entirely normal. When the *Freda* was ready, just as the
ice went, he challenged one of the jeerers, who had a fast cutter,
to race him on the Dvina and asked me as one who had seen
Thames barges in action to come with him. The other man took
up his challenge, but pointed out that the river, with the snow
melting up country, was coming down like a mill stream. The
*Freda*'s skipper was impatient to try his ship and the race was on.
We started in the smooth water of Muhlgraben and shot out into
the main river side by side to race up to the Riga bridge. We never
got there. If there had not been a strong northerly wind blowing
up the river we should both have been swept out to sea like corks.
At first both boats moved inch by inch up against the stream, the
water foaming round them. Then gradually the *Freda* drew
ahead and my skipper exulted, till he happened to look at the
shore and saw that, though roaring through the water, she was
not moving against the land and, as the wind began to drop, she
began to go astern. He had reefed before starting; now he set full
sail. The *Freda* remained exactly where she was, sailing like anything, while the other boat, also sailing extremely fast through the
water, went backwards until her skipper took his chance and shot
sideways into the Muhlgraben from which he had started. My
skipper was dancing with glee on the deck and as nearly as
possible capsized his ship. It was a famous victory, and the only
one I know in which a race was won by standing still.

The building of *Racundra* dragged on until I lost patience and
removed her, still unfinished, to the little harbour on the Stint See,
where an old sailor was looking after dinghies. As the Ancient
Mariner he became our crew on *Racundra* and also served as a
model for Peter Duck. He worked very hard and finished the
many jobs left undone by the builders in time for us to set sail on
August 20. The story of this delightful escape from politics is told
in *Racundra's First Cruise*.

After laying *Racundra* up for the winter very early I went to
Russia where I spent about a month. In December I went to
England, and in London met my wife and a couple of lawyers
to discuss arrangements for our divorce. Then I went to Barmouth
where the Collingwoods and Barbara were staying. I took with
me the diary-logbook which I kept while we sailed *Racundra*,
putting down as fully as possible the happenings of every day. I
told the Skald that I hoped sometime to make some sort of

account of sailing in the Eastern Baltic. He read it and urged me not to wait but to do it at once: 'You've got a book there ready-made.' I needed no further encouragement, and when I got back to Riga in time for Christmas the book was well advanced.

# CHAPTER XXXIX

## *The Curzon Ultimatum*

I finished *Racundra's First Cruise* at Kaiserwald before the end of January 1923 (it was published by Unwin later in the year) and then went to Russia. My concern was to pick up the threads of old acquaintanceships and to try and see what was happening in literature and the theatre. I attended, rather sceptically, meetings of 'organised' authors, which did not seem to be likely to result in the production of better books than can be written by authors not organised at all. I collected and read all the books in which my Russian friends found promise. I saw a horribly bad performance of *Tom Sawyer* at the Children's Theatre, besides even less interesting plays. I had talks with Litvinov and others, and I was delighted to see Radek's former secretary, the Brigadier, pushing a pram with her baby in the garden under the Kremlin wall.

Back in Riga, I made a translation of one of the books I had brought out of Russia, *A Week*, by Iury Libedinsky. This was the best of the short novels in which some of the younger writers were trying to show the revolution in terms of human beings. I do not think I could have found a better specimen of the new writing. The book had been attacked as 'counter-revolutionary' by the Communist papers and warmly defended by Bukharin. The author, however, presently became a member of the Communist party, became more and more involved in 'organisation' and joined with others in demanding that literature should toe the party line. I am old-fashioned enough to think that if literature is to be anything other than political journalism it must toe no line whatever. My translation was published in England and America but attracted little attention.

In the middle of March I left for England, where I saw the Collingwoods at Coniston and caught five trout at Lowick Bridge, stayed with Ted Scott in Manchester, caught fourteen trout at Bosley, and had a memorable beating at billiards from

308

John Scott. I returned to Riga at the end of April by way of Berlin. I saw pied flycatchers in the garden at Kaiserwald on May 4, had a squally cold sail on the Stint See, left Riga on May 6 and arrived in Moscow on the 8th to find yet another first-class crisis in Anglo-Russian relations. The supporters of Intervention had not yet given up hope. Curzon was Foreign Minister and he had sent a note to the British Mission in Moscow, to be delivered to the Russians, which had all the appearance of an ultimatum and indeed seemed intended to be a rejected ultimatum which, if it did not necessarily mean war, would have the result of breaking off even such trading relations as existed.

The note, in the most uncompromising language, made a number of unjustified and unjustifiable demands. What was serious, however, was something that was not in the note, and that was a peremptory instruction to R. M. Hodgson, the head of the Mission, to deliver the note without comment and not to discuss it in any way with the Russians. It was impossible not to think that, provocative as the note was, Curzon was deliberately making it more so by forbidding any sort of talk about it. I agreed with Hodgson in thinking that a break in relations was not inevitable, and also that the Russians, unable to have even a word with our representative in Moscow, would be bound to think that it was, and would therefore, having nothing to lose, delight Curzon by sending back a thoroughly uncompromising reply.

After dropping my luggage at the British Mission I went off at once to see the Russians. I found Litvinov, Bukharin, Zinoviev and Chicherin all in their different ways equally convinced that the British Government had determined to bring disagreement to the point of complete rupture. Russian public reactions were what was to be expected. There had been demonstrations in the streets. Curzon was hanged in effigy. It was clear that, thinking war inevitable, the Russians would compose a fighting reply rather than weaken their position in the eyes of their own people by making a peaceable gesture in vain. Yet the only way peace could be preserved was by making a gesture so peaceable that not even Curzon would be able to force a break.

I had talk after talk with Chicherin and Litvinov, who were already busy composing exactly the reply I feared. I urged them to throw it away and write another. They said they could not sacrifice the dignity of Russia by turning the other cheek to such a slap in the face as Curzon's note. I reminded them of the Bolshevik diplomat (Joffe) who wired from Berlin to ask if he must wear official dress at some state function, and of Lenin's instant reply, 'Wear a petticoat if you can get peace by doing so.'

They said, 'But it is perfectly clear that whatever we reply, short of a humiliating acceptance of the note *in toto*, we shall not get peace.' They believed the British Mission was packing its bags and eager to leave. They pointed out that they had been given no chance of talking with Hodgson. Curzon seemed to have created exactly the impasse that he needed, the impasse that was most certainly not wanted by the British Government as a whole.

I reported to Hodgson that so long as he was unable to see the Russians and tell them what I had told them, and what both he and I believed, nothing would prevent them from producing a reply that, while making inspiriting reading for revolutionaries, would slam the door on any new discussions, and throw things back to 1918. But Hodgson had had his instructions, to have no dealings with the Russian Foreign Office whatever. I spent hour after hour in earnest argument with the Russians. I have seldom drunk so much tea in the Kremlin in so short a time. In the end a few of them began to think that it might be possible to compromise if only there was any chance that the compromise would be accepted. It became obvious that the only thing to do was to disregard Curzon's instructions to Hodgson and to bring about the meeting that Curzon had forbidden. Again after much discussion, it was agreed that Litvinov would be prepared to go for a walk in the woods at a place outside Moscow, if I could persuade Hodgson to go for a similar walk in the same woods. Hodgson, to his great honour, knowing that he was risking his career, said that he 'was ready to go with me to spend an afternoon in the country'.

The place chosen was an estate with a fine old house that was being used as a rest home for officials. Hodgson and I drove out there and, walking in the woods, we met, by a remarkable accident, Litvinov, also out for a stroll. The *convenances* were well preserved. Litvinov and Hodgson put up quite a good show of surprise, and I left these two strangers together, and myself went to the old house, found a number of acquaintances from the various Commissariats and was immediately challenged to a game of chess by Krylenko, who was just finishing a game with Ganetzky. We had just ended our game when Litvinov and Hodgson came in for me. Krylenko and I got up from the battlefield and I introduced both him and Ganetzky.

Hodgson and I said our farewells to Litvinov, and, as we drove off on our way back to Moscow, Hodgson asked, 'What did you say were the names of your chess-players?' I told him and shall never forget the horror with which he looked at his own fingers. 'What?' he exclaimed, 'And I have shaken hands with that bloody chap.' 'Never mind his bloodiness,' said I. 'You have shaken much bloodier hands on the other side away in Siberia. And you may have saved a great deal of blood by being here today to shake his. Did you make anything of Litvinov?' 'He was very sceptical at first,' said Hodgson, 'but I went as far as I possibly could.' That night I was at the Commissariat of Foreign Affairs and in the Kremlin and knew that the Bolsheviks also had made up their minds to take the risk and to go a very long way. They replied to Curzon's ultimatum in a way that made a break in diplomatic relations impossible.* There was no break and I was presently back in Riga, making *Racundra* ready for a cruise among the Finnish islands.

This was one of the pleasantest of our voyages. We made a slow passage to the Moon Sound, through the narrow gap in the Rukeraga Reef to the deserted harbour of Rohukulla. Then, after looking at some shallow-draught sailing boats (said to be copied from South American whalers that have for a hundred and fifty years been used at Hapsal), we went on to Reval and thence to Helsingfors, after which, happily cut off from letters, newspapers and all politics whatsoever, we took, now the inner, now the outer channels through the Finnish islands. We had a very fine grass-snake with us, and, though loth to part with him, we endowed him with an island very thickly populated by frogs. We ourselves lived for the most part on eggs that tasted of seaweed, milk that tasted of seaweed, and the fish that we caught while at anchor. The Gulf of Finland is fed by such large rivers that it is not very salty. The fish we caught were mostly perch and pike and very much better to eat than the same fish caught in ordinary fresh water. Here, in the Gulf, pike behave like salmon. In the winter when the streams are frozen, they go, like salmon, to the sea, and in the spring they come up the streams to spawn, such of them as evade the humans who are waiting for them with spears, traps and nets,

* Cf. E. H. Carr's *History of Soviet Russia*, in which he says that the Russians at once accepted all conditions; the exact opposite to the truth, showing that the author knew nothing of Hodgson's courageous meeting with Litvinov, and of how, at the very last moment, one note was substituted for another.

to make 'golden caviare' of their roe and to dry good white fillets of pike-flesh in the sun. When the pike-run is on, you may see the pike alive in tubs in Reval market, and watch a housewife carrying one home still kicking in her shopping basket.

We brought *Racundra* back to Reval in September and, as I found urgent messages from the *Manchester Guardian* asking me to go into Russia, and a series of southerly gales set in, I arranged to lay her up there for the winter. We unrigged her, took everything out of her, and, with Eggers, her designer, watched her lifted from the water by a huge floating crane, watched her swinging high above our heads and set down on the quay as tenderly as if she were an egg-shell. A wooden cradle was built for her. She was roofed in with planks to protect her from the snow. Evgenia and the Ancient went off by train for Riga and I left for Petrograd and Moscow to arrange with the Russians for the articles they were to write for an Economic Supplement to the *Manchester Guardian* that was being edited by J. M. Keynes. In Moscow I was given unexpected fishing lessons by the gigantic Colonel Mackie whose first arrival I could never forget. We had come in together and on the platform of the Moscow station he had watched for some minutes four Russian porters trying very unhandily to carry one of his two enormous trunks. He could not bear the sight. 'You give that to me,' he said and swung one trunk up to his shoulder. 'Now the other.' Then, with a trunk on each shoulder, chatting to me as if he had no burden whatever, he strode down the platform quite unconscious of the flabbergasted onlookers. Mackie was a skilful bait-caster and on the tennis court at the British Mission he taught me how to use a short steel rod and one of the free-running American reels that have to be braked with the thumb. He could throw his spinner or plug into a bucket at the full length of the court and could have done it at greater distances if there had been more room. I still have the little Blue Grass reel he gave me, and I profited by his Moscow lessons well enough to catch a salmon in the Eden with it when I came back to the North of England.

# CHAPTER XL

# *Death of Lenin*

Whenever I arrived at the British Mission, where I found much more comfortable lodgings than elsewhere, I used to be greeted with the enquiry, 'Well, and what is going to happen now?'

In 1924 I was asked that question on January 14 when I turned up with chattering teeth after an extremely cold journey from Riga. 'Nothing this time, I hope,' I replied. Less than a week later we were stunned by the sudden news of Lenin's death. I had been in the Kremlin that morning and had heard there that he had at last taken a decided turn for the better. He had been out driving. He had laughed with the children of the village where he was staying. There seemed to be hope of a complete recovery. Then, suddenly, he was dead.

No one who was not there at the time can realise quite what that meant. For the revolutionary leaders it was like the removal of the keystone of an arch, although his long illness had accustomed them to being without him. For the ordinary folk, even for the bourgeoisie who seven years before had regarded him as the personification of all that they feared and hated, he had become a symbol of permanence. While he was there they could hope for something like a quiet life. With Lenin gone, anything might happen: revolts, revolution, everything thrown back once more into the melting pot. I walked sadly through the wintry streets, thinking of my talks with him, thinking that I should never again see him edging his chair round the table in little jerks while he argued, remembering him speaking in the old Soviet in Petrograd, delightedly observing that the revolution had outlasted the seventy days of the Commune and was now fairly to be called a revolution and not a revolt, imperturbably forcing his opponents to face plain facts, and giving them the time to take in those facts while he sat quietly writing in a notebook until he felt he had given them long enough, when, as he had expected, plain facts had brought most of his opponents round to agree with him.

I walked through the streets and saw that people were weeping as they walked. Lenin was dead.

On the 23rd I went to the Saratov Station when they brought his body to Moscow. Many whom I knew were there and Chicherin gave me a lift back into the town. He said that if Lenin had wished so to die as to shake the Soviet Government as little as possible he could not have contrived things better. This was so. The Government that had been functioning without him went on doing just that. No sudden change had to be made. Next day, one of the two million who passed through the great pillared hall in which he lay in state, I saw Lenin for the last time. I have never been able to bring myself to go into the tomb on the Red Square where, embalmed, he is still to be seen by pilgrims.

In the evening I went by appointment to see the nocturnal Chicherin and stayed talking with him till after three in the morning, our talk ranging to and fro over all Europe, but never once touching the subject of which both of us were thinking. Probably he was glad, just then, not to be talking with those others who would have been unable, that night, to talk of anything else. He rejoiced over the departure of Curzon, 'that invulnerable beast', and remarked on the un-Englishness of Curzon's character: 'I always noticed that Englishmen of position were extremely, almost fastidiously chivalrous, whereas this man when in the presence of people weaker than himself cannot prevent himself from bullying. He behaved so with Izmet Pasha; he behaved so with me, and I am told he tried to behave so when dealing with Colonial Ministers.'

Chicherin said that recent disputes in the Communist party had if anything strengthened the 'Old Guard' by giving them a fright lest too sudden a move towards democracy might lead to internal disintegration. 'For example,' said he, 'look at the sort of thing they are saying in the Higher Educational Institutions. One young lad said, "No one is indispensable. Given three months to acquaint himself with geography, any one of us could take Chicherin's place!"' He spoke with some disapproval of Trotsky: 'always an intellectual individualist ... forever making bad tactical mistakes ... Stalin is definitely out to lower Trotsky's prestige ... and has succeeded ... Trotsky in the Central Committee is really insufferable ... a combination of *enfant terrible* and genius ... and so autocratic.'

The day of the funeral was one of the coldest I have ever

known in Moscow. They greased the faces of the soldiers standing
guard and of those taking part in the funeral procession. The Chief
of Police was a Siberian who, boasting that no mere Moscow cold
could hurt him, did not share the precautions of the soldiers. He
lost the flesh from both cheek-bones and his chin from frost-bite.
In the Red Square, under the Kremlin wall, a mausoleum had
been built. Here, in a chamber, Lenin's body was to lie, under
glass so that for all ages pilgrims might come to see him. Close by,
on a high platform, in a cold that shrank the stomach and held a
dagger to the throat, stood the little group of leading Com-
munists. Trotsky was not there. He had left Moscow on his way
to a health resort in the Caucasus after a serious illness from which
he was still suffering. He could have returned to Moscow in time
for the funeral if the telegram brought to him in the train had not
told him that he was already too late (giving Saturday instead of
Sunday as the day chosen). Already, during Lenin's long illness,
his position had been weakened, and his absence threw an odd
light on that small group of Lenin's successors standing there on
that platform in the deathly cold afternoon of a January day. Few
people in Moscow who could walk took no part in that funeral.
Endlessly the columns moved through the archway into the great
square under the long narrow canopy of their own breath con-
gealing in the air above them. They moved slowly past the
mausoleum, close under the platform where that little group who
had worked with Lenin stood motionless in the cold.

There they stood, Zinoviev, Kamenev, Rykov, Joffe, Dzher-
zhinsky, Bukharin, and Stalin, then hardly known to the masses
of the people, who had not yet realised that for some years past
much steady work had been done to put an end to the 'Lenin and
Trotsky' tradition which still survived outside the inner circle of
the leaders. Trotsky was safely out of the way, though not yet
publicly thrown over. Much was to happen before 'Trotskyism'
could become the name for a heresy akin to high treason and
Trotsky himself could be banished to Alma Ata and later taken by
force to the Turkish frontier, exiled by the Revolution in which
he had once been second only to Lenin.

Stalin, Secretary of the Communist party, gradually working
his own men into secretaryships throughout the whole country,
thereby gaining unrivalled hold of the party machine, was not yet
ready to claim the place of leader. Anybody who on the day of
Lenin's funeral had proclaimed Stalin as Lenin's successor would

have been greeted with laughter. Many knew that Lenin on his
sickbed had tried to warn the party against letting Stalin have too
much power. Stalin could afford to wait. Lenin's successors were
to be Zinoviev and Kamenev. On that platform Stalin stood with
the men he was, when the right time came, to destroy. Did they
feel then, standing on that platform at Lenin's funeral, that the
ground under their feet, which had never been shaken by foreign
intervention and civil war, was, now that Lenin was dead, turning
into a quagmire? Almost every man on that platform died an un-
natural death. Zinoviev and Kamenev, leaders for a time, after
loyally helping in the elimination of Trotsky, found themselves
accused of some sort of treason, disgraced and shot. Joffe, a
sensitive, nervous little man, committed suicide. Bukharin, inexplicably, had helped Stalin in bringing about Zinoviev's and
Kamenev's downfall and death. Later his own turn came. He and
Alexei Rykov, Lenin's close friend, a simple-hearted and charming man (I remember his childish delight when, on his birthday in
the hungry period of the revolution, some friend had contrived to
make a little birthday cake for him with white sugar icing), and
the hard-working little Krestinsky who had done much to bring
some sort of order into the financial affairs of the state, were tried
together, also for 'treason'. It is said that Bukharin and Stalin had
been almost boisterously friendly after the death of their old
friends, Zinoviev and Kamenev.

It is also said that Stalin, secretly looking down on the Court
through a pane of blackened glass, heard Bukharin's 'Mark
Antony' speech and saw him walk out of Court, sentenced to be
shot. Stalin had no rivals after that, but became as it were a deified Caesar, referred to as 'Our Comrade, our Friend, our Father,'
the centre of a myth curiously like that which had at its centre
another 'Little Father' in the Tsar. History for the most part is
written by the victors and naturally puts them in a favourable
light, but there can seldom have been a more remarkable rewriting than that which began immediately after Lenin's death
and aimed at making people forget that Trotsky, not Stalin, had
directed operations during the October Revolution of 1917, and
that Trotsky, not Stalin, had made out of nothing the revolutionary army that won the civil war. A young man in Russia today
(any time after Lenin's death and before Stalin was embalmed and
put to join him in his mausoleum) would find it hard not to
believe that Stalin was not Lenin's right arm in 1917 and that he

and nobody else was Lenin's natural successor. Those who re-write history must see to it that no contradictory witnesses survive. Once history has been rewritten there is always a temptation to rewrite it again.

Lenin's funeral was on Sunday, January 27. On the following Saturday Hodgson went to the Commissariat of Foreign Affairs to present a note announcing British recognition of the Soviet Government, nearly seven years after it had been formed. For nearly seven years we had been doing exactly what the theorists of revolution had said we would, thereby confirming them at every turn. Intervention had fanned into flame the embers of a civil war that, but for us, would have ended almost the moment it began. The evils of that disastrous policy are with us yet, making it easy for those who wish to do so to persuade the normally peaceful-minded Russian people of our implacable hostility, and so to justify the policy of the iron curtain which is likely to have similar disastrous results for mankind. But then, on that second day of February 1924, recognition of the Soviet Government meant recognition that the policy of Intervention was not only dead but, so far as we were concerned, formally buried. It was a very happy day for me. 'My war', which had lasted for more than five years after the Armistice of 1918, was over. I was free to struggle back as best I could to my proper job.

There was a slight touch of comedy even over the ceremony of recognition. Chicherin, as I have said before, was a nocturnal creature, preferring to work in the quiet of the night and do his sleeping by day. He had been woken that day again and again by telegrams from Rakovsky and was asleep when Hodgson and William Peters came to the Russian Foreign Office and asked for the Commissar of Foreign Affairs. They were received by Litvinov, and when I saw Chicherin and Litvinov together in the evening, they were laughing at the thought that Chicherin, who of all men had been working and waiting for that moment, had 'overslept recognition'. Hodgson was as pleased as I was, the Russians not quite so pleased. Recognition was recognition and welcome, but, instead of making it the generous gesture it should have been, some fool in Downing Street saw to it that it was grudgingly done. For three years after recognition we had no Ambassador in Moscow but only a Chargé d'Affaires accredited to a Government that controlled one sixth of the world.

I returned to Riga on February 11, and four days later sailed for

England, only to be caught in the ice near the island of Bornholm. By the 19th ice had piled under the stern of the ship, and there was nothing to be seen but ice, except that in a dim mist six or seven miles away we could see just a hint of Bornholm. We played cricket on the ice in bright sunshine. On the 20th the German cruiser *Brunswick* cut a way through the ice and a party of German seamen with an officer, roped together, solemnly came over the ice to us and asked if there was anything we wanted. Our stores were running very low, since no more than a four-day voyage had been expected, and for some time we had been planning the meals we would have when we reached home. Breakfasts had suffered worst. We had run out of every kind of marmalade and jam. The captain suddenly faced by the Germans' very kind enquiry, tactlessly but truthfully replied, 'plum jam'. The German, who did not know that the captain had for two days bored us all by telling us about the plum jam he was accustomed to and missed so much, thought that the captain was laughing at him, and took a good deal of appeasing. The cruiser carved a way round us through the ice and we tried to get away in the lane she left, and reached a patch of open water off the south point of Bornholm, but were almost at once imprisoned again.

The wind shifted and the little patch of open water shifted with it. With each shift of wind we shifted too, hoping to avoid being trapped once more. Food ran out, and I went ashore with the mate and a sailor in a small boat, dodging the little bergs, landing on the ice and making our way ashore where we bought a sheep, and had hardly done so before the hoots from our steamer warned us that the wind had shifted again. We had a lively return voyage through the moving flock of boisterous little bergs but a great feast that night. Four days later a Danish ice-breaker cut a way through the ice and convoyed us to Copenhagen. Plates had buckled and the ice had damaged our propeller, but the captain, wishing to avoid the great cost of repairs in Denmark, decided to take the ship home as she was, and we steamed round the Skaw with the whole vessel vibrating, thanks to having only two efficient blades on her propeller. We drove across the North Sea in one day of bright sunshine and a second of blinding snow-squalls, found no pilot on station, and crept up the Thames on our fourth day out from Copenhagen. I saw the lawyers in London, spent a few days in Manchester, a day or two at Coniston, and was back in Riga on April 14.

A few days later we went to Reval to get *Racundra* ready for sea after the winter ashore. It was cold and when we went to visit our friends in Lodenzee we found still a lot of snow in the forest round the house. On May 8, my divorce being completed, the Master of *Racundra* was married to the Cook at the British Consulate in Reval.

After a slow but pleasant cruise back to Riga, with Lieutenant-Commander Gordon Steele, V.C. as extra hand, we both went to Russia and spent a month in and around Moscow. Back in Riga I was busy writing articles for the *Manchester Guardian*, driving once a week up into the Lettish hill-country with my friend John Chapman of the American Consulate in Riga to fish two delightful little rivers, the Amat and the Brasle, which were packed with trout and grayling. We used to spend the night in a peasant's hut, where the fleas were so hungry that we had no difficulty in getting up early and used to be fishing by 4.30 in the morning.

On August 1 we took *Racundra* for a leisurely cruise in the lower reaches of the Dvina, up and down Aa and up Bolderaa to that fascinating, mysterious, romantic and claustrophobic maze of shallow narrow channels winding between enormously tall and strong reeds for what feels like thousands of square miles. We lived mostly on eggs and the fish we caught. We sailed only for an hour or two at a time, as I had a lot of writing to do. By September 10 we were back in Stint See preparing to lay *Racundra* up for the last time, and on November 14 we said a sad farewell to her and to Riga, and sailed for England.

# CHAPTER XLI

# *Journalism v. Authorship*

On reaching London I went to the *Manchester Guardian* office where James Bone told me that C. P. Scott had sent a message asking if I would care to go to Egypt, where the Sirdar, Sir Lee Stack, had just been murdered, and report on the situation. I went to Manchester to see Scott and had a talk with Lloyd George, who said I should find Egypt child's play after Russia but very interesting. I took Evgenia to stay with my mother and on December 10 left London to travel overland to Venice.

On board ship between Trieste and Alexandria I had an extraordinary piece of good fortune in sitting next to Lady Downes at dinner. As undistinguished passengers, Lady Downes and I were not sitting at the captain's table. We spent the voyage talking mostly about fairy tales, and I assumed that she was, like many other English people, going out to Egypt for a winter tour. It turned out that Lady Downes and her husband, Sir Arthur, were both admirers of the *Manchester Guardian* and, when she heard that C. P. Scott had sent me to Egypt to see what was happening, she said at once that I ought to see Allenby, the High Commissioner, first of all. I said that I hardly supposed I could demand to see him. She then told me that she was quite sure there would be no difficulty about it, and that her reason for going to Cairo was to visit her sister who was Allenby's wife. When we arrived at Alexandria a launch with scarlet-uniformed kavasses and Field-Marshal Allenby's A.D.C. came off to meet her. The face of the captain, when he realised that this reception was not for one of the people he had chosen to entertain at his table but for a passenger with whom he had not troubled to exchange one word, was a sight not easily to be forgotten. This meeting was the beginning of a lasting friendship with the Downes family.

I had not been in Cairo twenty-four hours before I had word that I was expected at the Residency. I went there and found in

Lord Allenby's anteroom a group of officers. Several of them came over and spoke to me, with apparent surprise that I was going to put my head in the lion's mouth, and when an A.D.C. came in to say that Lord Allenby was extremely busy but I was to go in, they obviously expected me to be immediately ejected. I had heard before that his staff were devoted to, as well as terrified of, this soldier who had used the Old Testament as a military handbook during his Palestine campaign.

When I walked in, the enormously tall figure of the Field-Marshal slowly straightened itself. There was a cageful of small birds in the room, and among them one or two in which I was particularly interested. In about two minutes Egyptian politics had been swept away and we were deep in ornithology. He took me to see his aviary, still suffering from the tragedy caused by a snake that had found its way into one of the cages. The time flew by and it was well over an hour before he sent for Clark-Kerr, the Councillor, told him to put me in touch with the Egyptians, asked me to come to luncheon two days later and said goodbye. 'What on earth did you do to him?' said one of the awed officers still waiting in the anteroom. 'We thought he had eaten you.'

I enjoyed the chess-problem character of Egyptian politics in which no moral issues seemed to be involved. I liked hearing former Prime Ministers telling me what scoundrels other former Prime Ministers were, and I liked seeing them at the Mohammed Aly Club playing backgammon with each other as if each thought the others the best fellows in the world. I liked them for their own sakes, and for their unfailing humour. I liked seeing Nashat dodging from tree to tree through his own garden, because there was a good chance that somebody might take a pot shot at him. I liked the colossal Ziwar, temporary Prime Minister, for saying, glancing at his own enormous bulk, 'I fill the breach.' I saw everybody and everything.

And I learned too how different was C. P. Scott from any other editor. The *Manchester Guardian* had been taking a very strong line over the troubles in Egypt. Everything that I saw showed me that that line was wrong. C. P. Scott printed my articles with a note to say that they contradicted the policy of the paper, but if these were the facts, the policy would have to change, and change it duly did.

I made a number of new friends in Cairo and met an old one in Robin Furness, who had been at Rugby with me. I talked of fishing with Russell Pasha, and of Driffield Beck, which I was not to fish till twenty years later. I played a little billiards and saw the famous mongoose at the Turf Club. The year ended with the sight of my first hoopoes in the garden of Shepheard's Hotel.

Surprisingly, I had a little sailing in Egypt. In the middle of January 1925 I went duck-shooting on the Nile in a small centre-board dinghy, a delightful little boat. We were three. The other two were the guns, and when we sighted a flock of duck, it was my business so to sail up to them as to give both guns a chance when the birds rose off the water. We then picked up the victims and sailed on to find the flock once more. We were slightly impeded by Arab sportsmen who were shooting now and again from the banks and would then implore us to pick up their birds for them. I remember our two guns got forty-two duck and that these were of nine different species. But still more I remember the delight of sailing on that ancient river, with its strange craft, lateen-rigged with yards far longer than the masts, moving on opaque water rich with the mud of Africa and so very unlike the clear Baltic or the lakes at home.

On January 23 I left Cairo for the Sudan, travelling partly by river-steamer and partly by train. The river journey gave me some good memories: the ancient rock-dwellings of Primis, where high in the cliffs I could see doorways with stone fenders in them to prevent babies falling out; Abu Zimbel, the temple in the hill where, deep under the earth, I saw the morning light break the darkness of the inmost chamber, a piece of pure Rider Haggard; the ancient trading city on the bank from which the caravan roads led out over the sand of the desert; and places of more modern history, battlefields of the Mahdists that had been shown to me on the map when I was a small boy at school in Windermere.

At Halfa I was startled by a telegram from the Governor-General to say that I was expected to stay with him in Khartoum. I probably owed this to the kind forethought of Clark-Kerr, whom I cursed bitterly as I read the telegram. I need not have cursed. Sir Geoffrey Archer was as kind and helpful as everybody else. I should have found it almost impossible to get a room anywhere except at the palace, and it was made clear to me at once that if I did not see as much as could be seen in the time, the fault would be entirely my own.

The Sudan Government was a team of Old Blues, firmly carrying out a semi-Bolshevik policy, running a dictatorship on behalf of the native proletariat, the main object being to prevent exploitation of the native by would-be money-makers. Some of them were a little shocked at hearing this view of their activities, but agreed at once that their aims were exactly as I had described them.

Then came Omdurman and its market, and the Khalifa's bath, a very deep tank with, high on its walls, a pair of fine brass taps, looted at the time of Gordon's death from the Governor's Palace at Khartoum. No doubt they had been much admired. If Gordon's bath had brass taps, why shouldn't the Khalifa's have as much? So there they were, built into the tank and lacking nothing but a water supply.

By the end of February I was back in Manchester, quickly acquiring a sore throat answering questions on what I had seen. C. P. Scott arranged for me to see Lloyd George, and Molly Hamilton sent me to Ramsay MacDonald. It was a pleasant change to be talking about Egypt instead of about Russia.

We went to Windermere house-hunting, found nothing suitable at the price we could pay, and were on the point of giving up when one of the agents said he had a small cottage he did not think would do. He drove us to see it and we bought it the same day.

This was Low Ludderburn. It was a very old farmhouse, a cottage really, with two small rooms downstairs and the same, rather smaller, upstairs, very low ceilings and walls so thick that the stone staircase was built within the thickness of the wall. Outside there was a small stone terrace jutting out rather like the bridge of a ship over steeply dropping ground which early in the spring was covered with snowdrops, later with daffodils and later still with bluebells. The cottage was nearly six hundred feet above sea level, at the head of the valley of Cartmel Fell. There was a yard and some enormous very old yews.

At right angles to the cottage there was a grand old stone barn, built into the side of the hill so that the road over the fell passed it at the level of the upper floor; the gate of the hay-loft opened into the road, while the doors of the lower floor opened on to the yard. This building, unlike the cottage, was in a very good state of preservation, and Evgenia saw at once what a splendid workroom could be made of that upper floor.

From the terrace outside the cottage we could see forty miles away down into Yorkshire, to where the mass of Ingleborough rose above the nearer hills. Our water-supply was a small spring on the hillside above the cottage and when we went up to fetch water, we could see as far in the other direction, looking on to what I think the best panorama of Lake mountains, from Black Combe to Helvellyn and the high ground above the valleys of Lune and Eden.

The owner said that he could be out by the 12th of May, so we found lodgings at the farm of Hartbarrow, half a mile away, and I settled down to write my Egyptian articles and to do as much fishing as I could find time for. I did in fact get through a great deal of work at Hartbarrow, but, as usual, my diary mentions chiefly the fish.

On my last visit to Manchester I had complained to Ted Scott that the *Guardian* was not doing what it might for fishermen, where-upon he said 'You had better show us what you think we ought to do for them,' and gave me a column a week to do as I liked with. This gave me an excuse for fishing, and for several years I wrote a fishing essay a week. While Evgenia supervised a local jobbing builder and his mate turning the upper floor of the old barn into the finest workroom I have had in all my life, I managed to fish all the local rivers I had known as a boy: besides the Cumberland Derwent, the Hodder, the Ribble, the Dove, the Eden, the Eck at Inverchapel, and so on, a perfect orgy.

On September 15 Barbara Collingwood married Oscar Gnoss-pelius, whose family had known and been friendly with mine for many years, and in due course their only child became our courtesy niece.

I have never kept a full diary except for short periods such as the six weeks I spent in Russia in 1919. My diary records events in the shortest and most useless form for the writer of an auto-biography a quarter of a century later. It gives dates of arrival in Moscow, or Cairo or London but very little else. For the year 1926 I find entries like Feb. 25: London. March 3: Larches in bud. March 6: First daffodils. April 20: Swallows in the garden. April 24: Sheep broke in and ate our lupins. May 15: Eight trout in the Crake. Manchester, wrote a leader. July 30: Salmon (9 lb.) at Winderwath, and so on — merely pastoral.

But I do remember that some time during this year I put together a short history of the early years of the Russian Revolu-tion for the supplement to the *Encyclopaedia Britannica* that was edited by J. L. Garvin and went to see him at Beaconsfield. We went to Leeds where we saw Lascelles Abercrombie and stayed a few days with my mother, who had recently moved there in order to live next door to her youngest and favourite child, my sister Joyce. Then, suddenly, a telegram from C. P. Scott suggesting that I should visit China.

My arrival there began with the noise of a scuffle outside my cabin between rival representatives of the Canton Government, each of whom wished to invite me to Canton. That scuffle set the note of all that followed. There seemed to be no party among the Chinese, no group among the English, but knew exactly what I ought to say in the *Manchester Guardian* about the events that I had come to China to observe. This was the moment when the Chinese Nationalists had swept north to the Yangtze, armed largely with wooden rattles. Rival war-lords stored their booty for safety in British banks. British troops had been sent to China and every effort made by short-sighted people to bring about some sort of armed clash, so that war or something like it between England and the Nationalists should produce the shelving of the problem of the concessions which the Government at home made up its mind to solve. There was a danger lest the Chinese should be misled into thinking that the views of London were the same as those of Shanghai. My business was to listen to everybody who cared to speak and to give as accurate a picture as I could of a rapidly changing political scene.

I did the best I could and suffered a good deal from the well-meant but determined hospitality of British and Chinese business men, bankers, shippers, traders of all kinds, Chinese war-lords, British soldiers (much more moderate in their views than the business spokesmen), mandarins of the old regime, missionaries, poets, students, professors, politicians, advisers (Russian and English), consuls bellicose and the reverse, and some English diplomats who seemed to me to have a far more open-minded view of what was happening than was expressed by the English men of business. Never, even in Russia during the revolution, have I spent so many hours out of every twenty-four listening to enthusiasts talking politics. Never, before or since, have I had so continually to overeat if I did not wish to give offence. I had to learn to eat with chopsticks, and even to smack my lips when a Chinese war-lord picked a titbit from his plate with the chopsticks that had just left his mouth and, with polite hospitality, poked it straight into mine, to smack my lips and poke my chopsticks into his mouth with a similar titbit, as if we were two lovebirds feeding each other.

I was later to get a great deal of pleasure from using some of the war-lords as models for Chinese pirates, and in taking hints from Madame Sun Yat Sen herself for my portrait of the Chinese girl graduate who, while hankering for academic life in Cambridge, does, from her filial piety, keep in order her community of tough characters. And the dragon processions of *Missee Lee* are those that I watched delightedly in the streets of Hankow.

At the same time, in spite of this compulsory overdose of sharks' fins, bird's-nest soup, noodles and politics, I did enormously enjoy China. In Peking I visited my Aunt Edith, whom I had last seen in 1894, when, with my Aunt Jessie, she was setting off to China as a missionary, and I had said enviously how lucky she was to be going to China. She replied, rather severely, that she was not going there for pleasure. Aunt Edith, now a very frail old lady, living in a charming room on the ground floor with latticed windows and a door opening into the garden, spoke of the goodness of her Chinese friends and of the devotion with which they were nursing her and of the happiness she had found in China. These aunts were in Peking during the Boxer Rising and had been decorated for heroism. One of them had had a Boxer arrow through her bonnet during the siege.

Back in England in April 1927, I saw Lloyd George, who suggested that I should make a book of my Chinese articles. C. P. Scott approved. Unwin published it as *The Chinese Puzzle* and Lloyd George, not so much on my account as to please C. P. Scott, wrote a preface. It is completely out-dated now.

Soon after my return I was encouraged by a letter from publishers I had had no dealings with before, saying that they would like to include *Racundra's First Cruise* in their Travellers Library. I was delighted, as I always looked upon the book as the first sign of escape from the political writing in which I had been engulfed for so long. I agreed at once (and so did Allen & Unwin, the original publishers). This was the beginning of my long association with Jonathan Cape Limited.

I was again writing my weekly column in the *Manchester Guardian* and fishing at least once a week, trying to fish as many different rivers and to use as many different methods as possible. Whenever I went to London I used to go with Francis Hirst to Droxford where he had some fishing on the Meon. We fished by day and played chess in the evenings. I was never sure which I enjoyed more.

Colonel Kelsall, who regularly went fishing with me, lived in a house across the valley, a rather long way by road but well under half a mile as the crow flies from Ludderburn, and, having no telephones, we devised a system of signals. White signals showed up well on the darkish grey wall of his barn, while black signals were equally visible against the whitewashed gable-end of our cottage. The signals, triangular, square, and diamond-shaped, were afterwards of great use in *Winter Holiday*. On the subject of fishing we could say anything we wanted with these signals: 'ARE YOU GOING FISHING?' 'WHICH RIVER?' and in the depth of winter, going to fish for grayling, 'HAVE YOU ANY WORMS?' Kelsall, a great precisian, used to present me with a beautifully typed new copy of our code ('All previous issues cancelled') and pasted his own copy on one of two wooden boards hinged together to open like a book and, when not in use, kept padlocked. There was to be no leakage at his signal station. The fish never had a chance of learning beforehand what was planned for them.

In October Evgenia slipped on a wet stone in the garden, fell and broke her ankle. When she was allowed to get up and hobble on crutches, I advertised in the *Fishing Gazette* for an hotel or lodging where she would be able to fish from the window. The only reply came from *The Rose Revived*, an ancient inn at Newbridge, so called because it was the oldest bridge over the Thames. It was a delightful little tavern with a sign showing a rose being revived in a glass of sherry. My friend Hugh Sheringham who lived not very far away dropped in once or twice. As angling editor of the *Field*, he had written about fishing for so long that he no longer took any pleasure in the sport itself and gave it up altogether.

I think I should say here that I have never claimed to be a good fisherman, but only one who thoroughly enjoys fishing. Going fishing I have never thought to catch more fish than anybody else, luckily, for I should seldom have succeeded. Then, too, in the matter of enjoyment I am fortunate in that no sort of class-consciousness affects my pleasure. I have had great pleasure fishing for salmon, sitting as it were on the strong supporting stream. But I have also had great pleasure sitting on a wicker basket, one of a row of fishermen on the tow-path beside a still canal, watching for the slight quiver of the float that should signal a roach mouthing my maggot. It is now too late for me to catch every kind of English fish, but I have caught all but a very few, beginning with minnow, loach and stickleback, going on through coarse fish: roach, rudd, tench, bream, carp, perch, pike, chub, eel and, once only, a barbel. And then the game fish: salmon, trout, char and grayling. I have not caught a vendace or a shad or a sturgeon. Nor have I caught any very big fish. My most notable was a perch 3lbs. 2oz., before which a plumber stood in a Hampstead lodging unable to tear himself away, muttering reverently 'The FISH of a LIFETIME!' I was over sixty before I caught a twenty-pound salmon; my biggest brown trout, caught in 1955, was only 3¼lbs. and my biggest sea-trout, caught in 1956 in daylight on one of my very small (⁷⁄₁₆″) Port and Starboard flies, was 5½lbs.

Like Sheringham, I soon found that, with an article to write every week, the actual fishing became just a preparation for the writing, a mere dull duty, no longer any pleasure. But I was luckier than he in that after a few months I was able to stop writing my articles and to become once more a fisherman enjoying fishing for its own sake. I do not believe anybody has had happier days fishing than have been mine in the twenty and more years that have passed since I stopped writing about them.

Though fishing from the window of the inn was not possible, and even from the very muddy and slippery banks was very difficult, Evgenia sat outside watching other people fish. There were some interesting fishermen in the inn from time to time. Francis and Helena Hirst came for a week-end. The ankle mended and we were back at Ludderburn at the beginning of November. On the very last day I caught my one and only barbel.

Fishing with Kelsall for grayling in the middle of December at Appleby we had to break the ice at the edge of the river, go into the water to unfreeze our waders, and dip our rods to prevent the fine lines from freezing solidly to the rings. On one of those days the Eden was frozen across where it runs through the town and there was tobogganing down the steep main street from the Castle.

It was always our habit to greet the New Year out of doors and I remember the last night of 1927 hearing at midnight the bells of Cartmel, as we stood on the fell above the cottage with the snow deep under our feet.

In January 1928 it became known that there had been changes in Russia. Radek was out of favour and exiled; Trotsky also, and it was said that, in spite of years of detraction that had followed Lenin's death, he was still so popular that those in power, fearing a demonstration in Trotsky's favour, staged a sham departure for him, so that his actual departure, next day, should pass unnoticed. The result of these rumours was a telegram from C. P. Scott suggesting my going to Russia. I left for Moscow and got there on February 3 with a raging headache and feeling most unwell generally. The main question that interested C. P. Scott was answered at once. The solidity of the Soviet regime had not been shaken by the disagreements among the party leaders. Changes there had been, but no hint of disintegration. Changes in China had been more serious. As refugees in Moscow I found some of the leaders whom I had seen all-powerful in Hankow, among them the Chens and Madame Sun. Before I started on my return journey they entertained me at a tremendous Chinese banquet, enlivened by white wine very much fortified, sugary champagne, vodka and port. It made me feel more ill and more than ever anxious to be at home.

I was back at Ludderburn on March 6 and spent the rest of the year writing for the *Manchester Guardian*, fishing, sailing a small dinghy on Windermere, and falling ill at ever-shorter intervals.

In November, visiting Manchester, I lunched with Allan Monkhouse, and I remember his saying that the unsuccessful author could be known by the multitude of his publishers. We began counting our own, and I think I beat him by one, he having ten publishers and I eleven. He was literary editor of the *Guardian*, besides being a playwright and a most industrious novelist. Privately I became more than ever determined to escape from journalism before it was too late.

Whenever something happened in one of 'my countries' calling for a leading article, I used to be summoned to Manchester by telegram, and went there by the first available train, writing a rough draft in the train, doing the final draft in the library at the end of the long Corridor and then spending the night at Ted Scott's. All along the Corridor were small offices holding the various sub-editors, and presently I began to suspect that the Scotts were considering turning me into one of the rabbits in these safe comfortable hutches. This notion gave urgency to the question, was I or was I not to give up any idea of returning to the writing of books? Had I already left it too late to get back to writing what I had always hoped to write?

# CHAPTER XLII

## Swallows and Amazons

1929 was for me the year of crisis, a hinge year as it were, joining and dividing two quite different lives. It was the year in which, at last, I felt myself released from the obligation to go on with the work that had come to me with the war. Feeling free from that obligation I seem to have run amuck with liberty. To refuse a career offered by the *Manchester Guardian* must have seemed to C. P. Scott something very like sacrilege. Ted Scott, on the other hand, knew that I had never given up the hope that sooner or later I should get back to writing books, and he was too good a friend not to understand and to astonish his father by showing that he understood why, instead of welcoming the opportunity of becoming a full-time employee of the paper, I saw his offer as a warning and felt that once in the Corridor I should never be able to escape.

Ted told his father that my real interest was in books, not politics; but it was political articles that C.P.S. wanted from me. Finally C.P.S. told me that he planned for me eventually to succeed Monkhouse as literary editor, but that meanwhile I was to go to Berlin as resident correspondent. This was exactly what I wished to avoid. It was one thing to get a telegram asking for a leading article on some subject I was supposed to know something about. It would be quite another thing to be tied to a newspaper office. I told him I did not know German. He said that, after Russian, I should find German easy. On March 2 I lunched with him and he proposed a salary that seemed to me enormous. I went home to share a decision that would affect my wife as much as myself, and we foresaw that if I were to accept that offer I should once again be hopelessly involved in controversial politics, which of all things I most loathed, and that, if I were again to become so involved, I should never be able to get out. By March 19 Evgenia and I had made up our minds and I gave three months' notice to the *Manchester Guardian*, ending the existing arrangement, as I was sure I should not be able to do what was wanted in Berlin. On March 24, after a couple of days' sailing, with a weight off my shoulders but with no prospects whatever, I began the writing of *Swallows and Amazons*.

I had for some time been growing intimate with a family of imaginary children. I had even sketched out the story of two boats in which my four (five including the baby) were to meet another two, Nancy and Peggy, who had sprung to life one day when, sailing on Coniston, I had seen two girls playing on the lake-shore. For once I had without difficulty shaped the tale into scenes and even found the chapter-headings. The whole book was clear in my head. I had only to write it, but dreaded the discovery that after all these years of writing discursively I was unable to write narrative. I well remember the pleasure I had in the first chapter, and my fear that it would also be the last. I could think of nothing else and grudged every moment that had to be given to other activities. I wrote on plain paper with holes along one edge, so that the sheets could be clipped into a loose-leaf quarto binding. Night after night I used to bring it in a small attaché case from my workroom in the old barn to the cottage, so that I could reach out and lay my hand on it in the dark beside my bed. When I had fifty pages in that loose cover I felt that I had gone so far with it that this time I should be able to write the whole story. I decided to take the risk of offering it to a publisher. If he seemed willing, I would go on. If not, delightful as was the prospect of writing it, I should feel that I must work on at that other writing for which I knew I had a market. We were too poor to take a greater risk.

Jonathan Cape, whom I had met years before, and now met again at Molly Hamilton's, had seen the weekly articles that I was writing for the *Guardian* and made a remark that was prophetic in a way he did not expect. What he said was: 'Isn't it time that you were putting together some books to support you when you grow old?' What he proposed was that I should collect a volume of essays for him, and then another, until he had published a series of them. I went up to town in April, taking with me the typescript of *Rod and Line*, a selection from my fishing papers which I hoped I could persuade him to accept as the first of my volumes of essays. I also took with me on half a sheet of note-paper the title and a list of the chapter-headings of *Swallows and Amazons*. I did not want to show him any of the first draft of the book if I could help it, though I had shown some of it to Molly Hamilton and been enormously encouraged by her liking it.

Cape agreed at once that *Rod and Line* should count as the first of the volumes of essays, but said that what he really wanted was a collection of such essays on general subjects. With some diffidence I told him about *Swallows and Amazons* and showed him my half-sheet of paper. He glanced at it. 'That's all right,' said Napoleon Cape. 'We'll publish it and pay one hundred pounds in advance on account of royalties. But it's the essays we want.'

Now the *Guardian* had had two highly distinguished writers of 'Saturday Articles', G. W. E. Russell who every Saturday for many years contributed a paper under the general title of 'Collections and Recollections', and Arthur Ponsonby who wrote a weekly essay under the general title of 'Casual Observations'. Ponsonby, more and more involved in Parliamentary activities (he was eventually made a Baron and led the Labour opposition in the House of Lords), had resigned and asked the Editor to look for a successor. Ted had asked me if I would like the job if it were offered to me. There was some discussion as to whether it would be better to entrust the Saturday articles to one writer or to several. I had heard no more of this, and my three months' notice ran out on June 19.

On June 21, which was a Saturday, I had gone down to Droxford from London to fish the little Meon with Francis Hirst who was coming down by a later train. Hirst arrived and was putting up his rod when he suddenly asked, 'What do the *Manchester Guardian* want you for? I thought you had resigned. Something has happened there. Ted Scott rang me up on the telephone this morning and asked if I knew where you were. He wouldn't give me a message for you, but asked me how he could get hold of you.' As it was a Saturday and Ted was certainly not in Manchester, there was nothing to be done, so I went on with my fishing. We both did fairly well, as always on that delightful little river, and we played our usual level games of chess. Back in town on the Monday I telephoned from the London office to Manchester. Ted would say nothing on the telephone except that he had written me a letter. It was quite clear that something serious had happened. Next day I knew. C.P.S. had formally retired and Ted was Editor. Could I come to Manchester on the way back to Windermere and how soon could I begin to write the Saturday articles?

I was in Manchester on the 30th, and late that night, when the paper had been sent to press, John Scott, who in normal times was never at the office in the evenings, came in with a bottle of champagne, and we three, alone in the Editor's room at the end of the empty Corridor, celebrated Ted's succession. For a long time Ted had borne more than his share of the burden of editorship, but C.P.S. had clung to authority too long, and Ted, besides editing the paper, had had to be continually alert and ready to resolve difficulties of the most fantastic kind. I will mention as an example the night preceding a General Election, when C.P.S. had come in and unexpectedly remarked that nothing much seemed to be happening and that he wondered what subject Ted would find for his leading article. Even after his retirement, the old man retained the title (invented for him by Ted and John in consultation) of Governing Director and used gleefully to tell people, 'I can still sack the lot.' He had been a great editor for well over fifty years and was eighty-three when, at last, he allowed his son to take the chair as well as the work of editorship.

At the time when I was given the writing of the Saturday articles I was more than half way through *Swallows and Amazons*. On May 19 I had come to the end of the very rough first draft. Ted and I were alike mistaken in thinking I should find the writing of the Saturday articles easy. On the contrary, they brought *Swallows and Amazons* immediately to a standstill. The same old trouble of thirty years before showed itself again. I could not at one and the same time write stories and essays. Mine is a stiff and woodenish mind unable to vault from groove to groove. Further, the essays were taking a great deal more time than they were worth. I used to spend as much as three days in writing and rewriting. Then, the moment one of them was on the way to Manchester, I was worried nearly off my head in planning the next. I envied my two essay-writing friends, Robert Lynd and Ivor Brown, either of whom could at any moment sit himself in a chair, light a pipe, finish an essay before his pipe needed refilling and be able without revision to telephone it to the printer. I wrote on such subjects as 'Dust', 'Sitting down to Think', 'Winding up a Clock' and whatnot. It was all that I could do to pump out an essay a week, with an occasional leading article and some reviewing for Garvin's *Observer*. And meanwhile *Swallows and Amazons* had dried up at its source.

It might never have started again if it had not been for a

General Election in Egypt. This gave me the excuse for an Egyptian journey and a sea-voyage. The noble Ivor Brown took over the Saturday articles and I sailed for Egypt at the end of November. I had not been too well for some time, and I suspect that the new editor had planned that voyage as much for my health's sake as for the needs of his newspaper. I had left only one or two articles finished and when Ted saw me off at the docks he told me not to worry about others until I came back. The voyage started badly. On two successive nights it was so rough that the water-cistern above my wash-basin was emptied over my pillow, but by the time we were steaming down the Portuguese coast *Swallows and Amazons* had started again and I was enjoying myself prodigiously, in spite of catching a cold made much worse when, after leaving Marseilles, there was a Fancy Dress Ball on board, and two young married people spent a lot of trouble rigging me out as a very décolletée and much bejewelled dowager.

The Egyptian elections were as amusing as I had expected them to be. Thanks to Robin Furness I had a ringside view. I met all my old friends and found that not one of them bore me a grudge for the uncomplimentary articles I had written about Egyptian politicians five years before. On the contrary, all the retired Prime Ministers, gossiping over their coffee and backgammon, urged me to do the same again and to tell the truth about their enemies (with details they were eager to supply). Their own exposure they were prepared to bear for the sake of seeing their enemies' beards in the dust. But going from village to village, which meant an endless series of ceremonial coffees with turbaned sheikhs, preparing the way for colossal feasts at most irregular hours, was altogether too much for my miserable inside and before Christmas I was again in a very poor way. This meant that once more *Swallows and Amazons* was forging briskly ahead.

I was back in England in the beginning of February 1930, moderately ill, and took a clear month to make a final revision of *Swallows and Amazons*, before settling down again to crackle thorns under the pot with the Saturday articles and reviews for the *Observer*. Cape was still wanting to make a book of essays out of the articles, but I did not like them well enough, though I hoped they might improve when my much-loved story was safely at the printer's. In April Evgenia went off to stay at Malvern for a fortnight and I took the complete typescript to London. I hardly liked to let it out of my hands. I had a hope, just half a hope, that this time, at long last, I had stumbled on the way to write my sort of book. Fifteen years had passed since last I had written a story long enough to be called a book. Seven years had passed since *Racundra's First Cruise*, and that had been matter of fact and not fiction. *Rod and Line* had been a book about fishing. My books about Russia and China had been political, so that I never counted them as books at all. If I could not write stories now, I should never write them and must count myself a failure. *Swallows and Amazons* was to settle my fate. It was as if that book were the first I had ever written, and when, after last-minute corrections, I parted unwillingly with the typescript, I felt as I had not felt since that long-ago summer of 1904. Ridiculous, perhaps, but so it was.

The next day Constant Huntington of Putnam's astonished me by reminding me of *Old Peter's Russian Tales*, asking if I would care to do some translation from the Russian and offering the colossal sum of £1,000 if I would translate *And Quiet Flows the Don* by Sholokhov. Ivor Brown had published two stories of mine in the *Pall Mall Magazine* and had said that I was wasting time by not writing more. Sturge Moore was asking for more fairy stories. It almost looked as if Evgenia and I would not be risking starvation if I were to give up newspaper work altogether.

But I knew very well that *Swallows and Amazons* was the real touchstone. Molly Hamilton had liked the chapters she had seen. Jonathan Cape seemed undismayed. But I myself was as timorous about it as I have been over each of its successors. I must have been a great nuisance to my friends who, after all, knew nothing about it. They were extremely kind, Lascelles and Catherine Abercrombie, Tom and Mary Sturge Moore, Robert and Sylvia Lynd, all bidding me be of good cheer and rejoicing on my behalf that I was trying to get away from politics before it was too late. Only Francis Hirst demurred. We had a good week-end together fishing and playing chess as usual, and he, incurable politician, could not understand why I should want to get away.

I settled down again to write the Saturday articles, went to Manchester, where Ted and I, at a music-hall, wept together watching George Robey in 'Sixty Years a Queen'. I wrote a leader on the Poet Laureateship, then vacant, another rejoicing in Masefield's appointment, a long article on Walter Scott's Letter-books, a leader on the Egyptian treaty negotiations, and much else, filling in time until the proofs of the book should arrive.

They came at the beginning of June, and the first early copies of the book itself a month later. The day before, I had had a telegram from Ernestine Evans of Lippincott's, to say that they would publish it in America. I went up to London to see her about this, and also to see Hugh Sheringham, for whose *Book of the Fly Rod* I had promised to write a chapter. I was ill in the train going up, ill again two days later, and sufficiently frightened by violent pains to go and see a doctor. He diagnosed duodenal or gastric ulcers and told me to give up smoking as soon as I could and to eat nothing but fish. I spent a grimmish, rather light-headed day watching Surrey and Lancashire playing cricket at the Oval. That was Saturday. On Monday *Swallows and Amazons* was published. On Tuesday I was a good deal worse. My doctor said that I must choose between an operation, which he thought best avoided if possible, and a long cure. I went back to Windermere, wrote three Saturday articles on end, began an afternoon's fishing in the Leven, but had to give up on account of pains and sickness.

# CHAPTER XLIII

## *The Turn of the Tide*

Molly Hamilton was leaving England for a lecture-tour in America, and with extraordinary kindness she invited Evgenia and me to camp in her flat in Adelphi and enjoy its view over the river while I let my doctor work his will. We were just in time. I was again fainting without warning, as, years before, I had fainted in Petrograd. A divan-bed was fixed up for me in the sitting-room. I managed one more review for the *Observer* and then, lying on that divan, went through the horrid routine of living on hourly doses of bismuth, milk and olive oil, and learning how good coffee smells when you are not allowed to drink it. Fright had made it easy to give up smoking. I had smoked only two pipes one day, instead of my usual ounce of tobacco, one pipe the next, and did not smoke again for five years. Three weeks later I had a whole night without pain, my first for a very long time.

Apart from illness my time in Molly's flat was delightful, except for my poor wife, who for two solid months was bound by the clock, as she had to pour the medicines into me at regular hourly intervals. As soon as I was fit to see people, we had the gayest time we had had for years. The Abercrombies, Ivor and Irene Brown, Huntington, James Bone and his friends, Dan Macmillan, Robert Lynd, P. P. Howe, and Ric Eddison, with whom I had shared a governess in nursery days in Yorkshire. It was well worth while being ill, to be thus petted by old friends. And Sylvia Lynd wrote a very kind review of the book, and Lascelles and Catherine, bless them, told me that I need not worry about it as it was the thing they had always known I could do, and Ric declared himself its champion, and here and there appeared 'good' reviews and, though it sold extremely slowly, Jonathan Cape said he wanted another.

And then, perhaps best of all, Lascelles brought me the proofs of *The Sale of St Thomas*, the first part of which he had written as

337

long ago as 1911 and the later parts only this year. He read the whole poem to me, the finest of all his dramatic poems, and then he showed me my own name at the beginning of it, and I felt like 'Lawrence of virtuous father, virtuous son', endowed by Milton with immortality. Nor must I forget kind Hafez Afifi, a chess-player and a friend since my first visit to Egypt, now a Pasha and Egyptian Ambassador, who came with an Oriental retinue and filled my room with flowers as if I had been a prima donna or a corpse.

Evgenia and my friends were certainly petting me as if I were a prima donna, but I did not feel at all like a corpse and, after the first horrible days of extreme weakness, was enjoying that curious feeling of levitation that comes with convalescence. I have had, thanks to various misfortunes, my fair share of delightful con-valescences, during which life seems a tune played with the finger-tips on a spinet instead of with a fist on a grand piano. I have seldom had more pleasure in the actual work of writing than I had in those first days without an invisible fiend twisting a corkscrew through my solar plexus, days spent lying on that divan writing an article for the *Guardian* which Ted wanted for the centenary of William Hazlitt's death.

My doctor was triumphant and told me I could now eat any-thing, and the Hirsts found us rooms in a hotel near them out at Notting Hill. We moved there and a week later that infernal corkscrew was busy again, and I went back to a modified diet of milk and fish to tame it. On going home to Ludderburn, things once more improved. I was a feeble creature, but Francis Brett Young, who was then living at Esthwaite Lodge, let me fish his rod at Levens Hall, on the Kent, where I could potter about on the bank without wading. I caught a dozen sea-trout on a simple fly dressed with a grey partridge hackle, a blue silk body ribbed with silver and a few fibres of Golden Pheasant tippet for tail, and thought myself all but cured. Then came news that the Junior Literary Guild in America had taken a considerable edition of *Swallows and Amazons*, which made it seem almost safe to risk another year of living on our very small savings and to write another book. I began the rough draft of *Peter Duck*, instantly fell ill again, went up to London for more X-ray examinations and was told that there had been 'a complete relapse to the July condition'. It was now the end of November. P. P. Howe sent me to see a friend of his, Dr Forest Smith of St Thomas's. He made an identical diagnosis but suggested a different treatment, no food or drink that had been in contact with aluminium, and an alkaline powder after every meal. 'And the nearer you get to fifteen stone the better.' I was then extremely scraggy and weighed ten-and-a-half stone.

I have followed his advice ever since and now weigh much too much, though I have never quite reached my fifteen stone. The year thus came to a hopeful end. *Swallows and Amazons*, my pet book, had been published and though in England it sold at first extremely slowly (it was two years before it had earned more than the advance of £100), both Cape and Lippincott wanted another story. I had put *Peter Duck* aside, but I had another waiting to be written, and it was with cheerful hearts that Evgenia and I went up on the hill behind Ludderburn to listen for bells ringing in the New Year of 1931. We heard the Cartmel bells, far away but clear, and as we went down again to the cottage, I remember that an owl and a wild duck were also awake.

I was half way through the rough draft of *Swallowdale* by the end of February. There was already a full synopsis of *Peter Duck*, but for several reasons I had to write *Swallowdale* first, even though that story lets out that the children by then knew all about the old sailor. That spring, besides writing reviews I was also busy with an article on Defoe for the *Manchester Guardian*. In April we went sailing on the Broads, the next best thing to going to sea. *Swallowdale* was finished by the end of July. It sold in England very slightly better than *Swallows and Amazons*, but the first book was also finding readers. Our savings were melting away, but on taking the omens we thought we could take the risk of one more year and the writing of *Peter Duck*.

It so happens that worry stirs up duodenal ulcers, and that ulcers incline their owner to worry. And there was plenty to worry about in other things beside our shrinking bank account. Every few days I was having another attack of the twisting cork-screw, and it seldom happened that I slept through a night without having to get up to cure the familiar pain with the equally familiar powders. Robin Collingwood's Rugby friend Ernest Altounyan had for a long time been urging us to visit Syria, where he and his father were running a hospital. His children had identified themselves (regardless of sex) with my characters and were writing to say that I ought to come and see what they were really like, and when he wrote that he could guarantee to cure my miserable insides, we made up our minds to risk nearly the whole of such capital as we had and to go to Aleppo. We arranged for the building and taking out with us of a sailing dinghy to leave there by way of repaying hospitality. We shut up Ludderburn and booked passages for ourselves and the dinghy in the *Scottish Prince* that was to leave Manchester on January 8, 1932.

Ted Scott saw us off from Salford Docks. He had been growing ever keener on sailing since that first holiday on the Norfolk Broads when, for a few days, he had been able to forget the newspaper. We had been planning some day to share a sea-going boat, and in the meantime he had been doing a lot of what he called his 'homework' in reading books about coastal navigation. He meant to buy a small dinghy like my own, so that he and his son Dick could sail on Windermere. I had been looking round for a suitable boat and had heard of one that was fitted with air-tanks, so as to be unsinkable. We were talking of this to the last minute.

We had a delightful voyage, with mostly fair weather, so that on all but one or two days I was able to work at *Peter Duck* and, moreover, found in the captain's stateroom some pilot-books that were exactly what I needed. As always, I lost my pains at sea, and by the time we were plodding down the Portuguese coast, looking at the Burlings and Cintra, I was finding it hard to believe in that old corkscrew that on land for so long I had seldom been able to forget. It was Evgenia's first sea-voyage since leaving the Baltic and though we had left hardly any money in the bank we were full of trust that Aleppo would work a final cure, and so were able to forget finance and enjoy every minute. We called at Tunis for long enough to go out to lunch with my Cairo friends the Downeses in their Moorish house at Sidi-bou-Said. We watched the little bright-painted boats racing at Valetta, though we resisted the temptation to take our dinghy from its crate. At Alexandria we saw other friends and had the usual miserable time in shifting ourselves and our luggage and the crated boat from the *Scottish Prince* to a Khedivial Mail steamship that was calling at Cyprus, Marsina and Alexandretta. In Cyprus we saw Limassol and Larnaca and the old citadel at Famagusta, and Evgenia was able to eat oranges as she picked them off the trees (as she had always hoped to do) and I was delighted by the noblest chameleon I have ever seen whom I met walking in a trench. We came thus to Alexandretta, where we were met and taken over the Beilun Pass and so to the Plain of Antioch and Aleppo.

The dinghy was taken from its crate by the river Amuk and sailed very well on those waters, which are like the Broads, except for snow-mountains in the distance, grey limestone hills on which the shepherds tap continually with their sticks, to warn the snakes to get out of the way, fields of asphodel and tiny iris, and the occasional sight of camels that would seem odd in Norfolk. The little boat was still afloat there when, years later, that territory was given back to the Turks, who thus, without asking for it, acquired a minute addition to their fleet.

When we were there the Amuk was still Syrian, and that bit of country was well suited to the local brigands, who could hold up traffic on the road from Alexandretta and then disappear with their booty into the hills and over the Turkish border. The local inhabitants accepted these conditions and made the best of them. Thus, the farmer of the land where our Aleppine friends kept their boats was a cousin of one of the brigand chiefs, and it was felt that all parties had behaved well when, one day when we were fishing there, we were warned to be out of the way by four o'clock as the brigands had planned a descent on the road a little later. We did as we were told and in Aleppo learned how fortunate we had been, as by half-past five that afternoon the brigands had been in complete control of the road and, as usual, had got away with their gains.

The French were then in nominal control of the country and we heard how, on another occasion, they had called an anti-brigand conference of military and police chiefs in Aleppo, and how the brigands had held up their cars on the road, compelled the occupants to undress and sent them on to attend their conference in a state of nakedness. Humour of this kind was relished by the population and few but their victims had any but good words for the brigands.

The fishing was chiefly for cat-fish, and where the local fisher-men brought their catches ashore the banks were littered with the hideous, decaying heads of these creatures, which were cut off on the spot the moment they were landed, lest their ugly faces with their long barbules should frighten customers from buying their quite edible bodies. I caught no big ones, but was startled by the head of one of them which showed on the surface (so large that I thought it was a water-buffalo), snorted like a bullock and disappeared.

In Aleppo, in a room in a turret, high above the Turkish

cemetery, I wrote over three hundred pages of *Peter Duck*, sometimes reading snatches of it to the children who used to ask 'How
many pages?' when I came down from my eyrie. But the main
object for which we had risked bankruptcy in coming to Aleppo
was not achieved. Far from being a place for the cure of duodenal
ulcers, Aleppo was for many reasons the exact opposite. Inocula-
tions against various diseases made me much worse, and, as the
weather grew warmer and the mosquitoes more active we were
told for the first time that every member of the household had
had malaria. The stock of dried milk we had brought with us was
dwindling. My corkscrew was every day twisting into my solar
plexus. Work became more and more difficult, and it was clear
that I should find no cure in Syria. We were sorry to leave Dora
and her children and there were tears when we left, but it was
with heart-felt relief that we boarded an Italian steamer at
Alexandretta and once more enjoyed the miraculous effect of
sea air.

We landed at Famagusta and learned that the same *Scottish
Prince* in which we had sailed from England was somewhere off
the north coast of Cyprus, loading locust-beans. We crossed the
island to Kyrenia, a delightful place with an ancient castle, an
ancient monastery, and a harbour far too small for the *Scottish
Prince*. She was anchored outside and sent a boat ashore for us.
There followed an enjoyable time that might have been designed
to put right the evil effects of Aleppo. The beans were at various
places along that north coast, and the *Scottish Prince* anchored offshore while Cypriot lighters brought cargo alongside. But the
lighters could not work on that open coast if there was an onshore wind. The *Scottish Prince* would steam in when the wind
was offshore, anchor and take aboard a few lighter-loads of beans,
and then the wind would swing round and blow onshore, the
lightermen would stop work, and we would steam off to sea to
wait for the next change of wind, when we would come in again,
anchor as before and wait for the lighters. Sometimes we would
go ashore in one of the ship's boats and visit a village. We
interested the villagers as much as they interested us, and our walks
turned into processions. We were invited into houses where
every bit of furniture was occupied by silkworms while human
beings were content with the floor. Old ladies tried to show us
how to spin, walking with us, talking volubly and never stopping
their distaffs, spinning like tops beside them. Other old ladies

showed Evgenia their ovens, knowing without being told that she too was a passionately interested cook. I think one of the schools was given a holiday lest the children should miss the spectacle, for going ashore rather late after working to finish a chapter of *Peter Duck* I met Evgenia and the captain, who had visited a village, coming down to the shore at the head of an admiring column.

In Aleppo I had heard from Ted Scott that he had bought a small boat on Windermere and that he would be ready for a holiday on the Norfolk Broads as soon as we got back. I have my own last letter to him from Syria, telling him how glad I was that he too was a shipowner and telling him not to get drowned till I was there to fish him out. From Cyprus I had written again making final arrangements for our Broads cruise and telling him when we expected to dock at Rotterdam. We were a long time leaving Cyprus, and had a pleasant voyage through the Mediterranean, while I wrote a good many pages of *Peter Duck*, steamed up the Channel, getting glimpses of the English coast, and came at last to Rotterdam. The agent there came aboard with the captain's mail and the captain gave me a telegram. Ted Scott was dead. He had been drowned in Windermere a few days after I had sent my last letter to him from Cyprus.

It was as if our world had come suddenly to an end. I have never had a closer friend than Ted. We had no secrets from each other. Better than anybody, except perhaps his wife, I had known of the difficulties of those last five years and of his extreme loneliness in the office. Better than anybody, except my wife, he had known of our much smaller difficulties. I felt now that I ought to have joined him in Manchester instead of sticking to my books. Worse, I could not get rid of the thought that I had killed him. But for me he would never have taken to sailing. Sailing had proved to be for him what I had hoped it would be, the one thing that let him forget the office in Manchester. I had never seen him happier than when we were sailing together. And this was the end of it. I had been the one to make the enquiries that had ended in his buying himself a boat. I had learnt that the boat had air-tanks and was unsinkable. It had not sunk. It had capsized in a squall, but it had remained afloat. Dick, who was with him, stayed with the boat and was picked up almost at once. Ted died because he was too good a swimmer. He had left the boat to swim ashore and in the cold water of April had had a heart attack and died. But, if I had not set him sailing, he might have been alive today.

For many weeks I could think of nothing else and my book obstinately hung fire. Our cottage at Ludderburn had been burgled while we were away (the silly thief was caught when he was found putting Chinese coins into a slot-machine). It was a very grim summer. We had spent nearly all we had in going to Aleppo and not getting me cured. During June and July I finished the book. The two earlier ones were selling steadily though very slowly and Cape raised the advance on account of royalties to £150 for the new one. It went to the printers on August 3.

Meanwhile I had tried for the first time to do my own illustrations. In *Peter Duck* the pictures were supposed to have been made by the children themselves to illustrate the story they had themselves invented, so the bad drawing did not matter very much, and at least one of the drawings, Roger's picture of a night scene, which was perfectly black all over, was quite easy. This was the beginning of what afterwards became a habit. I had much disliked the excellent drawings made by professional artists for the earlier books because, though very good drawings, they did not seem to me to illustrate the stories but were merely skilful exercises by accomplished technicians. After the *Peter Duck* experiment, Cape suggested that in future I should be my own illustrator. I agreed but on sound trade union principles said that I should expect to be paid at professional rates, and so I have been ever since, and my bad drawings have come to seem part of the books, as indeed they are. In the end I did pictures for the first two books as well, and must admit that I have had a great deal of pleasure out of doing so, though the actual process would have been much less painful if at an earlier age I had learnt how to draw. Of course I have always had Nancy Blackett to take some of the blame for my scratchy line and uncertain anatomy.

On October 1 W. G. Collingwood died. I have told a little of what I owe to him. Mrs Collingwood, my dear aunt, had died before him. He had had a stroke and then another, with loss of memory and partial loss of speech. His death was not like Ted's. He had completed a full and generous life and left behind him books that will surely never be forgotten. Ted died on the very threshold of his career, when only those who knew that already for five difficult years he had been in actual though not titular control of the *Manchester Guardian* realised that he was as great an editor as his father had been before him. No one could regret for Mr Collingwood's sake that he was released from a life in which, since he could no longer work, he could find no happiness. But, with both the Collingwoods gone, that old life of Lanehead, the lovely life that they had allowed me to share, was over.

*Peter Duck* was published on October 12 and I went off with a fishing rod to Haverthwaite, by way of taking omens, and was startled into hopefulness by catching a salmon. Then two reviews appeared almost on the same day, one a very generous one by Hugh Walpole in the *Observer* and the other, anonymous, by someone who had evidently liked the book very much, in *The Times*. A few days later Cape's partner, Wren Howard, wrote to tell me that *Peter Duck* was already being reprinted. The turn of the tide had come just in time to save us and to justify Evgenia's courage in risking financial disaster. Presently the sales of the first two books began to catch up with those of *Peter Duck*, and I knew I could afford to write another.

No. Not that photograph. Not the C.I.D. man, bootlegger or political tough and hi-jacker, but a benevolent baldheaded one, something like this

# Postscript

I used to laugh at young men who wrote their autobiographies at the age of twenty-one or twenty-five. I now think that they are wise to write them before they have many mistakes to regret. The writing of an autobiography at sixty-five, seventy-three, seventy-six, knowing that there is no time in which to put right the errors of the past, is like a rehearsal for the Day of Judgment, and not an early rehearsal either but perhaps the very last. Few men can review their lives without misgiving. I have been fortunate in having such men among my friends, but I am not such a man myself.

Mine has not been a life of consistent effort towards a single end. It seems to me that I have been like a shuttlecock bandied to and fro by lunatics. I seem to have lived not one life but snatches from a dozen different lives. I have had a great deal of undeserved good fortune. The weakness that made possible my first marriage and so cost me my library and all else that I possessed at that time might have ended in my final shipwreck. Instead, to set against the misery that came from it, I can look back on more than thirty years of unclouded happiness with my second wife. In all that time I have felt firm ground under my feet instead of quicksands. But for her I should have been dead and unable to write this book. And but for her resolute courage in taking the risk of extreme poverty I should never have dared to take the step that gave me, towards the end of my life, the twenty years in which I have been able to write those books that may seem to some children an excuse for my existence. Further, but for her relentlessly honest criticism, they would be worse books than they are.

A.R.

# Epilogue

by Rupert Hart-Davis

The tide had indeed turned. Steadily increasing sales of the books removed all worries about money. The autobiography ends in 1932, but Ransome had another thirty-five years to live. From his notes and the accurate memory of his widow this brief account of the final years has been compiled.

Despite almost continuous illness, several operations, and half-a-dozen house-movings, he wrote and illustrated another nine children's books between 1933 and 1947. Each one was published within a month or two of its completion, and if necessary the author travelled to Edinburgh to correct the proofs at the printer's.

In 1933 he first broke his ankle; then, on a sailing holiday with Charles and Margaret Renold on the Norfolk Broads, he collapsed in agony after attempting to hoist sail. Renold, though inexperienced in such matters, navigated the boat to Wroxham, where the local doctor immediately called in a specialist, Mr Blaxland of Norwich. He operated that night for acute appendicitis. Convalescence at St Mawes in Cornwall enabled the Ransomes to see a lot of Claude Worth, the yachting expert.

At Ludderburn a neighbouring farmer gave them a silver-grey tabby cat, which soon produced three similarly coloured kittens. The Ransomes were so delighted with their appearance that they drove all the way to London to exhibit them at the Cat Show at the Crystal Palace, where they were 'highly commended'. The mother and one kitten were given away, but the other two, Polly and Podge, stayed for life. Ransome recorded how:

> At Ludderburn they often brought in small dead rabbits as trophies of the chase, only to have them instantly thrown out. This puzzled them, and one day, while we were sitting

at lunch, I glanced out and saw Polly and Podge coming along together under our yew-trees, with a live rabbit hopping along between them. If the rabbit tried to turn right, Polly headed it off. If it turned left, Podge was ready for it. It was like watching well-trained dogs shepherding a refractory sheep. They brought that rabbit right into the house, and right up to my chair, so that I was able to pick it up by its ears, carry it out and release it, while they were otherwise rewarded at home.

In 1935 came a sad farewell to Ludderburn, with its superb view and unparalleled work-room. It was much too primitive; the damp climate did not agree with Evgenia; they both longed for a sea-going boat of their own; and sea air always improved Arthur's internal troubles. After many visits to the East Coast they rented Broke Farm at Levington, near Pin Mill, on the Orwell river. A local man from Kendal moved their furniture down to Suffolk; he had never been south before, never out of sight of the hills. When he had finished unloading in the late evening, Arthur said 'You'd much better stop the night and not drive all that way back without a rest.' 'Nay, Mr Ransome,' said the man with a shudder, 'I want to get back to England.'

Sailing now took up a lot of their time. They bought a seven-ton cutter which they renamed *Nancy Blackett*, and with a strong young man as crew Arthur sailed her from Poole to Harwich and Pin Mill through appalling storms. Regular sailing greatly improved Arthur's health, and he soon came to know those East Coast waters as intimately as the Lakes of his childhood. In 1936 they sailed to Flushing and back as a reconnaissance for *We Didn't Mean to go to Sea*.

In 1937 Arthur was the first recipient of the Library Association's Carnegie Medal for the best children's book of the year (*Pigeon Post*, 1936). He was presented with it at Scarborough by the Archbishop of York, and he recorded:

It was a very fine day, and a large round medal, and I enjoyed meeting Temple, whom I had last seen shouting with laughter in the quadrangle at Rugby about forty years earlier. He talked very well about detective stories and grew red in the face with indignation as he spoke of one or two constructors of such tales, who, in his opinion, did not play fair.

Later in the year Arthur again strained himself hoisting sail and was operated on for umbilical hernia by Mr Blaxland at Norwich. In the nursing home he and Evgenia were busily planning a new boat which was to be specially built to their own design, when Arthur suffered an embolism, and his life was saved only by the prompt attention of the invaluable Blaxland.

1938 was mostly occupied by the boat, which was built by Mr King of Pin Mill and named *Selina King*. Arthur was so absorbed by the whole process that for a time he planned to write a book entirely about the building of a boat.

I saw *Selina*'s lines laid down on the floor of the loft. I watched the making of the moulds and Mr King's careful picking of the grown timbers that were to go into her. He and I went together to pick the elm for her yard-wide keel and saw the great tree lifted by a crane, laid on trolleys and driven in to meet the screaming saw that cut horizontally through the tree's entire length. Then the cut piece was lifted and we saw the top of the keel-to-be laid bare. You can never tell what may be in an elm until you cut it. The foreman of the timberyard was with us, and, as the keel was bared and we saw the dark splash of bad wood in the middle of it, he said but one word, 'Coffins', and the tree that might but for that dark spot have sailed the seas was condemned to hold bones underground.

Two trees were cut through and condemned before we found the perfect keel. Then there was the iron keel that was to go below it. For that a wooden mould had to be made, and when it was made we were at Cocksedge's foundry, to see the great cauldron of molten iron slowly tipped and the fiery stream poured from its lip. We saw the three-and-a-half-ton iron keel come from Ipswich and, with half the population of Pin Mill, helped to manhandle it into Mr King's shed. Then came the moment when the wooden keel was resting on the iron one, with stem and stern post, both of which we had seen in the raw, sticking up at each end, and the long double row of timbers, so that the boat was like an unclothed skeleton.

In August Arthur took time off to accompany a small boy to the Oval, where they saw Hutton make his record score of 364, and in September *Selina King* was launched, just before the Munich Pact.

In 1939 they left Broke Farm, which had become too noisy, and moved to nearby Harkstead Hall, a square brick farmhouse with roses and cedars in the garden. They were still only a few minutes away from their anchorage at Pin Mill and continued to enjoy the freemasonry of the little port and its sailing community. A new friend was Dick Stokes, director of Arthur's old family firm Ransome & Rapier. Arthur was charmed by the contradictions in this delightful man, who was a Catholic capitalist, Labour Member for Ipswich, and large employer of labour. They disagreed about almost everything but much enjoyed each other's company.

When the war came Arthur offered his services to the Admiralty, but they had no use for a 'middle-aged crock', and in any case, as he neatly put it, he had 'no stomach for the fight'. Sadly he sailed *Selina King* to Lowestoft, where she was laid up for the duration. The Battle of Britain, though it provided plenty of aerial action above, left them unscathed, but all Arthur's illustrations for *The Big Six* were destroyed by enemy action. Undeterred he swiftly produced another set in their place.

With sailing impossible, and warlike activity all round, they felt like drones in a hive, and when they realised that they might be turned out of Harkstead Hall at twenty-four hours' notice, they migrated once more to the Lakes. All they could find to buy was a bungalow called The Heald on the shore of Coniston Water. There was no garden and only home-made electric light. Arthur was able to do a little fishing, and he enjoyed playing chess with the military historian Liddell Hart, who was living nearby, but Evgenia detested the place at first sight, and one day in a local hotel dining-room she said loudly, 'I shall sell the damned place for what we paid for it the moment the war's over.' A man at the next table came over and said, 'I should like to take you at your word.' They shook hands on the deal, and sure enough in 1945, when they had endured the place for almost five years, the obliging man turned up, cheque-book in hand.

Failing to find a house in Suffolk, they moved on to London, where Jonathan Cape lent them his flat until they found one of their own in Weymouth Street. They sadly sold *Selina King*, now deemed too heavy for Arthur to handle, and bought a new boat which they named *Lottie Blossom* and kept on Chichester harbour. The London flat was nice enough, but neighbours' radios made it difficult for Arthur to write, and in 1948 they were back in the

Lakes, having bought Lowick Hall, on the river Crake, south of Coniston. There was a lot to be done. 'Plaster, dust, bad drains, decrepit water-pipes, rotting floors, leaking roofs, etc. But Golly what a place!' Arthur reported on June 21. He much enjoyed being Lord of the Manor, and Evgenia fell in love with the house and garden, but the estate was too big for them, they had constant trouble with tenants and farmers, and after two years they sold the place at a heavy loss and moved back to London, to a flat in Hurlingham Court, right on the river beside Putney Bridge.

It was now that the Garrick Club began to play an important part in Arthur's life. He had been elected in 1943, proposed and seconded by Daniel Macmillan and Ivor Brown, and had used the club intermittently during the Weymouth Street years. Now he became a regular attender. Every Thursday he travelled from Putney to Garrick Street, first by underground and later by taxi, arriving in time for lunch, spending the afternoon playing chess or billiards with any opponent he could find, and returning home after dinner.

Here I must introduce a personal note. I first met Arthur early in 1933, when I became a director of Jonathan Cape Ltd, and we became friends immediately. He had been brought up to call men by their surnames, and it was not until 1952 that he first called me Rupert. His inhibitions had by then been conquered by the easy-going camaraderie of the Garrick. By the time I knew him he had lost the lean and hungry look of his youth and was large and pink-faced. People often roused his wrath by saying how well he looked when in fact he was suffering greatly.

When I started my own publishing business after the war, Arthur took an excited interest from the beginning, remembering his own early days in the trade, and even bought a few shares. One day in 1947 I was discussing with my partner David Garnett whether we couldn't publish a nautical book to please our other partner Edward Young, who had commanded a submarine. 'What about circumnavigators?' I said. 'Captain Cook?' David said 'Slocum?', but that famous sailor was only a name to both of us. At that moment the telephone rang. It was Arthur, anxious to apologise for something. 'I'll forgive you', I said, 'if you'll tell me about Slocum.' 'Joshua Slocum', said Arthur, 'wrote the best sailing book in the world, and if you republish it I'll write you an introduction for nothing.' 'Done,' said I.

He was as good as his word, and in 1948 *Sailing Alone around the*

*World* (of which we sold 30,000 copies, plus 180,000 to book clubs) was the first volume in the Mariners Library of reprinted sailing books, which finally contained almost fifty volumes. Arthur acted as godfather and nanny to the series. No title was included without his approval; his own *Racundra's First Cruise* appeared as No 38; and he wrote introductions to *Down Channel* by R. T. McMullen (1949), *The Cruise of the Teddy* by Erling Tambs (1949), *The Falcon on the Baltic* by E. F. Knight (1951), *The Cruise of the Alerte* by E. F. Knight (1952), *The Cruise of the Kate* by E. E. Middleton (1953) and *The Voyage Alone in the Yawl Rob Roy* by John Macgregor (1954). Arthur wrote later, 'These were all much belated pieties, and the republishing of those books gave me a very great deal of pleasure.' He refused any sort of payment, so I gave him a set of the big Oxford Dictionary, which in due course he generously bequeathed back to me.

Early in 1952 Arthur underwent a prostate operation. His convalescence was long and slow, but he was cheered later in the year by the award of an honorary D. Litt from Leeds University. He could only just stand, and his fellow-graduand, the painter and writer Wyndham Lewis, was almost blind. Their wives watched with apprehension as the two men were ushered on to the rostrum and stood on its extreme edge; but all was well, and in his diary Arthur copied out the words of Dr Johnson, 'Every man has a lurking wish to be thought considerable in his native place.'

In 1953 the Ransomes sailed *Lottie Blossom* to Cherbourg, stayed there a week, and returned through a violent storm. Next year they repeated this exploit, storm and all, but that was the finish; *Lottie* was laid up, and next year sold. Arthur's sailing days were over.

In 1957 he was operated on for strangulated hernia, and had just recovered when he stumbled and fell down the stone steps outside Cape's office in Bedford Square. This apparently trivial accident started a train of misfortunes, from which he never fully recovered. Severe pains in the back were treated by an injection so violent that he was paralysed for two days, and then in worse pain than ever. His complaint was diagnosed as sciatica, lumbago, rheumatism and slipped disc; he was seen by one specialist after another, treated by a succession of masseurs and physiotherapists, and given every kind of drug. He was in bed first at home, then in a Harley Street nursing home, then in hospital, where he was treated for rheumatoid arthritis. After nine months of this he was

unable to move, and begged to be taken home to die. Home he
went, by ambulance and stretcher, and his life seemed almost at
an end. But miraculously he rallied, could soon walk without
sticks, and by October was convalescing at Pagham in Sussex.

In 1959 he published his last book, *Mainly about Fishing*, which
he felt he owed to the memory of his father, 'who had wanted to
write a book on fishing but died before he had time to do so'.

In 1960 the Ransomes bought the little derelict farmhouse in
the Lakes which they had rented for the last four years as a holiday
cottage. Repairs and alterations took longer than expected, and it
was not until November 1963 that they moved into their last
home, Hill Top, Haverthwaite, near Newby Bridge. They both
loved the house, and the buzzards, redstarts and deer by which it
seemed to be surrounded, but it was remote and comparatively
inaccessible, with no help available, and the folly of the move
became more and more apparent as Arthur grew steadily weaker
and less mobile.

By the time a few close friends assembled for his eightieth
birthday in January 1964 he was confined to a wheel-chair on the
upper floor of the house. Evgenia struggled on bravely, but in
October 1965, when Arthur had lost his memory and could do
nothing for himself, she moved him to the Cheadle Royal
Hospital, outside Manchester. There he lingered on for twenty
months, not noticeably unhappy and only occasionally conscious
of his surroundings. He died peacefully on June 3, 1967, and lies
buried, surrounded by his beloved hills, rivers and lakes, in the
lovely valley of Rusland. Evgenia, who died on March 19, 1975,
aged eighty, is buried beside him. By one of life's little ironies
Rusland is only one letter short of the German for Russia.

# Check List of Books
# by Arthur Ransome

(The dates in brackets are not on the books).

*The Souls of the Streets* 1904
*The Stone Lady* 1905
*Pond and Stream* (1906)
*The Child's Book of the Seasons* (1906)
*Things in Our Garden* (1906)
*Highways and Byways in Fairyland* 1906
*Bohemia in London* 1907
*A History of Story-Telling* 1909
*Edgar Allan Poe* 1910
*The Hoofmarks of the Faun* 1911
*Oscar Wilde* 1912
*Portraits and Speculations* 1913
*The Elixir of Life* 1915
*Old Peter's Russian Tales* 1916
*Aladdin and his Wonderful Lamp* (1919)
*Six Weeks in Russia in 1919* 1919
*The Soldier and Death* (1920)
*Racundra's First Cruise* 1923
*The Chinese Puzzle* 1927
*Rod and Line* 1929
*Swallows and Amazons* 1930
*Swallowdale* 1931
*Peter Duck* 1932
*Winter Holiday* 1933
*Coot Club* 1934
*Pigeon Post* 1936
*We Didn't Mean to go to Sea* 1937
*Secret Water* 1939
*The Big Six* 1940

*Missee Lee* 1941
*The Picts and the Martyrs* 1943
*Great Northern?* 1947
*Mainly about Fishing* 1959

# Index